JESUS yesterday, today, for ever

Graham Jackman

Other books by Graham Jackman:

The Language of the Cross: Reflections on the Atonement
Luke's Pauline Narrative: Reading the Third Gospel
The Word Became Flesh: A Theme in John's Gospel
Re-reading Romans in context
"As dying, and behold, we live": The Merz brothers and the Third Reich*

In German:

Die Sprache des Kreuzes: Überlegungen zum Erlösungswerk
„Das, was du bist, das sei auch ganz": Die Brüder Merz und das Dritte Reich

In French:

Petit Vocabulaire Biblique*

Available from Lulu (www.lulu.com) or *Amazon

Copyright © 2023 by Graham Jackman. All rights reserved.

ISBN: 9798853472532

Except where indicated otherwise, all Biblical quotations are from the New Revised Standard Version Bible: Anglicized Edition, copyright 1989, 1995, Division of Christian Education of the National Council of the Churches of Christ in the United States of America. Used by permission. All rights reserved.

Cover photo by Jeremy Thomas on Unsplash (https://unsplash.com)

Contents

Foreword vi

Introduction 1

Chapter 1. 'The Day Before Yesterday' 9
'In ... through ... by' *10*
'The image of the invisible God' *13*
'Before the foundation of the world'. *15*
A shared identity?. *18*

Chapter 2. Jesus in the Old Testament...23
Jesus and Adam. *24*
Where else do we recognise Jesus in the Old Testament? *30*
How is Jesus foreshadowed in the Old Testament? *32*
The Servant *35*
Understanding Old Testament prefiguring of Jesus *44*
Why 'Jesus in the Old Testament'?. *53*

Chapter 3. Preliminaries: Birth, Childhood – and 'Christology'...........58
Introduction *58*
A. The question of 'Christology' *59*
Jesus: a human child. *63*
B. Jesus' Childhood. *67*
The birth narratives *67*
The Gospels and Jesus' childhood. *72*
Jesus' early years. *74*
C. Growing up in Nazareth: the contemporary context. *76*
The religious scene *77*
The political scene. *85*
Socio-economic conditions *86*
Political unrest. *88*
Summing up. *90*

Chapter 4. Baptism and Temptation..93
Baptism *94*
Temptation *103*

Jesus – yesterday, today, for ever

Chapter 5. Outline of Jesus' Ministry 116
Length and timing 116
Jesus and John the Baptist 117
Visits to Jerusalem 121
The Gospels: thematic rather than chronological 122
Tentative conclusions 124
The disciples 129
The women 133

Chapter 6. The Mission of Jesus 136
The message 138
Jesus' dealings with individuals 143
The underlying problem 147
The shadow of the cross 159
Where is the man Jesus in all this? 162
A revelation of God 170
'In his image' 173

Chapter 7. From Caesarea Philippi to Jerusalem 174
At Caesarea Philippi 175
The Transfiguration 183
Towards Jerusalem 185
Coming to Jerusalem 190
In Jerusalem 195
Preparing for the future 200

Chapter 8. The Passion – and After 204
The authorities 204
The disciples 209
'It is finished' – Jesus and his suffering 218
And afterwards? 228

Chapter 9. The Glorified Lord 234
The risen Jesus 235
Excursus: Jesus as 'Lord' 243
A new mission 246

Chapter 10. The Risen Lord and his People 262
Jesus the 'pioneer' 262
Images of the church 266
Caring and protecting 273
'Indwelling' 284
The very present Jesus 292

Contents

Chapter 11. 'And for ever' … Jesus in the Future................................ 296
Jesus and the world of the future.. *297*
Meeting Jesus.. *305*
Afterword.. 313
The humanity of Jesus... *313*
A continuing identity?... *315*
Crucial – in more senses than one *316*
Two key moments: baptism and Caesarea Philippi...................... *317*
Jesus for us – today and for ever.. *319*
Bibliography 321

Foreword

One or two of the few people to whom I have dared mention that I was trying to write about Jesus responded in ways that effectively asked why I was doing so. The only answer that I can give is similar to that allegedly given by people proposing to climb Everest: because Jesus is there! Having written about various specific New Testament books or issues, I wished to try to sort out my understanding of the one who is at the heart of everything, the one whom Christians call Lord – and, in doing so, to give expression to my personal sense of reverence and thankfulness to him.

Books about Jesus usually focus on his earthly life – not surprisingly, since it is from that period that most of our knowledge of him comes, though many of their writers put question marks against much of what the contemporary sources, the Gospels, tell us about him. Yet for the believer, that earthly life is only one phase in a life which, though it begins in Bethlehem and Nazareth, not only reaches forward into our present and on into immeasurable futures, but is also rooted in immeasurable ages *before* his brief period on earth.

This book is therefore not another 'life of Jesus'. It is, moreover, neither essentially devotional nor academic in intention and character. Rather, it is my attempt to think as coherently as I could about the Biblical presentation of the different phases of what I have called, for want of a better term, Jesus' 'career'. Beginning 'before the foundation of the world', it follows the Biblical story of Jesus, from his prefiguring in the Old Testament, via his earthly ministry and his present role as Lord over his church, through to his future revelation in his majesty as 'king of kings and lord of lords'.

A further motivation for this look at Jesus was a vague unease with the ways in which Jesus is spoken about, not least in Christadelphian discourse. Anyone who attempts to speak publicly about Jesus knows how difficult it is to do so without lapsing into sentimentality; it is still more difficult, though, to strike the right balance between his divine origins and his humanity. For the most part, it appears to me, the former predominates. Jesus is viewed largely as inerrant and omniscient – except with regard to the date of his second coming! His humanity is acknowledged only when he suffers hunger or is tired, when he undergoes temptation, usually thought of as the natural impulse to avoid the cross, and then in his crucifixion itself. The result, it seems

Foreword

to me, is a Jesus who, all doctrinal statements notwithstanding, appears to 'pass through this world some inches off the ground', to use John Robinson's phrase[1] – in fact, much closer than is comfortable to the Catholic notion of Jesus' 'two natures', which conveniently allows Jesus' words and actions to be attributed, now to his human, now to his divine, nature, at the expense of any idea of Jesus as a truly unified being. It has not been my purpose to address the question of the Trinity, though it is probably subliminally present at many points in the book. However, I have, perforce, dealt with it briefly in chapter 3 while discussing Jesus' birth and childhood. The section of Robinson's book from which the above quotation is taken is very helpful on this topic.

My attempts to think realistically about Jesus' humanity may not convince, but I hope they may encourage others to see Jesus truly as man. On this issue, as on almost everything else in the book, it is my wish and intention that readers, even where they do not accept my interpretation, should be stimulated to reflect for themselves about everything that Jesus is and means for believers – and, indeed, for all people.

In approaching Jesus' earthly life, I have not attempted to provide a 'blow-by-blow' account, but rather to characterise various aspects of his ministry under a number of thematic headings. I have drawn primarily on the Synoptic Gospels, and especially Mark, since they probably give us the most straightforward account of his life – though we must beware of underestimating both the literary artistry and the theological insight with which these Gospels are written. I have repeatedly found, though, that if one seeks for an explanatory or interpretive phrase to sum up some aspect of Jesus' life, it is usually John's Gospel that provides it. I have not made extensive use of the New Testament Letters in writing about Jesus' earthly life since they, inevitably, are speaking about Jesus in relation to the needs and problems of Christian believers two or three decades later. The Letters come into their own, of course, in chapters 9 and 10, where it is the risen, present Jesus in his relation to believers that I am attempting to characterise.

It perhaps needs to be emphasised that to focus on Jesus, as I have done, does not imply any diminution of worship and thanksgiving to the Father. What I have been trying to do is, rather, to understand the Son as his Father's emissary, whose every action, from his baptism on, is devoted to the realisation of God's saving will and the demonstration of his love for his erring yet wonderful human creatures. The massed heavenly choirs of Revelation rightly give praises to them both for their redeeming work: '*To the one seated on the throne and to the Lamb be blessing and honour and glory and might for ever and*

---

1 John T. Robinson, *The Priority of John*, London 1985, p. 366.

ever!' (Rev. 5:13). And to that, like the four living creatures, we say 'Amen!'

Acknowledgements

I am once again deeply indebted to David Dunstan for his help and for his expertise in preparing the text for printing and publication and especially for his help in designing the layout and the cover.

My sister, Joyce Ford, has again provided wonderful help and support as a checker and proof-reader, as well as providing valuable comments on the various chapters as they have been written. It scarcely needs to be said that responsibility for any errors or infelicities, whether of orthography, style or content, is entirely mine.

Finally, I am, as ever, grateful for the patient support of my wife Jenny. For virtually the whole time since I began to write, she has been suffering from a variety of painful and limiting health problems which have meant considerable changes in our lives – but no wavering in her support. In the circumstances, I feel all the more thankful for being able to undertake and complete the writing of this book. To spend so much time thinking about Jesus can only be enriching, and I hope that readers may feel similarly enriched.

Introduction

It was a profoundly fragmented world in which the disciples of Jesus set about the task of preaching the gospel after his resurrection. Beneath the superficial unity provided by the *pax romana* was a multiplicity of tribes and nations, devoted to a bewildering range of gods and cults, all suspicious of each other and mistrustful of strangers, and all bent on protecting their own interests, sometimes violently – much as they do today!

Within such a world, the development of a Christian community made up of people from many different races, yet bound together across the barriers of nationality and culture, was not far short of a miracle. Former pagans from Greece and Asia Minor collecting money and sending it to impoverished Jews in Jerusalem – who would have thought of such a thing?

Perhaps that is why Paul calls the will of God, by which these developments had occurred, a 'mystery' (*musterion*). He means by that, not something secret, known only to a few initiates, but rather something that had only now, after the coming of Jesus, been revealed. It was a mystery hitherto undreamed of that Gentiles now had access on an equal footing with Jews to the grace of God in Christ:

> *In former generations this **mystery** was not made known to humankind, as it has now been revealed to his holy apostles and prophets by the Spirit: that is, the Gentiles have become fellow heirs, members of the same body, and sharers in the promise in Christ Jesus through the gospel. (Ephesians 3:5-6)*

It was not all sweetness and light, of course; there were tensions at times between Christian Jews and those who had once been pagan. And, given that the Christian gospel had Jewish roots, it was profoundly troubling to many Jewish Christians to find themselves rapidly becoming a minority within what still seemed to them like an essentially Jewish preserve. Even harder to understand, though, was to see the vast majority of their fellow-Jews reject the message about the risen Jesus that they had themselves accepted, while Gentiles believed. To explain this Paul again has recourse to the term 'mystery'. In Romans 9-11 he contemplates the puzzling story of God's dealings with Israel, their failure as a people to grasp with both hands the salvation brought through Christ, and their seemingly paradoxical displacement within the young church by Gentile believers, which led, in the short term, to still more conflicts, within the church as well as outside it. But the story that Paul outlines in Romans 11 does not end there: he foresees the ultimate reconciliation of Israel to God and thus of Jews and Gentiles:

> So that you may not claim to be wiser than you are, brothers and sisters, I want you to understand this **mystery**: a hardening has come upon part of Israel, until the full number of the Gentiles has come in. And so all Israel will be saved; as it is written, 'Out of Zion will come the Deliverer; he will banish ungodliness from Jacob.' ... As regards the gospel they are enemies of God for your sake; but as regards election they are beloved, for the sake of their ancestors; for the gifts and the calling of God are irrevocable. (Romans 11:25-29)

All these puzzling developments were in fact stages in one great overarching story, part of God's intentions for the human race and for the earth on which they live. And in his letter to the Ephesians, Paul sums up that entire purpose and its ultimate outcome in one of the most important statements in the whole of the New Testament, in which the word 'mystery' again occurs:

> With all wisdom and insight he has made known to us the **mystery** of his will, according to his good pleasure that he set forth in Christ, as a plan for the fullness of time, to gather up all things in him, things in heaven and things on earth. (Ephesians 1:8-10)

God, Paul says, has a purpose, his 'good pleasure', which is moving towards its consummation 'in the fullness of time', which may mean 'the right time' or, more probably, 'when the times reach their fulfilment', as in the NIV. His intention is to 'gather up' all things under one 'head'. 'Gather up' is the NRSV rendering of the rare Greek verb *anakephalaiomai*; at its centre is the word *kephale* (head), suggesting that the verb means 'to bring together under a (single) head'.[1] The whole of God's creation, and particularly the world of men, now so fragmented and riven with conflict and competition, will ultimately become one harmonious whole. And at the heart of God's 'good pleasure' is Jesus; it is 'in him' that everything will be 'gathered up'. It is under him as

---

1   This is its sense in its only other occurrence in the New Testament: '*The commandments, "You shall not commit adultery; You shall not murder; You shall not steal; You shall not covet"; and any other commandment, are **summed up** in this word, "Love your neighbour as yourself"'* (Rom. 13:9).

Introduction

'head' that 'all things' will be brought together; in their relationship to him they will find their place in the unity and harmony of the whole.

The frequent use of the word *musterion* is a feature of both Ephesians and the parallel letter to the Colossians – 10 of its 27 occurrences in the New Testament are found in these two short letters – and it is clear from Paul's letters and from Acts, and from how much he endured to promote it through his preaching, how important the forwarding of the divine purpose was to him. The unity of the young church that Paul celebrates in Ephesians 2 is for him a kind of model of that final reconciliation, a foretaste of the restored wholeness that he foresees in chapter 1 of this letter:

> *But now in Christ Jesus you who once were far off have been brought near by the blood of Christ. For he is our peace; in his flesh he has made both groups into one and has broken down the dividing wall, that is, the hostility between us. He has abolished the law with its commandments and ordinances, that he might create in himself one new humanity in place of the two, thus making peace, and might reconcile both groups to God in one body through the cross, thus putting to death that hostility through it. (Ephesians 2:13-16)*

We return, though, to chapter 1 and to Paul's use of the rare word *anakephalaiomai*. There are two points of detail to be noted. First, the word 'head' (*kephale*) may well have two interrelated meanings, suggesting not only the supremacy of Jesus, as God's appointed ruler over all things, but also the idea of a 'source' – compare the English usage of 'head' for 'the source of a river'. Jesus will not only have authority over the completed whole – he will also be the source of its unity, its pattern, perhaps even its truest meaning. And as its 'source' he is also the *means* by which the process is to be realised.[2]

The second point to note is the prefix *ana*, meaning 'again'; this implies probably that the gathering together involves a restoration of a lost wholeness, the oneness that was lost when '*sin entered into the world*' (Rom. 5:12) and the human race as a whole sought to liberate itself from the tutelage of the Creator.[3] His use of this prefix seems to indicate that Paul, surveying the

---

2 The same dual meaning of the word 'head' can be seen later in Ephesians when Paul writes of the church: '*But speaking the truth in love, we must grow up in every way into him who is the **head**, into Christ, **from whom** the whole body, joined and knit together by every ligament with which it is equipped, as each part is working properly, promotes the body's growth in building itself up in love.*' (Eph. 4:15-16)

3 J.B. Lightfoot writes that the passage implies 'the entire harmony of the universe, which shall no longer contain alien and discordant elements, but of which all the parts shall find their centre and bond of union in Christ.' (J.B. Lightfoot, *Notes on the Epistles of St. Paul*, 1895, p. 322, quoted in *The New International Dictionary of New Testament Theology*, vol. II,

3

Jesus – yesterday, today, for ever

world of his time, divided into competing, sometimes warring peoples, nations, and cultures, was able to recognise the fundamental problem. When men and women fall away from God, they fall away also from each other as each individual and group pursues its own ends.[4]

Taken on its own, this passage from Ephesians 1 might lead us to focus primarily on Jesus' future role at the end of the process, when he will reign over God's restored, re-unified world. Or we might think that it is above all by his death and resurrection that Jesus draws everything together. But Paul is almost certainly speaking rather of a process unfolding through time, with Christ at its centre at every point.

It is in the context of this purpose that we shall undertake our look at Jesus. The aim of this book is not to provide yet another 'life of Jesus' but rather to try to understand and elucidate the role of Jesus in the unfolding gracious purpose of God. As the title suggests, this involves thinking about his 'career', for want of a better word, in its various stages through time. The meaning of two of the three terms in my title, 'today' and 'for ever', seems obvious: 'today' refers to Jesus as he is now, the risen and glorified Lord, while 'for ever' looks not only to the continuation of his present activity but also to what will follow upon his return and his role as ruler on his Father's behalf over a world delivered at last from the depredations of human greed.

But what of 'yesterday'? To what does that refer? Most readers will realise instantly that my use of these three terms echoes a verse from Hebrews 13: '*Jesus Christ is the same yesterday and today and forever*' (v. 8). The writer of Hebrews might simply mean by this that the risen, living Jesus will ever be the one of whose goodness they have had direct knowledge or experience in the recent past. The 'Lord' in v. 6 is almost certainly a reference to Jesus – why else would the writer then immediately speak of Jesus as he does in v. 8?[5] This enables the writer then to affirm that the Jesus who stood by their former

---

p. 163)

4 'Each person makes himself the centre of his universe ... seeing things from his selfish point of view; becoming his own God, and worshipping himself ... In the story of Eden the serpent says to the woman: "Ye shall be as gods". That is the temptation to which mankind has succumbed: we have put ourselves, each one individually, in the centre of our universe, where God ought to be. And when persons do that, it separates them both from God and from each other.' (D.M. Baillie, *God was in Christ. An Essay on Incarnation and Atonement*, 2nd Ed., London 1955, p. 204)

5 In Hebrews the word 'Lord' (*kyrios*) occurs seventeen times. Of these, twelve are part of Old Testament quotations, including five occurrences of the phrase 'says the Lord'. Of the remaining five, one refers to God himself (8:2), one is uncertain (12:14), while three definitely refer to Jesus as 'Lord' (2:3; 7:14, and 13:20).

Introduction

leaders will, in the present, sustain the recipients of the letter too – and will continue to do so always. In that case, the writer intends by 'yesterday' simply the recent past of this community of believers, whether in and around Jerusalem or elsewhere.[6]

Yet the letter as a whole enables us to see Jesus' 'yesterday' in a larger perspective. It repeatedly implies a continuity between the earthly Jesus before his crucifixion and the glorified, immortal Lord of the present and the future. Indeed, the writer's argument in chapters 2 and 4 would be meaningless without such continuity:

Because he himself was tested by what he suffered, he is able to help those who are being tested. (Hebrews 2:18)

For we do not have a high priest who is unable to sympathize with our weaknesses, but we have one who in every respect has been tested as we are, yet without sin. (4:15)

Such passages imply that, despite the most radical difference that we can imagine, between the mortal man Jesus and the risen, immortal Jesus of 'today', the living Lord Jesus is in essentials the same Jesus that their 'leaders' (v. 7) must have told them of: one who had not only healed the sick and shown such compassion to the weak and failing, but had also experienced in mind and body the kinds of pressures and apprehensions that might now tempt them to abandon their faith in Christ and revert to the traditions of their Jewish fathers.[7]

---

6 I am, provisionally, persuaded by the view of W.F. Barling, among others, that the letter was written to 'Hebrew' believers in and around Jerusalem not long before, or even during, the wars that engulfed Jerusalem in the years 66–70 AD. If that dating is correct, it might indicate that these former leaders and preachers could include Paul and Peter, who are generally thought to have been put to death in the middle 60s as part of Nero's wave of persecutions. Whether or not that is correct, the writer clearly does not count himself among that first generation of apostles of Jesus (see also 2:3-4). This seems to me conclusive proof, quite apart from questions of style and content, that Hebrews was not written by Paul, as is still so often asserted.

7 This is, in essence, the same reassurance that Jesus himself gave, according to John, to his bewildered, apprehensive disciples on the eve of the crucifixion. Though the Father will give them 'another helper/advocate/comforter' (*parakletos*) when he himself will have 'gone to the Father' (John 14:16), his next words confirm that the new *parakletos* is none other than himself in a new form: *'I will not leave you orphaned; I am coming to you. In a little while the world will no longer see me, but you will see me; because I live, you also will live. On that day you will know that I am in my Father, and you in me, and I in you. They who have my commandments and keep them are those who love me; and those who love me will be loved by my*

Jesus – yesterday, today, for ever

Hebrews as a whole asks us, however, to think even more widely than that; with its extended parallels between the ministry of Jesus and the entire Mosaic system focused on the tabernacle and temple, and also with specific Old Testament figures, it invites, even requires, the reader to 'find' Jesus in the Jewish scriptures. Like many other places in the New Testament, this letter teaches us to see Jesus at almost every point in the Old Testament in so many different ways, not yet personally present but anticipated, promised, predicted and prefigured in people, events, and rituals. So our consideration of Jesus 'yesterday' has to take account of this dimension also – perhaps we might call it 'the day before yesterday' – and to ask what 'the same' means in this wider context.

It is not just a matter of types and prefigurings, however. The writer's Old Testament quotations in Hebrews 13:5-6, from Joshua 1:5 and Psalm 118:6 (with echoes also of Psalm 27:1 and Psalm 56:4, 11), unequivocally refer in their original setting to the Father. Here in Hebrews, though, the focus on 'the Lord' in v. 6 and the direct reference to Jesus in v. 8 show that the writer extends their sense to encompass Jesus too. He does something similar back in Hebrews 1, where his quotation from Psalm 102 is likewise applied to Jesus (v. 10-12).

This has three implications: first, it suggests a parallel between Father and Son in terms of 'character' or 'behaviour'. The Old Testament emphasises again and again that God is not only eternal, 'from everlasting to everlasting', but also for ever faithful and unchanging in his love for his people. This idea is at the heart of God's self-revelation to Moses in Exodus 34:6-7:

> *The LORD, the LORD, a God merciful and gracious, slow to anger, and abounding in steadfast love and faithfulness, keeping steadfast love for the thousandth generation, forgiving iniquity and transgression and sin, yet by no means clearing the guilty, but visiting the iniquity of the parents upon the children and the children's children, to the third and the fourth generation.*

The words 'steadfast love and faithfulness' in particular, *hesed* and *emeth*, are again and again quoted – and appealed to – in the Old Testament as epitomising God's abiding mercy towards Israel – see, for example, the recurrent use of *hesed* in every verse of Psalm 136. The declaration in Exodus thus reveals the essential significance of his name Yahweh: that as he has been in the past and now is, so he will ever be in the future too. A similar constancy of love and care is now attributed to Jesus in v. 6-8. God himself is ever 'the same' – it is no coincidence that the phrase 'the same' occurs in both the two

Father, and I will love them and reveal myself to them.' (v. 18-21)

Introduction

Psalms quoted in chapter 1, i.e. in Psalm 102 and in the writer's implied application to Jesus of the lines from Psalm 118 (the Hebrew text of Psalm 102 contains no word for 'the same', but the LXX version introduces the same phrase *ho autos*, the definite article followed by the masculine third person pronoun, that we find in Hebrew 13:8). And just as God is ever 'the same', so, in some way, is Jesus.

A second implication, arising out of this use of these quotations and references by the writer to the Hebrews, is that the 'yesterday' of v. 8 embraces more than just the previous few decades since the beginning of Jesus' ministry. By invoking the rich legacy of Old Testament teaching about the eternal faithfulness of God, he suggests a continuity in relation to the person of Jesus that reaches much further back.

The third implication is still more far-reaching: the writers of the New Testament, seeking and finding more and more anticipations and prefigurings of Jesus in the Old Testament, came to see – or were guided to see – that they must be the result of divine intentions that precede everything that the Old Testament tells us. What I have called the 'day before yesterday' must therefore reach back before 'the foundation of the world', as they call it on numerous occasions. As far back as our human thinking is able to take us – and then still further! – Jesus was there in the mind and intention of God.

Our reflections on Hebrews 13, linked with other passages in the same letter, have effectively defined for us the different 'stages' in Jesus' 'career', as I have called it, that we shall need to think about, here listed in reverse order:

- 'For ever': an unending vista of eternity stretching away into the future;
- A 'today': his present exalted status as Lord;
- A 'yesterday': the time of his earthly ministry;
- A 'day (or perhaps a time) before yesterday': the Old Testament age when Jesus, though not yet personally existing, is prefigured and anticipated in Israel's history and its scriptures;
- A time 'before the foundation of the world' when he is already part of his Father's loving purpose, even before it begins to unfold.

About the first and the last of these we can only speak tentatively, given the lack of clear, specific scriptural evidence. And while Jesus figures prospectively in the Old Testament *'in many and various ways'*, as Hebrews puts it (1:1), this is very different from the detail that we have of Jesus' earthly ministry, different too from the evidence that the New Testament provides about his present status and activity. It is therefore, inevitably, the second and the third

Jesus – yesterday, today, for ever

of these five stages, as listed above, that will mainly occupy us.

But we must begin at the beginning, or even before the beginning, for it is in thinking about what the biblical writers say about that earliest phase, 'before the foundation of the world', that we understand how he who underwent such extraordinary change, could yet remain 'the same'.

Chapter 1

'The Day Before Yesterday'

How far back do we have to go to find Jesus' origins? According to Micah, a very long way indeed: *'But you, O Bethlehem of Ephrathah, who are one of the little clans of Judah, from you shall come forth for me one who is to rule in Israel, whose origin is from of old, from ancient days'* (Micah 5:2). The word translated by the NRSV as 'ancient' is the Hebrew *olam*, which throughout the Old Testament refers to what lies beyond human reckoning of time, both future and past. Mostly translated in the KJV as 'ever' in the phrase 'for ever', it is also rendered as 'perpetual' and 'everlasting', notably in the phrase 'from everlasting to everlasting'. It is, of course, God, Yahweh, who is described in this way:

> Blessed be the LORD, the God of Israel, from everlasting to everlasting. (Psalm 41:13)

> Before the mountains were brought forth, or ever you had formed the earth and the world, from everlasting to everlasting you are God. (Psalm 90:2)

> ... your throne is established from of old; you are from everlasting. (Psalm 93:2)

> But the steadfast love of the LORD is from everlasting to everlasting on those who fear him, and his righteousness to children's children (Psalm 103:17)

Yet Micah uses this word in speaking of one who is yet to be, who 'shall come forth', and in a passage recognised by Israel, according to Matthew, as speaking of the coming Messiah. He is thus at once 'already' and 'not yet'.

We can perhaps understand this better if we look at Proverbs 8: *'The LORD created me at the beginning of his work, the first of his acts of long ago. Ages ago I was set up, at the first, before the beginning of the earth'* (v. 22-23). Here we again meet the word *olam* ('ages ago'). Trinitarian commentators have sometimes seen in this passage a parallel to John 1:1-3 and identified the speaker in this passage, 'wisdom', with the *logos* in John – and thus with the eternally pre-existent Son, as it is supposed. It is sufficient to notice that later in the same chapter God is said to have 'created' or 'brought forth' wisdom to disprove the notion of a 'co-eternity' of Father and Son asserted in the Athanasian Creed; the attribution to the *logos* of John 1:1 of an individual, personal identity is likewise contrary to the writer's intentions.[1]

The speaker in Proverbs 8 is clearly a personification of the abstract quality of wisdom, which in the preceding verses has been defined as the basis of a right relationship with God and right behaviour (v. 13) but also as prudence in practical affairs (v. 14-16) and as the source of prosperity and success in the world (v. 18-21). In the rest of the chapter, wisdom is traced back to God as its source, which probably means that it originates with him in the sense that he defines and embodies it, for it is described as present at, and even participating in, his work of creation (v. 27-30). 'Wisdom' is thus the essential quality of the 'plan' or 'creative intention' which God possessed before the creation was begun.

In this sense, these verses do indeed resemble the opening of John's Gospel: *'In the beginning was the word, and the word was with God, and the word was God'*. If we put these verses alongside Micah 5:2 we are led to the conclusion that the one who was later to be born, as Micah says, is part of this wisdom – indeed, that he is the content, or perhaps the very essence, of this wisdom, so that when he is born, that 'wisdom' (or the 'word') 'became flesh', as John goes on to say. The implication is clear: the entire creative intention of God is focused on a being already envisaged and thus present within the mind of God. He is as yet unborn but is later to be born at Bethlehem. In that sense, the words spoken about 'wisdom' later in the chapter can be seen as applicable to him too: *'appointed from eternity, from the beginning, before the world began'* (v. 23 NIV).

'In ... through ... by'

These passages in Micah and Proverbs were written hundreds of years before the birth of Jesus, but the ideas that they convey are confirmed in the passage in the New Testament which most clearly speaks of the relationship between Jesus and the creative purpose of God. In fact, they are not merely confirmed, but expanded and explained in the light of what Paul had come to understand about the Lord whom he worshipped:

> *He is the image of the invisible God, the firstborn of all creation; for in him all things in heaven and on earth were created, things visible and invisible, whether thrones or dominions or rulers or powers – all things have been*

---

1 I have sought to elucidate the Prologue of John's Gospel and particularly the meaning of *logos* in what I believe is a more scriptural sense in my *The Word Became Flesh*, pp. 108-134.

'The Day Before Yesterday'

created through him and for him. He himself is before all things, and in him all things hold together. (Colossians 1:15-17)

Leaving aside for a moment the two opening phrases of this complex passage, we need to consider the implications of the various prepositions used: 'in him' (*en*), 'through him' (*dia*), 'for him' (*eis*):

- The phrase 'in him all things … were created' takes us back to the origin of things: it seems to indicate that everything that God made owes its existence to its relationship to Jesus, as if all things were subordinate parts of a totality of which he is the centre and epitome. It is that relationship that 'justifies' or explains their existence. 'In Christ' is Paul's favourite way of speaking of the 'rationale' behind every action of God in the realisation of his purpose, as the opening of Ephesians illustrates:

  *Blessed be the God and Father of our Lord Jesus Christ, who has blessed us **in Christ** with every spiritual blessing in the heavenly places, just as he chose us **in Christ** before the foundation of the world to be holy and blameless before him in love. He destined us for adoption as his children through Jesus Christ, according to the good pleasure of his will, to the praise of his glorious grace that he freely bestowed on us **in the Beloved. In him** we have redemption through his blood, the forgiveness of our trespasses, according to the riches of his grace. (Ephesians 1:3-7)*

- 'Through him' might be said to suggest the *process* by which things come into being: it implies that everything had to be 'tried' in terms of its fitness for its place within the Christ-shaped whole and shaped by the requirements of that whole.

- The use of the preposition *eis* in the phrase 'for him' implies movement towards a goal: things first conceived in relation to Jesus and shaped by the aptness for the purpose to be achieved through him will finally achieve their destined place within the totality under him. Paul's use elsewhere of the image of the 'cornerstone' in Ephesians 2:20 reflects a similar idea: the cornerstone determines the angles and dimensions of the whole building.

So these three prepositional phrases comprehend a movement from an original conception via a progressive unfolding through to an ultimate realisation, with the as yet future Jesus Christ as the measure and decisive factor throughout.

There are two further New Testament passages that we need to consider

Jesus – yesterday, today, for ever

in relation to Paul's language in Colossians. In 1 Corinthians 8:6 Paul writes: *'yet for us there is one God, the Father, from whom are all things and for whom we exist, and one Lord, Jesus Christ, through whom are all things and through whom we exist'*. Catholic commentators in particular argue that there is here a

> … direct parallel between the "one God" the Father … and the "one Lord" Jesus and conclude that Jesus is not on the same side as "all" other created things. He is somehow on the Creator side of the dividing line. In the words of Joseph Fitzmyer, Jesus is here depicted by Paul as "the pre-existent mediator of creation".[2]

In support of that claim, the same writers urge that similar language to that used here about Jesus is used elsewhere about God: *'For from him and through him and to him are all things. To him be the glory forever. Amen.'* (Rom. 11:36). Yet here again it is instructive to look at the prepositions used. In 1 Corinthians 8, Paul says that all things are 'from (*ek*)' the Father, and that mankind, or perhaps the believers in Christ, are 'for (*eis*)' him, destined for him. By contrast, the sentence about Jesus uses twice the preposition *dia*. In the quotations from Romans, three prepositions are used: 'from' (*ek*), 'through' (*dia*), and 'to' (*eis*). That 'all things' can be said to be 'through' and 'for' both Father and Son is unproblematic and has no Trinitarian implications. The decisive point is the use of the preposition *ek*, which refers to a source – it is the preposition used, for example, in the genealogy of Jesus in Matthew 1 when the mother is referred to (v. 3, 5, 6, 16). Things can be 'through Christ' and also 'for Christ', in the sense that we have been suggesting – but they are not 'of Christ' in this sense of origins. He is not the source from which they come, and to which they owe their very existence. That is true of both the physical creation of heaven and earth and the new creation. Paul sums it up in 2 Corinthians: *'All this is from (ek) God, who reconciled us to himself through (dia) Christ'* (2 Cor. 5:18). In his first Letter, John repeatedly describes believers as 'born of [*ek*] God' (e.g. 1 John 4:7; 5:1).

A connection is also made between the as yet unborn Jesus and God's creative work in the opening verses of Hebrews, where the writer says that God 'appointed' Christ *'heir of all things, through whom he also created the worlds'* (Heb. 1:2). It is important to notice here that 'worlds' (or 'universe' in some translations) is actually a word concerned not with material things but with time, *aiōn*. The sense appears to be that the succession of ages, the stages in

---

2 Brant Pitre, Michael P. Barber, John A. Kincaid, Paul, *A New Covenant Jew*, Grand Rapids, Michigan, 2019, p. 119. The quotation from Joseph A. Fitzmyer is from his *First Corinthians*, AYB 32, New Haven, 2008, p. 343.

'The Day Before Yesterday'

the unfolding creative purpose of God, were shaped and directed in relation to the Son, who is to be the ultimate heir of 'all things'. So we encounter here the same sequence as in Colossians: 'in him' from the beginning through to 'for him' at the culmination. For good measure, the next verse corresponds to the 'through him' in Colossians: '*… he sustains all things by his powerful word. When he had made purification for sins, he sat down at the right hand of the Majesty on high …*' The entire movement from beginning to consummation is borne by him, specifically by his redeeming work in crucifixion.

It is, then, not hard to see that the passage in Colossians 1 is a more detailed expansion of Paul's words in Ephesians 1 that we quoted in the Introduction: '*to gather up all things in him, things in heaven and things on earth*'. But what of its opening, '*He is the image of the invisible God, the firstborn of all creation*'? The phrase 'the firstborn of all creation' confirms the line of thought that we have been exploring. The word 'firstborn' (*protōtokos*) can obviously refer to priority in time and in many cases does. From this, some have concluded that Jesus existed before all the other works of God's hands – though this view has, for those who think in this way, the unfortunate consequence that he is seen as 'created', a notion which they strenuously deny. Yet it is apparent throughout the Bible that to be 'the firstborn' was not a matter of simple priority in time: it also implied a position as privileged heir of the father's authority and the right to a 'double portion' of his possessions. In several striking cases it is not the firstborn in a temporal sense that accedes to this position: Isaac is preferred to Ishmael, Jacob to Esau, and Ephraim to Manasseh, while Joseph is elevated above a whole set of elder brothers. In a similar fashion, God simply designates Israel as his firstborn (Exodus 4:22); when he does the same for David, the language has obvious Messianic overtones: '*He shall cry to me, "You are my Father, my God, and the Rock of my salvation!" I will make him the firstborn, the highest of the kings of the earth*' (Ps. 89:26-27). So Paul's words in Colossians give no grounds for thinking that Jesus must have in some way pre-existed the rest of the creation: Paul is referring to the pre-eminence over all of the creation that God has conferred on him – everything is indeed 'through him' and 'for him', as v. 16 says.

'The image of the invisible God'

But what of the opening phrase, 'the image (*eikōn*) of the invisible God'? The notion of 'image' carries at least three complementary meanings:

- *Resemblance:* Jesus faithfully reflects the character and the intentions of God. As Hebrews puts it, he is '*the reflection of God's glory and the exact imprint of God's very being*' (Heb. 1:3); Jesus himself says simply: '*Whoever has seen me has seen the Father'* (John 14:9).

- *Manifestation*: Jesus reveals the otherwise invisible God to mankind. Paul puts it like this: *'For it is the God who said, "Let light shine out of darkness," who has shone in our hearts to give the light of the knowledge of the glory of God in the face of Jesus Christ'* (2 Cor. 4:6). God brings his Son into being not for himself only but as a means to make himself known to other human beings. The implication is that he desires more 'children' than this one.

- *Representation*: Jesus represents God – in two ways. First, all that had been in the mind of God as idea and purpose, to use our human terms, is now expressed in outward, visible form in the 'language' of the created world, in 'flesh', as John puts it. Secondly, as his unique Son, His 'one and only' as John describes him (John 1:14),[3] he is to share and to exercise the authority of the Creator over the rest of his creation.

The verses in Colossians that we have been considering were written, of course, with hindsight, as Paul reflects on what he has come to know and understand about the Jesus who appeared to him on the road to Damascus. The language of v. 16-17 links Jesus to the intimations that we find in the Old Testament about God's ultimate purpose and the role in it of one yet to be born. This suggests that v. 15 too points to the divine intentions that lay behind and preceded the creative work of God.

How, then, should we read the following verses in Paul's argument?

He is the head of the body, the church; he is the beginning, the firstborn from the dead, so that he might come to have first place in everything. For in him all the fullness of God was pleased to dwell... (Colossians 1:18-19)

Some commentators read this as a restatement of the previous verses and conclude that v. 15-17 too refer to the 'new creation', of which Jesus is in an obvious sense the 'firstborn'. Yet why would Paul repeat himself in this way? And why, in particular, would he repeat that Jesus is the 'firstborn'? It seems altogether more likely that the opening word 'and' implies a logical consequence or confirmation of what has already been said: that the position that Jesus holds in the 'new creation', of which his own resurrection is indeed the 'beginning', reflects his central position within the larger overarching purpose of God from its beginning, before all time, in the mind of God. For, as Paul

---

3 This, rather than 'only begotten', is almost certainly the meaning of *monogenes* in all its New Testament occurrences (John 1:14, 18; 3:16, 18; Heb. 11:17; 1 John 4:9).

'The Day Before Yesterday'

says, if he is pre-eminent in relation to the totality of created things, then, *a fortiori*, he must also have the 'first place' in the new creation – who but he could hold such a place? And on the other hand, Jesus' present pre-eminence demands that we grasp and recognise his centrality in God's entire purpose from the very beginning of things. The final sentence, v. 19, confirms what we have already understood to be the sense of the phrase 'image of the invisible God': that everything that God is is displayed in Jesus.

'Before the foundation of the world'

All that we have said so far is extremely general in nature, asserting simply that everything that God purposed to make and to do since the beginning was to find its meaning in the one who was to come, whom we now know to be Jesus. But do the scriptural passages that look back to this time 'before the foundation of the world' permit us to say anything more detailed about what the coming one was to be like – what he was to do and be, and therefore also what the goal and purpose of God's vast creative undertaking was?

The phrase 'before (or 'from') the foundation of the world' occurs ten times in the New Testament – the word for 'foundation' in all these cases is not *themelios*, a 'foundation' in a structural sense, as in Jesus' parable of the houses built on rock or sand (Matt. 7:24-27), but rather *katabolē*, which re-fers to a beginning in time, the initial action in starting to build. Two of these passages, Matthew 13:35 and Luke 11:50, simply confirm the idea that there was such a pre-determined divine intent. The others, though, shed light on the 'content' of the divine purpose – in two or three ways. First, and most explicit, are Peter's words in 1 Peter:

> *You know that you were ransomed from the futile ways inherited from your ancestors, not with perishable things like silver or gold, but with the pre-cious blood of Christ, like that of a lamb without defect or blemish. He was destined **before the foundation of the world**, but was revealed at the end of the ages for your sake. (1 Peter 1:18-20)*

Given the preceding verse, the natural sense of the final sentence is that be-fore the foundation of the world the purpose of God involved the need for a 'redemption' of men and women, and that this redemption would in some way depend on the death of Jesus. This has, of course, momentous implica-tions for our understanding of God's eternal purpose: first, that the process of redemption and restoration through Christ was no 'plan B', invented after the original intention was frustrated by the failure of men and women to fulfil their part, as the story of Eden in Genesis 3 explains. On the contrary, the 'fall' of mankind was itself foreknown and allowed for from the beginning –

Jesus – yesterday, today, for ever

but so was God's redemptive grace by which that failure was to be overcome. Paul's survey of 'salvation history' in Romans 11 concludes with an insight that confirms this understanding; his outburst of praise in the next two verses aptly sums up how extraordinary, by human standards, this gracious purpose was and is:

> *For God has imprisoned all in disobedience so that he may be merciful to all. O the depth of the riches and wisdom and knowledge of God! How unsearchable are his judgments and how inscrutable his ways! 'For who has known the mind of the Lord? Or who has been his counsellor?' (Romans 11:32-34)*

The route from 'beginning' through to the consummation was from the first destined to include what might look like a 'detour' via a fall and a restoration – but one in which all mankind would be finally knit together with God neither as slaves, nor as deserving high-achievers able to boast of their performance, but as loving children of a gracious father.

A second implication is that the one 'in whom' and 'for whom' all things were created, was not only destined to have 'first place' above everything else but also for a time to take last place, giving himself sacrificially so that others might finally be incorporated into the fully realised divine purpose. This helps to explain, and gives additional point to, the idea that we have seen in Colossians that everything was to be 'through' him.

Thirdly, if we go back to the words of Peter, quoted above, we notice the references to 'you': though God's purpose focused on the one through whom everything was to be realised, yet it visualised from the beginning, or even before the beginning, a whole family of creatures who would be drawn into and share in that final realisation. We find the same idea expressed in several places in the New Testament:

> *Come, you that are blessed by my Father, inherit the kingdom prepared for you **from the foundation of the world**. (Matthew 25:34)*

> *… he chose us in Christ **before the foundation of the world** to be holy and blameless before him in love. (Ephesians 1:4)*

> *This grace was given to us in Christ Jesus **before the ages began.** (2 Timothy 1:9)*

Two verses in Revelation may be added to this list:

'The Day Before Yesterday'

> *... everyone whose name has not been written **from the foundation of the world** in the book of life of the Lamb that was slaughtered. (Revelation 13:8)*

> *And the inhabitants of the earth, whose names have not been written in the book of life **from the foundation of the world** ... (Revelation 17:8)*

Translations of 13:8 vary according to whether the phrase 'from the foundation of the world' is deemed to qualify the phrase 'written in the book of life of the lamb' or 'that was slaughtered'; the parallel with 17:8, where the slaughter of the Lamb is not mentioned, seems to confirm that the first of these readings is the right one. But this very uncertainty aptly illustrates how inextricably the role of Jesus involves and incorporates in him many others. In these passages, the phrase 'before the foundation of the world' implies a kind of 'predestination', but with the focus not on the question: '*who* is predestined?', but rather on '*to what* are they predestined?'. The answer is perhaps best expressed by Paul in Romans: '*For those whom he foreknew he also predestined to be conformed to the image of his Son, in order that he might be the firstborn within a large family* [or: *among many brothers*]' (Romans 8:29). Since the Son represents the epitome of the whole and is instrumental in its realisation, it is natural that he should also be the pattern for each individual who is included within it.

It is noticeable that the language of these New Testament passages that refer to Jesus as foreknown has become markedly 'warmer' and more intimate as we have progressed. The last one that we have to consider forms in that respect also an appropriate climax:

> *Father, I desire that those also, whom you have given me, may be with me where I am, to see my glory, which you have given me because you loved me **before the foundation of the world**. (John 17:24)*

In God's foreknowledge, even before the world existed, the one who would be central to everything that he would do was not merely his instrument for the achievement of his purpose: he was already 'loved' – delighted in as one with whom God could share a relationship of mutual love, one who would reflect his own being and thereby draw others into that relationship. The prayer in John 17, in which these words occur, is the supreme example of this process taking place, as Jesus permits his disciples to glimpse that relationship from the inside and thus to be initiated into it.

What Jesus says here in John 17 about himself helps us to grasp the implications of John's language elsewhere in his Gospel: it is no mere linguistic gesture when John writes: 'For God so loved the world that he gave his one and only Son, that whoever believes in him shall not perish but have eternal life' (John 3:16 NIV).[4] The words imply a personal love on God's part, analogous somehow to that of a human parent for his or her child, however hard we may find it to ascribe such emotion to the eternal, omnipotent Creator. Similarly, the phrase 'one and only Son' in this verse and in John 1:14 and 18, points to God's delight in his future son, even 'before the foundation of the world'.

Our look at passages in Old and New Testaments has, I hope, helped us to see the centrality of Jesus in everything that God has created and has done. As the Father 'imagined' him, to use the language of human planning and envisioning, he was the very essence and epitome of the whole, so that everything was made and done 'in him', deriving its meaning from him. He is also the decisive means through which the purpose is worked out and reaches its fulfilment; and it is also 'in him' that everything will finally cohere in a harmonious totality that will fully reflect and give glory to God, its 'architect'. None of this required his pre-existence in the conventional sense – indeed, to posit that he was personally present from the beginning, or even before the beginning, is to reduce the extraordinary, perilous process by which the consummation will finally be attained to a charade. For how can it be 'in him' and 'through him' if he stands apart from the whole, from all eternity God, as the creeds of Nicea and Athanasius alike assert?

A shared identity?

There is, however, one passage in the Letter to the Hebrews that is widely understood to proclaim the 'co-authorship', as it were, of Jesus in the act of creation. In chapter 1 the writer declares the superiority of Jesus over the angels of God, quoting two Old Testament passages in support of his argument:

> Of the angels he says, 'He makes his angels winds, and his servants flames of fire.' But of the Son he says, 'Your throne, O God, is forever and ever, and the righteous sceptre is the sceptre of your kingdom. You have loved righteousness and hated wickedness; therefore God, your God, has anointed you with the oil of gladness beyond your companions.' And, 'In the beginning, Lord, you founded the earth, and the heavens are the work of your hands; they will perish, but you remain; they will all wear out like clothing; like a cloak you will roll them up, and like clothing they will be changed. But you are the same, and your years will never end.' (Hebrews 1:7-12, quoting Psalm 45:6-7 and Psalm 102:25-27)

---

4 The Greek *monogenēs*, translated here as 'one and only', does not mean 'only begotten', as rendered by the KJV and some other versions.

'The Day Before Yesterday'

The first of these two quotations presents no difficulty: it says that Jesus has been anointed and glorified – in other words, he has acceded to a status and a glory which he previously did not possess – for a specific reason: *because* he 'loved righteousness'. It thus emphasises that Jesus has attained to a position that was always his by 'birthright' but that he has achieved only now.

The second quotation, however, introduced with no further explanation and therefore apparently also relating to Jesus, appears to describe him as somehow a co-participant in God's work of creation itself. To some ears, that assertion might sound like a confirmation of the traditional Trinitarian conception of Jesus, which, at least in its most extreme formulation in the so-called Athanasian Creed, describes him as 'coeternal and coequal':

> ... The Father uncreated; the Son uncreated; and the Holy Ghost uncreated. The Father unlimited; the Son unlimited; and the Holy Ghost unlimited. The Father eternal; the Son eternal; and the Holy Ghost eternal.

Yet the New Testament knows nothing of such notions. Not only do its birth narratives of Jesus declare him to have a beginning, but more importantly still, its entire message turns on the fact that Jesus has been subject to change. In Hebrews itself, we find in chapter 1 the following: *'When he had made purification for sins, he sat down at the right hand of the Majesty on high, having* **become** *as much superior to angels as the name he has inherited is more excellent than theirs'* (v. 3-4). The same thought is found in the next chapter too: *'... we do see Jesus, who* **for a little while** *was made lower than the angels,* **now** *crowned with glory and honour'* (2:9). Far from sharing the eternal, timeless being of God, Jesus has been subject to change, from one form of existence to another – the very presence of the word 'become' signals the difference: Jesus *becomes*, but the father *is*.[5] If Jesus' exaltation was pre-ordained – as Hebrews 1:4 indicates, Jesus 'became' what he was destined to be, with his 'name' or title, 'son', taking on its full, latent meaning through his glorification – then there exists a kind of continuity between before and after, despite the radical discontinuity implied by the change that he underwent through his resurrection. But that is very different from the changelessness of the Father's eternal being.

In what sense, then, can the writer apply the words of Psalm 102 to Jesus, as he appears to do? The simplest way is to understand these words as Colossians 1 has taught us to: that Jesus is somehow involved in God's creative work, not

---

5 This transformation, from a lower mortal condition to godlike immortality, is also spoken of elsewhere: *'God put this power to work in Christ when he raised him from the dead and seated him at his right hand in the heavenly places ...'* (Eph. 1:20)

as active agent but as model and guiding principle. However, we can perhaps understand these verses better by thinking about them in terms of 'identity'. New Testament writers often apply to Jesus Old Testament words that originally referred, quite unequivocally, to the Father; it is as though the identity of the Father is extended to encompass the Son, so that what may be said of the Father can also be attributed to the Son. One obvious example is found in Philippians, where the title 'Lord' is applied to Jesus in Paul's re-reading of Isaiah 45:23:

Therefore God also highly exalted him and gave him the name that is above every name, so that at the name of Jesus every knee should bend, in heaven and on earth and under the earth, and every tongue should confess that Jesus Christ is Lord, to the glory of God the Father. (Philippians 2:9-11)

This sharing of divine titles is common in the New Testament. Thus, for example, in Revelation 1 we find: *'"I am the Alpha and the Omega," says the Lord God, who is and who was and who is to come, the Almighty'* (1:8); but in Revelation 22 Jesus is recorded as saying: *'See, I am coming soon; my reward is with me, to repay according to everyone's work. I am the Alpha and the Omega, the first and the last, the beginning and the end'* (22:12-13). These words identify the Son with the Father, while at the same time omitting the words which distinguish God from any other. So here in Hebrews, the writer is suggesting that Jesus, now sharing the title of 'Lord' with his Father, is caught up in his eternal purpose in a way that lifts him out of the time-bound physical creation – or possibly the temporary nature of the old covenant and of all human institutions (see Heb. 8:13; 2 Cor. 5:17; Rev. 6:12-14). We see the same extension of identity in operation when Paul applies to himself words originally written about the 'Servant' in Isaiah, i.e. about Jesus:

Then both Paul and Barnabas spoke out boldly, saying, 'It was necessary that the word of God should be spoken first to you. Since you reject it and judge yourselves to be unworthy of eternal life, we are now turning to the Gentiles. For so the Lord has commanded us, saying, "I have set you to be a light for the Gentiles, so that you may bring salvation to the ends of the earth."' (Acts 13:46-47)

A simple illustration from the book of Ruth may perhaps be helpful: the Moabitess Ruth says to her future husband Boaz: '... *spread your cloak over your servant, for you are next-of-kin'* (Ruth 3:9). 'Cloak' translates the Hebrew *kanaph*, which in all but about 20 of its 108 occurrences in the Old Testament refers to the wings of a bird or of the cherubim – that is how the NRSV

'The Day Before Yesterday'

translates it in the preceding chapter: *'... the God of Israel, under whose **wings** you have come for refuge!'* (Ruth 2:12). Ruth, a foreigner in Israel and in today's terms something like an immigrant, perhaps even an asylum-seeker, first finds a new identity in Israel by embracing its faith in Yahweh, exchanging her identity of pagan idol-worshipper for membership of Israel; henceforth she will be identified with the God of Israel. Then her status as childless widow and poor seeker of refuge is exchanged for that of wife of the obviously wealthy Boaz. Henceforth, she shares in Boaz' status: what he is, she is – like his cloak, his identity has been 'spread out' and extended to encompass her.

It is this way of thinking, foreign to a modern Western mind, that enables us to grasp how the writer to the Hebrews can quote Psalm 102 in relation to Jesus without implying any *personal* pre-existence of Jesus. From the resurrection and glorification, when he 'went to the Father' (cf. John 13-17 *passim*), he, as the first of many, is taken up into this widened divine identity. That is why Micah is able to say of the coming one that his *'origin is from of old, from ancient days'* (5:2). Jesus himself adopts a similar way of speaking in John 8, when he shocks his adversaries with the statement: *'Very truly, I tell you, before Abraham was, I am'* (John 8:58). Puzzling as we may find this notion of a shared identity, yet it in fact reflects the fundamental principle of the whole of God's work and his ultimate intention for the world. Zechariah's final picture of Jerusalem includes this detail:

> On that day there shall be inscribed on the bells of the horses, 'Holy to the LORD.' And the cooking pots in the house of the LORD shall be as holy as the bowls in front of the altar; and every cooking pot in Jerusalem and Judah shall be sacred to the LORD of hosts. (Zechariah 14:20-21)

God draws everything in the city, even such menial items, into his being – it is what an earth filled with God's glory implies. Its fullest realisation is summed up in Paul's phrase in 1 Corinthians 15: *'... that God may be all in all'* (1 Cor. 15:28).

Our survey of the relatively few passages in Old and New Testaments that refer to Jesus' place in God's purpose from 'before the foundation of the world' has shown that the New Testament writers, building on the various hints and intimations in the Old Testament and reflecting on their knowledge and experience of Jesus, not only grasped how fundamental Jesus was and is to the whole purpose of God, but also recognised that his suffering, death and resurrection are at the heart of it. Jesus' disciples had at first been quite unable to understand that the *'Christ of God'* (Luke 9:20) must suffer; the travellers to Emmaus spoke for them all in expressing their disappointment at what

Jesus – yesterday, today, for ever

they thought was a fatal blow to all their hopes: '... *we had hoped that he was the one to redeem Israel'* (Luke 24:21). But with the help of Jesus' repeated insistence (Luke 24:26, 44, 46), they came to realise that his death was, on the contrary, necessary. Nothing had gone wrong: the extraordinary shift from crucifixion to resurrection was in fact the vital, defining moment in '*the whole purpose of God'* (Acts 20:27).

With hindsight, of course, they and we realise that it could not be otherwise. The eternal God was not likely to have been 'making it up as he went along'. An event so unparalleled and momentous as the resurrection of Jesus must have been the decisive turning point in God's purpose, and Jesus himself must therefore always have been the focus and key to everything that God had done and would do. That realisation found confirmation in the new creation that emerged from Jesus' resurrection: his central position in the church was seen to confirm and to illustrate his role as the focus of the old creation, as we saw in Colossians 1. But it did more than that: it foreshadowed his central, unifying position in the as yet future unified and perfected creation towards which God is working and that Paul foresees in our quotation from Ephesians 1:9-10.

I referred in the Introduction to the fact that my title echoes the language of Hebrews 13:8: '*Jesus Christ is the same yesterday and today and forever'*. But how could the writer assert that Jesus who 'became', as we saw in Hebrews 1, could 'remain the same' across all ages? We have already noted that it cannot be a matter of an unchanging nature, i.e. of a form of life and a mode of being that remains constant throughout, or even of an unchanging kind of relationship to others, for Jesus passes from mortality to immortality and from humiliation to glory. Nor can the continuity be simply one of character and disposition, for he possesses these only from the time of his birth – or even from his coming to adult consciousness – important though that continuity is from then on, as our consideration of Hebrews 13:8 showed. Thinking about Jesus from 'before the foundation of the world' perhaps provides the answer: what unites all these phases in Jesus' 'career' is his place in the overarching purpose of God – the role that he fulfils and the things that are achieved through him – in order that the goal that Paul sets out in Ephesians might finally be achieved.

Chapter 2

Jesus in the Old Testament

Since the time of the apostles, Christians have proclaimed that Jesus' earthly life was anticipated and foreshadowed in the Old Testament. From the first century until the present time, writers and scholars have drawn attention to Old Testament texts that they believe to be relevant to Jesus.[1] The publisher's blurb inside the front cover of the more recent of the two books by Richard Hays mentioned in footnote 1 (below) sums up the prevailing opinion: 'The claim that the events of Jesus' life, death, and resurrection took place "according to the Scriptures" stands at the heart of the New Testament's message.'

It is obviously not my intention here to consider all the links between Jesus and the Old Testament that have been suggested by others – that would be neither possible nor desirable. I hope rather to consider which elements of Jesus' life and significance are foreshadowed in the Old Testament and in what form are they represented there – in other words, to see whether, how far, and in what way Jesus is present in the 'yesterday' of the Old Testament. Of necessity, this will have to be done in rather summary fashion; however, that brief overview will be book-ended by a more detailed look at two of the most important anticipations of Jesus – Adam at the beginning, and Isaiah's 'Servant' at the end.

However, I should also like to reflect on some questions that are seldom asked, as far as I am aware – the fact that there are such links between Old and New Testaments seems largely to be taken for granted. What kind of reading process is it that enables readers of the Old Testament to find there so many anticipations of the life and ministry of Jesus? Why is it that the Old Testament seems to lend itself to such a way of reading? And how does the

---

1 Recent works of this kind include the following: G.K. Beale and D.A. Carson (eds.), *Commentary on the New Testament Use of the Old Testament*, Grand Rapids, Michigan/Nottingham 2007, and three works by Richard B. Hays: *Echoes of Scripture in the Letters of Paul*, New Haven/London 1989; *Reading Backwards*, Waco, Texas 2014/ London 2015; and *Echoes of Scripture in the Gospels*, Waco, Texas 2016.

Jesus – yesterday, today, for ever

presentation of Jesus in the Old Testament that Christians claim to find there relate to our consideration in the previous chapter of his place within the purpose of God since 'before the foundation of the world'? Any answers that one may give, particularly to the second of these questions, will inevitably be tentative, even speculative, for these are questions that are not really considered in the scriptures themselves. In suggesting even such tentative answers I shall therefore be attempting, as it were, to second-guess the divine intentions behind this feature of them. Nevertheless, reflection on these questions can, I think, help us in our attempts to understand the place of Jesus in God's purpose, and perhaps even to know God better – and that is ultimately the goal of all biblical study.

Jesus and Adam

Our search for Jesus in the Old Testament in fact begins in its opening pages, in the story of the creation and of Adam. That is not surprising: the account of creation, especially as we find it in Genesis 1, is, after all, the first stage in the realisation of the *'good pleasure that he set forth in Christ'* before the foundation of the world which we have been considering. If we approach these chapters of Genesis bearing in mind what we noted earlier about God's intentions, we can scarcely fail to be struck by the correspondence with what is said about Jesus in the passages that we looked at previously.

- Like Jesus, Adam was made 'in the image of God' (Gen. 1:26, cf. Col. 1:15), the visible expression of God. The narrative of Genesis 1 suggests that, having made all the other living creatures, all capable of producing their young 'after their kind', the Creator himself wished to have beings that would in some quite unique ways be like *him*. Unlike the animals, though, each generation of which is similar to the preceding one, the man and woman that God created did not and could not share his unique divine power, so they could not be 'after his kind'. But they could be 'in his image' in their moral and spiritual nature; this is how the divine family was to 'be fruitful and multiply' (Genesis 1:28) – not by genetic or biological means, but by learning to know and understand God through his words and actions and by seeking to be like him. In the New Testament, the same fundamental process is in view, though now their likeness with God was to be arrived at primarily through their encounter with Jesus and through seeking to be like him, as he was like God.

- As well as being in a literal sense the 'firstborn of all creation', Adam [i.e. the first man and woman] was destined to be God's representative on earth. The unique creature 'man' that God had created was to *'have dominion'*

Jesus in the Old Testament

over all the other creatures, on behalf of the Creator, acting as his 'steward' in caring for the world that God had made – or at least, to care for one small part of it during what was presumably some kind of 'probationary period' (Gen. 1:26-28).

- In a sense, therefore, everything that God had made was 'in him', 'through him' and 'for him' in the way that we considered in chapter 1: Adam was the creation that was to give the rest of God's world its point and meaning. He alone could respond consciously to the Creator and reflect him back to himself so that the world could become *'filled with the knowledge of the glory of God'* (Habakkuk 2:14). Accordingly, everything was made so as to reflect this unique creature. The notion of the 'Goldilocks' zone, i.e. that the earth is uniquely habitable for mankind, is testimony to this profound consonance between these human creatures and the world that God had made for them.

- Man's failure to fulfil the role that is ascribed to him in chapter 1, presented in the form of the Eden story in Genesis 3, might appear to represent also the failure of the entire purpose of which he is the centre, yet we have already noted that this apparent setback was from before the beginning anticipated. As we saw in Chapter 1, Peter wrote that Jesus was destined before the foundation of the world to die like a sacrificial lamb so that human beings might be *'ransomed from the futile ways inherited from [their] ancestors'* (1 Pet. 1:18). If, then, the statements in Genesis 1 about God's unique human creation are to be realised, that must be achieved through a new, a counter-Adam, or as the New Testament puts it, the *'last Adam'* (1 Cor. 15:45).

The link between Adam and Jesus, as between foreshadowing and reality, was clearly recognised by the writers of the New Testament. Luke traces the genealogy of Jesus back to Adam, whom he describes as the *'son of God'* (Luke 3:38), while Paul draws explicit parallels and contrasts between the two, in 1 Corinthians, mentioned above, and also in Romans 5. A probable third such parallel and contrast also occurs in Philippians: *'Christ Jesus ... though he was in the form of God, did not count equality with God a thing to be grasped, but emptied himself, taking the form of a servant, being born in the likeness of men'* (Philippians 2:6-7) – the phrase 'the form (*morphe*) of God' is probably an echo of the Genesis expression 'in the image of God'.[2]

---

2   It has come to be understood, even by many theologians of a Trinitarian persuasion, that these words should be read and understood, not in relation to some imagined divine

Jesus – yesterday, today, for ever

Son of man

It seems highly likely that Jesus too was hinting at this relationship by his choice of the term 'son of man' when referring to himself – it occurs 69 times in the Synoptic Gospels and a further 12 times in the Gospel of John. Just what does this much-discussed expression mean, and why did Jesus choose to use it so frequently? In his treatment of this phrase, Oscar Cullman makes three important points:

- The Greek phrase in the New Testament *ho uios tou anthrōpou* is derived from the Aramaic *barnasha*.

- The first element in this word, *bar* (son), 'is very often used in a figurative sense. For "liar" the Aramaic idiom is "son of the lie"; sinners are "sons of sin"; a wealthy man is a "son of wealth". The genitive in the construct state following *bar* thus designates the classification to which one belongs.'[3]

- 'Accordingly, *barnasha* refers to one who belongs to the human classification; that is, it means simply 'man'.'[4]

The phrase therefore suggests one who is in some way the quintessential man, one who sums up in himself the whole of humanity and their destiny. And since Adam was and is in a Biblical context that essential man, Jesus' use of the expression 'son of man' makes the link between himself and Adam obvious. For Jesus' contemporaries who had some knowledge of the Old Testament, that link must have been still more obvious, for its Hebrew equivalent is *ben adam*, which occurs over 100 times in the Old Testament, all but about 15 of them in Ezekiel.

The title 'son of man' thus brings together the two prototypes of humanity, the one the model of our collective and individual failure, the other the model or 'firstborn' of the realised intention of God. The parallel and correspondence

status of a pre-existent Jesus prior to his birth, but rather in the Adamic context. For an example of a commentator coming to this understanding, see James D.G. Dunn's *Christology in the Making*, 2nd edition, London 1989, pp. 114-121 (part of a chapter entitled 'The Last Adam').

It is perhaps not without significance that in their recent book on Paul, three Catholic scholars dismiss this 'Adamic' reading of Philippians 2 as 'ultimately unconvincing'. They completely ignore the prominent place of Adam in Paul's writings in Romans 5 and 1 Corinthians 15; a link to Adam would sit ill with their preferred view of Christ as pre-existent and 'God' – see Brant Pitre, Michael P. Barber, John A. Kincaid, *Paul, A New Covenant Jew*, pp. 105-107.

3 Oscar Cullman, *The Christology of the New Testament*, London 1959, p. 138.

4 *Ibid.*

Jesus in the Old Testament

between the two that the New Testament highlights consist, however, almost entirely in their dissimilarity. In Romans 5 Paul points up the parallel, but it is one in which Jesus is the positive to Adam's negative:

> *Yet death exercised dominion from Adam to Moses, even over those whose sins were not like the transgression of Adam, who is **a type of the one who was to come**. But the free gift is **not like** the trespass. For if the many died through the one man's trespass, much more surely have the grace of God and the free gift in the grace of the one man, Jesus Christ, abounded for the many. (Romans 5:14-15)*

The same is the case in 1 Corinthians also:

> *For since death came through a human being, the resurrection of the dead has also come through a human being; for as all die in Adam, so all will be made alive in Christ. (1 Corinthians 15:21-22)*

> *'The first man, Adam, became a living being'; the last Adam became a life-giving spirit … The first man was from the earth, a man of dust; the second man is from heaven. (1 Corinthians 15:45, 47)*

Paul's language, setting a fallen man over against a life-giving one, here confirms something that we recognised in Chapter 1: that the realisation of God's purpose in creation would be achieved via a detour through failure and fall, and that the coming one would be not only its head and crown but also the vital means by which the goal would be attained – the phrase 'through him' in Colossians 1:16 may well have just this sense. Jesus' choice of the title 'son of man' is an indication of the depth of his understanding of God's purpose and of his own role within it.

However, the 'son of man' title does more than simply point to the parallel between Jesus and Adam: it contains within itself an indication of the process by which God's intention for his creation is to be achieved, notwithstanding the seeming disaster of Eden. Two Old Testament passages are of decisive importance for our understanding of this, one in Psalm 8 and the other in Daniel 7. Daniel's vision of the 'son of man' in the second of these sees him as what one may think of as the climax of the historical process; his appearance is preceded by the appearance of forms symbolising four human regimes, probably representative of all human regimes, a winged lion, a bear with tusks, a winged leopard, and finally one of indeterminate species but *'terrifying and dreadful and exceedingly strong'* (v. 7). The fact that supposedly human societies are represented not merely by beasts, but by beasts that bear no resemblance to actual creatures found in the natural world, emphasises how far removed such kingdoms were and are from the order of the world as God created it and intended it. So far was and is the human race fallen from the noble status for which it was made.

However, the state of things in which such terrible beasts may flourish is not for ever; finally, they are judged and found wanting. And then a 'son of man' figure is brought before God's judgment seat and is granted *'domin-ion and glory and kingship, that all peoples, nations, and languages should serve him'* (v. 14). We easily recognise this as the realisation of God's eternal pur-pose, when, as we saw in Chapter 1, all things are finally 'for' the coming one. However, it is also the realisation of God's creative intentions for humanity, as they are declared in Genesis 1. For though the 'son of man' appears at first to be an individual, later verses in Daniel 7 speak of him as a people: *'the holy ones of the Most High'* (v. 18, 22) and *'the people of the holy ones of the Most High'* (v. 27). Regrettably, this link to Adam is frequently ignored in critical discussion of this passage, often in favour of later Jewish speculation about a 'heavenly man' who descends to earth – this despite the obvious link with the all-too earthly creature, man.[5]

It is, however, Psalm 8 that provides the most complete understanding of what 'son of man' means, or at least implies. Significantly, the entire psalm is a meditation on the meaning of Genesis 1 and especially of God's determina-tion that the human beings that he has created should 'have dominion' over God's earthly creation. In the psalmist's eyes, man is puny and insignificant by comparison with the beauty and magnificence of the heavens: *'When I look at your heavens, the work of your fingers, the moon and the stars that you have established; what are human beings that you are mindful of them, mortals [liter-ally 'the son of man/Adam']* that you care for them'? (v. 3-4). Yet, he says, God has made them

> ... *a little lower than God, and crowned them with glory and honour. You have given them dominion over the works of your hands; you have put all things under their feet, all sheep and oxen, and also the beasts of the field, the birds of the air, and the fish of the sea, whatever passes along the paths of the seas.* (v. 5-8)

The psalmist is, in effect, asking how it can possibly be that human beings can ever attain to, or be worthy of, the honour and the authority that the words of Genesis appear to destine them for. The answer to that question comes when the writer to the Hebrews re-reads the psalm in the light of Jesus:

---

5 One example is John Ashton's *Understanding the Fourth Gospel*, Oxford 1991, pp. 337-368.

Jesus in the Old Testament

> *Now God did not subject **the coming world**, about which we are speaking, to angels. But someone has testified somewhere, 'What are human beings that you are mindful of them, or mortals, that you care for them? You have made them **for a little while** lower than the angels; you have crowned them with glory and honour, subjecting all things under their feet.' Now in subjecting all things to them, God left nothing outside their control. As it is, we do **not yet** see everything in subjection to them, but we do see Jesus, who **for a little while was made** lower than the angels, **now** crowned with glory and honour because of the suffering of death, so that by the grace of God he might taste death for everyone. (Hebrews 2:5-9)*

The writer makes one essential move in his reading of the psalm: he introduces into it the element of *time*: instead of being an essentially static statement about the world and mankind, the psalm acquires a prophetic dimension. This is seen at two key points: first, his introduction to the quotation relates it to 'the coming world', i.e. the fully realised world envisaged in God's creative purpose. Secondly, he interprets the Greek *brachus* ('a little') in v. 7 and v. 9 in a temporal sense, enabling him to discern three separate time levels: a past when Jesus 'was made lower than the angels' (v. 9), a 'now', when he is 'crowned with glory and honour' (v. 8, 9), and a future which is 'not yet' (v. 8), when all things will be 'put under him'.[6]

The writer to the Hebrews thus re-reads Psalm 2 as a highly compressed summary of Jesus' progress from human lowliness, via the abasement of crucifixion, to his present exaltation and his future rulership, i.e. 'yesterday, today and for ever'. He also implies that Jesus is the ultimate realisation of God's statement about man in Genesis 1: he is the kind of man that God had had in mind and had desired Adam to be, one who would be like himself and be part of the divine family. So far, he is also the only one, but the final clause makes clear that the course which his existence takes, from lowliness to glory, is not his alone, and not only *for* him: it is the means by which others too may escape from the humiliation brought about by sin and achieve instead the destiny envisaged in Genesis 1 – the 'through him' of Colossians 1 is again brought to mind.

Adam thus forms the link between Jesus as we encounter him in the New Testament and what we have seen in the previous chapter about the intentions

---

6   Of the five other occurrences of *brachus* in the New Testament, apart from the two here, one is used in a similar temporal sense: in Luke's narrative of Peter's denial, we find: '*A little later someone else, on seeing him, said, "You also are one of them." But Peter said, "Man, I am not!"*' (Luke 22:58)

that lay behind the creation. However, the relationship between Adam and Jesus is in one important sense different from all the others that we shall be considering: the New Testament writers recognise a parallel between them, as we have seen, but a parallel in which there is no resemblance, only contrast. Elsewhere, their writings invoke, or at least evoke, the Old Testament scriptures because they recognise some likeness, however incomplete. There may be other Old Testament figures who are entirely unlike Jesus, as Adam is, but none of them is brought into direct relationship with him.

It is not difficult to see why Adam is exceptional in this respect: the narrative of Biblical history, more specifically of 'salvation history', begins with Abraham. The preceding eleven chapters of Genesis comprise essentially a series of disasters resulting from the one great disaster of Eden. N.T. Wright describes Abraham and his family as 'the Creator's means of dealing with the sin of Adam, and hence with the evil in the world':

> Abraham emerges within the structure of Genesis as the answer to the plight of all human kind. The line of disaster and of the 'curse', from Adam, through Cain, through the Flood to Babel, begins to be reversed when God calls Abraham and says 'in you shall all the families of the earth be blessed'.[7]

We can therefore hardly expect to find any glimmerings of hope in the one with whom that disastrous course of events began.

Where else do we recognise Jesus in the Old Testament?

Our treatment of the rest of the Old Testament, with the exception of Isaiah's 'Servant', is inevitably brief. The following list includes aspects of Jesus' life and experience, far too numerous and varied to be discussed individually, that either the New Testament writers or later Bible readers claim to be prophesied or otherwise foreshadowed in the Old Testament, together with the Old Testament contexts in which they are said to be found – I make no comment on the plausibility of these parallels:

His early life
  His birthplace (Mic. 5:2)
  Galilee (Is. 9:1-2)
  His names (Is. 7:14; Joshua)
  Gifts brought (Is. 60:1-6)
  Stay in Egypt (Hos. 11:1)
  Slaughter of children (Jer. 31:15)

---

7   N.T. Wright, *The New Testament and the People of God*, London 1992, p. 262.

Jesus in the Old Testament

Miraculous birth (Sarah; Rebekah; Rachel; Hannah)

Jesus' ministry
Ministry of John the Baptist (Is. 40:1-5)
Baptism (Ps. 2:7; Is. 42:1)
Temptation (Israel in wilderness)

His teaching
Law and prophets *passim*
Release (Is. 61:1-2)
Warnings: Sodom, Nineveh, Flood (Luke 17:26-29; Matt. 12:41)
Olivet prophecy (Dan. 9:26-27; 11:31; Is. 13:9-13)
Use of parables (Ps. 78:2-4; Is. 6:9-10; 28:9-13; 29:10-12)
Vineyard (Is. 5)
Lost sheep (Ezek. 34)

Actions, events
Miracles of healing (Is. 29:18; 35)
Stilling the storm (Ps. 65:6-7; 89:9; 107:23-30)
In the temple (Ps. 69:9; Jer. 7:1-15; Mal. 3:1-3)
Meals (Is. 25:6)
Transfiguration (Ex. 33:18-34:9; 1 Kings 19:8-18)

The Passion
Entry into Jerusalem (Zech. 9:9; 2 Kings 9:13)
Last Supper (Passover; Ex. 24:6-8)
Betrayal (Ps. 41:9; Zech. 11:12-13; Mic. 7:1-6)
Submission (Ps. 40:6-8; Is. 50:5, 7)
Deserted by followers (Zech. 13:7)
Trial (Is. 53:8)
Physical abuse (Is. 50:6)

Manner of death
Lifted up (Is. 52:13; Num. 21:5-9)
His clothes divided (Ps. 22:18)
Offered drink (Ps. 69:21)
With criminals (Is. 53:9)
No bone broken (Passover; Ps. 34:20)
Mocking by onlookers (Ps. 22:7-8)
Physical suffering (Ps. 22:14-17)
Mental and spiritual anguish (Ps. 22; 69; Lam. 3:1-20)
Dying (Ps. 31:5)

Resurrection (Ps. 16:9-11; 17:13-15; 118:17-18, 21-22; Is. 52:15; 53:10-12)

It scarcely needs saying that this list is anything but exhaustive. It consists of the most obvious Old Testament passages that appear in one way or another to presage Jesus' coming, ministry and death, including many that the Gospels themselves direct the reader to. Despite its obvious incompleteness, it offers abundant evidence of the way in which so many aspects and details of Jesus' life can be seen to be anticipated in the Old Testament – not all in one place, but scattered across many of its books.

How is Jesus foreshadowed in the Old Testament?

Having attempted to compile a list of Old Testament anticipations of Jesus, we need to consider the question *how?* – in what ways and in what contexts do they occur? Looking at the list above, we can, I think, identify at least four different categories.

Overt prophecies

First, and most obvious, are many overt prophecies of Jesus' role in the unfolding purpose of God. These include such passages as Isaiah 7:14; 9:6-7; 11:1-9; 32:1-17; Jeremiah 23:5-8; Ezekiel 34:23-31; 37:24; Psalm 2; 110; Daniel 7:13-14. Passages like these focus, not on the person or the experience of the coming one, but rather on the functions that Israel's expected 'saviour' or 'anointed one' was to fulfil and the benefits to Israel and to mankind that he will bring: deliverance, judgment, justice, benign kingship. They also include most of the titles ascribed to Jesus (e.g. Immanuel, Shepherd, Son of Man, Branch, Son of David, Prince of Peace, priest). Passages like these were naturally well known in Israel and helped to shape expectations of the 'Messiah', even if the details, the role and even the very titles attached to him remained vague and contradictory – expectation of this kind is exemplified for us by Luke in the figures of Simeon and Anna in Luke 2. The emphasis in such passages on the beneficial results of his coming was doubtless one of the reasons why there was no notion of one who would behave and ultimately suffer as Jesus did. We will consider towards the end of this chapter the question of how the Old Testament came to be understood so differently.

Isolated phrases or verses

The most marginal – but in some ways the most illuminating – of these parallels are the apparently isolated phrases or verses in the Old Testament that New Testament writers – and many subsequent expositors – seize upon, such as Psalm 34:20: '*He keeps all their bones; not one of them will be broken*', or Ho-

Jesus in the Old Testament

sea 11:1: *'When Israel was a child, I loved him, and out of Egypt I called my son'.*[8] How ought we understand such connections made by the Gospel writers in particular? Are they simply seizing upon a phrase that seems to anticipate events in Jesus' life? Or are they highlighting for their readers that Jesus, especially in his suffering, summed up in himself the fate of many earlier righteous people who suffered at the hands of the ungodly – and that their experience was in some way analogous to his?

Psalm 34:20 is a particularly interesting example. It is widely understood that John's allusion to this verse, *'These things occurred so that the scripture might be fulfilled, "None of his bones shall be broken"'* (John 19:36), combines Psalm 34:20 with a reference to the instructions for the observance of Passover (Exodus 12:46). So it looks as though this is far from being merely a convenient verbal link; John links Jesus' fate both to Israel's national deliverance and, in the Psalm, to that of a single righteous man. Once again, though, it is only the coming of Jesus and his experience among men that creates the connection and brings to light a meaning within the text that no reader before Christ could have arrived at.

'Types'

In a third category are the many *'typological'* elements in the Old Testament, i.e. events and rituals in which different facets of the functions that Jesus was to fulfil are indirectly anticipated. Among the *events* we might include the following:

- The ark in which Noah and his family were saved from the Flood
- The miraculous birth of Isaac
- The sacrifice of Isaac
- The treatment of Joseph by his brothers
- The provision of light, water and bread to Israel in the wilderness (e.g. Exodus 13:21-22; 15:22-26; 16; 17:1-7)
- The crossing of the Red Sea and the provision of the brass serpent
- The giving of the Law at Sinai – the five blocks of Jesus' teaching in the Gospel of Matthew are held by many to be intended as a parallel to the five books of the Pentateuch
- God's self-revelation to Moses at Sinai (Exodus 34:6-7, cf. John 1:14,

---

8 Despite the persuasive arguments of Richard Hays in his *Echoes of Scripture in the Gospels* (Waco, Texas 2016), I am not totally convinced that *every such* reference in the Gospels to Old Testament language is more than an essentially verbal echo.

the Transfiguration)

- David's victories and his reign from Zion
- Solomon's reign of peace and his construction of the temple

Among the *rituals* we might include

- The Passover (Exodus 12)
- Sacrifices, especially sin offerings and burnt offerings
- The sealing of the covenant (Exodus 24:5-8)
- The Day of Atonement (Leviticus 16)
- The consecration and work of priests (Melchizedek; Leviticus 8-9)

Unlike the prophecies just mentioned, these events and rituals did not and could not lead to expectations on Israel's part: it was only with hindsight, sometimes with Jesus' guidance, that his disciples were able to discern in these 'types' aspects of the roles that Jesus was to fulfil – the Gospel of John in particular brings many of them to our attention. Similarly, Paul in 1 Corinthians 10:1-11 invites us to view the whole of Israel's physical and spiritual journey from Egypt to Canaan as an extended allegory of salvation and of the believer's journey from sin and death to life in God's 'promised land'.

Another kind of 'type' occurs when elements of Jesus' life and personal experience, or sometimes the whole trajectory of his life, and especially the passage from smallness to greatness or through death to life, are foreshadowed in the *lived experience* of major Old Testament figures. The most obvious are perhaps the life-stories of Joseph, Moses, David, and Jeremiah; all of them endure hardship in the course of their service to God and to their fellows, but all are borne up and preserved by his providential care. In addition, there are events in the story of Israel which correspond to aspects of Jesus' life, with Israel's conduct usually the negative to Jesus' positive, as is also the case with Adam.[9]

First-person voices

While some of these parallel life-stories, and especially that of Joseph, are indeed striking, the most remarkable of all the Old Testament anticipations of Jesus are those in a fourth category, those in which *a first-person voice* addresses us directly. For this reason, the cases of David and Jeremiah stand out by virtue of the precious insight that they provide into Jesus' inner life. Jeremiah's complaints and his Lamentations almost demand of us that we ex-

---

9 N.T. Wright has repeatedly argued that Jesus is, as it were, the final and true version of 'the Israel of God' – see, for example, *Paul and the Faithfulness of God*, pp. 815-816.

Jesus in the Old Testament

plore the parallels – and especially the contrasts – with Jesus, while David's outpourings of his feelings in such psalms as 22, 40, and 69, appear to take us inside the mind of Jesus, especially at times of trial and stress, in a way that the New Testament nowhere offers.

Other psalms too achieve a similar effect, even if not at such length or in such detail; two of the best examples are Psalms 116 and 118, part of the Hallel, the group of psalms sung especially at Passover and particularly associated with the Exodus. One can scarcely fail to think of Jesus when one reads the words of the unknown writer of Psalm 118, especially v. 14-18:

> *The LORD is my strength and my might; he has become my salvation.*
> *I shall not die, but I shall live, and recount the deeds of the LORD.*
> *The LORD has punished me severely, but he did not give me over to death.*
> *(v. 14, 17-18)*

When passages like these are read in the light of the story of Jesus, the voice of David or Jeremiah, for example, appears to us to be speaking for Jesus too. It is as though some inspiration, at once poetic and divine, leads David in particular to employ a language and an imagery to express his feelings which might be thought over-dramatic at times but which are subsequently found to be fully appropriate to the experiences of a man undergoing the torture and the public shame of crucifixion. As a result, Jesus' involvement with humanity and his solidarity with all mankind come powerfully to the fore.

Once again, though, it is only an awareness of the story of Jesus' life that enables the reader to discover in them other potential layers of meaning that the writer probably had not dreamed of. We shall return to the broader question of how all these anticipations and foreshadowings of Jesus in the Old Testament 'work' at the end of this chapter.

The Servant

Having begun this overview of Old Testament anticipations of Jesus with Adam, we conclude it now with Adam's polar opposite, the 'Servant' in Isaiah's prophecy. Among all the passages and forms in which Jesus may be said to be present in the Old Testament, these 'Servant' passages are, I suggest, unique. There are five such passages – I include 61:1-7 as well as the four normally regarded as part of the sequence, 42:1-9; 49:1-12; 50:4-11 and 52:13-53:12. Their uniqueness as intimations of Jesus lies in several features of them. Taken together, their very length means that they encompass the whole course of Jesus' life, providing more detail than any other prophecy about Jesus or any foreshadowing of him. In addition, though, they include, in formal terms, all but one of the categories that I have been attempting to distinguish above:

chapter 42 resembles in some measure prophetic passages such as are found in Isaiah 9 and 11; together, they present the whole trajectory of a life, from birth (49:1) to glorification (49:7; 52:15; 53:12); and in chapters 49, 50 and 61 we hear a first-person voice, speaking of his experiences and revealing his attitude towards his mission.

The content of these five passages also provides a uniquely comprehensive picture of the servant's mission. Chapters 42 and 49 focus primarily on his worldwide mission: to bring Israel back to God and to renew the covenant, but also to be a light to the nations, to establish justice and righteousness in the world, and to bring God's salvation to the world. Chapters 42, 50 and 61 emphasise the task that he is to perform for individual people: to comfort the poor, the oppressed and marginalised. The movement noticeable in these chapters from the worldwide to the individual and from the external to the personal reaches its climax in chapter 53, which focuses on the most profound need of humanity: reconciliation with God through the overcoming of the barrier of sin.

A particular, and completely unique feature of the content of the passages is that they not only provide indications, in growing detail, of the experiences and the suffering of the servant himself but also link them to his mission. Thus, the first passage includes the lines:

... a bruised reed he will not break,
and a dimly burning wick he will not quench;
he will faithfully bring forth justice.
He will not grow faint or be crushed
until he has established justice in the earth;
and the coastlands wait for his teaching. (Isaiah 42:3-4)

'Bruised' in the first line and 'be crushed' in the fourth represent the same Hebrew word *ratsats*, while 'dimly burning' and 'grow faint' translate cognate Hebrew words, *keheh* and *kahah*; he will treat with gentleness those who are 'fainting' or oppressed but will himself 'burn dimly', or even be 'quenched' and bruised. Just how the two are related is not made explicit, but these lines imply that his 'bruising' will be incurred in the course of his service – and perhaps even be the means by which relief and comfort are brought to the oppressed.

The second and third passages shed light on the servant's suffering more overtly. Chapter 50 in particular relates the brutality and the humiliations to which he will be subjected by the will of God, whose servant he is:

Jesus in the Old Testament

> *The Lord GOD has opened my ear, and I was not rebellious, I did not turn backward. I gave my back to those who struck me, and my cheeks to those who pulled out the beard; I did not hide my face from insult and spitting. (Isaiah 50:5-6)*

That the suffering and humiliation are an essential part of his mission which God has entrusted to him and not merely incidental to it, is implicit also in chapter 49, where the servant, despite all setbacks, continues to believe *'that my right is with the Lord, and my recompense with my God'* (v. 4). In the later verses of this passage, the Lord confirms that he will sustain and preserve his servant, carrying him through from humiliation and degradation to triumph and exaltation:

> *Thus says the LORD, the Redeemer of Israel and his Holy One, to one deeply despised, abhorred by the nations, the slave of rulers, 'Kings shall see and stand up, princes, and they shall prostrate themselves, because of the LORD, who is faithful, the Holy One of Israel, who has chosen you.' (Isaiah 49:7)*

These allusions to the servant's physical and mental sufferings culminate in the fourth, climactic passage in chapters 52-53. It confirms that his suffering is indeed by the will of God who sent him (*'Yet it was the will of the LORD to crush him with pain'* – v. 10) and provides reassurance of his ultimate exaltation:

> *See, my servant shall prosper; he shall be exalted and lifted up, and shall be very high. Just as there were many who were astonished at him – so marred was his appearance, beyond human semblance, and his form beyond that of mortals – so he shall startle many nations; kings shall shut their mouths because of him … (Isaiah 52:13-15)*

> *Therefore I will allot him a portion with the great … (Isaiah 53:12)*

This passage also confirms the link, intimated from the beginning, between the hardship and suffering borne by the servant and the purpose of his mission *'… he was wounded for our transgressions, crushed for our iniquities'* (53:5) – this is to be the means by which men are to achieve *shalom* (v. 5), both personal wholeness and peace with God. Moreover, it gives assurance that this saving mission will not fail; not only will many be 'made righteous' as a result of it, but he will himself enjoy the satisfaction of seeing its outcome:

> *… he shall see his offspring, and shall prolong his days; through him the will of the LORD shall prosper. Out of his anguish he shall see light; he shall find satisfaction through his knowledge. (v. 10-11)*

This brief overview of the content of the sequence of 'servant passages' demonstrates that the reader who approaches them with eyes trained by a knowledge of Jesus' mission in the New Testament is able, not only to discern in some detail the whole course of his mission, including even his resurrection, but also to grasp its purpose. Small wonder, then, that these passages resonate throughout the New Testament. When Jesus' disciples were repeatedly told in Luke 24 (in v. 7, 26, 44, and 46) that 'it was necessary' (Greek: *dei*) that he should suffer and then rise and enter his glory, it must surely have been these passages above all that were explained to them. They must also have been at the centre of Peter's thoughts when he wrote of *'the sufferings destined for Christ and the subsequent glory'* (1 Peter 1:11). That in turn may explain why the Gospel compiled by Mark, Peter's 'interpreter' or 'translator', according to early Christian sources, has at its heart the 'mystery' of a crucified Messiah, just as he is portrayed in Isaiah's paradoxical story.

There are, though, other features of the Servant passages that we need to consider if we are to appreciate how remarkable they are. We noted earlier the use of a first-person voice foreshadowing and merging with the voice of Jesus, notably in the Psalms; but here we encounter a whole symphony of voices. In each passage, a voice or voices speak to us, making of these passages a kind of drama, with orchestrated voices enacting the story of Jesus. In chapter 42, the voice, ostensibly God's, that addresses Israel – or all mankind – and the reader throughout the second half of Isaiah, from chapter 40 onward, presents his 'servant' to us, as if with pride in him and with admiration: *'Here is my servant, whom I uphold, my chosen, in whom my soul delights'* (42:1).

In the second passage, however, we hear the voice of the Servant himself; he too addresses all people: *'Listen to me, O coastlands, pay attention, you peoples from far away'* (49:1). At the end of the passage he describes for his audience what his task is:

> *Thus says the* LORD: *In a time of favour I have answered you, on a day of salvation I have helped you; I have kept you and given you as a covenant to the people, to establish the land, to apportion the desolate heritages; saying to the prisoners, 'Come out,' to those who are in darkness, 'Show yourselves.'* (Isaiah 49:8-9)

In the intervening verses, however, he speaks of his own attitude towards his calling, of his doubts as to its effectiveness, which are finally outweighed by his trust in the God who called him:

> *And he said to me, 'You are my servant, Israel, in whom I will be glorified.' But I said, 'I have laboured in vain, I have spent my strength for nothing and*

Jesus in the Old Testament

*vanity; yet surely my cause is with the LORD, and my reward with my God.'
And now the LORD says, who formed me in the womb to be his servant, to
bring Jacob back to him, and that Israel might be gathered to him, for I am
honoured in the sight of the LORD, and my God has become my strength ...*
(Isaiah 49:3-5)

It is a passage without parallel in the New Testament: nowhere else do we
hear of such feelings on the part of Jesus.

In chapter 50 it is again the voice of the Servant that we hear; he speaks first
of the Lord's instruction that was to prepare him for his mission, but in the
central verses, 5-7, he describes his pain and the humiliation inflicted on him
by those to whom he was sent. It is worth noting the tenses in this passage: the
Servant describes his decision to obey the Lord and his consequent suffering
in the past tense (v. 5-6), but his assertions of his confidence in God and the
certainty of his vindication (v. 7-9) are in the present tense. This creates the
impression that the passage is portraying the Servant at the very climax of his
career as he faces his accusers and prepares to endure his crucifixion. So, if
we read this passage as prospectively about Jesus, we are here again granted
an extraordinary insight into his mind at the time of his supreme trial, paralleled only by Psalm 22 – but nowhere in the New Testament. The final verses,
v. 10-11, may be spoken either by him or God, but whoever the speaker is,
these words represent an appeal to Israel, or to mankind, to heed the Servant's
message and his suffering. In terms of the unfolding drama of these Servant
passages, they are in effect an anticipation of the preaching of Christ crucified
and then vindicated in resurrection that began on the Day of Pentecost.

That brings us to the most astonishing of all these passages. At the beginning, we again hear the voice of the Lord, reflecting on both the certain
success of the Servant's mission and on the extraordinary reversal, from the
depths of humiliation to the height of exaltation, that is at its heart (52:13-
15). It is worth noting in v. 13 the phrase: *'he shall be exalted and lifted up and
shall be very high'.* The words 'exalted' (Heb. *rum*) and 'lifted up' (Heb. *nasa*)
are the same pair that are used in Isaiah's vision back in chapter 6: *'I saw the
Lord sitting on a throne,* **high** *and* **lofty'** (6:1); they also occur in Isaiah 2, where
they apply not to God but to the presumptuous self-glorification of men: *'For
the LORD of hosts has a day against all that is proud and* **lofty**, *against all that is*
lifted up *and high'* (2:12). In chapter 57, however, the same two words are
linked with the idea of extreme lowliness:

For thus says the **high and lofty** *one who inhabits eternity, whose name
is Holy: I dwell in the high and holy place, and also with those who are*

39

contrite and humble in spirit, to revive the spirit of the humble, and to revive the heart of the contrite. (Isaiah 57:15)

How will the high and lofty one descend to the level of the humble and lowly? Given the position of this verse, coming shortly after the Servant passages, one can scarcely avoid the conclusion that it is through his Servant, who becomes for a time the lowest of the low, that he thus condescends. The full implications of this high-low tension are revealed only in John's Gospel, where Jesus, almost certainly taking his cue from Isaiah's words, speaks of his impending crucifixion as a 'lifting up' (John 3:14; 8:28; 12:32, 34). There is here a kind of double irony: crucifixion was indeed a 'lifting up', albeit not as high as in the popular imagination, but one intended by its perpetrators to be the most extreme form of humiliation that would leave the criminal exposed to the derision and insults of the people. But for Jesus, and for John, the humiliation was his glory, hence truly an exaltation. Instructed by John, therefore, we recognise in Isaiah 52:13 a double meaning, encompassing both the depths and heights of the servant's career.

God is again the speaker at the end of this fourth servant passage, in verses 53:11-12, confirming the success of the Servant's mission and declaring his intention to glorify him because of his faithful service. But what of the earlier verses in this chapter? It is here that, to our astonishment, a new voice is heard, one that says 'we'. It is the voice of those who, not having heeded the Servant's *words*, have finally understood his *actions* – and repent of both their former blindness and the sins that necessitated so drastic a remedy. It is thus a confession both of sins and of faith, and therefore also a vindication of the Servant's self-sacrifice and of the strategy of the Lord in sending him:

For he grew up before him like a young plant, and like a root out of dry ground; he had no form or majesty that we should look at him, nothing in his appearance that we should desire him. He was despised and rejected by others; a man of suffering and acquainted with infirmity; and as one from whom others hide their faces he was despised, and we held him of no account. Surely he has borne our infirmities and carried our diseases; yet we accounted him stricken, struck down by God, and afflicted. But he was wounded for our transgressions, crushed for our iniquities; upon him was the punishment that made us whole, and by his bruises we are healed. All we like sheep have gone astray; we have all turned to our own way, and the LORD has laid on him the iniquity of us all. (Isaiah 53:2-6)

It is an astounding confession, all the more so for being found here in the Old Testament, centuries before Christ was preached.

Jesus in the Old Testament

It is not easy to determine whose is the voice that speaks in verses 7-10, but it seems most likely that it is that of a commentator, presumably the prophet himself, lamenting before God, the 'you' of v. 10, the terrible fate of the Servant, but also confirming the success of his mission.

The usual view of the Servant passages limits them to four, as we noted earlier, and sees chapter 53 as the climax and the *dénouement* of the Servant's story. Yet though we have scarcely mentioned it since the beginning of this section, it seems right, in fact, to include in the sequence the opening of chapter 61 also. Here again we hear the voice of the Servant actually performing his mission:

> *The spirit of the Lord God is upon me, because the Lord has anointed me; he has sent me to bring good news to the oppressed, to bind up the broken-hearted, to proclaim liberty to the captives, and release to the prisoners; to proclaim the year of the Lord's favour, and the day of vengeance of our God; to comfort all who mourn; to provide for those who mourn in Zion – to give them a garland instead of ashes, the oil of gladness instead of mourning, the mantle of praise instead of a faint spirit. (Isaiah 61:1-3)*

It might appear at first sight that this should come earlier in the sequence, for it shows the Servant doing what was said of him in chapters 42 and 50 – speaking words of comfort and grace to the oppressed, the blind, the prisoners and the weary. However, its position suggests to me that what we see in chapter 61 is the Servant who, having learned – perhaps by having read and understood the rest of the sequence – what his mission is and what terrors it involves, has nevertheless embraced it, as he himself says in chapter 49 in particular. So his voice is now heard, not in soliloquy, as in chapters 49 and 50, but actually commencing the task to which he has been called. When it is viewed in this way, we readily grasp why Luke placed this passage at the beginning of his account of Jesus' ministry (Luke 4:16-21): after wrestling for forty days with the enormity of what was asked of him, Jesus has grasped it, has identified himself with the Servant, and now announces himself as such to the people of Nazareth, representatives for the moment of the whole of Israel – and of mankind.

Our look at the content and the form of the Servant passages has highlighted their uniqueness as compared with all the other ways in which Jesus is foreshadowed in the Old Testament. That impression is confirmed and deepened when we consider them in their *context* – or, more precisely, their detachment from their context.

First, they have no 'typological' dimension: they do not relate to any

Jesus – yesterday, today, for ever

actual event or existing ritual that then becomes a model of a future, greater event. Secondly, while they include in chapters 49 and 50 extended passages of first-person speech, these are not attributable to any other speaker, as in the Psalms and Jeremiah; instead, they remain, in their Old Testament context, disembodied, unattached to any previously known individual. This is another way of saying that the person and the events foreshadowed in the Servant passages are completely without precedent; they speak of someone and something such as the world had never seen before. To that extent, they can perhaps better be compared with passages of more straightforward prophecy of the kind that we find in Isaiah 2 and 11, for example. Yet by virtue of their detail and especially their 'inwardness' – their focus on the inner life of the Servant – they are 'in another league'. Not for nothing do we find in this section of Isaiah the repeated declaration that God is about to do 'a new thing' (43:19) or 'new things': *'From this time forward I make you hear new things, hidden things that you have not known'* (48:6; see also 42:9).

It is instructive also to view the Servant passages in their context in Isaiah 40-66. The earlier chapters, 40-48, focus on Israel's need for deliverance from captivity in Babylon, while in the later chapters the emphasis appears to shift onto a more universal plane and to a more spiritual form of captivity. But these 'Servant' passages, far from arising naturally out of what precedes them, appear to sit within their context almost as a foreign body; the transitions at the beginning are abrupt and unexplained, while the exultation that follows in chapters 54-55 is not explicitly linked to what has gone before in chapters 49-53. There are links, of course, but they are rather those of absence followed by presence, or of negative followed by positive. Thus in chapter 41, the Lord says:

> *But when I look there is no one; among these there is no counsellor who, when I ask, gives an answer. No, they are all a delusion; their works are nothing; their images are empty wind. (Isaiah 41:28-29)*

There is a divinely appointed deliverer, *'one from the north ... summoned by name'* (41:25; 45:4), Cyrus, of course, who will set Israel free from Babylon; he is even God's 'anointed' (45:1). But he serves only a limited purpose – he is no servant such as God really seeks: *'I call you by your name, I surname you, though you do not know me ... I arm you, though you do not know me'* (45:4-5).

There is also Israel, of course: *'Israel, my servant, Jacob, whom I have chosen, the offspring of Abraham, my friend; you whom I took from the ends of the earth, and called from its farthest corners, saying to you, "You are my servant ... "'*

42

Jesus in the Old Testament

(41:8-9). But the Lord is forced to conclude that this servant has failed miserably and is himself now in need of saving and redeeming:

> *Listen, you that are deaf; and you that are blind, look up and see! Who is blind but my servant, or deaf like my messenger whom I send? Who is blind like my dedicated one, or blind like the servant of the* Lord*? He sees many things, but does not observe them; his ears are open, but he does not hear. The* Lord *was pleased, for the sake of his righteousness, to magnify his teaching and make it glorious. But this is a people robbed and plundered, all of them are trapped in holes and hidden in prisons; they have become a prey with no one to rescue, a spoil with no one to say, 'Restore!' (Isaiah 42:18-22)*

At the end of chapter 48, just before the second Servant passage, the sense of what might have been for Israel is explicit. The section from v. 12, addressed directly to Israel, seems to begin with an assertion of God's saving action through his chosen deliverer from Babylon, Cyrus, who is probably the 'he' of v. 14-15:

> *Listen to me, O Jacob, and Israel, whom I called: I am He; I am the first, and I am the last. My hand laid the foundation of the earth, and my right hand spread out the heavens; when I summon them, they stand at attention. Assemble, all of you, and hear! Who among them has declared these things? The* Lord *loves him; he shall perform his purpose on Babylon, and his arm shall be against the Chaldeans. I, even I, have spoken and called him, I have brought him, and he will prosper in his way. (v. 12-15)*

But deliverance in military and political terms is not enough – there is a larger obstacle to be overcome. Had Israel truly returned to the Lord, they would have returned from Babylon, enjoying spiritual blessings like those of the Exodus:

> *Go out from Babylon, flee from Chaldea, declare this with a shout of joy, proclaim it, send it forth to the end of the earth; say, 'The* Lord *has redeemed his servant Jacob!' They did not thirst when he led them through the deserts; he made water flow for them from the rock; he split open the rock and the water gushed out. (v. 20-21)*

But Israel had proved unwilling, incapable of such a change, and the blessings held in store for her remain might-have-beens:

> *Thus says the* Lord*, your Redeemer, the Holy One of Israel: I am the* Lord *your God, who teaches you for your own good, who leads you in the way you*

should go. O that you had paid attention to my commandments! Then your prosperity would have been like a river, and your success like the waves of the sea; your offspring would have been like the sand, and your descendants like its grains; their name would never be cut off or destroyed from before me. (v. 17-19)

The chapter therefore ends on a negative note *'"There is no peace," says the* LORD, *"for the wicked"'* (v. 22) – and then, in the void left by Israel's failure, we suddenly hear the Servant's voice: *'Listen to me, O coastlands, pay attention, you peoples from far away!'* (49:1).

The way in which these servant passages are set without explanation or smooth transition in the text of Isaiah illustrates what was said earlier about Adam as the negative counterpart of Jesus. The redemption of which Israel and the whole human race stand in need is not provided by anything that rises as it were naturally from the events that the prophet refers to. There is thus a 'Christ-shaped hole' in the Old Testament. But here in Isaiah the hole is wonderfully filled by the as yet mysterious figure of the Servant. The way in which he is at once integrated and not integrated into the unfolding drama of Israel's restoration and redemption illustrates aptly the relationship between Old Testament foreshadowing and New Testament fulfilment.

Understanding Old Testament prefiguring of Jesus

What readers do

There are so many more ways in which aspects of Jesus' life, experience and mission can be recognised in the Old Testament. However, we wish now to consider the significance of this unparalleled phenomenon, the prominence of the apparent prefiguring of Jesus in the Old Testament. This question has two major dimensions, one subjective and the other essentially objective. The subjective aspect involves asking *how?* – what is the process which enables readers, both in the New Testament and ever afterwards, to find Jesus there? That leads us then to the 'objective' dimension and the question *why?* – why are there in the Old Testament so many elements, statements, events, rituals, and voices, that make possible and even invite such readings, and how does the presentation of Jesus in the Old Testament relate to our consideration in the previous chapter of his place within the purpose of God since 'before the foundation of the world'?

Christian readers rarely consider how extraordinary it is that a body of writings that had been pored over for centuries by Jewish religious leaders and scholars who were searching for predictions concerning the expected redeemer of Israel was suddenly found to contain predictions and anticipations

Jesus in the Old Testament

of an entirely different kind of anointed one – not merely in a few places but in a great many, in almost every Old Testament book. In the final chapter of his Gospel, Luke provides a model of how this process of re-reading (or re-hearing) and re-understanding operates. He describes what happened when the women went to the tomb where they expected to find the lifeless body of Jesus:

> ... *suddenly two men in dazzling clothes stood beside them. The women were terrified and bowed their faces to the ground, but the men said to them, 'Why do you look for the living among the dead? He is not here, but has risen. Remember how he told you, while he was still in Galilee, that the Son of Man must be handed over to sinners, and be crucified, and on the third day rise again.' Then they remembered his words ...* (Luke 24:5-8)

The women are enabled to achieve a new and fuller understanding of what Jesus had spoken of repeatedly when his words are brought into relationship with their present experience. This simple example illustrates a fundamental principle of reading and understanding: any utterance, written or spoken, is always understood (or misunderstood!) within a specific context, and a changed context may modify our understanding, revealing additional layers of hitherto latent meaning or making comprehensible what was previously mysterious[10] – and no context was ever more fundamentally changed than that of these women, faced with an empty tomb and the bewildering news of Jesus' resurrection.

Throughout the rest of Luke 24, the same fundamental principle is extended beyond the recent spoken words of Jesus to the by now ancient text of the Hebrew scriptures – and it is Jesus himself who provides the impulse for this process. He teaches his disciples that his death, far from being a mishap, had rather been 'necessary', supporting his claim by *'opening their minds to understand the scriptures'*, referring to *'the law of Moses, the prophets and the psalms'*, i.e. to all three major sections of the Jewish Old Testament. In fact, Luke provides no less than three descriptions of an experience essentially analogous to that of the women at the tomb, in each case using the metaphor of 'opening' and thus revealing:

> ... *he **interpreted** to them the things about himself in all the scriptures.* (v. 27)

---

10 For a summary of theories of reading and understanding, see my *Re-reading Romans in Context* (2004), pp. 238-253.

*... Then **their eyes were opened** ... **he was opening the scriptures** to us? (v. 31-32)*

*'These are my words that I spoke to you while I was still with you – that everything written about me in the law of Moses, the prophets, and the psalms must be fulfilled.' Then **he opened their minds** to understand the scriptures ... (v. 44-45)*

One cannot but think that Luke must have appreciated the irony as he describes the Emmaus disciples reporting quite accurately – to Jesus, of all people – the events that he, Luke, has been narrating in the preceding chapters, yet unaware of the sequel in this chapter which completely transforms their significance (v. 19-24).

This was no isolated experience, however: during the first decades of the new Christian community, Jesus' disciples underwent a similar process of enlightenment as the stunning events of Jesus' life, death and resurrection compelled them to read familiar Old Testament passages with new eyes. Their use of the Old Testament is not confined to passages that can be seen to have direct relevance to Jesus – in Galatians 3 and Romans 4, Paul uses Old Testament texts, events and people to support his argument about the new relationship of Jews and Gentiles to the gospel, while in Romans 9-11, for example, Paul's many quotations and allusions to Deuteronomy, Isaiah and Hosea in particular have to do rather with the often-puzzling course of 'salvation history'. However, it is the prefiguring of Jesus himself in the Old Testament that predominates; the apostles' conviction is summed up in Paul's words: '... that Christ died for our sins in accordance with the scriptures, and that he was buried, and that he was raised on the third day in accordance with the scriptures ...' (1 Cor. 15:3-4).

It is often suggested or implied that Israel in Jesus' day 'should have' recognised him through the way in which he fulfilled Old Testament 'types' and prophecies. Yet in fact, it is only through the confrontation of prediction and reality that the meaning of both is grasped. We only see what we are looking for; the women who went to Jesus' tomb needed to be reminded, to bring together the sight before their eyes – an empty tomb – and Jesus' words about his death and rising again. Only then did they 'remember'. Prior to Jesus' resurrection, no such confrontation was possible, hence none was able to realise what was happening among them or to understand what their Old Testament scriptures actually meant. Jesus is recognised there only retrospectively – through 'reading backwards', as Richard Hays has called it.[11] It is only our

---

11   Richard B. Hays, *Echoes of Scripture in the Gospels*, Waco, Texas 2016, p. 5. In what fol-

Jesus in the Old Testament

knowledge of Jesus, his person, his life and his role in God's purpose, that makes visible within the language and the myriad people and events of the Old Testament the outlines of Jesus.

In the early days, immediately after Jesus' resurrection, the apostles used the Old Testament primarily as a source of 'proof texts', referring mainly to what I have categorised as 'prophetic passages' (see above) to support their message and to explain the significance of Jesus' life, death and resurrection, probably drawing on the teaching that Jesus had given in the days between his resurrection and his ascension (Acts 1:3). In proclaiming Christ to a Jewish audience, they could obviously appeal to no other authority. They also emphasised the notion of 'fulfilment' – notably in Matthew's Gospel, in John's account of the Passion, and in Paul's letters to the Romans and Galatians – showing in particular that the hitherto unthinkable notion of a crucified lord and redeemer was not merely not unthinkable after all but was, in fact, foretold. For Paul in particular, this assertion of continuity between Israel's story in the Old Testament and the death and resurrection of Jesus served an apologetic function: it was vital to his demonstration that the strange twist in the unfolding story of 'salvation history' by which Gentiles accepted the 'Jewish' Messiah while Israel did not, far from being a breach of faith towards Israel on God's part, was, on the contrary, envisaged from the beginning.

Prefiguring

However, the Letters and the Gospels illustrate that they also began to see Jesus in passages in two others of my categories, in isolated phrases or sentences and, above all, in typological prefiguration. Such 'prefiguring' in an Old Testament event or person has traditionally been spoken of as a 'type', with the parallel in the life of Jesus as the 'antitype', following Paul's use of the Greek *tupos* in Romans, for example: '*Adam, who is a* **type** *of the one who was to come*' (5:14). The word occurs also in 1 Corinthians 10, though it is important to note that for Paul it is not a simple matter of a parallel or a foreshadowing: in this passage (1 Cor. 10:6, 11) and elsewhere, *tupos* carries the additional meaning of 'example', as for example in Philippians 3:17, 1 Thessalonians 1:7 and 2 Thessalonians 3:9.

The identification of this kind of prefiguring depends not on a simple one-to-one similarity, but rather on the recognition of a pattern. Richard Hays argues in his *Reading Backwards* that this was the case with the disciples at Emmaus: '... the puzzled Emmaus disciples have all the facts but lack the

---

lows, I am considerably indebted to this and to the other books by Hays that are listed in the Bibliography.

Jesus – yesterday, today, for ever

pattern that makes them meaningful'. What they lacked, he suggests, was 'a figural interpretation of the Old Testament's Psalms and stories.'[12] Earlier in the same book he explains what he means by this term, which he derived from the great German literary critic Erich Auerbach: 'Figural interpretation establishes a connection between two events or persons in such a way that the first signifies not only itself but also the second, while the second involves or fulfils the first.' The comprehension of the interdependence of the two events or persons is not simply a process of comparing and aligning facts but rather, Auerbach asserts, 'a spiritual act', or, in Hays' words, 'an act of imaginative correlation', more akin to poetic understanding than to the sciences or mathematics.[13]

It is, moreover, an act in which the revealing of meaning works in two directions: if the Old Testament 'type' enables us to see something about Jesus that we might otherwise not have seen, it too gains in significance and depth by being brought into relationship with Jesus. So understood, the process of reading and grasping the typological significance of Old Testament figures is far from being a kind of game or academic exercise; the ancient text is 'actualised' – brought into the present, where it addresses us, the present-day readers, with its original meaning enriched through having been brought into relationship with Jesus. Moreover, it does so powerfully and effectively: '... true reading both presupposes and produces the transformation of readers.'[14]

One of the most obvious warrants for reading in this way is Paul's use of Exodus figures in 1 Corinthians 10:

> *I do not want you to be unaware, brothers and sisters, that our ancestors were all under the cloud, and all passed through the sea, and all were baptized into Moses in the cloud and in the sea, and all ate the same spiritual food, and all drank the same spiritual drink. For they drank from the spiritual rock that followed them, and the rock was Christ. Nevertheless, God was not pleased with most of them, and they were struck down in the wilderness. Now these things occurred as examples [tupos] for us ... (v. 1-6)*

Two conclusions are suggested by the 'figural', i.e. typological reading of this passage:

- Paul sees an essential continuity between the story of the Israel and the present experience of the church;

---

12 Richard Hays, *Reading Backwards*, Waco 2014/London 2015, p. 14.

13 Erich Auerbach, *Mimesis*, quoted by Hays in *Reading Backwards*, p. 2.

14 *Echoes of Scripture in the Letters of Paul*, p. 148

Jesus in the Old Testament

- Israel's story therefore addresses us, today, with the force of these exemplary events enhanced and deepened by the link with Jesus.

It is important, though, to notice two further points about this. First, that it is the present-day believer's experience of salvation that makes possible and determines the parallel: believers' awareness of the presence of Jesus with them, supplying them with all that they need for their new life and their journey towards the land of promise, transforms their understanding of what was happening when Israel journeyed towards theirs. Second, it is the recognition of the 'figural' resemblance that makes possible the identification with Jesus as 'the rock', not the other way round.

Pre-existence?

The above quotation from 1 Corinthians 10, and especially the phrase '... *and the rock was Christ'* has, of course, frequently been seen – by literally minded readers – as evidence for the pre-existence of Jesus. It is much more probable that Paul had by this time arrived at the conclusions expressed in Ephesians 1:9-10 and Colossians 1:15-17 that we looked at in the previous chapter: that Christ was from 'the beginning' the very centre and focus of God's creative and redemptive purpose and therefore informs the entire process, though actually existent only from the point of his birth. That awareness naturally gave a particular direction to the poetic imagination and enabled them to recognise the more easily the patterns and 'figures' that the death and resurrection of Jesus drew their attention to.

One passage in the New Testament makes this explicit:

*Concerning this salvation, the prophets who prophesied of the grace that was to be yours made careful search and inquiry, inquiring about the person or time that the Spirit of Christ within them indicated when it testified in advance to the sufferings **destined** for Christ and the subsequent glory. It was revealed to them that they were serving not themselves but you, in regard to the things that have now been **announced** to you through those who brought you good news by the Holy Spirit sent from heaven – things into which angels long to look!*

*... You know that you were ransomed from the futile ways inherited from your ancestors, not with perishable things like silver or gold, but with the precious blood of Christ, like that of a lamb without defect or blemish. He was **destined** before the foundation of the world, but was **revealed** at the end of the ages for your sake. (1 Peter 1:10-12, 18-20)*

'Destined' (*proginosko*) actually means 'known before', to God himself, of course, but then also dimly glimpsed by the prophets whose words spoke of Jesus in his sufferings and his glory, arousing their curiosity and expectation. But only 'you', i.e. Peter's readers, have had those prophetic intimations 'announced' clearly to them (v. 12), and only now, in these 'last times', has the one who was known to God and dimly glimpsed by prophets been 'revealed' or 'made real' for you. That 'revelation' having been made, it became possible for the apostles to turn back to the earlier stories of Israel and read them anew, glimpsing the foreshadowing of Christ at so many points. The Trinitarian reading of such passages replaces poetry and imagination with questionable metaphysics, forfeiting in the process the spiritual and moral richness that flows from the kind of reading that we have been discussing.

Similarity and difference

The quest for 'types' almost inevitably focuses on resemblances, whether in a particular individual or event or in the patterns formed by sequences of events. In view of the enthusiasm for 'types' among some Bible-readers, however, we do well to note Hays' caveat:

> ... typological correlations can be of various kinds ... we have to ask what Paul is doing with the typology in each particular case. Some typologies create antithetical correlations ... and others create positive correlations ... These broad characterizations can only be a matter of degree, since all typologies, being metaphorical, spring from a perception of likeness between dissimilar entities. Thus even the most antithetical typology must contain elements of likeness, and even the most positive typology must contain elements of contrast. Otherwise, the figure would not work at all.[15]

Even where we are able to see some kind of resemblance between Jesus and a person or event in the Old Testament, it is important to register and to highlight the difference between them. Even in its most heroic figures, those set before us as examples of faith, we can hardly fail to observe how their early promise ends in some kind of failure. The pattern of *Joseph's* life, for example, with its descent into the depths, not once but twice, followed by an ascent to dizzying heights, may resemble that of Jesus, yet the later phase of his life is less glorious. It is hard to see in Joseph's policy of concentrating the ownership of all the land in Egypt in the hands of Pharaoh while reducing the people of Egypt to the status of servitude – but sparing the priesthood from these measures (Genesis 47:13-26) – any resemblance to Jesus' attitude towards the

---

15 *Echoes of Scripture in the Letters of Paul*, p. 101.

Jesus in the Old Testament

dispossessed. *Gideon* begins as a divinely chosen leader of Israel against the Midianite invaders, yet later encourages a return to idolatry in Israel (Judges 8:22-27), has multiple wives, and establishes a dynasty that proves disastrous for Israel (Judges 9). *Solomon* the wise turns into an idolater, a man whose wives and concubines are counted in hundreds and whose lavish life-style sows the seeds of rebellion and division in Israel (1 Kings 11).

Most tragic of all is the story of *David*, the 'man after God's own heart'. His fall from grace through his adultery with Bathsheba and the virtual murder of Uriah are bad enough, but his repentance and humble submission to their evil consequences might be thought finally to outweigh them and, for the reader, are almost more valuable than his earlier virtuous conduct. What is really disappointing – and most signally contrasted with the pattern of Christ – is his vindictiveness towards Joab, his long-time accomplice, and the foolish Shimei, to whom he had once granted forgiveness (1 Kings 2:5-9). It is as though the deeply engrained pattern of all-too human behaviour reasserts itself against the pattern of Christ into which he had been introduced.

Disappointments such as these lead to the melancholy conclusion that we recognise Jesus in the Old Testament precisely through his *absence*. The 'tragedy of Israel', their failure and fall, is a reflection of that absence; were human history to continue for ever without him, it could lead only to the endless repetition of their failure and fall, albeit in other circumstances. I referred earlier to a 'Christ-shaped hole' in the Old Testament, and, looking back with eyes enlightened by him, that, above all, is what we notice. In fact, we frequently recognise Jesus in the Old Testament precisely because of the dissimilarity; indeed, it seems to me that this statement is true above all in this sense of his absence. Francis Watson is, I think, saying something like this when he writes, commenting on Paul's treatment of the Law of Moses:

> If the promise speaks directly of God's unconditional future saving action, although without naming Christ, the law speaks of this divine saving action only by the highly indirect route of showing that salvation cannot be attained through human agency.[16]

It is instructive in this context to return to the two extreme cases that we considered earlier, Adam and the 'Servant'. In thinking about the former, I suggested that his relationship to Jesus was entirely one of contrast – there is no resemblance to be noted, only dissimilarity, except for the decisive, determining force of their lives. Adam above all leaves a void that needs to be

---

16 Francis Watson, *Paul and the Hermeneutics of Faith*, 2nd edition, London/New York 2016, p. 328-9.

Jesus – yesterday, today, for ever

filled if the human race is to have a future – and it is Jesus who fills it. That is why Paul especially sets Jesus over against Adam as his opposite. He speaks of Jesus as the 'last Adam' but he might have well described him as the 'counter-Adam', the one whose life is to undo all the negative consequences that flow from Adam's life.

Isaiah's 'Servant' is Adam's polar opposite, not only in his behaviour, but also in a formal, literary sense. There are few Old Testament figures who resemble Adam in being presented in a wholly negative fashion – and there is certainly none who resembles the Servant. Neither Adam nor the Servant can be regarded as a 'type' since they represent, within the pages of the Old Testament, opposite models or ideas of humanity. All other Old Testament figures move between these two poles, tugged hither and thither by the competing forces that they represent, reflecting now something of the one, now something of the other. There is, however, this fundamental difference between them: Adam, male and female (Gen. 1:27), was real, all too real; the Servant, by contrast, seems like a dream, a vision of a man like no other, an unrealised possibility. As Jesus himself said to his disciples, until he came, no one had ever seen one like him: *'Blessed are the eyes that see what you see! For I tell you that many prophets and kings desired to see what you see, but did not see it, and to hear what you hear, but did not hear it'* (Luke 10:23-24).

Before moving to the second aspect of the issue of Old Testament prefiguring of Jesus, it is perhaps advisable to comment briefly on the way in which we speak about these correspondences. I have, earlier in this chapter, gone so far as to list examples of such prefiguring and to analyse them into categories. Yet I have to emphasise that I have throughout been conveying not indisputable facts but the conclusions that I have personally come to – aided, of course, by the thoughts and reflections of others. It is, I think, vital not to speak of any resemblance that we have discerned as though it were objective fact: that 'this *is* that', or that 'this *means* that'. The reading process that I have been attempting to describe is essentially subjective: it arises out of a cognitive process that works through intuitive impulses which, as Hays observes, bring it closer to the reading of poetry than to scientific or mathematical reasoning.

In attempting to convey to others our new insight or understanding, we do well, therefore, to emphasise its subjective nature, avoiding any suggestion that our conclusions are objectively 'true' and therefore binding on anyone but ourselves. It is damaging to the life of a religious community when every act of interpretation, no matter how implausible, is presented as unchallengeable fact rather than possibility – the more so when that 'fact' comes buttressed by the prestige or even the authority of one or other of the

52

community's founders or prominent leaders.

Why 'Jesus in the Old Testament'?

We have been looking so far, in our attempts to understand the significance of the foreshadowing of Jesus in the Hebrew Scriptures, at what I described as the subjective dimension – how all these types and shadows 'work' from the point of view of the reader. We turn now to the 'objective' dimension: how and why are there within the Old Testament so many features – events, rituals, people, prophecies, phrases, etc. – in which those with eyes trained by their acquaintance with Jesus are able to recognise aspects of his life, teaching and experience?

The first thing to say is that all the 'types', parallels and prophecies are *not* the product of a divine maker of jigsaw-puzzles who delights to create patterns and interlocking pieces for his own amusement and as a diverting challenge to his children – an impression sometimes created when the quest for 'types' becomes, seemingly, an end in itself, when dubious parallels are drawn, and names, numbers and words are manipulated to 'make them fit'. It is not to satisfy our delight in games and puzzles that the Old Testament was given to us, and we should not treat it like a vast cryptic crossword!

The nature of man

If we try, cautiously and humbly, to view the question in relation to God, several reasons appear fairly obvious. First of all, if he created man in line with the intentions that he had for them 'from the foundation of the world', as we explored in chapter 1, then even after the Fall, the descendants of Adam must have retained capacities and qualities that he possessed. To be a child of Adam is to resemble him not only in the negative sense but also in the potential with which he was created. It seems therefore inevitable that among all his children throughout the generations – and even apart from any direct divine intervention – there should arise individuals and situations in which some elements of God's vision of man would find at least partial realisation, thus foreshadowing in some measure the perfect realisation of God's intentions in Jesus. The whole history of Israel, and of mankind as a whole, still bears, even in our fallen condition, the stamp of the true man that God desired. The amazing achievements of human intelligence and ingenuity, their artistic creativity, *and* their capacity for love and selflessness all testify to mankind's origins in God's creative act.

From this flows a further reflection: human history of necessity reflects the divided, contradictory nature of humanity, with the result that individual human beings' experience is a reflection of both the good and the bad in it. It is thus no accident that the lives of prominent individuals, whose stories we find in the Old Testament, repeatedly illustrate those contradictory impulses in ways that find their fullest expression in the experience of Jesus. The trajectories of human lives reveal patterns of falling and rising, or of rising and falling, that we see in their most extreme form in the life of Jesus. The Old Testament thus teaches us that Jesus is not just joined to humanity in the way that Luke's genealogy illustrates (Luke 3:23-38); he is embedded in or, perhaps better, interwoven with, the whole of human history and the patterns of individual lives. In particular, his life sums up the fate of the good man in an evil world; still more particularly, it recapitulates the story of all God's emissaries to his people. Jesus himself repeatedly likens himself to the prophets, whose fate, he realises, he is going to share (e.g. Matt. 23:31-37).

This principle, the centrality of Jesus to everything that God does, is not applicable only to human lives. If God's entire purpose is, as we saw in the previous chapter, 'through Jesus' and 'for Jesus', then it follows that events in the history of both the people and individuals, and also rituals and laws that God prescribed for Israel, must bear a relationship to him in some way, even if only in contrast to him. The detailed instructions about the Aaronic priesthood. the complex process of their consecration, and their elaborate dress are in some ways anticipations of Jesus but, much more obviously, they point to the difference between this ultimately unsatisfactory form of mediation between man and God and the one true mediator and saviour. This is, of course, the argument of Hebrews 9-10.

The nature of God

The Jesus-pattern that readers repeatedly find in the Old Testament also shows us something fundamental about God himself. It is not simply a question of that foreknowledge that Peter speaks of in his opening chapter of his Letter and that we referred to above. If God has in some way shaped and directed the lives of certain individuals who figure in the Old Testament, then we might expect that he will have done so consistently, in accordance with his own nature. The Jesus-pattern is surely the evidence that it is so – in two senses. First, we are able, in the light of what we know of his purpose before and in creation, to recognise his purposefulness in working out his declared intentions. Secondly, we see a consistency in his dealings with human beings and in his treatment of individuals, which are realised in and through the actions of men and women. In the final pages of the Old Testament, we find the assertion: 'I the LORD [i.e. Yahweh] do not change' (Mal. 3:6); much earlier, in Exodus 34, he describes the characteristics that are summed up in his name, emphasising consistency both in steadfast love and in judgment (Ex. 34:6-7).

Jesus in the Old Testament

And as quintessential man, Jesus is not excepted from those patterns; as part of humanity, he suffers as men suffer, 'with blows inflicted by human beings' (2 Sam. 7:14), as Nathan says to David.

It is sometimes argued, usually on the basis of Romans 3:25, that the forgiveness and grace received from God by those who lived before the coming of Jesus, thus all the Old Testament figures with whom we are familiar, actually flowed from the death of Jesus. This way of thinking about the relationship between Jesus and the Old Testament seems to me far too mechanistic. Was David, for example, forgiven because of Jesus' sacrifice? It was, surely, for his repentance, as he himself understood (see 2 Sam. 12:13 and Ps. 32:1-2, 5), on the basis of what he knew and believed about God, not because of some event about a thousand years later, of which he knew little or nothing.

That is not to say, however, that there is no connection of any kind between Jesus and incidents of this kind. It seems to me rather that this episode in David's life illustrates the consistency of God that we have been considering: the grace that men found with him throughout Old Testament times was of the same fundamental character as that finally expressed in Christ – Paul's quotation from Psalm 32:1-2 in Romans 4:6-8 confirms this. This link between David, for example, and the gospel of God's grace in Christ is, in fact, another example of 'figural reading': Paul's and our knowledge of Jesus enables us to view David's story with new eyes and to recognise the fundamental pattern of God's freely given forgiveness.[17]

For Israel's – and for Jesus' – sake

Fundamentally, however, the outlines of Jesus that are to be discerned in the Old Testament are there for man's sake, more specifically, for Israel's sake. The Hebrew scriptures contain, on the one hand, the history of a family, then of a people, in which we find vivid, unforgettable examples of human behaviour, both good and ill. In particular, we see that even the best men have 'feet of clay', as we noted earlier. On the other hand, the reader encounters from time

---

17 Similarly, it is our knowledge of Christ and the redemption through him that enables us to recognise that he is foreshadowed in various Old Testament rituals, such as the Passover and the Day of Atonement. Notice how the writer to the Hebrews fastens on to the detail of the law concerning sin offerings: only in the case of sin offerings for a priest or for the whole people was some of the blood brought into the tabernacle and the carcase burned 'without the camp' (Lev. 4:1-21). Accordingly, we read in Hebrews: *'For the bodies of those animals whose blood is brought into the sanctuary by the high priest as a sacrifice for sin are burned outside the camp. Therefore Jesus also suffered outside the city gate in order to **sanctify the people by his own blood**.'* (Heb. 13:11-12). We may, I think, be sure that it was the manner of Jesus' death that alerted the writer to this parallel, not the other way round.

Jesus – yesterday, today, for ever

to time intimations of a world other and better than the one that they have known, and of a coming one who would be instrumental in its realisation. It seems to me that God wished to evoke in his people both a realisation of their need of him and a longing for the better world – or, in religious language, repentance and faith. Not for nothing does Paul write that the Law was *'our disciplinarian until Christ came'* (Gal. 3:24). I do not believe that this means that Israel should have recognised Jesus as 'the Messiah' when he came: the *paidagogos* (KJV: 'schoolmaster') was a trusted slave charged with the moral education of a child, taking them to school and keeping them out of mischief. This suggests that the function of the Law, indeed of the Old Testament as a whole, was to develop the moral and spiritual sensibilities of Israel so that when the redeemer came, they would be the more open to his teaching and example. In figures like Simeon, who was *'looking forward to the consolation of Israel'*, and Anna, one of those who were *'looking for the redemption of Jerusalem'* (Luke 2:25, 38), we see examples of the fruit of the 'pedagogue's' work. People like them may have glimpsed fragments of the coming one in different parts of the Old Testament, but what they probably saw above all, I suggest, was his absence – that Christ-shaped hole that I have already referred to. When Jesus read from Isaiah 61 in the Nazareth synagogue and then declared *'Today this scripture has been fulfilled in your hearing'* (Luke 4:21), he was announcing that their looking and waiting were now over – the hole was at last being filled.

When Jesus in Luke 24 teaches his disciples how to read their scriptures anew, he is also pointing to what we must take to be a further divine intention behind the hidden presence of Jesus in the Old Testament: God was providing, for Israel and for subsequent readers, grounds for faith in himself, in his consistency and faithfulness to his promises – but also for faith in his Son. Jesus' list of the 'witnesses' that testify to him includes the following: *'You search the scriptures because you think that in them you have eternal life; and it is they that testify on my behalf'* (John 5:39). Three chapters further on, he is more explicit: *'Your ancestor Abraham rejoiced that he would see my day; he saw it and was glad'* (John 8:56). Looking back from a post-resurrection perspective, John is pointing to what Israel might have seen, had they been able to read their scriptures in the way that Jesus did. For he is the ultimate, perfect reader of the Old Testament: all these Old Testament parallels provided instruction for him. We shall have more to say about this in the next chapter, but it is clear from the Gospels that his knowledge and uniquely insightful understanding of the Old Testament shaped not only the man Jesus but also his mission, as his reading from Isaiah 61 makes clear.

Jesus in the Old Testament

Written – to be read

As one looks at the various facets of the presence of Jesus in the Old Testament, one is forced to a further conclusion, so fundamental that it is often overlooked: that the correspondence between Jesus and all these ways in which he is prefigured in the Old Testament is not so much a relationship with people and events in earlier times as *with the written account of them*. We cannot 'get behind' the written narrative to the raw material, the 'as it really was' of history. One often hears easy talk of 'the hand of God' at work in the affairs of both individuals and nations, as though he manipulated them to create the patterns that we delight to discover. But it is the act of narration, the process of shaping, selecting and omitting required for the telling of any story, that creates the pattern. And writings in which the Spirit of God has a hand are likely to reflect God's character and his intentions for mankind.

This implies that the writings were ultimately shaped by the as yet future Jesus – not by his own personal agency, but by the sheer fact of his centrality to everything that God has done and is doing. These writings were so influenced by the all-knowing Creator that they reflect him. Perhaps this is what is meant by Peter's phrase *'the Spirit of Christ within them'* (1 Peter 1:11). It is, for example, the omission of much that doubtless did not fit that makes Joseph come to resemble Jesus in some ways.

This realisation helps us to understand more fully what John means when he writes that *'the word became flesh'*: it was not just God's one initial 'word' or intention that was finally realised in Jesus, but also all the types and parallels created in the countless words of the prophets, chroniclers and poets of the Old Testament. As we said before, we should not be surprised that Jesus' disciples, and all the wisest and most learned in Israel, were so much less clever than we and failed to recognise the pattern: it was only the lived embodiment of the pattern that at last enabled it to shine out from amid the chaos and confusion of all that had gone before.

And so at last, all the shards of the coming redeemer, scattered throughout these writings, came together in the man Jesus – to whom we now turn.

Chapter 3

Preliminaries:
Birth, Childhood – and
'Christology'

INTRODUCTION

Any attempt to write about Jesus naturally focuses on his time on earth. Although he was anticipated and prefigured in the Old Testament, everything that we find there is, of necessity, only an outline of the actual man Jesus of Nazareth. But equally, however much the life of the believer is lived in relationship to the present risen and glorified Jesus, it is from the earthly Jesus, whose actions and words are, to some extent at least, known to us, that we are able to learn who he is, what he taught, and what his will for himself and for us actually is. The Gospel accounts also 'earth' Jesus in another sense: they prevent our imposing on him our subjective visions. Jesus is frequently 'hijacked' for every possible kind of cause, whether social, political or spiritual, often in ways that have little to do with the figure that we encounter in the Gospels. Their narratives curb our tendency to fashion him according to our particular needs or in the likeness of our 'experience', real or imaginary.[1]

That is why our title emphasises continuities: that the Gospels' Jesus was the authentic realisation of Old Testament predictions, *and* that the present risen Jesus, though exalted, unimaginably powerful and glorious, is fundamentally the one of whom we read in the Gospels. We have seen in the previous chapter that the Jesus of the Gospels shapes the way in which we now read the Old Testament – he is only there in as far as we are able to discern

---

1 I have listed in the bibliography some of the more recent books on Jesus. Those that I have personally found most helpful include Maurice Casey's *Jesus of Nazareth*, NT Wright's *Jesus and the Victory of God*, William Barclay's *The Mind of Jesus,* and Hans Küng's *Jesus* (a section of his much larger book *On Being A Christian*).

Preliminaries: Birth, Childhood – and 'Christology'

elements of him, or the outline of his 'career', in people and events in the history of Israel. Similarly, what the living, exalted Lord Jesus of this present time is and does, and what he will be in the future, when all things are finally brought together in him and under him, all of this must be consonant with what he did during his brief life on earth, however different the glorified Jesus might be in his mode of existence and the powers available to him. Much as the Old Testament 'types' gave some idea of the expected Messiah, so too the Jesus of the Gospels 'foreshadows' the risen Lord. Within the narrow compass of an earthly human life are to be glimpsed the seeds, as it were, which come to full flowering after his resurrection.

A. THE QUESTION OF 'CHRISTOLOGY'

It is not my intention to deal at length with the debates about the nature of Jesus and his relationship to the Father that have troubled the Christian community almost from the beginning. It is, however, impossible to write about Jesus without touching on these issues and, more importantly, without making clear – or as clear as is possible on so complex a question – what the assumptions are which underlie everything else that I shall say about him. It might be thought strange to include these issues in a chapter concerned mainly with Jesus' early life, before his ministry began; in fact, however, it is precisely here, before the powers imparted to him at his baptism through the descent of the Spirit on him could have their effect, that the nature of Jesus can best be considered.

Debates among Christians concerning 'Christology', i.e. the nature of Jesus, have in the course of the centuries taken various forms. Over the last 250 years approximately, the issue has been the subject of a sporadic debate usually referred to as 'the Quest for the Historical Jesus'. This quest has gone through several phases – it is fashionable to speak of a 'first quest', a 'new quest', and a 'third quest' – all claiming to seek to rediscover Jesus as he actually was, or even, who Jesus really was.[2] The first phase of the quest was driven primarily by historical scepticism – doubts as to the reliability of the Gospels and a rejection of the supernatural elements in Jesus' story. In the later phases of the quest, however, the issue was somewhat different: fundamentally, it

---

2 Summaries of the 'quest' and its various stages can be found in the works by Maurice Casey and NT Wright mentioned in note 1. Two other useful and reasonably succinct sources are Gerd Theissen & Annette Merz, *The Historical Jesus. A Comprehensive Guide*, London 1998, translated by John Bowden from the German original, *Der historische Jesus: Ein Lehrbuch*, Göttingen 1996 and James D.G. Dunn's *Jesus Remembered (Christianity in the Making*, vol. 1), Grand Rapids, Michigan 2003 (Part 1).

Jesus – yesterday, today, for ever

was driven by the apparent contrast between what are usually called 'the Jesus of history' and 'the Christ of faith', which was deemed to indicate that the 'real Jesus' was very different from the Christ worshipped in Christian churches.

That question was, however, much older; it was, in essence, a resumption of the Christological disputes that engulfed the Christian church in the early centuries of its existence. To grasp the relationship between the mortal Jesus of the Synoptic Gospels and the risen Lord on whom the faith of Christians is now focused was difficult enough, but the question was made immeasurably more complex, not to say insoluble, by the growing tendency in the second to the fourth century to view Jesus as having pre-existed and being in some sense 'God'. How did, how could, the man Jesus of Nazareth relate to the 'eternal Son'? Was it possible to reconcile the former's mortal, human existence with the allegedly eternal, divine nature of the latter?

The answers given to that question reflected a tendency not to see Jesus as a real human being at all – God, it was felt, could not really have revealed himself in a truly human body. The 'Docetism' that, towards the end of the first century, probably caused John to write his first Letter was an early form of such thinking. Other, later forms include the thesis of Apollinarius in the fourth century that, while Jesus possessed a human body and a human 'soul', the divine Logos had taken the place of a rational human mind; later still, in the fifth century, the 'Monophysites' claimed that the human nature of Jesus was absorbed by the divine, so that he had only one 'physis' or nature.

All these different versions of Christ viewed him essentially 'from above', with the supposed divinity of the eternal Son given priority over the claims of his humanity. The result is in every case that Jesus is viewed as 'a human being in whom God did the thinking and talking'.[3]

The church as a whole finally rejected all these one-sided Christologies in favour of an agreed solution, set out at the Council of Chalcedon in 451 AD, which was actually no solution at all. In essence, the formula accepted at Chalcedon simply asserted both the human nature of Jesus and his supposed divine nature – simply placing them side by side and providing no explanation of how these apparently irreconcilable 'natures' could be reconciled. The following formulation is taken from the *Catechism of the Catholic Church*, published in English in 1994:

§ 464 The unique and altogether singular event of the Incarnation of the Son of God does not mean that Jesus Christ is part God and part man, nor does it imply that he is the result of a confused mixture of

---

3 Enda Lyons, *Jesus: Self-portrait by God*, Blackrock, Co. Dublin 1994, p. 18.

Preliminaries: Birth, Childhood – and 'Christology'

the divine and the human. He became truly man while remaining truly God. Jesus Christ is true God and true man.

A further paragraph purports to explain how this reconciliation of opposites is deemed to work:

> § 475 Similarly, at the sixth ecumenical council, Constantinople III in 681, the Church confessed that Christ possesses two wills and two natural operations, divine and human. They are not opposed to each other, but cooperate in such a way that the Word made flesh willed humanly in obedience to his Father all that he had decided divinely with the Father and the Holy Spirit for our salvation. Christ's human will 'does not resist or oppose but rather submits to his divine and almighty will.'

It is evident, I think, that not much remains of genuine humanity in one who, it is claimed, possesses both a human and a divine will, despite the strenuous, not to say desperate, assertions that Jesus is 'true man'.

One further conclusion relating to 'Christology' can be drawn from the narratives of Jesus' childhood which we shall consider shortly: the Gospel writers devote little attention to the theoretical, abstract issues that later gave rise to the often bitter arguments and schisms between Christians. Why is it so? It suggests that they were not greatly concerned with questions of Jesus' essential nature; the language of the theorists of the early centuries – 'person', 'substance', 'hypostasis' and the like – is foreign to them. Faithful to the Jewish tradition from which they, as well as Jesus, came, their focus is on *function*, on practical *ethical and spiritual* realities rather than on 'being'. Saying that Jesus is 'God with us' or that 'the word become flesh' are for them not 'ontological' statements, i.e. statements about Jesus' essential *being*: rather, they mean for them that in Jesus human beings were able to see how God acts towards his human creatures, and that Jesus was God's agent, acting to realise the purpose that he had long before declared. The anguished arguments of theologians over many centuries arose from the abandonment of Old Testament, Jewish traditions of thought in favour of a traditionally Greek focus on essences and substances, in other words, from a shift from *functional* to *ontological* preoccupations. For the Gospel writers, Jesus is 'God with us' and the word becomes flesh only when he begins his ministry, not while an infant in a manger or a small boy in Nazareth. The clearest demonstration of this is found in Mark: the 'gospel of the Son of God' (Mark 1:1) begins only when Jesus, now aged thirty, comes to be baptised by John (Mark 1:9).

However, the question of Jesus' humanity is not a problem confined to

Jesus – yesterday, today, for ever

Trinitarians. Even if we are non-Trinitarian, hampered by neither historical scepticism nor traditional Christian doctrine, it still remains difficult to
form a picture of the historical Jesus. The 'quest' was provoked precisely by
Christians' tendency even today to 'read back' their understanding of, and relationship with, the risen Lord into their view of the man Jesus of Nazareth –
a case of the 'continuity' that I referred to earlier being stood on its head. This
led, and still leads, many to view the Jesus of the Gospels as though he were
already the all-powerful, omniscient Lord of the present rather than as the
man of Nazareth; they tend to maximise the miraculous dimension of Jesus'
ministry and to attribute to him a god-like inerrancy and certainty in the realisation of his mission. The portrait of Jesus that we find in John's Gospel, viewing Jesus explicitly from a post-resurrection perspective and emphasising his
seeming omniscience, has been particularly influential in Christian thinking
about Jesus, whether Trinitarian or not, as Raymond E. Brown suggests.[4]

This way of thinking has the effect of making Jesus a man in name only,
except for those moments in the Gospels when he is said to be tired (e.g. John
4:6) or hungry (e.g. Mark 11:12), and when he utters his anguished prayer
in Gethsemane. Otherwise, he becomes a kind of 'god in human form' who
floats through the story, his feet barely touching the ground, it seems. Some
of the ways in which the Jesus of the Gospels is spoken of are not too different from the famous phrase in which Ernst Käsemann, one of the 20th century theologians associated with the 'New Quest', described Jesus in John's
Gospel: as 'a God striding over the earth.'[5]

The problem is compounded by the way in which John's words in chapter
1 are often understood: the phrase *'the word became flesh and lived among us'*
(1:14), especially when associated with Christmas, is taken to mean that the
baby of Bethlehem was 'the word become flesh', somehow a heavenly being
from the moment of birth. John's intention is surely quite different: he is referring to the totality of the life, death and resurrection of Jesus – that is where
'we have seen his glory'.

Views like these are, I believe, fatal to any sense of the essential likeness of
Jesus to the rest of mankind, however much we may assert his true humanity.
We may *say* that he was *'one who in every respect has been tested as we are'* (Heb.

---

4 Raymond E. Brown, *A Crucified Christ in Holy Week*, Collegeville 1986, p. 57 (quoted in
Lyons, op. cit., p. 186).

5 "Even if this heavenly being genuinely touches ground on the path of his parabola and
does not, as many in both ancient and modern times have interpreted him as doing, pass
through this world some inches off the ground, there can be no doubt that he is not in the
fullest sense 'one of us.'"(John A.T. Robinson, *The Priority of John*, London 1985, p. 366).

Preliminaries: Birth, Childhood – and 'Christology'

4:15), but to think or speak about Jesus in the way that I have been describing is not so far removed from the Trinitarian picture of Jesus. Simply to assert blandly that Jesus is both 'son of man' and 'Son of God' is not much of an improvement on the doctrine of 'two natures' unless we attempt to understand what the two terms mean and how they may be reconciled with each other. To do this means above all that we must begin by taking his humanity with full seriousness.

Jesus: a human child

What do we actually mean when we speak of 'humanity', apart from the basic question of human parentage? To anticipate what we shall see in the next section, the little that the Gospels tell us about Jesus' early life is shaped primarily by theological preoccupations: the need to persuade readers that Jesus of Nazareth is indeed the Jewish Messiah and the Son of God. Yet even in their brevity, these accounts allow us to identify in Jesus the basic elements of human existence, which, leaving aside the purely physiological, I take to include at least the following:[6]

A life before God

Luke writes that Jesus '*grew ... in favour with God and man*' (Luke 2:52); this tells us that he lived 'facing God', aware of his presence, conscious of his duty to please him and his own need of God's approval. In short, he lives as *a creature before his creator*. It is out of this awareness that prayer grows; the many references that we find in the Gospels to Jesus at prayer are the clearest possible evidence of this creature-creator relationship that he shared during his earthly life with all other human beings – and which is incompatible with notions of Jesus' eternal co-existence and equality with God the Father.

Finite rather than infinite

The fact that Jesus was born at a particular time and in a particular place, and that he was, for example, subject to his parents (Luke 2:51), illustrates that, like all human beings – and by contrast with the infinite, omnipotent and eternal God – he was limited in relation to time and place and in his powers and abilities.

A life in time

Both Matthew and Luke begin with a birth narrative, to which a genealogy of Jesus is attached. So Jesus' life begins where we all begin, being born by a human mother. These narratives then make it clear that Jesus' life, like that of

---

6   My list is based upon that of Enda Lyons in his *Jesus: Self-portrait by God*, Blackrock, Co. Dublin 1994

all human beings, was time-bound, following a path of growth and development and then moving inexorably towards its end. Luke's brief references to Jesus' childhood and adolescence confirm this: *'And the child grew and became strong ... And Jesus grew in wisdom and stature'* (Luke 2:40, 52).

Learning

The human relationship to time means more than simply growth, decline and death: it includes also *mental* development. Luke says that *'the child grew in wisdom'*; the very word implies a progressive increase in knowledge and understanding, a gradual widening of what he knew and understood. This in turn indicates that, far from being omniscient, there were things that Jesus did not know. Even during his ministry we see him asking for information, and Luke's account of his visit to Jerusalem at the age of twelve describes Jesus *'sitting among the teachers, listening to them and asking them questions'*. There were things of which he was ignorant or which he did not understand. It is important for us to recognise this seemingly banal fact: that Jesus knew and understood more and better later than he did earlier, that he once 'thought like a child' but later 'put away childish things'. All human beings pass through a similar process, inherent to which is that we change our minds as we come to understand more, that we pass through periods of perplexity or uncertainty before coming to new conclusions, that we abandon one set of intentions for others, doubting, learning from mistakes.

Moral and spiritual development

The word 'wisdom' in Luke 2:52 implies that the learning encompasses not only factual knowledge and rational understanding but also moral and spiritual awareness. We move from a child's innocence, through to the wisdom (we hope!) of old age. This is what all human beings experience, and if we are to take seriously the humanity of Jesus, as we must, then one is forced to the conclusion that Jesus too probably experienced something similar – in short, that he had a mental life akin to that of other human beings. There seems, moreover, no reason not to assume that that process of change and development continued throughout his life.

Moral freedom – the life of the will and the emotions

Time is the essential dimension of our entire mental life in another sense too. Despite our tendency to look back to the past, aided by our amazing capacity for memory, human life is essentially lived facing forward: the life of the will and the emotions is made up of such feelings as hoping, aspiring, fearing, imagining, desiring, making plans, intending, choosing between possibilities and also regretting. Leaving aside the complexities of the subject, it is the

Preliminaries: Birth, Childhood – and 'Christology'

common experience of human beings that we are free to make such choices. Jesus' humanity surely means that his mental life was similar; when he separated himself from his family and the other people with whom they were travelling and returned to the temple during the visit to Jerusalem recorded in Luke 2, he made a choice and took a decision, just as we do. Only a free agent can praise, honour and obey God; and it is essential to our view of Jesus that we acknowledge this to be true of him too.

A life among other human beings

Luke tells us that Jesus *'was obedient to [his parents]'*. The initial socialisation of the child normally takes place through his or her relations with parents and, in some cases, with siblings. So it was in Jesus' case too. But Luke's phrase, *'grew ... in favour with God and man'*, also indicates that as he grew, his circle of acquaintances grew too; he learned to live among other human beings, knowing them and being known by them and beginning to establish his place and his unique identity in the world. If Jesus had been from childhood the uniquely omniscient being, already aware of his divine origins, that he is often held to be, how could he have related to others honestly and authentically? To reveal who he was would have incurred, one may suppose, either derision or suspicion and rejection, not the favour that Luke mentions. Equally, how could other people in Nazareth have remained totally unaware of the 'otherness' of this unique being in their midst? Yet of any awareness of his uniqueness there is in the Gospels no trace;

> *'Where did this man get these things?' they asked. 'What's this wisdom that has been given him? What are these remarkable miracles he is performing? Isn't this the carpenter? Isn't this Mary's son and the brother of James, Joseph, Judas and Simon? Aren't his sisters here with us?' (Mark 6:2-3)*

Imperfection

It may appear inappropriate to speak of 'imperfection' in relation to Jesus, yet by implication he later did so himself: When addressed as 'Good teacher', he replied: *'Why do you call me good? No one is good but God alone'* (Mark 10:17-18). No one, not even Jesus, was the 'finished article' – at least until he said on the cross *'it is finished'*. All human beings are conscious of conflicting elements within themselves: passions, instincts, impulses and appetites that are frequently at war with each other but especially with our more reflective, rational capacities (cf. James 4:1; Romans 7:14-20). The decision to return to the temple that we referred to above, despite the anguish that it was bound to cause for his parents, is perhaps an example of Jesus' 'unfinished' condition, resulting from an unresolved conflict of this kind.

Jesus – yesterday, today, for ever

Historical and cultural determination

All human beings, because they exist in time, bear the mark of the time and place in which they live: they speak the local language, adopt, at first at least, the norms, traditions and practices of the surrounding society, and share its knowledge of the world. What this may have meant in Jesus' case we shall need to consider further later, but the visit to Jerusalem at the age of twelve, already referred to more than once, provides a simple illustration: Jesus went because it was the common practice in the family and in the devout Jewish environment in which he grew up. There may be other reasons too, but the simple fact of cultural conditioning cannot be discounted.

The evidence that we have been able to adduce from Luke's few verses about Jesus' childhood is obviously sparse, yet it is sufficient to indicate that the child Jesus was in every respect fully human. Though he was, by virtue of the manner of his conception and birth, a unique creature, 'son of God', his childhood appears to have shown no trace of anything outside the range of human behaviour and experience. He was not yet, in any practical, recognisable sense, 'God with us' or 'the word made flesh' – that is, surely the conclusion that we must draw from the Gospel writers' almost complete omission of this phase of his life. When the story of Jesus' life begins in earnest, it therefore comes almost as a surprise: we move from the 'ordinariness' of Jesus' childhood to the extraordinary events of his ministry. But that ordinariness should remind us that the gospel narratives are relating the words and actions of one who truly is a human being, albeit one endowed now with remarkable, God-given powers: the central figure in the story has a mental life similar to our own. He has to learn, think, decide, choose; he experiences doubt, anxiety and uncertainty – those nights in prayer were, surely, not devoted solely to sweet meditation.

It is here that the continuity that we have already referred to is of particular significance. We saw in the previous chapter that the figure of Adam is one of the ways in which Jesus is most clearly foreshadowed in the Old Testament, albeit in an entirely negative, contrastive sense, and that this link is confirmed and underlined in the New Testament. And when we begin to read about him in the Gospels, we not only find him consistently referred to as 'son of man' but also placed, by Luke, in a genealogy that shows him integrated into a line of human descent that goes back to Adam. Later in the New Testament, in Hebrews 2, he is presented as the ultimate realisation of the destiny of 'man' as heralded in Genesis 1 and as the first of God's many 'sons and daughters'. It is simply not possible, without discarding an essential element of the architecture of the entire Biblical narrative, to make of Jesus one who descends to

Preliminaries: Birth, Childhood – and 'Christology'

us from heavenly realms and then, after a brief quasi-human life, returns to divine glory.

B. Jesus' Childhood

The birth narratives

As already mentioned, the Gospels' accounts of Jesus' early years are essentially theological rather than biographical in orientation. The continuity that we referred to in the introduction to this chapter is an essential theme in the birth narratives of Matthew and Luke, though the two accounts are very different from each other – Mark and John include no account of Jesus' beginnings at all. Matthew's account focuses on Joseph's role: it is he who receives an angelic visitation explaining the circumstances of Mary's pregnancy, relating it to an Old Testament prophecy and urging him not to break off their betrothal. Luke, by contrast, focuses on Mary's visitation, including detailed statements about the child's identity and future role, and on her humble, willing response to it, which Luke contrasts markedly with Zechariah's response to the announcement of another child, John the Baptist. There is a similar contrast between the visitors who come to worship the new-born child: in Matthew, they are 'wise men' from 'the east', presumably Gentiles, therefore, bringing gifts with an obviously symbolic significance, while in Luke they are local shepherds, people of the lowest social class, who would be deemed unclean, both ritually and, probably, hygienically.

Nevertheless, both accounts present Jesus as *the promised one*, foreshadowed not only in the Old Testament, as we saw in Chapter 2, but also in the various passages that we explored in Chapter 1 about one who would be the true man, through whom and for whom the purpose of God would come to its final realisation. In Matthew, this theme is introduced in the opening line, which links Jesus to the earlier figures, Abraham and David, and to the promises made in relation to them: *'An account of the genealogy of Jesus the Messiah, the son of David, the son of Abraham'* (Matt. 1:1). Luke's account similarly relates the forthcoming birth to Old Testament prophecies, though in more detail, and sees it as the continuation, or resumption, of 'salvation history', i.e. the story of God's loving purposes of salvation unfolding through time in the history of Israel. Accordingly, the announcement of the birth is marked by a sense of rejoicing, a note struck particularly in two 'songs', comparable to operatic arias, by the two already contrasted parents Zechariah and Mary, and also in two shorter songs, the angelic chorus in chapter 2 and then the *Nunc Dimittis* of the elderly Simeon.

Though the context in Luke's account focuses almost solely on *Israel's* hope of redemption and salvation – Anna, for example, speaks of the child in relation to *'the redemption of Jerusalem'* (2:38) – there are hints of a wider significance. In Luke, Simeon refers to *'all peoples'* and *'a light for revelation to the Gentiles'* (2:31-32), while in Matthew the universal implications of the birth are represented by the involvement of the 'wise men', presaging the commandment at the close of this Gospel to *'make disciples of all nations'* (28:19). Luke's genealogy in Chapter 3, reaching back to Adam, points in the same direction. By implication, therefore, the rejoicing at the birth of Jesus is that of all mankind at the coming of the one in whom human history will at last find its true fulfilment.

However, in Luke's narrative this continuity with the Old Testament is far from straightforward: his story begins at the heart of Israel and her traditional faith, in the Jerusalem temple, and the first person we encounter is Zechariah, a priest and representative of the existing order. But Zechariah and Elizabeth, the representatives of the old order, are childless and are likely to remain so: *'Both of them were righteous in the sight of God, observing all the Lord's commands and decrees blamelessly. But they were childless because Elizabeth was not able to conceive, and they were both very old'* (Luke 1:6-7). While this may seem to represent a comforting parallel to the condition of Abraham and Sarah, its significance in the context can hardly be missed: the old system is barren – the salvation and redemption, for Jerusalem and for the world, that Simeon and Anna were waiting and hoping for, will not come from this source. A new intervention of God, a new outpouring of his Spirit, parallel to the birth of Isaac, will be necessary, fulfilling the promise found in Isaiah: *'For I will pour water on the thirsty land, and streams on the dry ground; I will pour out my Spirit on your offspring, and my blessing on your descendants'* (Is. 44:3). For this, the narrative moves far away from Jerusalem, to despised Galilee and to a simple village girl. It is on her that the Spirit will be poured: *'The Holy Spirit will come on you, and the power of the Most High will overshadow you. So the holy one to be born will be called the Son of God'* (Luke 1:35).

Luke is suggesting, then, that the birth of Jesus, while representing fulfilment and continuity, also represents the most radical *discontinuity*. His genealogy of Jesus in Luke 3 points in the same direction: by presenting it in the reverse order, unlike Matthew, he implies that Jesus can be seen, not as the final fruit of a line stretching back to Abraham, as Matthew does, but rather as one who bears on his shoulders the crushing weight of a history of disobedience and failure stretching back to – Adam. By implication, then, Luke, who was, of course, a companion and disciple of Paul, is here presenting Jesus in Paul's terms as the 'second Adam' (as mentioned in chapter 2).

Preliminaries: Birth, Childhood – and 'Christology'

Like Paul, Luke sees both a parallel and a contrast between Adam and Jesus. The final verse of the genealogy describes Adam as 'the son of God': unlike Adam, Jesus will prove himself truly a 'son of God', but like Adam, he represents a beginning, or, more precisely, a new beginning, a new creation and a new humanity (Luke 3:38).

Son of God

However, these two accounts have something still more radical to tell us: they announce Jesus as a man, certainly, born to a woman and to be brought up and cared for by two human parents, but nevertheless a 'son of God' by virtue of the unique circumstances of his conception. It was a birth at once completely normal *and* utterly unique since the child has no human father. We have, of course, no idea what it means to say that Jesus was begotten by the Holy Spirit, as these two Gospels tell us, and we do well to avoid speculation. We should, though, not assume any kind of divine element in Jesus' genetic make-up or suggest that God was in some sense his biological father – such a suggestion brings us dangerously close to pagan tales of gods giving birth to children with human mothers. As we have just mentioned, Luke's genealogy describes Adam as 'son of God' (Luke 3:38), yet in the latter's case we would hesitate to suggest any genetic relationship. It is perhaps better to think in terms of a child born by the will and through the intervention of God and endowed with gifts and qualities that will fit him for the task that will later be his.

Christian readers of these stories are perhaps so used to the idea of Jesus as son of God that its extraordinariness scarcely registers. It is not so much the altogether supernatural nature of the event, which, incidentally, far outweighs all the other supernatural phenomena that surround it – the annunciations to both Joseph (Matthew) and Mary (Luke), the guiding star, the angelic appearance to the shepherds, for example[7] – but, above all, the idea that the Creator of all things, the eternal Lord of the universe, should choose to join himself in this way to such comparatively small and insignificant creatures as ourselves. We are inclined, as we think about it, to echo the psalmist's question: *'What are human beings that you are mindful of them, mortals that you care for them?'* (Ps. 8:4). The birth of the child Jesus obliges us to grasp that in God's eyes we are not insignificant – in fact, that the statement about the

---

7 Familiarity tends to mean that we barely notice the problems that these events pose for the modern reader: not simply their supernatural dimension but also the absence of any support for them in secular history, notably the difficulty in identifying the census that Luke refers to at the beginning of his second chapter. We also fail to notice the complete absence of any trace left by events so strikingly unusual in the world of that time.

Jesus – yesterday, today, for ever

creation of man in Genesis 1 really does mean what it says: *'God created hu-mankind in his own image'* (Genesis 1:27). As I have already said, it is fruitless to attempt to understand in any biological or genetic way what it means for a child to be born in the way that Matthew and Luke describe. That is not, however, a reason to doubt the truth of these narratives, however much that might go against the assumptions of human thought: what other way have we to explain how and why this child in due time grew up to be a unique human being, one without parallel in human history?

Reversals

The apparent contrast, particularly marked in Luke, between the completely Jewish colouring of the birth narratives and the universal reach at the end of these two Gospels is a hint of a third, less obvious theme: the story is not go-ing to proceed smoothly to its appointed end. The two accounts thus confirm what we have seen announced 'from the beginning' and foreshadowed in the Old Testament: that the coming one will attain to the lofty status predicted of him only through opposition and suffering. In Matthew, almost the whole of chapter 2 is overshadowed by the threat of violence against the child on the part of king Herod (Herod the Great), which necessitates first the flight to Egypt and then the family's move to Nazareth in Galilee. In Luke, there is no such threat to the young child; however, amidst all the rejoicing and the sense of glad anticipation that God is at last going to 'visit' and redeem his people Israel, suffering under Roman domination, we hear a different note in the words that Simeon addresses, in prose rather than verse, to Mary: *'This child is destined for the falling and the rising of many in Israel, and to be a sign that will be opposed so that the inner thoughts of many will be revealed – and a sword will pierce your own soul too'* (Luke 2:34-35).

These two narratives imply, then, that the way to the realisation of what is said of Jesus at the time of his birth will involve an extraordinary reversal of all the values and hierarchies of the existing order of things. We have al-ready noticed the switch in Luke 1 from Jerusalem, focus of all Israel's hopes, to the insignificant village of Nazareth in despised Galilee; and from a male priest, Zechariah, to a young peasant girl. This reversal is sustained in chapter 2, where the news of the birth is revealed, not to the great or to the religious leaders but to lowly shepherds, and then to a woman, Anna, and to an old man Simeon. A reversal of this kind is predicted in Mary's song in chapter 1, the *Magnificat*, which has already announced such a reversal: *'He has shown strength with his arm; he has scattered the proud in the thoughts of their hearts. He has brought down the powerful from their thrones, and lifted up the lowly; he has*

Preliminaries: Birth, Childhood – and 'Christology'

filled the hungry with good things, and sent the rich away empty' (1:51-53).[8]
This birth, then, is the vital stepping stone to the ultimate accomplishment of the creative intention of God 'from the beginning'. The child is to fulfil a dual role: he is to be the first exemplar of the perfected humanity envisaged by Genesis, the man 'in the image of God'; at the same time, by realising that intention, he will be God's supreme revelation of himself to mankind and his instrument in working out his saving purpose for humanity. Matthew's account confirms this when it is said that Jesus is to be called *'Emmanuel'*, which means, as Matthew tells us, *'God is with us'*. (Matt. 1:23).

John's Prologue

While Mark and John contain no reference to Jesus' early life. John, however, does include a prologue, the first eighteen verses of Chapter 1, in effect in place of a nativity story. It tells us nothing about Jesus' birth or early life; instead, John's description of him as 'the word become flesh' (1:14) links up powerfully with the ideas that we have explored in chapters 1 and 2 and, in particular, echoes Matthew's reference to 'God with us'. John's simple phrase thus brings together at least three fundamental ideas about Jesus:

- He is – or, more accurately, is going to be – the realisation in a human life of the whole purpose of God, i.e. of everything that the Old Testament says about the coming one and about God's intentions in his creative work right from 'the beginning'. The opening phrase, *'In the beginning'*, is clearly a deliberate echo of the opening of the creation story in Genesis 1.

- He is the ultimate self-revelation of God – the expression in v. 1, *'the word was God [or 'divine']*, implies that, as the *New English Bible* puts it, *'what God was, the word was'*.

- In him God speaks to mankind; he is his 'last word' to us, the creatures who are, uniquely, *'in his image'* and thus able to hear and respond to him.[9]

John's Prologue, though profoundly different from the nativity stories in Matthew and Luke, helps us to recognise what the Gospel writers are attempting above all to do in their different openings. These sections of the Gospels

---

8 I have dealt more fully with the the the relationship between beginning and ending in Luke and the theme of reversal in my *Luke's Pauline Narrative: Reading the Third Gospel* (2019).

9 John's Prologue is discussed at some length in my *The Word Became Flesh: A Theme in John's Gospel* (2016).

Jesus – yesterday, today, for ever

have a dual focus. On the one hand, they look forward to the eventual outcome of Jesus' ministry, death and resurrection: his future role as saviour and king. On the other hand, they look back: Matthew traces his descent from Abraham and David and sees his coming as the fulfilment of promises, while John's gaze is fixed on 'the beginning' and even 'before the beginning'. They thus form a kind of hinge between past and future – which is, in fact, what Jesus' earthly life as a whole is.

The Gospels and Jesus' childhood

Readers of the Gospels are often puzzled by the scarcity of information about the life of Jesus prior to the beginning of his public ministry. There is so much that readers, especially believing readers, would like to know about him as a child and young man, yet all we find, after the nativity accounts in Matthew and Luke, are a few verses in Luke, including an account of his visit to Jerusalem with his parents at the age of twelve. Two obvious reasons can be suggested for the Gospels' perhaps puzzling silence about Jesus' early life, quite apart from the limitations on length imposed by the space available in a single scroll:

- The Gospel writers simply deem Jesus' life prior to the beginning of his ministry to be unimportant, or, perhaps better, irrelevant to the needs of the reader. The saving mission of Jesus, they imply, begins with his baptism. When, after Jesus' ascension, Peter proposes that a replacement must be found for Judas Iscariot, he describes the necessary qualifications for the role as apostle like this: *'So one of the men who have accompanied us during all the time that the Lord Jesus went in and out among us, beginning from the baptism of John until the day when he was taken up from us – one of these must become a witness with us to his resurrection'* (Acts 1:21-22). In Acts 10, summarising the ministry of Jesus, Peter essentially repeats the same idea: *'That message spread throughout Judea, beginning in Galilee after the baptism that John announced'* (Acts 10:37). Similarly, in his farewell discourses in John, Jesus says: *'You also are to testify because you have been with me from the beginning'* (John 15:27) – the 'beginning' of the events to which the apostles are be witnesses is the time of his calling of his disciples, which, according to John 1, is closely related to Jesus' baptism by John the Baptist. The way in which Mark begins his Gospel is explicit: after his bombshell of an opening sentence, *'The beginning of the good news of Jesus Christ, the Son of God'* and two Old Testament quotations, Mark launches immediately into his account of John the Baptist's work, culminating in the baptism of

Preliminaries: Birth, Childhood – and 'Christology'

Jesus.

- As we saw in the previous chapter, a Graeco-Roman *bios* was very different from our contemporary notions of biography. It contained no trawl through the minutiae of the childhood of their subject for clues to his or her psychological make-up; as Richard Burridge comments, 'Against this background, the gospels' concentration on Jesus' public ministry from his baptism to death does not seem very different.'[10]

What is the effect of the extreme reticence of the Gospels concerning Jesus' early life? First, they provide virtually no link between the past, God's creative intentions from the beginning and his promises to Israel that are evoked in the opening birth narratives, and Jesus' ministry when it begins. The effect is to make the story of Jesus' ministry as much of a surprise to the unsuspecting reader as it was to the people of Israel, whose conception of the 'coming one', if they had one, laid the same emphasis upon rulership and victory that we find in Matthew's and Luke's birth narratives. By that very surprise, these accounts challenge us, as Jesus' contemporaries were challenged, to rethink in the light of that life our understanding of what God had promised and what his intentions were. Jesus' life, as we encounter it in the Gospels, is thus the decisive criterion for everything that we think or say about God's eternal purpose.

However, the Gospel accounts may also disappoint the reader's expectations in another way. They have described the rejoicing of Luke 1 and the extraordinary events of Luke 2; the birth narratives of Matthew and Luke have so far been rich in Old Testament echoes and symbolism, in celebration of the fulfilment at last of God's promises, and in extraordinary events. Moreover, the child who has been born is destined for decisive and glorious roles in the unfolding purpose of God. So what kind of wonderful child will he be? Was he obviously different from other children? Was he better behaved, more intelligent? Did he from the beginning possess special powers? Did everyone know that he was different, special – and did he himself know? The clearly supernatural events included in the narratives of Jesus' birth and childhood can lead to the assumption that similar events must have continued to mark his young life. It is all too easy to allow the imagination to run riot – to imagine Jesus as some kind of child prodigy, as was done in the early centuries of Christianity, in works such as the *Infancy Gospel of Thomas* and the *Infancy Gospel of James*, both probably from the second century AD.

---

10 Richard A. Burridge, *Four Gospels, One Jesus? A Symbolic Reading*, London 1994, pp. 6-7.

Yet following the presentation of Jesus in the temple (Luke 2:38), there is a virtual silence – just fourteen verses in Luke 2. They begin and end with two generalised descriptions:

When Joseph and Mary had done everything required by the Law of the Lord, they returned to Galilee to their own town of Nazareth. And the child grew and became strong; he was filled with wisdom, and the grace of God was upon him. (v. 39-40)

Then he went down to Nazareth with them and was obedient to them. But his mother treasured all these things in her heart. And Jesus grew in wisdom and stature, and in favour with God and men. (v. 51-52)

It appears to be a childhood of surprising normality, not to say ordinariness, interrupted only by an account of the visit to Jerusalem when Jesus is already twelve years old, marked by an incident which in any other childhood would be regarded as a minor childish escapade.

There is thus an apparent mismatch between, on the one hand, the roles ascribed to Jesus and the lofty things said about him even before his birth and, on the other, this ordinariness. It is not that the Gospel writers intended to direct our attention to this normality: the brevity of these passages simply reflects their priorities. Their situation, like that of their original readers, was radically different from ours. They needed to convince a sceptical world that the man from Nazareth was, however surprising it might seem, truly the Son of God, now risen from the dead. Today, the reverse is the case: believing Christians for the most part accept Jesus' divine origins – what they need is to grasp and to allow for his genuine humanity.

What this means, of course, is that our desire to have some picture of Jesus as a child and as a young man is not merely idle curiosity: it bears upon the most fundamental of all issues surrounding Jesus, his status as 'son of God', to which we have already alluded. In that context, the 'mismatch' that we have noted is itself a comment on the vexed question of the relationship between his divine, i.e. supernatural, roles and his ordinariness, i.e. between his humanity and his unique status as 'son of God'.

Jesus' early years

What picture are we able to construct of Jesus' childhood, based on the sparse information available to us? Much will inevitably be no more than conjecture, but Luke's brief statements do allow us to draw certain conclusions. The statement in v. 41 of chapter 2 that Jesus' parents went to Jerusalem every year at Passover tells us instantly that Jesus was brought up in a home charac-

Preliminaries: Birth, Childhood – and 'Christology'

terised by Jewish piety – the fact that they also took Jesus to be circumcised as an eight-day-old baby and then dedicated him to God in the temple (Luke 2:21, 22-24; cf. Lev. 12) had already indicated this. That in turn suggests that Jesus probably attended the synagogue in Nazareth regularly, and that what he heard or was taught there was reinforced, possibly even repeated or expanded, by his parents at home. It is likely to have been a home in which the traditions of Jewish piety were observed as Joseph and Mary sought to fulfil the commandment of Deuteronomy 6 to *'impress them [the commandments] on your children'*. Robert Aron in his book on Jesus' 'obscure years' describes them like this:

> For Joseph, and thus for Jesus, there was no action, however familiar and banal, that was not the object of a blessing. The world in which a Jew lives is one that is completely sacred. Even its apparently most secular aspects are linked to the divine … Thus, around the child Jesus, a whole universe dedicated to the divine revealed itself within the framework of the family home. He is accompanied by the sacred in his home at every moment; it colours his every action and accompanies his every childish thought.[11]

The phrase in Luke 2:51, *'was obedient'*, tells us something else: that he was indeed 'brought up', just as all human children are – he needed to be taught how to behave appropriately, at first in the home, along with the siblings that we hear of later (see Mark 6:3). This is confirmed in both v. 40 and 52 by the presence of the word 'grew', which in fact renders two different Greek words. In v. 40, *auxanō* is the normal word for natural growth in plants and animals; this verse is speaking of a natural process of physical development, suggesting that he became a sturdy, healthy child, but also of mental development; 'wisdom' may imply development of his intellectual powers but perhaps also an unusual degree of thoughtfulness and of moral and spiritual awareness.

How, one wonders, did his parents behave towards him? Did they treat him differently from the other children born later? I imagine that they were wise enough to show no favouritism – the stories of Jacob's and David's families are a powerful warning against it – but they may, like all sensible parents, have treated all their children differently according to their differing characters and needs. Did Mary at some point tell Jesus about the circumstances of his birth? If she did, how could she possibly treat him in the same way that she treated her other children? Luke's phrase in v. 51, *'His mother treasured all these things in her heart'*, may well mean that she did not. She might well,

---

11   Robert Aron, *Les Années Obscures de Jésus*, Paris 1966, pp. 70, 72.

Jesus – yesterday, today, for ever

though, have told him as he grew up that he had been dedicated to God by his parents, rather as Hannah had given her special child to God (Luke 2:22-24; cf. 1 Sam. 1:22-24). It may have been no more than the Law's requirement for a firstborn child, but perhaps in this case it was taken seriously by Mary and Joseph – we remember that Mary's song in Luke 1 closely resembles Hannah's song in 1 Samuel 2.

The word for 'grew' in v. 52 is *prokoptō*, which means not just growth but 'progress' or 'advancement', again both physical ('stature') and mental ('wisdom'). However, the original meaning of the word may tell us something more: it refers firstly to the process by which metal is lengthened by being hammered out. It conjures up the idea of Jesus being shaped by the forces acting upon him – being 'malleable', in fact – suggesting a social dimension to his development as he responds to the circumstances and the people that surround him. That might refer in the first place to his learning through his experience of family life: working out how to cope with younger siblings and with other village children of his own age – did they perhaps make fun of him because of his seriousness? Or was he faced with the kind of insinuations implicit, perhaps, in his adversaries' comment later in his life: *'They said to him, "We are not illegitimate children; we have one father, God himself"'* (John 8:41). We may think of him also experiencing and coming to appreciate the unconditional love of parents, grasping through Joseph's strengths and weaknesses in the role what a father can and should be.

C. Growing up in Nazareth: the contemporary context

I suggested earlier that historical and cultural determination is an essential feature of human existence: Jesus was a real man, living in Israel at a particular time in history, and even when still quite a young child he will have begun to absorb unconsciously the habits, attitudes, and assumptions of life around him. We find evidences of his familiarity with all these things in his later teaching.

It is not my purpose to deal extensively with the background to Jesus' life; much useful information can be found in the works listed in the footnote below.[12] But we need to ask ourselves what kind of environment it was in

---

12 Information on Israel in the time of Jesus may be found in the following works, among others: Maurice Casey, *Jesus of Nazareth*, London & New York 2010; Joel B. Green & Lee Martin McDonald (eds.), *The World of the New Testament*, Grand Rapids, Michigan 2013; J. Julius Scott Jr., *Jewish Backgrounds of the New Testament*, Grand Rapids, Michigan 1995; Gerd Theissen & Annette Merz (eds.), *The Historical Jesus. A Comprehensive Guide*, translated by John Bowden, London 1998 (original title: *Der historische Jesus: Ein Lehrbuch*, Göt-

Preliminaries: Birth, Childhood – and 'Christology'

which he grew to manhood. It is not easy for readers of the New Testament to realise how different the Israel of Jesus' day was from the Israel of which we hear in the Old Testament. Several centuries lie between the last events that figure in the Old Testament, the visits of Nehemiah to Jerusalem, the book of Malachi, and Esther's interventions in the affairs of the Persian empire, all placed somewhere around the middle of the 5th century BC, and the time of Jesus.

The religious scene

The synagogue

Apart from his parents, probably the most powerful influence upon Jesus as a boy must have been what he learned in the synagogue. The development of the synagogue was a major consequence of the disasters that had befallen Israel in the previous centuries, above all the destruction of Jerusalem, the end of the kingdom of Judah and the Babylonian exile. With the disaster of 586 BC, Israel had forfeited the three pillars of her national life: the land, the Davidic monarchy, and Jerusalem and the temple.[13] How, then, could their worship be continued without their city and their temple? This question was answered by the building of the second temple, described in Ezra, and then by the construction of Herod's magnificent but short-lived replacement. But much else, too, that Israel did in the years after the exile, right down to Jesus' day, was driven by the ambition to reconstruct Israel's spiritual and religious identity and to learn from this national disaster. Those efforts were, at least in part, not without success: idolatry, at least, was never again a serious danger to Israel's faith.

However, perhaps the most important, and probably the most effective of these attempts at reconstruction was the development of the synagogue, which is thought to be a result of the experience of exile and the need to survive it. Despite the continued veneration for the temple, once rebuilt, and the continuing desire to mark the major feasts in the Jewish calendar, the synagogues, found throughout Israel and in Jewish areas in the *diaspora*, 'developed as the centre of Hebrew life after the loss of traditional institutions'[14] and played a central part in a profound change in the character of religious life in Israel. It was a lay institution, in the hands of local elders rather than priests, and all males, even quite young boys, were able to participate in its services,

---

tingen 1996).

13   Scott, *Jewish Backgrounds*, pp. 108-112.

14   *Ibid.*, p. 139.

which consisted essentially in the reading of the Law and the Prophets and in prayer, though by the time of Jesus they often included also some kind of 'homily' or exposition of the scriptures. Scott sums up the character of religious life in Israel as a result of all the changes triggered by the loss of the temple in 586 BC as follows:

> The significance of the temple in Intertestamental Judaism was ... largely symbolic and sentimental. It was the visible centre of religious life and the pride of the nation. Nevertheless, in fact, its role and function were in decline ... The centre of Judaism had moved from temple and ceremony to morals and ethics. The piety and thought of such groups as the Pharisees were based on the law, not merely the temple and the ceremony of the law. The actual centre of Jewish religious life had moved to the synagogue.[15]

We have, then, to think of the synagogue, with its services, its reading from, and exposition of, the Old Testament being at the centre of Jesus' young life. It will have been no matter of habit or routine, either: Isaiah describes the coming one like this:

> *The spirit of the LORD shall rest on him, the spirit of wisdom and understanding, the spirit of counsel and might, the spirit of knowledge and the fear of the LORD. His delight shall be in the fear of the LORD. (Isaiah 11:2-3)*

Perhaps this is what Luke meant by the 'grace' of God that rested upon him – not, I think, some miraculous power or knowledge, but a mind wonderfully insightful when he hears the scriptures read and expounded and a capacity to retain and memorise what he has heard. From this, there surely must have developed, as he grew, a strong sense of the reality and nearness of God, a delight in what he came to know and understand about him, and an awareness that he had been 'given to God' virtually at birth.

Literacy

Some scholars believe that Jewish children, and especially boys, learned to read at some kind of elementary school attached to the synagogue, enabling them to read the scriptures and participate in synagogue worship. More recently, however, doubts have been cast on the level of literacy in Jesus' day. Estimates vary wildly: Maurice Casey asserts that 'When they grew up, Jesus and Jacob [i.e. James] will have become, like Joseph, adult male Israelites who

---

15 Scott, *Jewish Backgrounds*, p. 155.

Preliminaries: Birth, Childhood – and 'Christology'

read from the Torah in Hebrew…'.[16] Scott, by contrast, describes a quite limited form of education and literacy, focused almost solely on the ability to read the Hebrew scriptures and relying heavily on rote-learning, repetition and memorisation, while Catherine Hezser estimates literacy in Roman Palestine, i.e. the world of Jesus, at 3 percent, or slightly higher![17] Kent L. Yinger writes: 'Oral repetition and memory, versus written lessons, were undoubtedly the primary medium of instruction … The vast majority of the Jewish population was non-literate and without formal education'[18] Chris Keith, from whose book some of these estimates are taken, comes to a similar conclusion: 'Most people in the time of Jesus could not read or write'.[19]

It seems likely, then, that the instruction that Jesus received at the synagogue was probably fairly rudimentary and would not attain to what Keith calls 'scribal literacy'. How, then, was he able find his place in the Isaiah scroll and then read from it, as Luke suggests he does later (Luke 4:16-17)? One can conceive of the possibility that someone in his environment who did possess such learning might have noticed this boy's remarkable interest and understanding and taught him far more than the synagogue could offer, aided by the grace that was upon him to quicken his understanding. Some such instruction may have been the answer to the question posed about him in John 7: '*How does this man have such learning [i.e. grammata – 'letters'], when he has never been taught?*' (John 7:15). Though he had not the formal qualification of a scribe, many of those who met and heard him clearly thought that he had – they called him 'teacher' and compared his teaching favourably with that of the scribes.

---

16 Maurice Casey, *Jesus of Nazareth*, p. 161.

17 Catherine Hezser, *Jewish Literacy un Roman Palestine*, Tübingen 2001, p. 496 (quoted in Keith, *Jesus against the Scribal Elite* – see note 19 below).

18 Kent L/ Yinger, 'Jewish Education', in *The World of the New Testament. Cultural, Social, and Historical Contexts*, ed. Joel B. Green & Lee Martin McDonald, Grand Rapids, Michigan 2013, pp. 325-329 (here p. 328).

19 See Chris Keith, *Jesus against the Scribal Elite. The Origins of the Conflict*, revised edition, London/New York 2020, pp. 19-24. Part of the difficulty of this topic are the differing meanings attached to the notion of 'literacy'. At one end of the scale lies what Keith calls 'scribal literacy' – the ability to read the text of the scriptures in the original language, to compare texts, to find one's place in scrolls without chapter headings or verse numbers, and to interpret them. At the other end would lie the ability to decipher a limited number of well-known passages, possibly in Aramaic, while in between would be the kind of literacy that enabled, for example, business men to cope with their accounts or tradesmen to understand information vital to their trade

Jesus – yesterday, today, for ever

Jewish 'sects'

It seems unlikely that the young Jesus will have been directly affected by another consequence of Israel's recent history, the increasing influence of Hellenism, i.e. Greek language and culture, as a result of the conquests of Alexander the Great in the 4th century BC.[20] This imposition of Hellenism in Israel reached its peak in the second century, when the Seleucid monarch, Antiochus IV, began a determined drive to Hellenize Israel, culminating in the desecration of the temple which finally provoked the Maccabean uprising. Yet while the resistance movement led by the Maccabees succeeded in freeing Israel from Seleucid rule, they were far from being opposed to all features of Hellenistic culture: '... Hellenism ... remained as a permanent feature in Judaism afterwards. The Hasmonean dynasty, especially the later rulers, were sympathizers or even outright supporters.'[21] Greek culture and language permeated the Judean aristocracy, especially in the major centres, and Greek was widely spoken – 'culture' refers not only to Greek language but also to such things as institutions, education, entertainments, styles of dress and architecture, and to more intangible things such as philosophy, ways of thinking, values and priorities. Scott includes the astonishing statistic that '... 40 percent of the pre-A.D. 70 burial inscriptions in Jerusalem are in Greek'.

The Gospels give no real hint of the degree of influence enjoyed by Greek culture because Jesus appears to have confined his ministry to the Aramaic-speaking countryside and small towns in Galilee, apart from his various visits to Jerusalem, apparently avoiding Sepphoris and Tiberias in Galilee, where Greek language and culture flourished.

Even in Nazareth, though, Jesus will have become aware of one consequence of the influence of Hellenism, the development of the three competing Jewish sects or 'sects of philosophy', as Josephus calls them.[22] The *Sadducees* were the heirs of the most moderate and more aristocratic sections of the resistance movement led by the Maccabees. Though they had originally been part of that opposition, they were not unsympathetic to a 'modernising' – and therefore Hellenizing – of Jewish culture. In religious terms, they were closely associated with the temple and its rituals – the high priests in the 1st century came from among the Sadducees – and they were strongly represented in the Sanhedrin (see Acts 4:1; 5:17). In religious terms, the Sadducees gave supreme importance to the written Law, the 'books of Moses', rejecting the

---

20   Scott, *Jewish Backgrounds*, pp. 112-120.

21   *Ibid.*, p. 117.

22   Josephus, *Antiquities of the Jews*, XVIII, 1; *The Wars of the Jews*, II, 8.ii.

Preliminaries: Birth, Childhood – and 'Christology'

traditions and teachings of 'the fathers' which together comprised the 'oral law'. This focus on the Pentateuch accounts for their rejection of the idea of resurrection, which the New Testament attributes to them on more than one occasion (Matt. 22:23; Mark 12:18; Luke 20:27; Acts 23:8).

Given their largely aristocratic roots and their close association with the temple, it is not surprising that the Sadducees sought to work with, rather than against, the Roman occupiers, however disliked they might be. The collaboration of the high priest with Pilate at the time of Jesus' trial and crucifixion is indicative of the positions of both parties: each needed the other, no matter how much they disliked each other. The arrest, trial and crucifixion of Jesus are therefore probably attributable primarily to the influence of the Sadducees; his 'cleansing' of the temple was clearly seen as a threat to the religious *status quo*, while his sheer popularity among 'the people' was deemed to constitute a threat to the fragile political settlement with the Romans. Their anxieties on that score are aptly summed up by John:

> So the chief priests and the Pharisees called a meeting of the council, and said, 'What are we to do? This man is performing many signs. If we let him go on like this, everyone will believe in him, and the Romans will come and destroy both our holy place and our nation.' (John 11:47-48)

Jesus may not have encountered Sadducees directly until he went to Jerusalem at the age of twelve, but even in remote Nazareth, he will certainly have met with the influence of *Pharisees*. They are widely believed to be the 'descendants' of the *Hasidim* ('pious ones'), who, following in the footsteps of Ezra, sought after the return from exile to lead Israel back to the study and the diligent observance of the Law. They were characterised by their zeal for both the written and the oral law, which went hand in hand with their rejection of the Hellenistic influence in Jewish life and worship and their consequent hostility to the Roman occupiers. If the Sadducees were the party of the well-to-do in Israel, the Pharisees were a movement much closer to the ordinary people and generally enjoyed wide public esteem for their evident piety. A typical Pharisee was not an office-holder but simply one dedicated to the task of calling Israel back to its original vocation as the holy people of God, separate from all other peoples. In their zeal, they tried to impose upon all Israelites the observance of purity laws that the Law itself required only of the priests, and in their own lives to 'build a fence around the Law' by going beyond what the Law required, as Jesus' parable of the Pharisee and the tax-collector illustrates (Luke 18:9-14).[23] However, their role as self-appointed

---

23   The phrase is Kenneth Bailey's in his *Jesus through Middle Eastern Eyes*, Downers Grove,

guardians of Jewish law and tradition left them vulnerable to the twin dangers of hypocritical self-righteousness and scorn for others less zealous than themselves that are devastatingly satirised by Jesus in this parable. It seems likely that already as an adolescent in Nazareth he had begun to notice these failings.

The young Jesus will almost certainly have had no direct experience of the third 'sect', the *Essenes*. They are thought to have developed from the most radical opponents of the Seleucids during the Maccabean period, who later withdrew entirely from public life to form separate communities where they could practise an ascetic, monkish manner of life, based on the extreme interpretation of the Mosaic Law prescribed by a figure known as 'the teacher of righteousness', thought to have been a high priest driven from office by a Maccabean (i.e. illegitimate) high priest. Regarding the priesthood and the temple worship in Jerusalem as totally corrupt, and rejecting all compromise with foreign, i.e. Roman rule, they saw themselves as the only true Israelites, whose duty it was to make atonement by their practice of righteousness for the sins of the people as a whole. It is generally accepted that the Dead Sea scrolls found at Qumran belonged to an Essene community living in that region of the Judean desert.

The Jesus of the Gospels is obviously aware of the religious debates then current in Israel and is able to enter into them – itself an astonishing feat for a young man from a small village who has not benefited from the kind of training reserved for the few who were striving to achieve scribal status. At the same time, his perceptive mind, sharpened by his growing understanding of the Law and the influence of God's grace upon him, surely helped him to recognise the weaknesses in the arguments and the inconsistency of those who *'load people with burdens hard to bear, and [themselves] do not lift a finger to ease them'* (Luke 11:46). Indeed, one senses in him later an indignation with the way in which the religious class made 'righteousness' an almost unattainable goal for ordinary people: *'For you lock people out of the kingdom of heaven. For you do not go in yourselves, and when others are going in, you stop them'* (Matt. 23:13). It seems likely that the roots of that indignation are to be sought in Jesus' early years, when he was moving about in Galilee, seeing human life as lived by the ordinary people, many of them the 'sinners' so easily dismissed by the 'righteous'.

Aged twelve in Jerusalem

The only detail concerning Jesus' early life that the Gospels provide is Luke's

---

Illinois & London 2008, p. 348, in the context of his discussion of this parable.

Preliminaries: Birth, Childhood – and 'Christology'

account of Jesus' visit to Jerusalem with his parents at the age of twelve. Most interpretations of this event, and particularly of Jesus' words when he is chided by his parents (v. 48), are based upon the assumption that he is already aware of both his identity as unique son of God and his future mission. His words, *'Did you not know that I must be in my Father's house?' –* or, in other versions: *'about my Father's business' –* (Luke 2:49), are taken to be an expression of that awareness. I am far from certain that Jesus did possess such knowledge at this stage. There are two considerations that seem to me to argue against an interpretation based on that assumption. First, it would have amounted to a repudiation of Joseph as father, which would have been even more hurtful than the thoughtlessness, arising from his enthusiasm, that had led him to stay behind. Secondly, Luke's comment, *'But they did not understand what he said to them'* (v. 50), seems to imply that not even Mary took Jesus' words to mean what many subsequent Christian readers have taken them to mean, i.e. as a reference to God as his father in the most literal sense. That may confirm my impression that she had not spoken to Jesus explicitly about the manner of his conception; it may even indicate that the extraordinary events of a dozen years earlier were no longer at the forefront of her mind. It is Luke, writing, of course, with hindsight, who recognises a deeper meaning in these words, which, on my reading of the passage, escaped all three of them.

So what *did* Jesus mean? His words are, in the first place, an answer to Mary's reproach, as if to say, 'Where else would you expect me to be?' The word 'must' (in Greek, the word *dei*, which plays so significant a part in Luke's Gospel) may imply a strong sense of inner impulsion, or it may suggest a duty, a claim on him that he must heed. Might these words not express his recognition, entirely without any pressure from others, of his duty to do what Jewish boys both then and today are expected to do – to take on himself 'the yoke of the Law' at about this age? It is, I think, not without significance that it is at the age of twelve that Jesus goes to Jerusalem with his parents, apparently for the first time: it was the moment when it was fitting for such a boy to go. As to the phrase 'my father's (house)', this too could be the language of any truly pious Jewish boy, acknowledging that God was the father of all Israelites and that he has claims upon their attention and their time that take precedence over everything – as Jesus himself later taught (Luke 14:26).

And what of Jesus' time in the temple? Jesus may well have come to Jerusalem full of anticipation: that he would see at last the glories of Herod's gleaming new temple, hear explanations of the scriptures from teachers more learned than those who taught in the Nazareth synagogue, and visit at last God's dwelling place in Israel, there to experience a form of worship that

83

Jesus – yesterday, today, for ever

corresponded to his own sense of what befitted his God. It seems likely that the reality of Jerusalem was profoundly disappointing. One may surmise that Jesus, with his deep understanding of the scriptures and his strong sense of the holiness and the love of God, found the rituals of the temple anything but impressive. Twenty or so years later, his view of the way in which the temple was run and of the kind of teaching offered by the learned scribes was scathing, as Matthew 23 in particular reveals.

Did he converse with the teachers of the Law already possessed of a full self-consciousness as divine Son and Messiah, as many assume? It appears to me more likely that it was the kind of situation that any who have ever taught an exceedingly perceptive boy or girl of Jesus' age will recognise: the quick, penetrating intelligence of the young that sees through the tired, standard answers and justifications offered by the adults, asking deceptively simple questions that lay bare the inadequacies of the conventional answers. One can readily imagine him asking the scribes, the supposedly authoritative exponents of the scriptures, the same kind of penetrating questions that he later posed to his adversaries:

> 'How can they say that the Messiah is David's son? For David himself says in the book of Psalms, "The Lord said to my Lord, 'Sit at my right hand, until I make your enemies your footstool.'" David thus calls him Lord; so how can he be his son?' (Luke 20:41-44)

Or might he have asked the Ethiopian's question, one that Jesus may well have pondered frequently: *'About whom ... does the prophet say this, about himself or about someone else?'* (Acts 8:34)? The text of Luke 2 perhaps implies that he was able to answer his own questions better than the teachers, for he appears both to ask and to answer: *'... they found him in the temple, sitting among the teachers, listening to them and asking them questions. And all who heard him were amazed at his understanding and **his answers**'* (v. 46-47).

Luke concludes this episode which another enigmatic phrase: *'Then he went down with them and came to Nazareth, and was obedient to them'* (v. 51). It may mean simply that he continued to live a normal life as the eldest son, subject to his parents' training and discipline as before. Or is there in the word 'obedient' a suggestion that in the episode in Jerusalem he had not behaved towards his parents quite as he should have done? I do not think we need to be troubled by the thought that to acknowledge that possibility would mean accusing him of sin. It would simply be a recognition that he was still a child.

The political scene

The visit to Jerusalem may well have contributed to Jesus' knowledge of the

Preliminaries: Birth, Childhood – and 'Christology'

world around him in another way too. Seeing the evidences of Roman power, with a strong force of soldiers based in the Fortress of Antonia dominating the entire Temple Mount, as was usual at Passover time, he would have been confronted as never before with the reality of foreign hegemony over Israel.[24] The fall of Jerusalem in 586 BC, when the kingdom of Judah was conquered by Babylon, not only marked the beginning of the *diaspora*, the dispersal of Israelites throughout many lands but also the end of an even nominally independent Israelite/Jewish state. Except for the 100 years, approximately 160–63 BC, between the Maccabean wars and the conquest of Israel by the Romans under Pompey, Israel was under foreign domination. So throughout Jesus' life, control rested with the Roman occupiers, though they usually preferred to rule through local puppet figures. Herod the Great had been one such, but after his death Rome divided the land three ways between his sons. However, the evident unsuitability of Herod Archelaus had led to Judea and Samaria coming under the direct control of the Roman procurator, who at the time of Jesus' birth was, of course, Pontius Pilate. The Roman procurators gave the Jews considerable autonomy; in Judea's case, power was exercised mainly through the high priest, an office which since the days of the Maccabees had become increasingly politicised and was held by Roman appointees rather than by the descendants of Aaron. Roman power remained largely in the background, being directly employed only when there was any hint of rebellion against Roman rule and Roman taxation. However, the presence of Roman soldiers in Jerusalem was a reminder to Jesus and to everyone where ultimate power lay.

He may also have come to understand, as never before, the difference between Judea and his homeland of Galilee – and the relationship between Jews and Samaritans. Galilee had been separated politically from Judea since the division of Israel in the 10th century BC, and following the death of Herod the Great had come under the figurehead rule of Herod Antipas, with a third son of Herod the Great, Philip, ruling in Ituraea and Trachonitis (see Luke 3:1). Moreover, it was separated physically from Judea by the territory of Samaria. Following its re-conquest by the Maccabees in 104 BC, Galilee had been 'rejudaized' through resettlement by Jewish incomers. Kenneth Bailey asserts that Nazareth was a 'settler town' as a result of this policy – and probably 'a conservative all-Jewish town' in consequence, as the reception that Jesus receives there in Luke 4:16-30 suggests.[25]

---

24 This suggestion is made by Robert Aron in his *Les Années Obscures de Jésus*.

25 Kenneth E. Bailey, *Jesus Through Middle Eastern Eyes*, p. 152.

Galilee had a large non-Jewish minority, both in its coastal regions and in the two major towns of Tiberius and Sepphoris, and was surrounded on three sides, north, south and east, by non-Jewish territories. Despite its relative economic wealth, the result of its agricultural resources, Galilee was looked down upon by 'Judeans' as 'Galilee of the Gentiles', while Galileans were held to be less sophisticated 'country cousins' who spoke a distinctive, accented version of Aramaic (Matt. 26:73):

> ... even an impeccably Jewish Galilean in first-century Jerusalem was not among his own people; he was as much a foreigner as an Irishman in London or a Texan in New York. His accent would immediately mark him out as 'not one of us,' and all the communal prejudice of the supposedly superior culture of the capital city would stand against [Jesus'] claim to be heard even as a prophet, let alone as the 'Messiah', a title which, as everyone knew, belonged to Judea ... [26]

The Gospels indicate that even in 'backward' Galilee, Jesus was *au fait* with the political realities of the time: Roman hegemony, the rule of Herod Antipas, and even Herod Archelaus' journey to Rome to ensure his right to succeed Herod the Great as ruler over part of his lands (the parable of the 'minas' in Luke 19).

Socio-economic conditions

Jesus' understanding of the world around him will doubtless have broadened as he entered his teens – the visit to Jerusalem probably marked some kind of caesura, his beginning to take his place in the grown-up world. He will gradually have become familiar with all aspects of village and even national life: its religious life in the first place, since that was ostensibly the source of Israel's very existence and *raison d'être*, the contemporary political scene, and the popular culture of the day. As he grew up, and especially after he began to work alongside his father in his trade as a carpenter or jobbing builder – the word *tektōn* has a wider sense than simply 'carpenter' – Jesus will also have gained a wider experience of economic and social life in Nazareth and surrounding villages, perhaps even in larger towns too.

Galilee was above all an agricultural region, with the vast majority of its population living in small towns and villages and engaged in subsistence farming. Those living in the few major centres were generally better off, a factor which led to antagonisms between town and countryside. Much more significant, though, was the wide difference between the few rich people,

---

26 R.T. France, *The Gospel of Matthew*, Grand Rapids, Michigan 2007.

Preliminaries: Birth, Childhood – and 'Christology'

aristocratic landowners and some merchants, and the great bulk of the rural population, many of whom no longer owned their land and were instead tenants on the estates of often absentee landlords, run by a manager or 'steward' (see Jesus' parables in Luke 16:1-13 and 20:9-16). The parable of the 'Dishonest Manager' refers to debtors; debt obliged many small farmers to relinquish their lands and to become hired labourers on such estates, while others were forced into dependence on the patronage of some wealthy or powerful person or even some kind of bond service (the 'prisoners' that Jesus refers to in Luke 4:18 were probably such people). And as a result of the growing influence of Roman law rather than the Law of Moses, debtors could also face imprisonment (see Matt. 5:25-26).

The law of jubilees (see Leviticus 25) was intended to undo the inequalities that each fifty-year period of economic and financial activity in Israel – agriculture, trade, borrowing, etc. – inevitably produced, and to restore the land and the people to the condition of equality envisaged by the way in which the land had originally been divided up after Israel had taken possession of it. It must be doubted to what extent this law was actually applied; in the 8th century Isaiah inveighs against those who '... *join house to house, who add field to field, until there is room for no one but you, and you are left to live alone in the midst of the land!'* (Isaiah 5:8). The reforms introduced by Nehemiah (see Nehemiah 5:1-13) were an attempt to secure land for small farmers, and further measures for the same purpose were undertaken during the Maccabean period,[27] but as Scott comments, 'By the first century ... the safeguards for small landholders had been severely weakened if not actually overthrown. The threat of losing their land was a constant reality and many were in fact displaced'.[28]

The difficulties of the small landowners and tenant farmers were exacerbated by the various forms of taxation to which they were subject. In addition to the tithes imposed by the Mosaic Law but not always paid, they were liable to pay tribute and taxes imposed by Rome (see Mark 12:13-17), tolls and duties on various products and trade – collected at 'toll booths' such as that at which Levi the tax-collector was sitting (Mark 2:14) – and the temple tax (see Matt. 17:24-27). Religious contributions did not end there, though; 'Sacrifices, offerings, gifts for special occasions such as cleansing ceremonies and the like added to the religious economic demands.'[29]

---

27 Scott, *Jewish Backgrounds*, p. 241.

28 *Ibid.*, p. 241.

29 *Ibid.*, p. 238. Scott suggests that 'the total levy for religious duties could come close to 50 percent of the income of a working person.'

Jesus – yesterday, today, for ever

At worst, the dispossessed sank to the level of the underclass (referred to by some writers as 'non-persons' or 'expendables'), made up of slaves, beggars, women, children, invalids of various kinds.[30] For such people there was, of course, no form of social security, so that they became dependent on the charity of others, and their situation was aggravated by the fact that society in first-century Israel, like the rest of the Greco-Roman world, worked essentially on the honour-shame principle, in which status, high or low, did not depend on the individual's personal qualities but was attributed on the basis of such factors as 'religious purity, family heritage, land ownership ... vocation, ethnicity, gender, education, and age',[31] to which list we should probably add invalidity. These were the factors that caused people to be regarded as 'non-persons' or 'expendables'; when Jesus speaks, especially in Luke's Gospel, of 'the poor', he is probably using this as an umbrella term to cover all such people.

The number of references in Jesus' parables to economic and social conditions suggests he became acutely aware of the nature of the society around him. His teaching reveals a man familiar with every aspect of life: agricultural practices (e.g. the parables in Matthew 13 or the parable of the Lost Sheep), the absentee landlords (the parable of the Tenants of the Vineyard), the behaviour of the wealthy and powerful (the Rich Man and Lazarus). He must have registered the pressures on individuals and families of poverty and illness – the widows, the crippled, the dispossessed – and observed with growing sympathy and insight how human beings behave in particular circumstances, sometimes wisely, sometimes destructively.

Political unrest

One further feature of life in Israel in Jesus' time brings together the three areas of experience that we have mentioned: the religious, the political and the socio-economic. When David was a fugitive from the wrath of Saul, he took refuge in the cave of Adullam, where he was joined by *'Everyone who was in distress, and everyone who was in debt, and everyone who was discontented'* (1 Samuel 22:2). In Jesus' time too, it was from among men whom dispossession, penury and virtual slavery had driven to desperation that there emerged the bands of brigands which troubled Jewish society in the first century. As Josephus reports, their vengeful wrath was directed primarily at the rich, and sometimes also at the bureaucratic machinery that appeared to favour them.

---

30 *Ibid.*, pp. 244-246.

31 This list is taken from Joel B. Green, *The Gospel of Luke*, Grand Rapids, Michigan/ Cambridge 1997, p. 60.

Preliminaries: Birth, Childhood – and 'Christology'

However, behind such movements lay also political and religious motives. Few Jews relished the idea of being subject to Roman rule, not only because of the usual rejection of foreign domination but also out of religious convictions: it was improper, even sacrilegious, that the land that God had given to Israel should be ruled by strangers. Josephus' account of the divisions in Jewish religious life includes, alongside the three 'sects' already mentioned, a 'fourth philosophy' – though there was nothing 'philosophical' about it. Josephus is referring to those who resorted to violent uprising against foreign domination and foreign taxation. They include such groups as those known as 'Zealots' and also the 'Sicarii', a name relating to the short dagger that they concealed about their person and used mainly against other Jews whom they deemed to be insufficiently zealous or to have collaborated with the Romans. It is not surprising, then, that first-century Israel saw a series of uprisings against Roman rule.[32] It was probably movements such as these that sparked the final, fateful uprising against Rome in 66 AD. Such politically motivated brigands were those whom the Gospel writers refer to as *lestes*.

Judas of Galilee was perhaps the most influential of these figures, being followed by other members of his family and inspiring similar uprisings. He claimed that God was the only ruler of Israel and that no other should be recognised; he therefore rejected the payment of Roman taxes. It is no coincidence that he was a Galilean: it is widely held that Galilee in Jesus' day was perhaps the most rebellious region of Israel, having a long tradition of desiring political autonomy under God:

> Galilee had a tradition of political autonomy ... It's a kind of quasi-anarchistic ideal, that this loose tribal confederacy is ruled directly by God. And those ideas and that ideal continues to be alive and well in northern Palestine.[33]

Jesus must as a young man have heard about such things, but, despite the attempts of some writers to portray him as a *lestes*, there is no evidence of any such activity on his part. That did not stop the chief priests describing him to Pilate as a seditious rebel (see Luke 23:2). It is one of the great ironies of the story of Jesus that he comes to be identified with such violent men: for 'Barabbas was a *lestes*' (John 18:40), and so, presumably, were those who

---

32 These included notably the following: Judas of Galilee (c. 6 AD, cf. Acts 5:37), Theudas (44–46 AD; cf. Acts 5:36), the Egyptian (c. 52–60 AD; cf. Acts 21:38).

33 Allen D. Callahan, 'Galilee' on Frontline newsletter, Public Broadcasting Service (PBS):
www.pbs.org/wgbh/pages/frontline/shows/religion/portrait/galilee.html.

Jesus – yesterday, today, for ever

were crucified alongside Jesus (Mark 15:27).

Summing up

As we read the Gospels, we need to keep in mind that Jesus was not living in some kind of 'never-never land' untouched by political, social and economic pressures. He grew up in the world that I have been trying to describe, where, for well over a decade, his work brought him into contact with people whose lives were shaped by these pressures. It must have shaped him too: he was, surely, a man of his time, sharing its knowledge, its habits of thought, its way of life, however critically he may have come to view them. We may be sure that he well understood how things worked in this society – and where the message of the grace of God was most likely to fall on fertile soil.

What picture of Jesus himself emerges from the sparse evidence provided by Luke, our knowledge of first-century Israel, and our personal experience as human beings? We may, I think, imagine the young Jesus as a remarkably thoughtful, sensitive and understanding boy, dutiful and respectful towards his parents and unusually mature both emotionally and intellectually for his years. Some of his peers might well have envied him or laughed at him, but Luke's statement that he *'grew in favour ... with men'* probably implies that he was generally well thought of by those who knew him. Later, as a young man, he was doubtless kind and considerate, mature beyond his years, observant and of remarkable intelligence.

His intellectual development must have been accompanied by a growing *moral awareness.* As an adolescent and as a young man, he must already have begun to develop that insight into human behaviour that enabled John to write of him: *'[he] needed no one to bear witness about man, for he himself knew what was in man'* (John 2:25). He will have begun to observe human beings' proneness to self-interest, hypocrisy and self-deception – but also their capacity for love and selflessness and creativity – and to develop that judgment of his fellows that would later drive him to the conclusion that, with all their many faults, these strangely flawed creatures were worth saving.

Yet it must have been more than a matter of observation. How did he recognise and put names to their flaws? The New Testament writers insist that Jesus is 'like us', 'the second Adam', 'the man Christ Jesus'. The writer to the Hebrews goes further: he asserts that Jesus was *'like his brothers and sisters in every respect'* (2:17) and *'in every respect has been tested as we are, yet without sin'* (4:15). But as we know, temptations arise not so much through forces acting upon us from without, as through impulses from within ourselves – from wishes on the one hand, and from fears on the other. In his teaching, for example in the 'Sermon on the Mount', Jesus speaks of being angry and hating

Preliminaries: Birth, Childhood – and 'Christology'

(Matt. 5:22, 43), of coveting and lusting (5:28), of hypocritically playing to the gallery (6:1-4), of judging and condemning others (7:1 ff.). To be able to speak of these and other such things, Jesus must have known what they were – and knowledge of that kind can come only from personal, internal experience. We may learn the names for certain forms of behaviour that we observe, but we do not understand them until we have experienced these impulses and emotions. So, shocking as it may seem, we are, it seems to me, compelled to think of Jesus as himself knowing what it is like to lust, to hate, to feel envy, and all the rest of our unlovely human impulses. He must also have realised, from his own experience, how difficult it is to resist such impulses, how painful it is to 'pluck out an eye' or 'cut off a hand', to use his own language (Mark 9:42-47). So let us not assume that the inner conflict and struggles that we all experience were foreign to him. Indeed, how could they be if he really was '*in every respect ... tested as we are*'?

There must, though, have been a powerful spiritual awareness, a strong sense of the God that he heard about in the synagogue; he recognised him in the natural world around him – his analogies in the Sermon on the Mount suggest this – and he must have communed with him in whatever private moments his life allowed him. He may well have had a sense of mission, a desire to devote his life to God, without necessarily knowing about the unique task which he was later to perform. This awareness of God can only have sharpened the inner struggles to which we have referred.

We have already quoted Luke's statements that '*the grace of God was upon him*' and that he '*grew in favour with God*'. The tendency to allow our imagination to run away with us on the basis of these phrases and to ascribe to him all kinds of special knowledge and intimacy with God must be constrained by two things: first, the reactions to him as he begins his ministry, notably during his visit to Nazareth, do not suggest that anyone had noticed anything strange or abnormal about him. They saw him, no doubt, as an intelligent, thoughtful, wise, kind young man, but nothing that would have set him apart from all others.

The second constraint relates to our earlier consideration of his being 'the son of God', yet born to human parents. God entrusted the upbringing of his son to human parents and allowed him to develop in their environment, subject to the kind of influences that we have been exploring. From this, one can only conclude that it was his Father's will that he should truly be a man, with a human being's experiences, shaped, in part at least, by living alongside other human beings and with an emotional, social and intellectual make-up akin to theirs. It would hardly have made sense if he were to have been the recipient of special revelations or some form of direct contact with God that would set him apart from all his fellows. This is a further sign of the potential that God saw in humanity, fallen though they were and are; he caused his son to be born into their world and allowed him to be shaped by all his experiences of it.

Much of this chapter is essentially speculative in nature, yet it can scarcely be otherwise. I have simply been attempting to follow the promptings of what the Gospels do say, read in the light of the New Testament's insistence on Jesus' genuine humanity and on my own experience of what that means. I conclude, tentatively, that we should see the young Jesus as the best possible version of a human being, but without any explicitly supernatural elements. The consequence of that reading is to open up a much greater difference than is often assumed between that young man and the empowered Jesus that we see during his earthly ministry. Such a wide disparity is, however, required by the Gospels' account of the surprise of the people, not only that he possessed such healing powers, but also that the person they had known in Nazareth should have become this authoritative teacher and worker of wonders. It also heightens the importance of what lies between the 'ordinary' young man and his sensational ministry – his baptism and temptation, to which we turn next.

Chapter 4

Baptism and Temptation

Within the ministry of Jesus, his baptism is an extremely important event. As we saw at the beginning of the previous chapter, the New Testament writers are unanimous in taking the ministry of John the Baptist to be the 'beginning' of the story of Jesus. That clearly implies that Jesus' personal mission begins with his baptism by John; it is the first event in his adult life that they record.

It is therefore extraordinary that so little attention is often paid to the meaning of Jesus' baptism. There is so much that anyone trying to understand Jesus would like to know: what made Jesus leave Galilee and, with it, his work and family, and travel south to Judah to be baptised by John? And what was the purpose and meaning of his submitting to John's baptism in this way? These questions seem seldom to be asked; it appears to be assumed that he 'just knew' that he was to do this and that this was the time to begin his mission. If one takes the view adopted by many, which attributes to Jesus a quasi-divine knowledge and certainty at every point about what he should do, then perhaps questions like these *are* unnecessary. If, however, one is attempting, as I am, to think of Jesus as truly one like ourselves, with a mental life similar, though probably not identical, to our own, then questions like these become more pressing. As we pointed out at the end of the preceding chapter, this is the event that forms the link between Jesus, the carpenter-builder in Nazareth, and Jesus, the preacher and healer that we are to encounter in the Gospels – and which must therefore provide an explanation of how the former became the latter.

Given that importance, it is extraordinary, too, that it is narrated so briefly: just five verses in Matthew are devoted to it, three in Mark, and two in Luke – Luke does not even narrate the baptism itself but refers to it, in a participial phrase within a subordinate clause, as something that has already taken place. Luke's brevity makes apparent where the Gospel writers' interest lies – not on the act of baptism itself but on what happens immediately afterwards, the vision of the Holy Spirit descending like a dove upon Jesus, and then the voice from heaven. The account in John's Gospel goes still further in this direction: it is the Baptist who tells what has happened, rather than the narrator, and his attention is focused entirely upon the descent of the Spirit, which, he says, he had been told to expect as a sign identifying the one who would baptise with the Holy Spirit and who therefore is the promised *'man who ranks ahead of me'* (John 1:30).

Baptism

Nevertheless, before considering the meaning of the descent of the Spirit and the voice from heaven, we need first to think about the baptism itself. As its greater length implies, it is only Matthew's account that tells us anything more than the barest fact; it reports, before the baptism itself, a brief conversation between John and Jesus: *'John would have prevented him, saying, "I need to be baptized by you, and do you come to me?" But Jesus answered him, "Let it be so now; for it is proper for us in this way to fulfil all righteousness." Then he consented'* (3:14-15). John's words here seem to presuppose that he recognises Jesus and is aware of his role and status – John and Jesus were, after all, related, as Luke's account of the relationship between their mothers confirms. Jesus' reply and his acceptance of baptism by John are frequently interpreted as an expression of obedience to a divine command, exemplary for all subsequent believers. Perhaps more importantly, though, these words suggest that Jesus, whom John has just declared to be more righteous than himself, submits to an act symbolising repentance, thereby associating himself with the mass of his fellow-Israelites. That would make it the first step in that identification with sinners which ends with his hanging on the cross alongside two murderous political extremists.

Both these ways of understanding Jesus' words presuppose a prior understanding on his part of his role and mission, as well as some kind of prior acquaintance between him and John, as Matthew's account implies. Yet in John's Gospel, the Baptist says twice that *'I myself did not know him ...'* (John 1:31, 33), adding that only the descent of the Spirit, which took place *after* the baptism itself, enabled him to identify Jesus. Since John's father was a priest, we might assume that the family lived in or near Jerusalem in the south, at a significant distance from Galilean Nazareth, so it is quite plausible that the boys seldom or never met. Luke, in the Gospel that alone informs us about the family links between the two, provides a possible alternative explanation for the absence of any prior acquaintance and John's failure to recognise Jesus: having recorded John's birth, he continues: *'The child grew and became strong in spirit, and he was in the wilderness until the day he appeared publicly to Israel'* (Luke 1:80). This statement seems to suggest that from a fairly early

Baptism and Temptation

age John left the family home and lived in the Judean desert – his dress and diet, as described in the Gospels, indicate an austere, ascetic existence of this kind, as well as an obvious parallel with Elijah. It may well be that his elderly parents died quite early in John's life, making such a departure more readily understandable.

These factors have led some commentators to suggest that John might have lived for a time with an Essene community in this region, probably very similar to the one whose collection of scrolls was found at Qumran. John's preaching, with its call to repentance and emphasis on impending judgment, might be thought to bear some resemblance to the Essenes' rigorous quest for purity and their rejection of Israel's religious institutions based in Jerusalem.

Their brevity is, however, not the only puzzling feature of the Gospel accounts of Jesus' baptism. No less remarkable is the complete absence of any explanatory introduction. Matthew, for example, leaves Jesus at the end of his second chapter still a child, settled with his parents in Nazareth (2:23); the next mention of Jesus is: *'Then Jesus came from Galilee to John at the Jordan, to be baptized by him'* (3:13). Mark is even more extreme: apart from his opening statement about his Gospel (1:1), Jesus' name first occurs in v. 9: *'In those days Jesus came from Nazareth of Galilee and was baptized by John in the Jordan.'*

Why, then, did Jesus come to John to be baptised? One can conceive of several possible scenarios for this decision. At the other extreme from his 'just knowing', some might imagine an ordinary young man who, while going about his daily life, somehow hears of the work of a strange preacher down in Judea who is calling on people to undergo a baptism of repentance and decides that he should go too. However, such a view seems to disregard Luke's comment that Jesus *'increased in wisdom and in years, and in divine and human favour'* (Luke 2:52). Similarly, if Psalm 22 really does represent insight into the mind of Jesus, then it paints a picture incompatible with such a casual, almost accidental decision to travel south: *'Yet it was you who took me from the womb; you kept me safe on my mother's breast. On you I was cast from my birth, and since my mother bore me you have been my God'* (Ps. 22:9-10). As we observed in the previous chapter, what little we know about Jesus between his birth and the beginning of his ministry leads us to see in him a deeply thoughtful young man with a love of the Old Testament scriptures, extraordinary perceptiveness and a deep awareness of God. If, in addition to such characteristics, he knew that he had in some way been dedicated to God just after his birth, he might well have been looking and waiting for some sign as to what he should do, how he should serve the God he thought of as Father.

Jesus – yesterday, today, for ever

In that case, he would have been electrified by the news of what was happening down in the Judean desert, by the Jordan, and felt impelled to witness or to share in what was happening.

The fact that he had reached the age of thirty about this time (Luke 3:23), the age at which priests began their ministry (see Numbers 4), could have confirmed for him that this was the moment for his service to God to begin. To a faithful Jew, such as Jesus obviously was, John's activity in the desert must have seemed like the arising, at last, of a true prophet from God, calling on his people to abandon the corrupt, sinful ways that had so disfigured society in Israel in the century and a half since the Maccabean wars.

It is notable in this connection that both Matthew and Mark specifically remark that Jesus came 'from Galilee'. John's account suggests that Andrew and probably Peter too, both Galilean fishermen, were among the Baptist's disciples (John 1:41-42) but, given what both these Gospels say about John's ministry, the appearance of someone from Galilee must have been unusual: *'Then the people of Jerusalem and all Judea were going out to him, and all the region along the Jordan'* (Matt. 3:5); *'... people from the whole Judean countryside and all the people of Jerusalem were going out to him'* (Mark 1:5). Jesus' Galilean accent might perhaps have enabled John to realise who he was; more importantly, though, these details enable us to discount the notion that he came to John because large numbers from Galilee were doing so, They suggest rather a more or less individual decision on his part that led to his undertaking the lengthy journey south.

And what of the act itself? Was it, as Matthew's account seems to suggest, an act of submission to his Father's will by which he accepted his mission? Does its significance lie in his voluntary identification with sinners? Or was it truly an act of repentance in response to John's call? We have to remember that 'to repent' in the language of the Old Testament, expressed usually by the word *shuwb*, especially in Jeremiah, means to 'turn' or 'return'.[1] The very practical implications of the word are reflected in John the Baptist's demand for 'fruits worthy of repentance' and the specific instructions that he provides in Luke's account for specific groups of people. If it were the case that Jesus came with the mindset that I have suggested, prepared to devote himself in some way to the service of God, then his coming would truly be an act of 'turning': he had apparently given up his 'normal' past way of life in order to embrace another, even if he did not yet know exactly what it was to be. Indeed,

---

1 When we encounter the words 'repent' and repentance' (*metanoia*) in the New Testament, we should perhaps remember this essentially practical sense and not think only in the more psychological sense that *metanoia* suggests.

Baptism and Temptation

he might have concluded that his adult life hitherto had not matched up to his claim of dedication in Luke 2:49 – and that would truly have made his baptism an act of 'repentance'. The meaning of baptism as a passage through death to a new life is already anticipated in the radical change that it marked in the life of Jesus.

The heavens opened

As we have already noted, the Gospel writers all give greater attention to what follows the baptism than to the act itself. The scene is described briefly but is full of significance, and in all three Synoptic Gospels it includes three elements: the opening of the heavens, the descent of the Spirit upon Jesus in the form of a dove, and the voice from heaven.

Within the world-picture that pervades the whole of the Old Testament, the heavens are both uniquely the realm of God *and* the 'firmament' that divides what is above from what is below, not only in the physical sense of Genesis 1 (v. 6-8) but also in the moral and spiritual realm, as the barrier between human beings and God. The rare occurrences where the heavens are said to be opened therefore signify something momentous: on the one hand a revelation of things otherwise hidden from human view, and on the other a direct intervention of God in human affairs – when he is said to 'come down'. On some occasions, he 'comes down' without any explicit reference to the 'opening' of the heavens, whether to 'inspect' human behaviour (Gen. 11:5; 18:21), to reveal himself, either to Israel, as at Sinai (Ex. 19:18, 20) or to an individual such as Moses (Ex. 34:5; Num. 11:17, 25), or to act on behalf of his people (Ex. 3:8; Ps. 18:9; 144:5).

The two moments in the Old Testament that appear to relate most directly to what occurs at Jesus' baptism are the following:

> *O that you would tear open the heavens and come down, so that the mountains would quake at your presence … to make your name known to your adversaries, so that the nations might tremble at your presence! When you did awesome deeds that we did not expect, you **came down**, the mountains quaked at your presence. (Isaiah 64:1-3)*

> *In the thirtieth year, in the fourth month, on the fifth day of the month, as I was among the exiles by the river Chebar, **the heavens were opened**, and I saw visions of God. (Ezekiel 1:1)*

The first of these passages places the emphasis on God's self-revelation to Israel at Sinai in order to call on them to be his people and to seal that calling through the making of a covenant. So Isaiah is here expressing a longing for

Jesus – yesterday, today, for ever

a new self-revelation of God in decisive, redeeming action as at Sinai. Alone among the Gospel writers, Mark makes a clear allusion to this moment, for he echoes the violence of Isaiah's language: *'And just as he was coming up out of the water, he saw the heavens **torn** apart (schizo)'* (Mark 1:10), whereas Matthew and Luke opt for *anoigo* ('open'). Mark's record in particular thus emphasises the meaning of this event for God's people – that the ministry of Jesus, now about to begin, is a new intervention of God in human affairs through an act of self-revelation, leading to the inauguration of a new covenant with mankind. By contrast, the Ezekiel passage describes a private experience by which an individual is called to act as God's agent and intermediary, as was the case with Moses, Jeremiah and others.

The descent of the Spirit

Despite the echoes of Sinai in Mark's account, the events following the 'rending' of the heavens are focused on a single individual, as in the case of Ezekiel, rather than on a whole people. Matthew and Mark say that Jesus saw the Spirit's descent on him – there is no suggestion that others were aware of what happened, apart, that is, from John the Baptist, who himself says in John's Gospel that *'I saw the Spirit descending from heaven like a dove ...'* (1:32).

What was the meaning of the descent of the Spirit upon Jesus? We can best approach this, perhaps, by considering some of the Old Testament examples where God 'comes down' or when the Spirit comes upon a human being. In the case of Moses and of Ezekiel, and also of the other prophets, the individual is empowered or authorised to speak for God. Sometimes, that authority is confirmed by some kind of sign – Moses' rod is transformed into a serpent (Ex. 4:1-4), Isaiah's mouth is 'cleansed' with the burning coal (Is. 6:6-7). In other cases, though, the change was more internal, within the person himself: Bezalel and those who worked with him appear to have had their existing skills enhanced: *'See, I have called by name Bezalel son of Uri son of Hur, of the tribe of Judah: and I have filled him with divine spirit, with ability, intelligence, and knowledge in every kind of craft, to devise artistic designs, to work in gold, silver, and bronze'* (Ex. 31:2-4). The most radical change is that indicated in the case of Saul:

> *Then the spirit of the LORD will possess you, and you will be in a prophetic frenzy along with them and be **turned into a different person**. Now when these signs meet you, do whatever you see fit to do, for God is with you ...* *As he turned away to leave Samuel, **God gave him another heart**; and all these signs were fulfilled that day. (1 Samuel 10:6-9)*

The fact that Saul needed to become 'a different person' is, perhaps, an in-

Baptism and Temptation

dication of his unfittedness for his new role; nothing comparable happened when David was anointed because he already possessed many of the qualities needed, as did Bezalel.

These latter examples, involving the enhancing of existing qualities rather than total transformation, would appear to be the more appropriate model for what happened with Jesus. Isaiah's words are perhaps the best indication of what he experienced:

> *The spirit of the LORD shall rest on him, the spirit of wisdom and understanding, the spirit of counsel and might, the spirit of knowledge and the fear of the LORD. His delight shall be in the fear of the LORD. He shall not judge by what his eyes see, or decide by what his ears hear; but with righteousness he shall judge the poor, and decide with equity for the meek of the earth ... (Isaiah 11:2-4)*

These words seem to imply a more perfect understanding of the scriptures, a still closer relationship to God, and a yet greater desire to serve him, aided by a still more acute ability to understand and interpret what he experiences and an unerring sense of truth and right – just those qualities and faculties that we see in operation when Jesus during his ministry encountered all kinds of people and faced every kind of challenge from his adversaries.

Yet we must not underestimate the significance of what takes place here: one who had hitherto been 'the carpenter from Nazareth' becomes a preacher and healer, one whom his followers look up to as their teacher and master, and finally as their 'lord'; the one whose task it is to proclaim, and ultimately to initiate in his own body, the reign of God on earth

One detail of John's account of Jesus' baptism is indicative of the uniqueness of Jesus' case compared with all Old Testament precedents:

> *And John testified, 'I saw the Spirit descending from heaven like a dove, and it remained on him. I myself did not know him, but the one who sent me to baptize with water said to me, "He on whom you see the Spirit descend and remain is the one who baptizes with the Holy Spirit."' (John 1:32-33)*

This passage confirms that the Spirit did not merely 'descend' on Jesus but 'remained' on him, using the Greek word that is so important a part of John's vocabulary, *mēno*. The Old Testament tells us repeatedly that the 'word of the Lord came' to the various prophets, implying that there were also times when the Spirit did not rest upon them; John's account, by contrast, suggests a permanent presence of the Spirit with Jesus, from that moment until his death on the cross. This is perhaps part of what John means when he writes

Jesus – yesterday, today, for ever

a little later: *'He whom God has sent speaks the words of God, for he gives the Spirit without measure'* (John 3:34). Even before that, at the end of John 1, Jesus himself suggests something of the kind when he suggests an analogy between himself and Jacob's vision of a ladder in Genesis 28: *'Very truly, I tell you, you will see heaven opened and the angels of God ascending and descending upon the Son of Man'* (John 1:51). Though there is no reference to the Spirit here, the inference to be drawn is, I think, that Jesus will be a kind of link between heaven and earth, or between man and God. As long as he is there among men, heaven is, in a sense, permanently open – the 'rent' in the barrier between men and God is not simply momentary. This is perhaps another way of saying that God has not merely 'come down' for a brief moment but will henceforth be revealed and work his saving work among men through the one on whom the Spirit has now descended. The rending of the heavens and the 'descent' of the Spirit concern others beside Jesus, but only through him, the Son, for it is on him alone that it descends.

The various parallels with Old Testament contexts that we have been considering lead to one obvious, yet seldom noted, conclusion: that the events following upon Jesus' baptism are the equivalent in Jesus' life to the calling and commissioning experiences of the major Old Testament prophets. Looking at the cases of Moses, Isaiah, Jeremiah, and Ezekiel, the following table sets out seven elements in that opening experience: call, vision, sign, task, objection, reassurance, and some kind of empowerment commensurate with the task (the distinctions between them are not always clear, and not all are present in every case):

	Moses	Isaiah	Jeremiah	Ezekiel
Call	Ex. 3:4-6	6:8	1:4-5	2:1
Vision	Ex. 3:2-3	6:1-4	1:11-12	1:4-28
Sign	Ex. 4:2-9			3:1-3
Commission	Ex. 3:10, 15-22	6:9-10	1:14-17	2:3-5
Objection	Ex. 3:11, 13; 4:10, 13	6:5, 11 (?)	1:6-7	2:6-8
Reassurance	Ex. 3:18-22; 4:14-17	6:6-7	1:8, 18-19	3:8-10
Gift of Spirit	Ex. 4:11-12, 15-16	6:6-7	1:9-10	2:2; 3:12-14

If we set Jesus' baptism alongside this simple table, it is apparent that some of the essential elements are present: the vision, the sign, and the gift of the Spirit, while John's ministry might be thought to represent a 'call' – though one that Jesus, as far as we know, had himself to recognise and respond to. Equally apparently, at least at this stage, there is no objection on his part and therefore no reassurance.

Baptism and Temptation

The voice from heaven

But what of the task or commission? That comes, I suggest, in the words spoken by the voice from heaven. Two of the three Synoptic Gospels say that the words are spoken to Jesus himself:

And a voice came from heaven, 'You are my Son, the Beloved; with you I am well pleased.' (Mark 1:11, Luke 3:22)

Only in Matthew are these words spoken in the third person, as if to others than Jesus; it is noteworthy that John the Baptist makes no reference to any voice, suggesting, perhaps, that he did not hear it and therefore that it was audible only to Jesus.

Another feature of this event points towards a similar conclusion: we saw earlier that Mark's echo of Isaiah 64:1 suggests a parallel with events at Sinai. What was revealed at Sinai? Ultimately, the whole of the Law was given there, but the very first thing announced to Moses there was this:

This is what you are to say to the house of Jacob and what you are to tell the people of Israel: 'You yourselves have seen what I did to Egypt, and how I carried you on eagles' wings and brought you to myself. Now if you obey me fully and keep my covenant, then out of all nations you will be my treasured possession. Although the whole earth is mine, you will be for me a kingdom of priests and a holy nation.' (Exodus 19:3-6)

It is at once a call and the beginnings of a commission for Israel, but what happens here first is that God declares to Israel who they are and what they are to be. If we take the words spoken from heaven to be addressed, at least primarily, to Jesus, then it seems natural to assume that something similar occurs here, as the very formulation implies: *'You are ... '.* If Jesus came to John with both a sense of dedication and an uncertainty as to *how* he was to serve, as I have suggested, then we might reasonably conclude that God's call to him came, as it did for Israel at Sinai, in the form of this revelatory announcement of his identity.

But did he need such a revelation? As we noted in the previous chapter, it is usually assumed that Jesus already knew that he was God's Son, yet it seems to me, especially in view of the parallel with Sinai, that he is only now hearing just who he was and what his role was to be. This makes far better sense of the subsequent temptation: the repeated phrase, *'If you are the Son of God'* perfectly reflects the situation of one who has only now become aware of his exalted status and is reflecting on what possibilities it opened up and how he should exploit his privileges, especially in the face of what he had also learned

Jesus – yesterday, today, for ever

about the burden that he was to assume.

It might be thought that the few brief words reported by the Synoptic Gospels cannot represent any kind of commission comparable to that received by the prophets mentioned earlier. But to think this is to reckon without the uniquely quick, perceptive mind of Jesus, filled as it evidently was with the Old Testament scriptures that he will have heard, even if not read – for where would he have obtained copies of them? – so often during the past twenty-five years or so. For him, surely, these words will have evoked at least three Old Testament passages of the greatest moment.

'*You are my son*' echoes almost exactly the text of Psalm 2:7: '*You are my son; today I have begotten you,*' in which God promises to him kingship and authority. Many commentators see this Psalm as part of an enthronement ceremony in which David, or one of his descendants, is simply proclaimed king; from this the conclusion is sometimes drawn that what is happening here is that the man Jesus is being simply 'adopted' as Son of God. It goes without saying that this reading runs counter to the intentions of all the Gospel writers; nevertheless, the idea is not unhelpful in one respect, for it helps us to recognise that in these words the Father is now laying claim to his son, calling upon him to take upon himself the implications of his elevated status – and perhaps acknowledging with delight the act of 'turning' or 'repentance' that Jesus has just performed through his baptism. At all events, this particular phrase focuses attention on the kingly role due to be played ultimately by the Son; Jesus will doubtless not only have recognised the phrase but also recalled how the Psalm continued, with its promise of authority and rulership.

However, the addition to those words of the further phrase 'the Beloved' (*ho agapetos*) gives them a pathos not present in the psalm, for it is readily recognisable as an echo of Genesis 22:2: '*Take your son, your only son Isaac, whom you love*'. The similarity is even clearer if we look at these words in the Septuagint version: '*ton uion sou ton agapēton*' and set them alongside Mark's words, '*ho uios mou ho agapētos*' (v. 11): the two phrases differ only in the substitution of 'my' (*mou*) for 'your' (*sou*) and in the grammatically necessary switch from accusative to nominative case. As he heard and recognised this phrase, Jesus must surely have drawn the inference that the path that led to his kingship lay through an experience of danger and death or near-death analogous to the experience of Isaac on Mount Moriah – but also that he would ultimately be secure, precisely because of the love of the Father who might require this of him.

The third element in the words from heaven is perhaps even more significant: '*… with you I am well pleased*'. These words are generally taken to be a

Baptism and Temptation

quotation, or at least an echo of the first Servant passage: *'Here is my servant, whom I uphold, my chosen, in whom my soul delights'* (Is. 42:1).[2] Jesus will undoubtedly have recognised all the words and known their sources, but this last phrase was probably especially familiar to him. As Jesus grew to manhood he may well have wondered about the identity of the 'Servant', as many Jewish teachers had done, and one can imagine that the solutions provided by the teachers in the Nazareth synagogue will not have satisfied him. Whether this announcement from heaven simply confirmed what he had already grasped – that he was himself the Servant – or whether it told him something that he had hitherto not realised or had at most suspected, once that identification was grasped and acknowledged, it constituted the most awesome and challenging commission imaginable, greater even than those of Moses, Isaiah and Jeremiah, for example.

Temptation

As a form of 'call' or commission, the words spoken by the voice from heaven differed in one fundamental way from all the Old Testament examples: they told Jesus who he was and, in extreme brevity, what role he was to fulfil – but they gave no precise instructions as to what he was to *do*. There is nothing resembling the following from Jeremiah 2, for example: *'The word of the LORD came to me, saying: Go and proclaim in the hearing of Jerusalem, Thus says the LORD ...'* (Jer. 2:1-2). A closer parallel is perhaps the call to Saul of Tarsus, which similarly focused on the function that he was to fulfil but was likewise short on specific instructions: *'The God of our ancestors has chosen you to know his will, to see the Righteous One and to hear his own voice; for you will be his witness to all the world of what you have seen and heard'* (Acts 22:14-15).

The comparison with Paul may help us to understand what happened next. Though Acts makes no mention of it, Paul himself, in his account in Galatians, states quite explicitly what he did in response to the commission that he had received: *'I did not confer with any human being, nor did I go up to Jerusalem to those who were already apostles before me, but I went away at once into Arabia'* (Gal. 1:16-17). Paul gives us no indication of what he did during that stay in 'Arabia'; NT Wright suggests a parallel with Elijah:

> ... he, like Elijah, made a pilgrimage to Mt. Sinai in order to go back to the place where the covenant was ratified. He wanted to go and present

---

2   This connection seems well founded, despite the fact that the LXX rendering of this verse does not use the verb *eudokeō*, which is one of the regular LXX equivalents of the Hebrew verb *ratsah* and which occurs in the account of Jesus' baptism in all three Synoptic Gospels. Instead, the LXX uses *prosdechomai*, another of its equivalents for *ratsah*.

103

Jesus – yesterday, today, for ever

himself before the One God, to explain that he had been 'exceedingly zealous,' but that his vision, his entire worldview, had been turned on its head. And he received his instructions: "Go back and announce the new king."[3]

Both F. F. Bruce and Jerome Murphy-O'Connor, by contrast, think that 'Arabia' refers to the Nabatean kingdom, which stretched from the Syrian desert, east of Damascus, right down to the Sinai Peninsula and the north-western corner of the Arabian Peninsula, and that there Paul immediately began his work of proclamation to the Gentiles. Both writers suggest that it was this activity that aroused the ire of king Aretas IV, necessitating Paul's undignified escape from Damascus, referred to at the end of 2 Corinthians 11. I am not entirely convinced by either of these suggestions; anti-Jewish feeling among the Nabataeans may have been enough to explain the danger to Saul in Damascus even without any preaching, while Luke ascribes Paul's flight from Damascus to Jewish hostility as a result of his witness in the synagogue there:

> ... *immediately he began to proclaim Jesus in the synagogues, saying, 'He is the Son of God.' ... Saul became increasingly more powerful and confounded the Jews who lived in Damascus by proving that Jesus was the Messiah. After some time had passed, the Jews plotted to kill him ...* (Acts 9:20-23)

I find more persuasive the older view that Saul went into 'Arabia', wherever that was, in order to reflect on his experience on the Damascus road, to rethink his faith and his understanding of the Old Testament and to come to terms with the entirely new situation in which he now found himself. Bruce suggests that his three days of blindness in Damascus 'had been sufficient for his mind to be reoriented', but that seems to me far too short a time for so fundamental a reappraisal.

The purpose of this apparent digression is, of course, to suggest a parallel between Paul's time in 'Arabia' and Jesus' forty days in the wilderness. This period is usually labelled 'the temptation of Jesus', focusing on three specific challenges to him. Apart from these, the accounts of this period are very brief; Mark's is the shortest, giving no details, while Matthew and Luke insert into Mark's outline the details of the three temptations:

> *And the Spirit immediately drove him out into the wilderness. He was in the wilderness forty days, tempted by Satan; and he was with the wild beasts; and the angels waited on him.* (Mark 1:12-13)

---

3 Tom (N.T.) Wright, *Paul: A Biography*, San Francisco/London 2018, pp. 62-65 (here p. 64).

Baptism and Temptation

Then Jesus was led up by the Spirit into the wilderness to be tempted by the devil. He fasted forty days and forty nights, and afterwards he was famished. The tempter came and said to him ... Then the devil left him, and suddenly angels came and waited on him. (Matthew 4:1-3, 11)

Jesus, full of the Holy Spirit, returned from the Jordan and was led by the Spirit in the wilderness, where for forty days he was tempted by the devil. He ate nothing at all during those days, and when they were over, he was famished. The devil said to him ... When the devil had finished every test, he departed from him until an opportune time. (Luke 4:1-3, 13)

The conventional reading of the temptation makes it sound almost as though the purpose of the wilderness period was for Jesus to be subjected to a kind of formal test of obedience to God – that he is *'led by the Spirit'* into a lonely place to face his 'qualifying examination'. It seems to me far more plausible to see in his being 'driven' by the Spirit (in Mark's words) an inner compulsion arising out of the impact upon him of the call that he has now received. While Matthew's account might suggest that the 'tempter' came and spoke with Jesus only at the end of the forty days, when Jesus was very hungry, both Mark and Luke appear to say that the 'temptation' lasted throughout the whole period. From this we may conclude that the three temptations of which details are given were either a kind of final assault by this 'enemy', or that they represent the essence of Jesus' inner debate, summing up all the issues with which he wrestled continuously throughout, though they may perhaps have presented themselves in their sharpest form when Jesus was weakened through hunger. This implies that the 'temptation' was not just a generalised, formal test of obedience, but rather a period of intense reflection about the call that had come to him, much as, in my view, Paul's time in 'Arabia' was.

Luke's phrase, that the tempter *'departed from him until an opportune time'*, is sometimes taken to imply a link with Jesus' time of prayer in Gethsemane, before his crucifixion; if that is so, then it adds weight to the suggestion that these forty days were a time of similarly agonised reflection and prayer, during which he contemplated what lay ahead and asked for, and received, the strength of heart and will that would enable him to set out on his mission. It is far too easy to think of Jesus' acceptance of his mission as something predestined and inevitable, even automatic. It may have been, viewed retrospectively or from the standpoint of the divine purpose 'from the beginning', from 'before the foundation of the world', but for this thirty-year-old man with the emotional make-up, the drives and desires, and the imagination of a man, it must have represented, irrespective of what he knew of it before, a daunting,

105

awesome calling, involving not only dangers but also the loss of the life that he knew and the future that might otherwise have been his.

The three temptations

As we look at the accounts of the temptation, it becomes clear that Jesus spent his forty days in the wilderness reflecting intensely on the Old Testament scriptures that he knew so well and rethinking his understanding of them. Each of the temptations recorded in the Gospels turns on the meaning of specific passages and on the way in which apparently divergent texts could and should be reconciled with each other. The voice of 'satan' is, surely, that of Jesus as he weighs the meaning of a particular quotation – but then rejects the course of action that it might seem to justify by setting it against another passage. This was no mere game of quotation-swapping: it was a matter of life and death, for himself and for mankind. The answers that Jesus gives to the tempter spring from a profound understanding of how the scriptures as a whole fit together, which enabled him to discern which should take precedence and what would be a legitimate way of acting upon them.

The first temptation, arising, one supposes, out of the hunger that he will have begun to feel very soon after entering the wilderness, could have been inspired by his knowledge of the provision of manna for Israel in the wilderness. It is as if Jesus asks himself the question posed in Psalm 78: *'Can God spread a table in the wilderness? Even though he struck the rock so that water gushed out and torrents overflowed, can he also give bread … ?' (v. 19-20)*. If for Israel his firstborn (Ex. 4:22) he had *'commanded the skies above, and opened the doors of heaven … rained down on them manna to eat, and gave them the grain of heaven … sent them food in abundance'* (v. 23-25), then, surely, he could not wish his one and only son, whom he had but recently charged with so vital a mission, to perish from starvation. As Jesus himself taught later, *'Is there anyone among you who, if your child asks for bread, will give a stone?'* (Matt. 7:9).

By the answer that he gives, Jesus shows that this first temptation was perhaps the most fundamental of all: *'Man does not live on bread alone, but on every word that comes from the mouth of God'* (Matt. 4:4). At least five lines of thought on Jesus' part may be indicated by his choice of this quotation:

- The original context from which Jesus' answer was taken, Deuteronomy 8, viewed Israel's long years in the wilderness as a trial of trust and obedience: *'… in order to humble you, testing you to know what was in your heart, whether or not you would keep his commandments'* (Deut. 8:2). Jesus' use of words from this context imply that he understood that he too was being tested – that he was having to face up to and commit himself to the call

106

Baptism and Temptation

that had come to him at his baptism.

- The reference to the *'word that comes from the mouth of God'* may point back to the voice that he had heard at his baptism, with its threefold reference to the Old Testament. Jesus effectively declares here his intention to seek out and then to act upon the meaning of his Father's will for him as foreshadowed in the Old Testament – the very thing that he was seeking to do during this period of intense reflection.

- The source of the quotation, Deuteronomy 8:3, suggests that he perceived a link between himself and Israel as a whole – that it was his task to be what Israel collectively had failed to be, not only a true witness to the glory and the grace of God, but also, remembering the allusion to the Servant passages in the words from heaven, a truer and more faithful servant:

> But you, Israel, my **servant**, Jacob, whom I have chosen, the offspring of Abraham, my friend; you whom I took from the ends of the earth, and called from its farthest corners, saying to you, 'You are my **servant**, I have chosen you and not cast you off' … Who is blind but my **servant**, or deaf like my messenger whom I send? Who is blind like my dedicated one, or blind like the servant of the LORD? He sees many things, but does not observe them; his ears are open, but he does not hear. (Isaiah 41:8-9; 42:19-20)

- The inclusion in the Deuteronomy quotation of the word 'man' (*anthrōpos* in Matt. 4:4; *adam* in Deut. 8:5) suggests a still more profound and far-reaching meaning for this temptation. Jesus rejects here any claim to special treatment, despite his status as son; far from expecting any divine privilege, he aligns himself with humanity as a whole, as he had done at his baptism. The same applies, in fact, to all three temptations: Jesus answers with words originally addressed to all the people of Israel. This deliberate and explicit choice on Jesus' part justifies the view that it is the temptation in the wilderness that Paul had specifically in mind when he wrote to the Philippians that Jesus *'though he was in the form of God, did not count equality with God a thing to be grasped, but made himself nothing, taking the form of a servant, being born in the likeness of men'* (Phil 2:6-7) – we notice here the word 'servant' again. The phrases 'the form of God' and 'equality with God' could obviously be echoes of the repeated formulation in the temptation accounts, *'If you are the Son of God'*. Paul seems to have seen the wilderness temptations as the decisive moment in Jesus' rejection of self-glorification and his choosing the path of submission to the Father's will for him, embracing the mission that the voice from heaven had laid

Jesus – yesterday, today, for ever

upon him.[4]

- Still more important, perhaps, is the use of the word *adam*; it suggests a parallel – and a contrast – with Adam, who, as we saw in chapter 2, is perhaps the most important Old Testament prefiguring of Jesus. The use of this word – remembering that Jesus' internal debate will presumably have been conducted in Aramaic – may indicate Jesus' awareness that he faced a decision comparable to that of Adam and Eve. Would he take the path of rebellion chosen by Adam or submit himself obediently to the calling of his Father? Paul's use of the phrase 'equality with God' in the Philippians quotation points in precisely the same direction.[5] And if the words do carry that sense, then it would suggest that, as he wrestled with these Old Testament echoes, Jesus grasped how much depended on his decision – that it was his vocation to be the new 'counter-Adam' that we discussed in chapter 2, thus making possible the undoing of the consequences of Adam and Eve's fateful choice, reversing the flow of human history, and leading ultimately to a renewed and reconciled humanity in a world freed from all its present ills.

The Servant passages, brought to the forefront of his mind by the voice from heaven, would have helped to confirm these blessings that his acceptance and faithful realisation of his mission would bring to mankind: justice (or 'righteousness') established at last in the world (42:4); the light of God's mercy known to the nations (42:6); the restoration of a fallen Israel and their reconciliation with their God (49:5-6); his salvation reaching out to the farthest ends of the earth (49:6). It may be that he now for the first time grasped fully what the fourth Servant passage calls '*the fruit of the travail of his soul*' (Is. 53:11) and that he first saw in his mind's eye those ever-widening circles of men and women praising God that are imagined in the second half of Psalm 22 (v. 22-31) – and so was able to set them over against the suffering that appeared to be attached to the mission.[6] All this, and more, was implicit in that first temptation.

However much Jesus had known what to expect before coming to John, the

---

4 This is suggested in Tom Barling's fine exposition of this whole passage in Philippians in his *The Letter to the Philippians*, published by *The Christadelphian* in 1981, pp. 61-79.

5 See note 2 in chapter 2.

6 It was, surely, outcomes of this kind, rather than any purely personal consequences, that constitute '*the joy that was set before him*' which, according to Hebrews 12:2, enabled Jesus to '*endure the cross*', and '*disregard ... its shame*', not only at the last, in Gethsemane and after, but right from the beginning.

Baptism and Temptation

mission implicit in the words from heaven, heard within their Old Testament context, must have been the most profound challenge imaginable: they asked of this young man that he should leave his home, his family, and his life in Nazareth, and assume the task, not merely of preaching repentance to Israel, but also of becoming the focus of a new relationship between God and man – a mission which would lead him into great personal suffering, both mental and physical. We cannot know how Jesus was able to come to that decision – and it must ultimately have been his decision – but the implicit comparison with Gethsemane encourages us to think of prolonged, anguished wrestling in prayer, his mind, sharpened by the Spirit, able to visualise the immeasurable blessing that his calling would bring to mankind. At the same time, his deep sense of God's nearness and his love for him (into which the same psalm gives us unparalleled insight) must have made him desire above all things to fulfil the Father's wishes and further his purposes. And we may, I think, be sure that in his prayers he will have found – or received – the assurance that the Father would sustain and support him throughout his time of service – and beyond.

Not just 'whether' but also 'how?'

It would be possible, of course, to find echoes of this same fundamental debate in Jesus' mind in the two other temptations specifically mentioned by Matthew and Luke. For example, Jesus' response to the third temptation, *'Worship the Lord your God, and serve only him'* (Matt. 4:10), is not only a further expression of submission to the Father's will but also includes the significant term 'serve'. It seems to me, however, that they also provide evidence of an additional issue that preoccupied Jesus during his time in the wilderness. It was a question not only of 'whether' – whether he would embrace the calling brought to him by the voice from heaven – but also of 'how?' What did he actually have to do, how should he go about the task assigned to him? As we have said, the voice from above gave no specific instructions – yet the realisation of Jesus' mission of necessity involved a host of questions and decisions, including perhaps the following:

- What was to be the primary thrust of his proclamation – should he do as John had done, emphasising the imminence of judgment, or should he focus on the grace and forgiveness of God?

- Should he proclaim his own identity and call on men and women to accept him as their Messiah and Saviour?

- Where should he begin – at the centre of Israel's faith in Jerusalem or at

Jesus – yesterday, today, for ever

home in Galilee?

- To whom should he address his message first – should he seek to win the support of Israel's leaders, or should he speak to the ordinary people?

- What should he actually *do*? Should he seek to take over the leadership of Israel from its present corrupt establishment in Jerusalem, using the powers bestowed on him at his baptism?

- And how should he win the hearts and minds of men and women? Should he perform some spectacular act that would bring people to their knees before him in amazement? Or should he rather seek to win their adherence by relieving the drudgery of many lives by miraculously providing in abundance the necessities of life?

It is not difficult to see that the last two questions in this list, focused on his use of his newly received powers, are at the heart of the three temptations specifically mentioned by Matthew and Luke. The second of them, in Matthew's order, represents the apparently attractive idea that he might perform a stunning and spectacular feat that would convince everyone of his divine origins – and, of course, obviate the necessity of enduring suffering and rejection – while behind the third lay the impulse to take a short cut to kingship by making a grab for worldly power. Even the first temptation could have been triggered by such 'strategic' thinking: that he might make bread not just for himself but for all Israel, especially for the poor among them. That, surely, would establish his credentials as a new and greater Moses and secure the adherence of the mass of the population. The popular appeal of such an action on Jesus' part is all too clearly displayed in John 6.

Yet the voice from heaven did not leave him to face such questions alone. We looked in chapter 2 in some detail at Isaiah's 'Servant passages', observing that together they provide a picture of almost every aspect of the ministry of Jesus – and it was precisely Isaiah's picture of the 'Servant' that was evoked by the words from heaven, addressed to Jesus as he emerged from his baptism. It seems likely, therefore, that the heavenly voice was directing his reflections on the task that lay before him towards those passages. And the impulse to think in the terms suggested by the three temptations might well have derived from the Servant passages. Jesus could have found additional warrant for the idea of providing bread for the masses in Isaiah 49:

I have kept you and given you as a covenant to the people ... saying to the prisoners, 'Come out,' to those who are in darkness, 'Show yourselves.' They shall feed along the ways, on all the bare heights shall be their pasture; they

Baptism and Temptation

shall not hunger or thirst, neither scorching wind nor sun shall strike them down, for he who has pity on them will lead them, and by springs of water will guide them. (Isaiah 49:8-10)

A spectacular act, such as casting himself down from the temple, might have been justified by words in Isaiah 52:

Just as there were many who were astonished at him – so marred was his appearance, beyond human semblance, and his form beyond that of mortals – so he shall startle many nations ... (Isaiah 52:14-15)

Similarly, an attempt to seize power might have been thought required of him on the basis of Isaiah 42 and 49:

Kings shall see and stand up, princes, and they shall prostrate themselves, because of the LORD, who is faithful, the Holy One of Israel, who has chosen you. (Isaiah 49:7)

He will not grow faint or be discouraged till he has established justice in the earth; and the coastlands wait for his law. (Isaiah 42:4)

The way in which Jesus rejects these three temptations illustrates that the attempt to realise in his ministry the picture of the 'Servant' provided by Isaiah – or indeed any Old Testament passages – was no simple matter. The passages, all from Deuteronomy, on which Jesus bases his rejection illustrate that his thinking involved not simple obedience to commands but an extraordinarily perceptive understanding of how the widely differing prophecies and the foreshadowing of the Messiah in the Old Testament fitted together – what came first, which things were to be done by him and which were consequences, either of men's responses to him or of God's response to those responses. Jesus had clearly grasped that though men were to be amazed at him, and though kings were to prostrate themselves before him, it was not his business to make that happen by any grasping after such effects. That, and also the negative aspects of his calling, the suffering and the shame, could be left to other men and to God.

What could Jesus – and what can we – find by way of explicit instructions or descriptions of the Servant's actions?

He will not cry or lift up his voice, or make it heard in the street; a bruised reed he will not break, and a dimly burning wick he will not quench; he will faithfully bring forth justice. He will not grow faint or be crushed until he has established justice in the earth; and the coastlands wait for his teaching. Thus says God, the LORD ... I have called you in righteousness ... to open

111

the eyes that are blind, to bring out the prisoners from the dungeon, from the prison those who sit in darkness. (Isaiah 42:2-7)

The Lord GOD has given me the tongue of a teacher, that I may know how to sustain the weary with a word. Morning by morning he wakens – wakens my ear to listen as those who are taught.'(Isaiah 50:4)

Most explicit is the fifth passage in Isaiah 61:

... the LORD has anointed me; he has sent me to bring good news to the oppressed, to bind up the broken-hearted, to proclaim liberty to the captives, and release to the prisoners; to proclaim the year of the Lord's favour ... to comfort all who mourn. (Isaiah 61:1-2)

The focus in all these passages is on compassion, comfort, healing and a release from burdens for the marginalised in Israel – for the poor, the debt-bound, the oppressed, the sick and the over-burdened, with whose plight Jesus was by then very familiar, as we suggested in the previous chapter. It is the Servant's task both to proclaim and to enact these things, and, by both his words and his actions, to bring the good news of God's 'favour' (*ratson*); his mission will be like a 'year of jubilee' for Israel and, ultimately, for mankind, when all accumulated debts, of money and of sins, will be wiped out.

The Servant passages would also have given Jesus ample grounds for concluding that his mission might prove, or rather, might appear, unsuccessful; as we saw in chapter 2, one of them actually foresees the Servant reflecting on apparent failure: *'But I said, "I have laboured in vain, I have spent my strength for nothing and vanity... "'*– but that, like the consequences of his mission for the Servant personally and its ultimate outcome, could be, and had to be, left to God: *'... yet surely my cause is with the LORD, and my reward with my God'* (49:4).

It is evidently not the case, of course, that Jesus reflected only on these Servant passages during his forty days in the wilderness; his responses to the 'tempter', using texts from Deuteronomy, indicate that other passages were very much in his mind. One can imagine him thinking his way through everything that he had heard and learned in the synagogue, reviewing, modifying or rejecting what he had been told and perhaps even had himself thought about them, all the time praying for guidance in his understanding in a more or less continuous process of 'consultation' with God. But it is hard to resist the conclusion that the Servant passages played a predominant part in his reflections and shaped the way in which he came to understand what he was to do. The three named 'temptations' are, it appears to me, a kind of summary

112

Baptism and Temptation

of this lengthy process: the 'tempter', variously named 'satan' or 'the devil', represents the promptings of those alternative readings of the Old Testament that appeared to offer less painful and more flattering images of the role to which Jesus had been called. But his discerning spirit, his honesty and integrity would not permit him to entertain such notions, contrary as they were to the outline of the Messiah that emerged from his profound, prayer-driven contemplation.

Any attempt to reconstruct what may have been the thinking of Jesus at any time, let alone at one so critical as the wilderness period, is obviously conjectural and must be undertaken with caution and reverence. It is tempting, inevitably, to read back into this period of Jesus' life not only what 'Messianic' passages in the Old Testament suggest about Jesus' inner life and relationship to God, but also what we know of his ministry and especially of his Passion. It may be, for example, that I have ascribed too central a place in that process to the Servant passages. By attempting nevertheless to imagine what might have been happening during the 'temptation' period, I simply wish to emphasise that his decision, however much it lies outside our experience, must in some way be accessible to our thought and imagination, even if we are mistaken in the detail or in the weight that we attach to any particular factor. Even to attempt to understand Jesus' decision brings him closer to us, makes him more truly man – and deepens our love for him and our worship of him.

Perhaps the most compelling evidence for the importance to Jesus of the Servant passages is found in Luke's account in his fourth chapter of Jesus' visit to the synagogue in Nazareth. Jesus' deliberate choice of Isaiah 61 – '*He unrolled the scroll and found the place where it was written…*' – indicates how significant this particular passage was to him, while his omission of the phrase '*and the day of vengeance of our God*' from Isaiah 61:2 illustrates how carefully he distinguished between what his message was to be now and what it might need to be later. That Jesus leaves the quotation unfinished is a mark of the difference between his message and that of John; his will be first and foremost a message of grace and release. The imperative to respond in faith and the responsibility to God's judgment that it inevitably brings with it remain for the moment unsaid.

And why has Luke placed it here, right at the beginning of his account of the ministry and immediately after Jesus' time in the wilderness? This episode clearly interrupts the chronological order of Jesus' ministry; Luke himself indicates this, for he introduces the Nazareth scene by referring to Jesus' prior activities in Galilee: '*Then Jesus, filled with the power of the Spirit, returned to Galilee, and a report about him spread through all the surrounding country. He*

Jesus – yesterday, today, for ever

began to teach in their synagogues and was praised by everyone. When he came to Nazareth …' (Luke 4:14-16). He also later reports Jesus as saying: *'And you will say, "Do here also in your hometown the things that we have heard you did at Capernaum"'* (v. 23). It looks, therefore, as though Luke wishes us to see a direct link between the scene in the synagogue at Nazareth and Jesus' time in the wilderness; he shows him announcing publicly the outcome of his period of reflection and prayer: his acceptance of his appointed role, how he has understood it, and what he intends to do – probably in contradistinction to what he had been taught in this same synagogue as a child and young man. Jesus' words here remind one a little of a political candidate announcing his decision to stand and outlining his manifesto. The content of the programme, though, is very different – and so is the man!

'Shaliach'

It might be thought strange that the Father should not provide detailed instructions for the mission which he was giving to the Son. In fact, it is entirely in keeping with the way in which God uses human agents, which can perhaps best be described in terms of the Jewish concept of the *shaliach*, the empowered agent or plenipotentiary who is 'sent' by another to act on his/her behalf. A contemporary Jewish source describes it as follows:

- A person's *shaliach* is as he himself.

- … The *shaliach* does not abnegate his intellect, will, desires, feelings, talents and personal 'style' to that of the one whom he represents; rather, he enlists them in the fulfilment of his mission. The result of this in not a lesser bond between the two, but the contrary: the *meshaleiach* [i.e. the one who 'sends' the agent] is acting through the whole of the *shaliach* – not only through the *shaliach's* physical actions, but also through the *shaliach's* personality, which has become an extension of the *meshaleiach's* personality.

- The emissary's final achievement is attributed to the principal.

- The emissary's every action is attributed to the principal.

- The emissary completely embodies the principal.

- … while the goal is for the principal to be represented – in order to achieve this, the emissary must bring his own entire being into the mission.[7]

The role intended for human beings in Genesis 1:26-27 is fundamentally

---

7 http://www.torahofmessiah.com

Baptism and Temptation

similar, as is that played by Abraham's servant in Genesis 24, who, faced with the responsibility of choosing a wife for Isaac, devises his own plan of action (see Genesis 24:11-14). It is also, *par excellence*, the role of a son in the service of his father, and it is in these terms that Jesus speaks of his work in John's Gospel:

> ... *the Son can do nothing on his own, but only what he sees the Father doing; for whatever the Father does, the Son does likewise. The Father loves the Son and shows him all that he himself is doing. (John 5:19-20)*

It is, of course, also the kind of role that Jesus desires and anticipates for his disciples:

> *You are my friends if you do what I command you. I do not call you servants any longer, because the servant does not know what the master is doing; but I have called you friends, because I have made known to you everything that I have heard from my Father. (John 15:14-15)*

Reflecting on Jesus' time in the wilderness, one might well conclude that when Jesus says in John that *'My teaching is not mine but his who sent me'* (7:16), when he insists that he declares to Israel *'what I have seen in the Father's presence'* (8:38) and that he has *'told you the truth that I heard from God'* (8:40), he is not referring to some pre-incarnational experience with the Father, nor even to visionary experiences during his earthly ministry. He is speaking rather of the process of prayerful reflection and meditation on the Old Testament that had doubtless characterised his earlier life but which, sharpened by the Spirit, had been given new impetus in the wilderness by the pressure of his new calling. What he had learned, understood and internalised there, not least from Isaiah, would shape his ministry and determine the course of the rest of his earthly life.

Chapter 5

Outline of Jesus' Ministry

Length and timing

Despite the existence of four accounts of Jesus' life, it is remarkably difficult to form a clear overall picture of his ministry – of the 'when' and the 'where'. Like most writers of that age, the Gospel writers have not that concern for linear time and for precise details in relation to dates and places that has been an ever-more prominent characteristic of the Western mind over the past five centuries. Luke, who is generally held to be the best historian among the four, is punctilious enough to locate precisely the beginning of John the Baptist's ministry:

> *In the fifteenth year of the reign of Emperor Tiberius, when Pontius Pilate was governor of Judea, and Herod was ruler of Galilee, and his brother Philip ruler of the region of Ituraea and Trachonitis, and Lysanias ruler of Abilene, during the high priesthood of Annas and Caiaphas ... (Luke 3:1-2)*

Yet, as we saw in the previous chapter, even he is happy enough to dislocate chronology in order to be able to use Jesus' 'sermon' in the Nazareth synagogue as a kind of programmatic 'manifesto' for his ministry (Luke 4:16-30), even though he is obviously aware that Jesus has already performed amazing things elsewhere before arriving in Nazareth: *'And you will say, "Do here also in your hometown the things that we have heard you did at Capernaum"'* (v. 23).

As has often been noted, it is therefore difficult to determine the length of Jesus' ministry. From a reading of the Synoptic Gospels only, one might conclude that it took the form of a period of preaching and healing in northern Israel, in Galilee and surrounding areas, extending as far as the territory around Tyre and Sidon in the west and into Decapolis, across the Sea of Galilee, after which he made his way to Jerusalem for the feast of Passover, during which he was arrested and crucified. On that reading, Jesus' entire ministry might be thought to have lasted less than a year. However, John's Gospel, which, as far as dates and places are concerned, appears to be much more precise than

Outline of Jesus' Ministry

the Synoptics, presents an altogether different picture. John refers to no less than three Passover feasts: one early on (2:13), another in the middle of the Gospel (6:4), and then a third, at which, as in the Synoptics, Jesus is crucified (11:55; 13:1; 18:28). These details suggest a ministry lasting over two years at least, even if it is hard to see how the often-quoted figure of three and a half years is arrived at, unless it is derived from a somewhat speculative reading of Daniel's 'seventy weeks prophecy' with its reference to 'half of the week', i.e. three and a half days, understood as three and a half years (Dan. 9:27).

Jesus and John the Baptist

That is, however, far from being the only puzzle arising from the very different chronologies of John and the Synoptics. When did Jesus commence his public ministry? Both Mark and Matthew lead directly from Jesus' time in the wilderness to the beginning of his preaching activity in Galilee, which, they say, began after John was put in prison by Herod Antipas:

> *He was in the wilderness forty days, tempted by Satan; and he was with the wild beasts; and the angels waited on him. Now after John was arrested, Jesus came to Galilee, proclaiming the good news of God, and saying, 'The time is fulfilled, and the kingdom of God has come near; repent, and believe in the good news.' (Mark 1:13-15)*

> *Then the devil left him, and suddenly angels came and waited on him. Now when Jesus heard that John had been arrested, he withdrew to Galilee. He left Nazareth and made his home in Capernaum by the sea … From that time Jesus began to proclaim, 'Repent, for the kingdom of heaven has come near.' (Matthew 4:11-13, 17)*

Luke's account looks very similar, despite the insertion of the episode in Nazareth:

> *When the devil had finished every test, he departed from him until an opportune time. Then Jesus, filled with the power of the Spirit, returned to Galilee, and a report about him spread through all the surrounding country. He began to teach in their synagogues and was praised by everyone. (Luke 4:13-15)*

John's account could scarcely be more different. Jesus' period in the wilderness does not figure in his narrative; instead, Jesus appears to remain in the area where John was baptising (John 1:15-51) before travelling to Galilee, with a number of disciples, to attend the wedding in Cana (2:1-12). He then goes, still with a group of disciples (2:22), to Jerusalem for the Passover

(2:13-25); it is presumably during this visit that his memorable encounter with Nicodemus takes place (3:1-15). Jesus then remains in Judea and begins some kind of preaching and baptising ministry in '*the Judean countryside*' (3:22), probably not far from John's baptismal site. There is at least the suggestion, then, that for an unspecified time Jesus and some of his disciples are engaged in a ministry that parallels that of John – so much so that John's disciples appear to regard Jesus' activities as a threat to John's: '*Now a discussion about purification arose between John's disciples and a Jew. They came to John and said to him, "Rabbi, the one who was with you across the Jordan, to whom you testified, here he is baptizing, and all are going to him."*' (3:25-26). And all this precedes John the Baptist's imprisonment, as John is at pains to point out: '*John, of course, had not yet been thrown into prison*' (3:24).[1]

It is only after all this that Jesus again departs for Galilee (4:3) and, on his way through Samaria, meets the Samaritan woman at the well, as John records in his chapter 4. If we put John's account alongside the Synoptics, we might surmise that this journey to Galilee is the one referred to in Mark 1:14 and that John's arrest occurred before Jesus' departure from Judea. According to John, the move to Galilee was motivated by concern about the Pharisees' view of his activities (4:1-3), which might have made his continued presence in Judea unwise, at least for the moment. By contrast, Matthew and Mark are perhaps suggesting that the arrest of John the Baptist plays some part in the decision. Maurice Casey's interpretation of that decision is striking, though speculative:

> What would a normal person in Jesus' position have done, when Herod Antipas arrested and imprisoned John? One obvious possibility would have been to move to the relatively safe territory of Philip the tetrarch, out of reach of Herod Antipas. Another would have been to flee further north and then perhaps east ... Jesus did not do any such thing! He did the amazing and dangerous thing, he headed straight back into Galilee, the kingdom ruled by Herod Antipas, and openly and publicly preached the good news, that God would soon establish his kingdom.

---

1 This narrator's aside figures prominently in Richard Bauckham's thesis that John assumes on the part of his readers a prior familiarity with Mark and/or other Synoptic Gospels. He argues, convincingly, it seems to me, that John's purpose here is not to put Mark right or to substitute his own chronology of the ministry for that proposed by Mark, but rather to explain the relationship between the two accounts: 'The function of 3:24, for readers/hearers of Mark, is therefore not to correct Mark's chronology, but to place the events of John 1:19-4:43 between Mark 1:13 and Mark 1:14.' – Richard Bauckham, 'John for Readers of Mark' in Richard Bauckham (ed.), *The Gospels for All Christians*, Edinburgh 1998, p. 154.

Outline of Jesus' Ministry

In due course, some Pharisees brought him the [inevitable] news: "Herod wants to kill you".[2]

The notion that Jesus spent time in Judea with some disciples, engaged in a baptising ministry comparable to John's *before* he began to preach in Galilee, is at once surprising and puzzling. Why did he spend the first period after his baptism in this way? Ought we perhaps view it as a kind of 'apprenticeship', during which Jesus gains his first experience in his future role as teacher and preacher, possibly with the support of John the Baptist? The idea might seem implausible: would one on whom the Spirit has descended need such a 'trial run'? Yet if, as I have sought to do, we try to remember that Jesus is truly man and had spent his preceding years as a village craftsman, then the notion of a time of experiment and trial makes a good deal more sense. But in that case, why did Jesus then distance himself from Judea and from John, or at least John's disciples, and move northwards to Galilee? A number of possible reasons suggest themselves: Jesus may have wished to begin his ministry proper on his home territory. He may also have taken his cue from the Isaiah passage quoted by Matthew in his record of this move:

> *In the former time he brought into contempt the land of Zebulun and the land of Naphtali, but in the latter time he will make glorious the way of the sea, the land beyond the Jordan, Galilee of the nations. The people who walked in darkness have seen a great light; those who lived in a land of deep darkness – on them light has shined. (Isaiah 9:1-2; see Matthew 4:15-16)*

There may, however, be a further reason of a different kind. While John the Baptist may have been an invaluable mentor or at least model as he took his first steps as a public preacher, Jesus must, I think, have realised that his ministry was to have a quite different character. Apart from his references to the coming of one greater than himself, John's message appears to have been a stern one, emphasising the coming of judgment and the need to save oneself through repentance:

> *John said to the crowds that came out to be baptized by him, 'You brood of vipers! Who warned you to flee from the wrath to come? Bear fruits worthy of repentance ... Even now the axe is lying at the root of the trees; every tree therefore that does not bear good fruit is cut down and thrown into the fire.' (Luke 3:7-9)*

Though Jesus describes him later as 'more than a prophet' (Luke 7:26)

---

2 Maurice Casey, *Jesus of Nazareth*, pp. 180-181.

Jesus – yesterday, today, for ever

because of his role as his forerunner, his message was in other respects that of a typical Hebrew prophet in the Old Testament, bringing to Israel a warning of impending disaster and urging them to change their ways. Jesus implies, in the same passage, that John is part, though a distinguished part, of the old order: *'I tell you, among those born of women no one is greater than John; yet the least in the kingdom of God is greater than he'* (Luke 7:28). His own mission, by contrast, was to be the beginning of something new, characterised primarily by the announcement of God's grace, the 'year of God's favour' that he announces in the Nazareth synagogue, as we saw in the previous chapter. When challenged by Pharisees about his parable of the dishonest manager (Luke 16:1-13), Jesus says: *'The law and the prophets were in force until John; since then, the good news of the kingdom of God has been proclaimed, and everyone is urged to enter it'* (Luke 16:16 – this rendering from the *New English Translation*, supported also by the CSB and the CEB, makes much better sense than the '... everyone is forcing their way in' or similar that is suggested by most modern translations). These words make clear Jesus' awareness of the gulf that distinguished him and his message from even the greatest of the old world. It was a distinction that he made abundantly clear when challenged over the issue of fasting:

> *No one tears a piece from a new garment and sews it on an old garment; otherwise the new will be torn, and the piece from the new will not match the old. And no one puts new wine into old wineskins; otherwise the new wine will burst the skins and will be spilled, and the skins will be destroyed. But new wine must be put into fresh wineskins. (Luke 5:36-38)*

From this perspective, the move to Galilee makes perfect sense: Jesus was not only able to escape, at least for a short time, from the pressure of the Pharisees' scrutiny, but also to prevent any easy assumption that his activity was no more than a continuation, or even an imitation, of what John had been doing.

All this raises another question however: why do the Synoptic Gospels make no mention of Jesus' early ministry in Judea? According to John, he was accompanied there by 'his disciples' (John 3:22). It seems likely that some, at least, of the disciples referred to in John 1 were among them and therefore that Peter and Andrew, even if no longer with Jesus by this time, would be aware, then or later, of this stage in Jesus' life. In which case, why does Mark, the Gospel that probably was based on Peter's account of Jesus' ministry,[3]

---

3 The dependence of Mark's Gospel on the testimony of Peter was assumed by virtually all early Christian writers, beginning with the comments of Papias early in the second cen-

Outline of Jesus' Ministry

completely omit it? The most likely explanation is that the Gospel writers saw it as only a preliminary to, rather than as part of, Jesus' mission proper; the fact that even John, who alone is our source of information about this Judean period, includes no detailed account of any episodes from it, may be thought to confirm that explanation.

Visits to Jerusalem

The relationship of John to the other Gospels throws up a further puzzle concerning the chronology and shape of Jesus' ministry. As mentioned above, many episodes in John – indeed, most of the narrative – are linked to a Jewish feast, for which Jesus has apparently gone to Jerusalem. Sanders lists them as follows:

Passover (spring)	John 2:13
Weeks (Pentecost, early summer)	perhaps John 5:1
Booths (Tabernacles, autumn)	not mentioned
Passover	John 6:4
Weeks	not mentioned
Booths	John 7
Passover	John 11:55

Again one has to ask why these visits do not figure in the Synoptic Gospels. The answer may well be that the Twelve, who were probably the main sources for the three Synoptic Gospels, were simply not present; they are mentioned only in relation to the Passover in John 6 and to events that took place on their home territory in Galilee, of which the Feeding of the 5,000 at that Passover was one. They are also mentioned in John 9:2, which seems to be attached to the account of events at the Feast of Tabernacles that begins in John 7, at which they appear not to have been present! So it looks as though Jesus went to at least some of these feasts in Jerusalem alone – that certainly appears to be the case in John 7, where John says that he went '*not publicly but as it were in secret*' (7:10). Incidentally, this focus on events in Jerusalem not known to the Twelve is compelling evidence for the view that the writer of John's Gospel was *not* a Galilean fisherman and son of Zebedee, but rather a resident of Jerusalem, who was largely unknown to the 'Twelve.[4] It is not difficult to detect a somewhat strained relationship between the Galilean disciples and

---

tury.

4 For arguments in support of this thesis, see Richard Bauckham, *The Testimony of the Beloved Disciple*, Grand Rapids, Michigan 2007, and also Appendix A of my *The Word Became Flesh*.

John, the 'beloved disciple', for example at the Last Supper (John 13:22-26), when going to Jesus' tomb (John 20:1-10), and by the Sea of Galilee (John 21:20-23).

More importantly in the present context, it appears to imply that Jesus' ministry in Galilee may have been not one unbroken period of preaching but rather a series of lengthy, possibly seasonally determined periods of itinerant preaching, interspersed perhaps by periods at home. Matthew says that Jesus *'made his home in Capernaum'* (Matt. 4:13), which suggests that he had a base there, from which he made extensive forays into various parts of northern Israel and occasionally to Jerusalem. It is true, of course, that Jesus said that *'Foxes have holes, and birds of the air have nests; but the Son of Man has no-where to lay his head'* (Luke 9:58) and that the disciples claimed to have *'left everything and followed you'* (Mark 10:28), but neither statement requires an unbroken period on the road of over two years. The latter statement comes from the time when Jesus and his followers were on their way to Jerusalem for the final time, a journey for which they would presumably have had to leave everything in a more complete sense than before.

The Gospels: thematic rather than chronological

The conclusion that presents itself as a result of this review of the temporal aspects of Jesus' ministry is summed up by Maurice Casey: 'We must therefore be content without a chronological outline of the ministry, and without knowing how long it lasted.'[5] This does not imply any criticism of the Gospels; it is apparent that to the Gospel writers questions of chronology and coverage of the whole of Jesus' life were of lesser moment than thematic concerns, as they were to ancient historians and biographers in general. As noted earlier, Richard Burridge has shown that the Synoptics Gospels correspond broadly to the conventions of ancient biography (the Greek *bios* and the Roman *vita*).

This divergence from modern notions of biography and history is particularly true, of course, in the case of John. The list of feasts mentioned in John confirms that he includes in his Gospel only a tiny number of episodes in Jesus' ministry; after his arrival in Galilee in chapter 4, only one further incident is located there, the Passover-time feeding of the multitude in chapter 6. Similarly, despite the space devoted to time spent in Jerusalem, very few separate events are covered: the healing at the unnamed feast and the subsequent controversy occupy the whole of chapter 5, while the entire middle section, from 7:1 to 10:21, appears to be devoted to Jesus' visit to the Feast of

---

5 Maurice Casey, *Jesus of Nazareth*, p. 185.

Outline of Jesus' Ministry

Tabernacles in chapter 7. After that, John tells us only of events at the Feast of Dedication (10:22-39) and the raising of Lazarus (11:1-44). From that moment on, his movements before and after his two visits to Bethany (10:40-42; 11:54-57), the meal at Bethany (12:1-8) and his entry into Jerusalem (12:12-19) are all set against a background of conspiracy against him that leads to the plot to kill him (11:45-53; 12:9-11). John then devotes five chapters (13-17) to Jesus' final discourses to his disciples.

We might think that the Synoptic Gospels are quite different in this respect, yet they too appear in different ways to shape their accounts of Jesus' ministry in terms of various thematic concerns rather than coverage and chronological accuracy. To illustrate the point, consider the Gospel of *Mark*, which Matthew and Luke appear to have used as the basis for their accounts. Austin Farrer's analysis of the healings recorded there presents evidence suggesting that the choice of those individually recorded is far from random: he demonstrates that in the Galilean phase there a total of ten healings, including those of the two 'demoniacs' – two parallel sets of five, or 'handfuls', as Farrer puts it, while in chapters 9-10, up to the moment of Jesus' arrival in Jerusalem, there are a further two, making twelve in all, all Jewish. These additional two, after Caesarea Philippi, are the epileptic boy (9:14-29) and blind Bartimaeus (10:46-52). In addition, though, there is one healing outside Jewish territory, of a Gentile Syro-Phoenician woman (Mark 7:24-30) – placed, not accidentally, alongside Jesus' challenge to received notions of ritual purity (7:1-23) – to point forward to the coming opening to Gentiles.[6] Farrer's scheme seems the more plausible because he is able to show that the same 12+1 pattern is also found in Matthew, while in Luke he identifies the pattern in chapters 4-11 – and then a further 12+1 in chapters 13-18!

> In Galilee and Judaea Jesus heals twelve Israelites and one Gentile, as Mark had said; in the Samaritan region, between the first mention of Samaritan contacts (9:51-56) and the last (17:11-19), Jesus heals another thirteen persons, of whom one, the thankful leper, is said to be a Samaritan.'

The inference that Farrer draws seems plausible: twelve to represent the twelve tribes of Israel, just as there are twelve disciples, plus one Gentile, pointing to the as yet future incorporation of Gentiles into the new people of God.

---

6 Austin Farrer, *A Study in St Mark*, Woking/London 1951, and *St Matthew and St Mark*, Glasgow 1954. Most of Farrer's numerically based analysis I find over-complex and far from convincing, but his basic analysis of the healings seems to me quite persuasive.

Passage	Person	Disease	Passage	Person
1:21-28	Demoniac in synagogue	Possession	5:1-20	Gerasene demoniac
1:29-31	Peter's mother-in-law	Dangerous internal illness	5:21-24, 35-43	Jairus's daughter
1:40-45	Leprous man	Defilement	5:24-34	Woman with issue of blood
			7:24-30	Syro-Phoenician girl
2:1-12	Paralytic	Incapacity (foot/ears)	7:31-37	Deaf stammerer
3:1-6	Withered hand	Incapacity (hand/eyes)	8:22-26	Blind Bethsaidan

Other studies of Mark have similarly sought to uncover the deliberate structuring that underlies the apparently random order of the individual short sections of which Mark's account is made up. The Galilean ministry, from 1:16 to 8:26, for example, appears to comprise two parallel cycles of events (1:16-3:35 and 4:35-8:36), made up of the following five phases: healings – opposition – rejection – beginnings of a new people – premonitions of Jesus' death. Between the two cycles stands a series of parables (4:1-34) focusing on Israel's response to his coming and the effects of his teaching, i.e. the 'theory' for which the two cycles provide the 'evidence'.[7]

This kind of organisation is still more evident in *Matthew*. He has grouped the events of ministry around five blocks of teaching, each with a specific focus (ch. 5-7, 10, 13, 18, and 23 (or 24)-25), while ten of Mark's twelve plus one healings are all packed into chapters 8-9. As to Luke, we have already referred to his re-positioning of Jesus' visit to Nazareth apparently for thematic rather than chronological reasons. Though he departs from Mark to a considerable extent by including what appears to be an extended period of activity in Samaria on the way to Jerusalem (9:51-18:14), Farrer argues that he still retains Mark's twelve plus one arrangement of healing – but doubles it!

Tentative conclusions

These are, of course, no more than indications of the kind of structuring along thematic rather than chronological lines that have been discerned – or hypothesised – in the Synoptic Gospels. The overall effect is that it is impossible to form any kind of detailed picture of the geographical and chronological shape of Jesus' ministry. Nevertheless, a number of conclusions may be hazarded:

---

7 See, for example, Jerry Camery-Hoggatt's *Irony in Mark's Gospel. Text and Subtext*, Cambridge/ New York 1992.

Outline of Jesus' Ministry

- On his return to Galilee – irrespective of any prior activity in Judea – Jesus very soon took up residence in Capernaum, possibly in the house of Simon Peter (Mark 1:29; 9:33) and presumably because of its more central location: *'He left Nazareth and made his home in Capernaum by the sea' (Matt. 4:13); 'When he returned to Capernaum after some days, it was reported that he was at home'* (Mark 2:1). The reports in Mark 3 of his family's alarm (3:20-21, 31-35) may indicate a desire on their part to take him back to the quiet of Nazareth: *'When his family heard what was happening, they tried to take him home with them. "He's out of his mind," they said'* (3:31 NLT).

- Capernaum became the base for Jesus' preaching and healing mission, predominantly in the small towns and villages around the Sea of Galilee, particularly on its northern shore. The names are familiar to us from the Gospels: Bethsaida, Gennesaret, Chorazin, Magdala. At times, he went further inland, to Cana and Nazareth itself, and even as far as Nain, in the Plain of Jezreel (Luke 7:11-17). Jesus also crosses to the eastern shores of the lake, to areas such as the territory of the Gergasenes or Gadarenes, where Jews were probably in the minority. He may well have done this to escape the crowds that followed him, eager to see more miracles; Mark's account in his chapter 4 speaks volumes about the pressure that Jesus came under: *'On that day, when evening had come, he said to them, "Let us go across to the other side." And leaving the crowd behind, they took him with them in the boat, just as he was. Other boats were with him'* (Mark 4:35-36). The feeding of the 4,000 (Mark 8:1-10) is thought to have taken place here. One might also conclude from Mark 8 that Jesus went across the lake to these areas when distressed at the criticism and opposition he encountered from the Pharisees and others after the feeding:

    And immediately he got into the boat with his disciples and went to the district of Dalmanutha. The Pharisees came and began to argue with him, asking him for a sign from heaven, to test him. And he sighed deeply in his spirit and said, 'Why does this generation ask for a sign? Truly I tell you, no sign will be given to this generation.' And he left them, and getting into the boat again, he went across to the other side. (Mark 8:10-13)

- As we noted in chapter 3, Jesus' activities in Galilee appear to have been focused on the rural population living in small towns and villages; there is no reference in the Gospels to the two large centres in Galilee, Tiberias and Sepphoris. This may be a reflection of the cultural differences and tensions between town and country; the cities differed from the surrounding

Jesus – yesterday, today, for ever

countryside not only in their greater wealth but also as centres of Hellenistic culture and mentality. The contrast between city and countryside is illustrated by events in the Jewish War (66–70 AD): 'In contrast to the surrounding country ... Sepphoris remained loyal to the Romans and because of this for a while called itself "city of peace" (Eirenopolis)'. Why might Jesus have avoided the cities during his ministry? Two obvious reasons suggest themselves: one is proposed by Theissen and Merz:

> Given this difference of mentality between the city and the surrounding countryside, it is quite improbable that in his youth Jesus was decisively stamped by influences from Hellenistic culture through Sepphoris ... So it is not by chance that the Synoptic Jesus tradition is silent about the two largest Galilean cities. Sepphoris, only six kilometres from Nazareth, is no more mentioned than Tiberias, which is only sixteen kilometres from Capernaum. Neither city seems to exist. From this we may conclude that Jesus above all addressed the country population, which lived in the many smaller places.[8]

The other possible reason has to do rather with Jesus' own understanding of his role that we discussed in chapter 4. Luke places at the beginning of his account of the ministry the opening of the fifth and last of the Servant passages in Isaiah that we looked at in chapter 2: *'the* LORD *has anointed me; he has sent me to bring good news to the oppressed, to bind up the brokenhearted, to proclaim liberty to the captives, and release to the prisoners'* (Isaiah 61:1/Luke 4:18). There were doubtless plenty of poor and oppressed people in Tiberias and Sepphoris too, but in the villages of Galilee almost the entire population might be so described, as Jesus must have known only too well as a result of his working life among them. In addition, the second Servant passage placed its emphasis first on his mission to Israel: *' ... to bring Jacob back to him, and that Israel might be gathered to him'* (Isaiah 49:5), though it does go to speak also of being a light for the Gentiles. Thus everything about Jesus, his upbringing and experience on the one hand, and his knowledge of Isaiah's prophecies on the other, would have pointed him towards the Galilean countryside rather than towards the generally wealthier, more sophisticated Hellenised cities.

- The Gospels suggest that in the later stages of the Galilean ministry he ventured further afield, into areas that were not part of Israel's heartland, even

---

8 Gerd Theissen & Annette Merz, *The Historical Jesus. A Comprehensive Guide*, pp. 170-171.

Outline of Jesus' Ministry

if partly populated by Jews. One of these was the area known as Decapolis ('ten cities'), the territory surrounding ten predominantly Greek-speaking cities stretching south-east from the Sea of Galilee (Mark 7:31). Gadara, where Jesus healed the 'demoniac', was in the northernmost part of this region, and Mark says that this man proclaimed what Jesus had done for him 'in the Decapolis' (5:20). Another was the region of Tyre and Sidon on the Mediterranean coast, though probably not the cities themselves. It is clear that people, presumably Jews, from the area of Tyre and Sidon were among the crowds that came to see and hear Jesus (Mark 3:8; Luke 6:17), and Jesus himself visits the area on at least one occasion (Matt. 15:21; Mark 7:24). Both Gospels place this immediately after another dispute with Pharisee critics, this time over questions of purity rituals, again suggesting a desire on Jesus' part to be free for a time of such negative reactions. In addition, there was a single visit to the extreme north, to the area around Caesarea Philippi at the foot of Mount Hermon, where the 'Transfiguration' of Jesus took place (Matt. 16:13; Mark 8:27).

- The most obvious structural feature of Jesus' ministry is the one that enables us to speak of a 'Galilean ministry', namely, the clear division of the ministry into two major stages. All three Synoptic Gospel identify the visit to Caesarea Philippi, along with the Transfiguration that followed shortly afterwards, as marking a profound change in Jesus' activity which divides the ministry into two clearly distinguished parts. Almost immediately afterwards, apparently, Jesus began his journey southward to Jerusalem for the Feast of Passover at which he was to die. Matthew in particular makes this clear by introducing the new phase of Jesus' ministry with the same formula as he used at the beginning of the first stage: *'From that time on, Jesus began to show his disciples that he must go to Jerusalem and undergo great suffering at the hands of the elders and chief priests and scribes, and be killed, and on the third day be raised'* (Matt. 16:21) – compare *'From that time Jesus began to proclaim, "Repent, for the kingdom of heaven has come near"'* (4:17).

The first of the two passages just mentioned also indicates the three essential features that distinguish the second phase from the first:

- Jesus' eyes are now fixed on Jerusalem, whether or not he is already on the way – as we saw in discussing Luke above.

- He now begins to speak about the fate that awaits him in Jerusalem.

- As an inevitable consequence of these first two features, Jesus' attention is now focused primarily on his disciples – this is particularly clear in Mark 9-10 – because Jesus is presumably thinking about what lies beyond his death and resurrection, when they will have to take on responsibility for the continuation of his work.

Even in John's Gospel, so different in virtually every respect, we find a similar change of focus from 'the world' to the disciples. There, however, it is a change, not in time or place, but in thematic concerns. At the end of John 12, both the narrator, first, and then Jesus in effect draw a line under his public ministry and survey the outcome:

> *Although he had performed so many signs in their presence, they did not believe in him ... Nevertheless many, even of the authorities, believed in him. But because of the Pharisees they did not confess it, for fear that they would be put out of the synagogue; for they loved human glory more than the glory that comes from God ... 'I have come as light into the world, so that everyone who believes in me should not remain in the darkness. I do not judge anyone who hears my words and does not keep them, for I came not to judge the world, but to save the world. The one who rejects me and does not receive my word has a judge; on the last day the word that I have spoken will serve as judge ...' (John 12:37, 42-43, 46-48)*

There follow then, before the account of the crucifixion, five chapters in which Jesus devotes himself entirely to his disciples.

We do not know how long the journey to Jerusalem lasted; Luke devotes a large part of his Gospel to it, as noted above, though the geographical and chronological indications are less than specific – in Luke 10:38 Jesus is already in Bethany, very close to Jerusalem:

> *... he set his face to go to Jerusalem. And he sent messengers ahead of him. On their way they entered a village of the Samaritans to make ready for him. (Luke 9:51-52)*

> *Now as they went on their way, he entered a certain village (Luke 10:38)*

> *He was praying in a certain place. (Luke 11:1)*

> *Jesus went through one town and village after another, teaching as he made his way to Jerusalem. (Luke 13:22)*

> *On the way to Jerusalem Jesus was going through the region between Samaria and Galilee. (Luke 17:11)*

Everything about the incidents and parables that Luke includes in this

Outline of Jesus' Ministry

section, apart from the occasional references to Samaritans, suggests that, contrary to Farrer's hypothesis, Jesus is still in a thoroughly Jewish environment – it is, as Casey suggests, an 'extraordinarily static journey'![9] Perhaps we should conclude that when Luke refers to Jesus 'setting his face' to go to Jerusalem, he is referring not so much to geographical movement but rather to the direction of his thinking – of which, more in chapter 7.

The disciples

All three Synoptic Gospels include an account of Jesus' selection of his twelve disciples (Matthew 10:2-4, Mark 3:16-19 and Luke 6:13-16.)[10] It also emerges from all three that of the twelve men, just three or four (Peter, James, John and Andrew) form an inner group which Jesus takes with him to the mount of Transfiguration and Gethsemane and whose names appear more frequently, while the names of several others occur only in the original lists. The absence of any such account in John's Gospel is further evidence for the view that John, its writer, was not one of the Twelve and not a Galilean. There are many references to 'the disciples' in John – though none at all in chapters 5, 7, 8 and 10 – but the disciples named are different from any list elsewhere: *'Simon Peter, Thomas called the Twin, Nathanael of Cana in Galilee, the sons of Zebedee, and two others of his disciples'* (21:2). John's only references to 'the Twelve' occur in 6:67-71 and 20:24.

It is usually assumed that the expression 'the disciples' is simply a synonym for the Twelve, those whom Jesus specifically chose to 'be with him' (Mark 3:14) and who are listed in the passages mentioned above. In a number of places, however, there are indications that 'the disciples' refers to a larger group of followers, those from whom the Twelve were selected. Luke describes that selection as follows: *'And when day came, he called his disciples and chose twelve of them, whom he also named apostles'* (Luke 6:13; cf. Mark 3:13-14), and later adds *'He came down with them and stood on a level place, with a great crowd of his disciples'* (Luke 6:17). Matthew later appears to describe Jesus taking the Twelve apart from a larger company of followers: *'While Jesus was going up to Jerusalem, he took the twelve disciples aside by themselves, and said to them on the way ...'* (Matt. 20:17). One also wonders whether Matthew is referring to one of the Twelve when he writes: *'Another of his disciples said to him, "Lord,*

---

9   Maurice Casey, *Jesus of Nazareth*, p. 183.

10   I do not intend to comment on these lists, in respect of either the ordering of the names or the apparent discrepancies between them. These and other issues relating to the Twelve are discussed by Richard Bauckham in his *Jesus and the Eyewitnesses*, Grand Rapids, Michigan/Cambridge 2006, pp. 93-113.

first let me go and bury my father"' (Matt. 8:21). The most explicit evidence for the existence of a larger group comes in Luke 10, where, having previously sent out the Twelve to preach and to heal (Luke 9:1-6; Matt. 10:1-15; Mark 6:7-13), Jesus sends out a further seventy disciples to go to places where he himself expects to come later: *'the Lord appointed seventy others and sent them on ahead of him in pairs to every town and place where he himself intended to go'* (Luke 10:1). It is clear, too, that these seventy are endowed with the same powers and authority as the first twelve; not only are they told to heal (v. 9), but they report on their return that *"Lord, in your name even the demons submit to us!"'* (v. 17).

These missions may be seen as a form of 'training' for the disciples, preparing them for their future work as witnesses to Jesus when he would no longer be present. Yet, 'trainees' though they may be, the missions make of them fellow-workers with Jesus – this was the purpose for their selection: *'And he appointed twelve, whom he also named apostles, to be with him, and to be sent out to proclaim the message ... '* (Mark 3:14). Moreover, they were successful missions, as Jesus' response to their reports emphasises (Luke 10:17-24).

Both these passages quoted above, and especially Luke's phrase *'... sent them on ahead of him in pairs to every town and place where he himself intended to go'*, are significant in another sense, too. They suggest some kind of overall strategy for Jesus' ministry, some systematic attempt to 'cover' the whole of Israel, or of Galilee at least: *'... you will not have gone through all the towns of Israel before the Son of Man comes'* (Matt. 10:23). They also give added grounds for the suggestion made earlier in this chapter that the ministry might not have been one unbroken peregrination through the towns and villages of Galilee but rather a series of 'tours' through different areas, conducted according to some 'plan of campaign'. These missions also raise the question of what Jesus did while the disciples were away. Might they have been the times when he made some of those visits to Jerusalem that figure in John? – or did they enable Jesus to have some respite from his activities, and perhaps also meet and talk with specific individuals?

In addition to such missionary activity, the disciples, and more especially the Twelve, fulfilled a variety of roles for Jesus. They were, of course, the primary audience for his teaching, as Matthew makes clear at the beginning of his collected sayings of Jesus, known to us as 'the Sermon on the Mount': *'When Jesus saw the crowds, he went up the mountain; and after he sat down, his disciples came to him. Then he began to speak, and taught them ... '* (Matt. 5:1-2). At many other places, also, they are privileged witnesses of Jesus' actions and hear what he says in relation to them. In Mark in particular, we observe that

Outline of Jesus' Ministry

Jesus on several occasions provides additional information or explanation (Mark 4:10, 34; 7:17; 9:28; 13:3) – they are 'insiders', as against those 'outside' (4:11). At other times, they are effectively Jesus' servants: on both occasions when Jesus feeds a multitude, they receive the food from Jesus and distribute it to the crowd (Mark 6:41; 8:6) – a role which might be thought to foreshadow their later functions as leaders of churches. Similarly, Jesus asks two disciples to bring him his mount for his entry into Jerusalem, and later to locate and prepare the room for the Last Supper (Mark 11:1-2; 14:12-16).

At times, the disciples act as what we might call today 'minders' for Jesus. Thus, after a long day of teaching, Jesus suggests that they sail across the Sea of Galilee, perhaps to escape the pressure from the crowds, and Mark writes: *'And leaving the crowd behind, they took him with them in the boat, just as he was' (Mark 4:36)*. At other times, they attempt to protect Jesus from the unrelenting pressure; this is perhaps the motivation behind their attempts to prevent people bringing their children to Jesus: *'People were bringing little children to him in order that he might touch them; and the disciples spoke sternly to them'* (Mark 10:13), and their apparently harsh rejection of the Syro-Phoenician woman: *'And his disciples came and urged him, saying, "Send her away, for she keeps shouting after us."'* (Matt. 15:23). Yet, though Jesus speaks of them in the warmest of terms, elevating them to a level of unparalleled intimacy – *'And looking at those who sat around him, he said, "Here are my mother and my brothers! Whoever does the will of God is my brother and sister and mother"'* (Mark 3:34-35) – he rejects any attempt on their part to determine his course of action. Thus, when, on the morning after what appears to be Jesus' first day of teaching and healing in Galilee, the disciples seem to reproach him for having withdrawn to pray just when so many are waiting to hear and see him, Jesus sets aside their advice: *'And Simon and his companions hunted for him. When they found him, they said to him, "Everyone is searching for you." He answered, "Let us go on to the neighbouring towns, so that I may proclaim the message there also; for that is what I came out to do"'* (Mark 1:36-38).

The choice of the Twelve was in part a pragmatic issue: Jesus must have felt the need for a small group to share his ministry more closely with him and, probably, to be a source of support. They were also to serve as the guarantors of the accurate transmission of his message when he would himself no longer be present, a responsibility which they were uniquely able to bear as *'from the beginning eyewitnesses'* (Luke 1:2). As Jesus says to them in John 15: *'You also are to testify because you have been with me from the beginning'* (John 15:27). Probably, however, Jesus had something else in mind too: his reference to their future exaltation, *'sit[ting] on twelve thrones, judging the twelve*

Jesus – yesterday, today, for ever

tribes of Israel' (Matt. 19:28) suggests that they are twelve because they are to represent a new Israel: 'Jesus' appointment of the Twelve symbolized the claim that in his own ministry this messianic restoration of Israel had already begun in nucleus.'[11]

We need to note also how the Gospel writers, themselves probably closely identified with the Twelve in one way or another, make use of the disciples at times as figures with whom the readers are able to identify. Their reactions to their experience of Jesus in the earlier part of his ministry may well have served to articulate those of later believers; when, for example, Jesus stills the storm in Mark 4, the disciples' rhetorical question could well have been, and indeed still is, an invitation to a congregation to supply the answer: *'He said to them, "Why are you afraid? Have you still no faith?" And they were filled with great awe and said to one another, "Who then is this, that even the wind and the sea obey him?"'*

This reader/audience-related use of the disciples becomes more pronounced in the second part of Jesus' ministry, when, as we saw earlier, attention is focused primarily on them. Here, though, it is no longer a question of identification but rather of ironic distance. Already in his chapters 6-8, Mark highlights their incomprehension of Jesus' person and calling, symbolised in the healing, first of the deaf man with the speech impediment (Mark 7:31-35) and then of the blind man whose blindness is slow to yield to the light that Jesus brings (Mark 8:22-25):

> *But when they saw him walking on the sea, they thought it was a ghost and cried out; for they all saw him and were terrified. But immediately he spoke to them and said, 'Take heart, it is I; do not be afraid.' Then he got into the boat with them and the wind ceased. And they were utterly astounded, for they did not understand about the loaves, but their hearts were hardened. (Mark 6:49-52)*

> *They said to one another, 'It is because we have no bread.' And becoming aware of it, Jesus said to them, 'Why are you talking about having no bread? Do you still not perceive or understand? Are your hearts hardened? Do you have eyes, and fail to see? Do you have ears, and fail to hear? And do you not remember? When I broke the five loaves for the five thousand, how many baskets full of broken pieces did you collect?' They said to him, 'Twelve.' 'And the seven for the four thousand, how many baskets full of broken pieces did you collect?' And they said to him, 'Seven.' Then he said to them, 'Do you not yet understand?' (Mark 8:16-21)*

---

11 *Jesus and the Eyewitnesses*, p. 95.

Outline of Jesus' Ministry

In chapters 9-10, after the Caesarea Philippi incident and the Transfiguration, almost every incident draws attention, in one way or another, to their slowness of comprehension and the persistence of worldly attitudes, the *'things of man'*, as Jesus calls them at Caesarea Philippi (8:33). Again and again, Mark's irony invites the reader/hearer to recognise and reject the blindness and worldliness of the disciples' behaviour, as in the following examples:

When he had entered the house, his disciples asked him privately, 'Why could we not cast it out?' (Mark 9:28)

But they did not understand what he was saying and were afraid to ask him. (Mark 9:32)

John said to him, 'Teacher, we saw someone casting out demons in your name, and we tried to stop him, because he was not following us.' (Mark 9:38)

People were bringing little children to him in order that he might touch them; and the disciples spoke sternly to them. (Mark 10:13)

They were on the road, going up to Jerusalem, and Jesus was walking ahead of them; they were amazed, and those who followed were afraid. He took the twelve aside again and began to tell them what was to happen to him.' (Mark 10:32)

'Teacher, we want you to do for us whatever we ask of you.' And he said to them, 'What is it you want me to do for you?' And they said to him, 'Grant us to sit, one at your right hand and one at your left, in your glory.' (Mark 10:35-37)[12]

If Mark's account of Jesus' ministry really does derive from Peter's teaching, as tradition has it, one can only wonder at the absence of vanity that permitted so unvarnished a presentation of the disciples, and above all of Peter himself.

Yet, whatever the disciples' imperfections, there is no doubting the importance to Jesus of their companionship and support; it emerges clearly in his words during the Last Supper in Luke's account: *'You are those who have stood by me in my trials; and I confer on you, just as my Father has conferred on me, a kingdom...'* (Luke 22:28-29).

---

12 For a detailed study of the use of irony in Mark, see the work by Jerry Camery-Hoggatt referred to in note 8, above.

The women

It was not unusual in the Israel of Jesus' day for itinerant teachers to be accompanied by a group of followers, much like Jesus' disciples. It was probably very unusual, however, for women to figure among them. It is not clear just what role women played in Jesus' ministry – whether women were regularly among those who moved throughout Galilee and further afield with Jesus. However, Luke's testimony is unequivocal:

> Soon afterwards he went on through cities and villages, proclaiming and bringing the good news of the kingdom of God. The twelve were with him, as well as some women who had been cured of evil spirits and infirmities: Mary, called Magdalene, from whom seven demons had gone out, and Joanna, the wife of Herod's steward Chuza, and Susanna, and many others, who provided for them out of their resources. (Luke 8:1-3)

This passage affirms that women – and not just the odd one – did indeed accompany Jesus on at least some of his travels. In addition, all three Synoptic Gospels confirm that numerous women travelled with him when he went to Jerusalem to die (Matt. 27:55; Mark 15:41; Luke 23:49, 55).[13] Given the patriarchal nature of society in Israel, one must suppose, I think, that there were women whose family circumstances permitted them to absent themselves from their homes to follow Jesus – widows and unmarried women, presumably. Anything else would require a most unusual degree of emancipation! All three Gospels also say that these women gave financial support for Jesus and his disciples – they 'provided for them out of their resources' (Luke 8:3). Their importance for Jesus and for the subsequent development of the church is indicated by the fact that they, rather than the male disciples, note the place where Jesus' body is laid after the crucifixion and thus become the first witnesses of the resurrection.

Luke's reference to Mary Magdalene, quoted above, is particularly significant because it may shed light on the reasons why Jesus found so many adherents among women. The 'seven devils' probably refer to some severe form of mental disorder, from which Jesus had been able to release her, and this is probably indicative of Jesus' sympathy for women and his understanding of the societal and psychological pressures to which they were subject in a male-dominated world. If one examines a list of the encounters, and especially healings, to which the Gospel writers give particular attention, it becomes apparent that the majority are women, including the following: Mary

---

13 Again, it is not my purpose to comment on the various names mentioned. For a discussion of them, see, for example, Bauckham, *Jesus and the Eyewitnesses*, pp. 48-51.

Outline of Jesus' Ministry

and Martha, the Samaritan woman (John 4), the Syro-Phoenician woman, the woman taken in adultery, the 'sinful woman' in Luke 7, the widow of Nain, the woman with the issue of blood, and the crippled woman in Luke 13.

The Gospel writers do not dwell on the presence of women among Jesus' followers, but even the bare information that they provide enables us to see their importance for Jesus extended beyond the provision of financial support and the 'women's work' that one supposes to have been thrust upon them. In view of Jesus' evident friendship with Mary of Bethany and with Mary Magdalene, the presence of women at the cross when all his male supporters had deemed it to be too dangerous, and his sensitivity in dealing with the women like those in John 8 and Luke 7, Casey may be right to say that '... Jesus was emotionally and administratively more dependent on a small group of women than the Gospels tell us'.[14]

It is hard to imagine, even in today's world, how a group of followers accompanying Jesus and presumably living at times in improvised circumstances, might include both men and women. However, we do well to heed Maurice Casey's warning that we should not read back into first-century Galilee later rabbinical comments about women's roles and behaviour, as is often done by Christian writers seeking to 'talk up' Jesus' departure from contemporary practices and restrictions. As Casey points out, 'There is not ... any evidence that women attached to [Jesus] caused any scandal, nor is any kind of comment on such a matter attributed to [him]'. We may be sure that Jesus' adversaries would have seized upon anything that might have given even the slightest grounds for such a charge.[15]

There is so much that we do not know with any certainty about Jesus' ministry in relation to times, dates, places and people. A modern version of the Gospels would look very different from what we actually find in the New Testament. But their very resistance to our desire for factual, verifiable precision serves to remind us of the cultural gap between Jesus' time and our own. More importantly, though, the Gospel writers' way of telling the story places the emphasis where it belongs: not on the externals of Jesus' life and ministry but on what was going on within the story – on his mission and message and on the significance for us readers of the life, death and resurrection of Jesus of Nazareth.

---

14 Casey, *Jesus of Nazareth*, p. 195.

15 *Ibid.*, pp. 106-7.

Chapter 6

The Mission of Jesus

In this and the following two chapters, I shall be attempting to understand the significance of Jesus' earthly life: what he hoped to achieve as he went about teaching and healing, what the outcomes were, and what his activities reveal about him. We shall leave this last question, what Jesus himself was like, until the later part of the chapter, but one fundamental thing must be said at the beginning: that in everything that he said and did, Jesus had two 'audiences' in mind: on the one hand, those whom he wished to win for God, Israel and the other people who encountered him – including, by inference, those who *will believe in me through their [i.e. his disciples'] word ...'* (John 17:20) – and, on the other hand, the Father, of whose presence and scrutiny he is ever aware, whom it is his task to represent, and whom he seeks at all times to please. This factor is succinctly stated by Jesus in the particular style of John's Gospel when he says: *'And the one who sent me is with me; he has not left me alone, for I always do what is pleasing to him'* (John 8:29).

We saw in the previous chapter that there is a significant change in the ministry, at least as narrated by the Synoptic Gospels, after the incident at Caesarea Philippi – we will consider later why this might be so – so we shall in this chapter focus on the period before that time.

What was Jesus trying to do when he embarked upon his ministry in Galilee – after whatever preliminary activity there may have been down in Judea or by the Jordan, as we considered in the preceding chapter? It is an important question, yet strangely, it seems to be one that is seldom asked. So much attention is focused upon the death of Jesus that the impression is created sometimes that that alone was the goal of Jesus' coming, the preceding life being treated primarily as a source for devotional and exhortational themes. Indeed, so one-sided is believers' concern with the cross that one is tempted sometimes to ask whether everything that came before was merely a way of filling in time until the moment came for Jesus to suffer! It seems to me essential to recognise that Jesus suffered *because of* what he did and said during his ministry and to view the cross as 'the continuation of the ministry

The Mission of Jesus

by other means'.

We suggested in chapter 4 that Jesus' understanding of his calling was shaped above all else by Isaiah's 'Servant' prophecies. What specific 'mission' do we find outlined there? To summarise what we found when looking at the Servant passages in chapter 2 and in chapter 4, the first of these passages speaks in global terms:

> *... he will faithfully bring forth justice. He will not grow faint or be crushed until he has established justice in the earth; and the coastlands wait for his teaching ... I have given you as a covenant to the people, a light to the nations ... (Isaiah 42:3-4, 6)*

The second passage is more specific: while it reiterates what the first passage says, it adds at the beginning a more immediate objective: bringing Israel back to God:

> *And now the LORD says, who formed me in the womb to be his servant, to bring Jacob back to him, and that Israel might be gathered to him ... It is too light a thing that you should be my servant to raise up the tribes of Jacob and to restore the survivors of Israel; I will give you as a light to the nations, that my salvation may reach to the end of the earth ... I have kept you and given you as a covenant to the people, to establish the land, to apportion the desolate heritages; saying to the prisoners, 'Come out,' to those who are in darkness, 'Show yourselves.' (Isaiah 49:5-9)*

In these passages, we can distinguish several aims:

- The first of these two passages and the latter part of the second are concerned with ultimate outcomes of the Servant's work, establishing 'justice' or perhaps 'righteousness' throughout the world.

- The earlier part of the Isaiah 49 passage points to two more specific and more immediate objectives: first, bringing Israel back to God – this probably implies a spiritual renewal as well as a physical regathering – and thus 'restoring' them from a position of humiliation, and, second, bringing 'light' – the light of the knowledge of God and his grace – to the rest of the world.

- Alongside these long-term national or universal purposes, the first and third Servant passages also portray the Servant in his dealings with individuals, showing gentleness and compassion towards the 'weary' (50:4) and those who are 'bruised' and 'close to extinction' (42:3).

Jesus – yesterday, today, for ever

The message

'The kingdom of God has come near'

If we set these tasks against the Gospels' accounts of Jesus' ministry, it becomes apparent that two of these objectives, restoring Israel and bringing comfort to the unfortunate, were the immediate focus of Jesus' ministry, at least in its Galilean phase. How did he go about these tasks? Both Mark and Matthew begin their accounts of the ministry with a summary statement:

Now after John was arrested, Jesus came to Galilee, proclaiming the good news of God, and saying, 'The time is fulfilled, and the kingdom of God has come near; repent, and believe in the good news.' (Mark 1:14-15)

From that time Jesus began to proclaim, 'Repent, for the kingdom of heaven has come near.' (Matthew 4:17)

Perhaps the first thing to notice is Mark's phrase 'the good news [or gospel] of God'. Jesus called upon his hearers to acknowledge God as the supreme reality in their lives, to be aware of him before all else and to seek to do his will – in other words, to make God the centre of their lives, as he was in Jesus' own life. The phrase 'kingdom of God' (or 'kingdom of heaven', an expression that reflects Jewish use of the term 'heaven' in order to avoid having to pronounce the name of God[1]), which Mark uses in the same sentence and which occurs so frequently in the Gospels, is another way of expressing this: the word *basileia* means, first, the king*ship* of God, his authority over mankind and especially over Israel, and his claims upon their worship and obedience. Israel's scriptures, their prayers and temple rituals, all acknowledged this fact, but, as Jesus well knew, God was in fact honoured more in word and in ritual than in practical reality.

But things would not always remain so: God's intention was to reveal himself in action, exerting his authority and realising his will within the human world – his 'king*dom*' was going to 'come', in the way that Jesus expressed so succinctly in the Lord's Prayer: *'Your kingdom come. Your will be done, on earth as it is in heaven'* (Matt. 6:10). And, Jesus says, his kingdom is now 'at hand' or 'has come near', and Israel must prepare itself for that action and for the 'crisis' (Greek: *krisis* = 'judgment') that it would bring.

---

1 See, for example, Jesus' question to his critics: *'Did the baptism of John come from heaven, or was it of human origin? Answer me.'* (Mark 11:30). Jesus himself respects Jewish sensitivities by using 'heaven' instead of 'God', though 'God' is obviously the true antithesis of 'men'.

The Mission of Jesus

Repentance: a prophet's message

So Jesus' proclamation of God's kingship necessarily implied the command to 'repent'. As we noted in chapter 4, both the English word and the New Testament Greek word *metanoia*, meaning literally a change of mind or thinking, lack the force of the Old Testament Hebrew word that probably lay behind Jesus' words in Aramaic. *Shub* in Hebrew meant to 'turn round' or 'return' in all kinds of practical contexts – the word occurs over 2,000 times in the Old Testament. Israel must turn round, turn to face God, putting aside the other preoccupations that ruled their lives.

Restoring Israel by calling them back to God had been the function of almost all the prophets of the Old Testament, not least of Jeremiah, who uses the word *shub* repeatedly:

> **Return**, *faithless Israel, says the* LORD. *I will not look on you in anger, for I am merciful, says the* LORD; *I will not be angry forever* ... **Return**, *O faithless children, says the* LORD, *for I am your master; I will take you, one from a city and two from a family, and I will bring you to Zion* ... **Return**, *O faithless children, I will heal your faithlessness. (Jeremiah 3:12, 19, 22)*

This parallel reminds us that, in part at least, Jesus' task was that of a prophet. Not only was he frequently viewed, or at least discussed, in those terms (see, for example, Mark 6:15 and Luke 7:16), but he too compared himself with the prophets, perhaps above all with Jeremiah. When rejected in Nazareth, he commented: *'Prophets are not without honour, except in their hometown, and among their own kin, and in their own house'* (Mark 6:4); when warned about Herod's intentions, he replied: *'it is impossible for a prophet to be killed outside of Jerusalem.'* (Luke 13:33).

John the Baptist had been a prophet too, as both Jesus' comments about him and even his dress and manner of life emphasised, but, though he was forerunner to Jesus, his message was in one important sense different. He too called on Israel to repent, but that call came accompanied by warnings of impending divine judgment; even his references to the one greater than himself who was to come saw Jesus primarily as the one who would implement that judgment:

> *John said to the crowds that came out to be baptized by him, 'You brood of vipers! Who warned you to flee from the wrath to come? Even now the axe is lying at the root of the trees; every tree therefore that does not bear good fruit is cut down and thrown into the fire ... I baptize you with water; but one who is more powerful than I is coming; I am not worthy to untie the*

thong of his sandals. He will baptize you with the Holy Spirit and fire. His winnowing fork is in his hand, to clear his threshing floor and to gather the wheat into his granary; but the chaff he will burn with unquenchable fire.' (Luke 3:7-9, 16-17)

Jesus' call to repentance inevitably implied a judgment too, and the warning note becomes more dominant as his ministry proceeds, but his message focused primarily on a divine intervention in human affairs that would bring blessing. That God was going soon to assert his kingship was 'good news'. In fact, as Mark's expression has it, God was himself 'good news' (1:14): his will for men was good – that was one of the most fundamental features of Jesus' teaching, and for Israel perhaps the most surprising.[2] What lay ahead was therefore a display of God's favour, an offer of grace and forgiveness to wayward Israel, and, by extension, to mankind as a whole. Thus, despite the fact that the Synoptic Gospels use Isaiah 40 to introduce their account of John the Baptist's ministry (Matthew 3:3; Mark 1:3; Luke 3:4-6), it is above all Jesus who fulfils the commission that was originally given to Isaiah himself in Isaiah 40:

Comfort, O comfort my people, says your God. Speak tenderly to Jerusalem, and cry to her that she has served her term, that her penalty is paid, that she has received from the Lord's hand double for all her sins. (Isaiah 40:1-2)

The Sermon on the Mount

The way in which Jesus spoke about the kingdom of God may surprise us. At no point does he explain what the phrase means, though the word *basileia* ('kingdom') occurs frequently in his teaching, most frequently in Matthew. His hearers were, no doubt, familiar with the concept, which to this day is affirmed in many traditional Jewish prayers, beginning with the phrase 'Blessed are you, O God, our Lord, King of the Universe...', while the idea of a future time when God would exert his power and authority in order to redeem and restore Israel figures prominently in the writings of the Old Testament prophets. So Jesus was able to use the phrase, assuming that his hearers would grasp the basic meaning.

Instead, Jesus speaks often about two other aspects of the kingdom of God: *how* it will come, notably in the parables brought together in Matthew

---

2 The phrase 'the good news – or 'gospel' of God' (Mark 1:14) should probably be understood as a 'subjective genitive', i.e. 'God's gospel' or 'the gospel that God brings', but in the light of the overall impact of Jesus' ministry it seems not improper to read it also as an 'objective genitive', i.e. 'the good news about God'.

The Mission of Jesus

13, and how one may 'enter' the kingdom, in other words what kind of people are fitted for the kingdom. The first words of Jesus' teaching as recorded by Matthew strike this note immediately: *'Blessed are the poor in spirit, for theirs is the kingdom of heaven'* (Matt. 5:3). The 'Sermon on the Mount', in Matthew 5-7, is in fact the only extensive example in the Gospels of Jesus' teaching about the kingdom of God. In these chapters, Matthew appears to have gathered together and carefully arranged various sayings of Jesus on this topic, as he does with other aspects of Jesus' teaching in chapters 10, 13, 18 and 23-25.

The Sermon begins with the eight 'Beatitudes', which present a succinct portrait of the kind of person who is fitted for the kingdom, and then develops a fuller picture, focusing on a few major features:

- an obedience that comes from the heart rather than formal compliance with external forms (ch. 5) – here Jesus re-interprets some major features of the Mosaic Law to explain what God truly desires of his people;

- kindness to others that reflects the mercy and kindness received from God (5:38-48);

- genuineness in all forms of worship and law-observance; Jesus calls for an integrity in which words and actions are in accord. He accordingly appears to reserve his strongest condemnation for hypocrisy rather than any other form of wrong (6:1-18; 7:15-23);

- trust in God's care and provision for his people (6:19-34; 7:7-11).

The whole Sermon asserts the absolute priority of God's will in the life of his people, perhaps best summed up in the lines at the end of chapters 5 and 6:

'Be perfect, therefore, as your heavenly Father is perfect.' (Matthew 5:48)

'But strive first for the kingdom of God and his righteousness, and all these things will be given to you as well.' (Matthew 6:33)

The Sermon, with its mountain setting and being itself part of a Gospel that contains five blocks of teaching that are sometimes compared to the 'five books of Moses', may give the impression that it is, in effect, a new Law, and that Jesus required his fellow-Israelites to achieve some impossible standard of purity and piety. In fact, though, the very first thing that the Sermon does is to sketch a picture of people profoundly aware of their imperfections and sins and totally dependent on the mercy and grace of God; they are the 'poor in

Jesus – yesterday, today, for ever

spirit', the meek or humble who mourn over their weakness, who *'hunger and thirst for righteousness'* and long to be other than they are. In essence, then, the Sermon as a whole is effectively a picture of what repentant people look like. And it is to these people that Jesus promises an entrance into the kingdom of God.

It becomes clear, then, that, contrary to what is sometimes asserted about Jesus, he did not offer 'cheap grace', to use the phrase coined by Dietrich Bonhoeffer.[3] He asked of men and women *'everything'* but promises them in return *'a hundredfold now in this age—houses, brothers and sisters, mothers and children, and fields, with persecutions—and in the age to come eternal life'* (Mark 10:30).

In the Nazareth synagogue

It is instructive to compare the Sermon with the way in which Luke begins his account of the ministry; instead of generalised, summary statements of the kind found in Matthew 4 and Mark 1, he chooses a specific incident, Jesus' teaching in the Nazareth synagogue, based on a quotation from the fifth Servant passage (Luke 4:16-30; Is. 61:1-2):

> *'The Spirit of the Lord is upon me, because he has anointed me to bring good news to the poor. He has sent me to proclaim release to the captives and recovery of sight to the blind, to let the oppressed go free, to proclaim the year of the Lord's favour ... Today this scripture has been fulfilled in your hearing.' (Luke 4:18-19, 21)*

That he should choose this passage is evidence for the key role played by these passages from Isaiah in Jesus' understanding of his task, as I suggested in chapter 4.

As we would expect, Jesus' message corresponds broadly with Matthew's and Mark's opening statements: it refers to an impending display of God's grace to men and the coming of a new age, the 'year of God's favour', which it describes as 'good news', though, as is the case throughout Luke, the verb *euangelizo* is used rather than the noun *euangelia*.

Nevertheless, there are several differences: there is no call to repentance, though that was probably implicit in what Jesus said, and the emphasis is still more firmly placed on God's grace and the forgiveness of sins. The last phrase in the quotation from Isaiah, *'the year of the Lord's favour'* echoes the law concerning the year of Jubilee, with its cancellation of all debt and the

---

3 In *The Cost of Discipleship*, 1937, quoted by David Wenham in *Jesus in Context. Making Sense of the Historical Figure*, Cambridge 2021, pp. 153-154.

142

The Mission of Jesus

accompanying enslavement (see Leviticus 25:8-35), and promises God's 'favour', an evident reference to a grace that cancels every 'debt' of sin on Israel's part.

In addition, Jesus' quotation foregrounds the meaning of the 'year of God's favour' for *individuals*. The most important word in the quotation is 'release' (*aphesis*), which occurs twice; it refers to release from any and every form of bondage: physical (blindness), social (debt, enslavement), and spiritual (sin and guilt). Jesus is here fulfilling the picture in Isaiah 50 of the Servant *'speak[ing] a word in season to him that is weary'*.

There is still one further, and very significant difference. In using the Isaiah quotation, Jesus identifies himself as central to the coming of the age of God's favour and forgiveness. As we said when looking at the Servant passages in chapter 2, in Isaiah 61 the Servant himself speaks as one who is aware of his commission, has identified himself with it, and is now announcing himself to the people. And in describing himself as 'anointed' (*mashach*), he effectively declares himself to be the 'Messiah', the anointed one.

Jesus' dealings with individuals

Uniquely powerful and precious as these two 'set pieces', the 'Sermon' and the Nazareth episode, are, more characteristic of the way in which the Synoptics portray Jesus are the brief accounts of his meetings with all kinds of people. In these, Jesus is true to his word in the Nazareth 'sermon': in nearly all cases, leaving aside his critics and adversaries – we will consider these negative responses later – those with whom Jesus speaks individually are, in one way or another, the oppressed and the bruised. In his dealings with them, Jesus reveals extraordinary compassion, joined to a sympathetic understanding of the pressures that led to their plight, particularly in the case of women, who in fact outnumber men in such encounters, as we pointed out in the preceding chapter.

It is Luke, though, who most draws our attention to Jesus' compassionate, perceptive treatment of women. It is to him that we owe the touching account of his meeting with the 'sinful woman' in Luke 7, who displays her gratitude in so dramatic a way, despite the disapproval of Simon the Pharisee. Also unique to Luke are the encounters with the bereaved widow at Nain (also in Luke 7) and the crippled woman in Luke 13, whom he evidently notices even though she has made no attempt to approach him, and the story of Mary's aspiration to sit at his feet as a disciple, despite the disapproval of her sister (Luke 10). He defends these women against their accusers, where necessary, and enables them to regain a position of respect in society. Sadly, we cannot hear the tone of voice in which he spoke, but we can, I think, safely assume that his voice

Jesus – yesterday, today, for ever

and bearing during these encounters were gentle and encouraging.

Setting people free

Jesus' words in the Nazareth synagogue, with their focus on 'release', make it clear that he saw his contemporaries as 'bound' in one form or another; in Luke 4 he speaks of them as prisoners of war, held at the point of a lance – this is the meaning of the word *aichmalotos* in v. 18 – and in Luke 13 he describes the crippled woman as one 'in chains'. Jesus' ministry was thus a kind of battle, on God's behalf, against all the forces, social, physical, psychological and spiritual, which enslave men and women.

This is particularly evident in Mark's Gospel, which begins with a whirlwind of activity, marked by the repeated use of the word *euthos* ('immediately'). After what is said in v. 10-11, it is as if a deliverer has invaded the territory of a malign enemy to set free its captives. That is in fact the figure that Jesus himself uses to explain what he is doing: *'But no one can enter a strong man's house and plunder his property without first tying up the strong man; then indeed the house can be plundered'* (Mark 3:27), he says, echoing the language of Isaiah in the context of the Servant passages:

> Can the prey be taken from the mighty, or the captives of a tyrant be rescued? But thus says the LORD: Even the captives of the mighty shall be taken, and the prey of the tyrant be rescued; for I will contend with those who contend with you, and I will save your children. (Isaiah 49:24-25)

Mark's account of this deliverance begins in the most dramatic way possible, with the curing of a man with an 'unclean spirit' (Mark 1:23-26). Four chapters later, Mark gives us in the Gadarene demoniac a still more dramatic illustration of such bondage:

> He lived among the tombs; and no one could restrain him any more, even with a chain; for he had often been restrained with shackles and chains, but the chains he wrenched apart, and the shackles he broke in pieces; and no one had the strength to subdue him. (Mark 5:3-4)

This man was able to break the chains with which others had bound him, but nothing could be done to release him from those unseen internal fetters. In these two early examples, it is by the authority and power with which the Spirit had equipped him that Jesus is able to bring these two wretched individuals release, in the latter case leaving him *'clothed and in his right mind'*. There is a further example in Mark 9, where Jesus heals an epileptic boy; the symptoms are readily identifiable as epilepsy, but, in keeping with the thinking of the time, it is described as an 'unclean spirit' (v. 25). 'It' seizes, throws,

144

The Mission of Jesus

convulses the boy, reducing him to forms of behaviour in which, as with the Gadarene demoniac, all semblance of truly human life is lost until Jesus exerts the authority vested in him.

Healings

Dramatic as these events are, they are far outnumbered and outweighed in importance in all three Synoptic Gospels by Jesus' many healings of physical disabilities of various kinds, mainly during his Galilean ministry before the decisive Caesarea Philippi episode. This is particularly the case with the healing miracles in Mark, which have been the subject of extensive examination in the writings of Austin Farrer, referred to in the previous chapter. How, then, ought we understand the healing miracles in the context of Jesus' ministry?

- If the number of healings specifically referred to by the Synoptic Gospels suggests that they represent the whole of Israel, then the obvious implication is that all Israel is sick. The symbolism evokes the language of Isaiah: *'The whole head is sick, and the whole heart faint. From the sole of the foot even to the head, there is no soundness in it, but bruises and sores and bleeding wounds; they have not been drained, or bound up, or softened with oil.'* (Isaiah 1:5-6).

- The healings are an expression of Jesus' compassion towards people who were suffering. The Gospels tell us some nine times that he *'had compassion'* or was *'moved with compassion'*. The Greek verb used in most of these cases, *splagchnizomai*, does not include the notion of 'fellow-feeling' implied by the prefix *com* in the word 'compassion', but Jesus' responses in all these cases were probably a fruit, in part at least, of his wide experience of village and small town life in Galilee, where he will have seen every kind of human distress at quite close quarters.

- The healing miracles were evidence of the power and authority that had been bestowed on Jesus at his baptism by the descent on the Spirit upon him. Those who witnessed them use both these words to express their amazement:

  When the crowds saw it, they were filled with awe, and they glorified God, who had given such authority (exousia) to human beings. (Matthew 9:8)

  'What kind of utterance is this? For with authority and power (dunamis) he commands the unclean spirits, and out they come!' (Luke 4:36)

  For the most part, however, *dunamis* is used to refer to the actions themselves, often translated as 'works of power', though it is also used when

Jesus – yesterday, today, for ever

Jesus senses, after being touched by the woman suffering from haemorrhages, that 'power' had gone out of him (Mark 5:30; 8:46). It is characteristic, however, of an age in which every 'natural' phenomenon was attributed to an animate, even personal force, that for the most part his healings are attributed to Jesus' 'authority' – as if part of a struggle between two rival powers.

- These evidences of power and authority served to authenticate Jesus as Messiah and Son – or at least, they would have done if he had openly claimed any such identity.[4] That he did not explicitly do so left those who met him to draw conclusions for themselves, leading to the kind of puzzled questioning that the Gospels repeatedly report. What did Jesus expect people to conclude? It seems to me that for him the question of the correct title or identification was less important than that they should think in a similar way to the centurion whose slave Jesus had healed: *"'But only speak the word, and let my servant be healed. For I also am a man set under authority, with soldiers under me; and I say to one, 'Go,' and he goes, and to another, 'Come,' and he comes, and to my slave, 'Do this,' and the slave does it'"* (Luke 7:7-8). His reasoning takes him only so far, but he had grasped the essential: that Jesus' authority is derived, delegated, and that he therefore represents one greater than himself. As usual, John's Gospel gives direct expression to the sense that remains latent in the Synoptics: Nicodemus' opening words express the conclusions that everyone should have drawn, as a starting point, at least, to faith: *'... we know that you are a teacher who has **come from God**; for no one can do these signs that you do apart from the presence of God'* (John 3:2).

- As well as being signs of Jesus' role as divine emissary, the healing miracles were also signs and a foretaste of the kingdom of God. When asked by disciples of John the Baptist whether he really was *'the one who is to come'* (Luke 7:19), Jesus replies: *'Go and tell John what you have seen and heard: the blind receive their sight, the lame walk, the lepers are cleansed, the deaf hear, the dead are raised, the poor have good news brought to them. And blessed is anyone who takes no offence at me.'* (v. 22-23). It is usually thought that Jesus' words are an allusion to such passages as Isaiah 35: *'Then the eyes of the blind shall be opened, and the ears of the deaf unstopped; then the lame shall leap like a deer, and the tongue of the speechless sing for joy'* (Is. 35:5-6). It is important, though, to draw a further conclusion: if the 'kingdom of God' is a time and a realm in which God's will is done, then such acts of compas-

---

4 See chapter 7.

The Mission of Jesus

sionate deliverance are signs of God – of what he is like.

- Both the last two points are signs of Jesus' ambivalence about people's attitudes towards him. He clearly wished people to understand his works of healing as signs witnessing to his divinely given mission and of the authority with which he had been endowed, but he wanted also that they should be seen as coming from *God*. John's Gospel is full of statements pointing to this double 'testimony':

*Neither this man nor his parents sinned; he was born blind so that God's **works** might be revealed in him. (John 9:3)*

*The **works** that I do in my Father's name testify to me. (John 10:25)*

*'... even though you do not believe me, believe the **works**, so that you may know and understand that the Father is in me and I am in the Father.' (10:38)*

- Though the 'signs' in John's Gospel are *prima facie* signs of Jesus, I think it is more important and ultimately correct to see them as signs of *God* and of his benevolent response to all forms of human need. The Synoptics do not use the abstract, theologically loaded language of John, but their apparently simpler narratives point in the same direction – and show at the same time, just as John does, that Jesus wished men and women to grasp this too. Mark's Gospel in particular, the most enigmatic and the most sparing of commentary on the unfolding story, may be said to resemble John's Gospel, minus the discourses that accompany the signs. The gospel truly is *'the gospel of God'* (1:14), a new revelation of his kindness and mercy towards mankind, correcting the tendency to see him above all as a fearsome judge.

In the accounts of Jesus' healing miracles, we thus have confirmation of what was represented by the 'rending' of the heavens at Jesus' baptism: God is revealing himself through his agent Jesus – and what is shown is his concern for human beings, his creation. Again, it is the Gospel of John that provides the concise formulation of the truths that we otherwise find hard to recognise from the Synoptics' narratives: *'And this is eternal life, that they may know you, the only true God, and Jesus Christ whom you have sent'* (John 17:3).

The underlying problem

In addition to all these inferences that could relatively easily be drawn from them, Jesus' healing miracles also possess, as every reader soon becomes aware, another meaning, perhaps the most important one, on a quite differ-

Jesus – yesterday, today, for ever

ent, metaphorical level. We suggested earlier, with a reference to Isaiah 1:5-6, that the various forms of disability that Jesus dealt with, and especially the twelve specifically named healings, represented the 'sickness' of Israel as a whole. That sickness was, of course, neither physical nor merely social or psychological, as Isaiah's preceding verse indicates: '*Ah, sinful nation, people laden with iniquity, offspring who do evil, children who deal corruptly, who have forsaken the* LORD, *who have despised the Holy One of Israel, who are utterly estranged!'* (Is. 1:4).

The forces that 'bound' the people that Jesus met were manifold – physical disability, poverty, social exclusion, psychological disturbance, moral failing – but, as the call to repentance made clear, behind and beneath all these lay one essential enslaving force: human sin, the drives within their own personality and in the surrounding society that impelled them, often against their better judgment, to act in ways contrary to the will of God and destructive of true human life.

This metaphorical use of physical infirmity runs right through the Bible. It is well understood, for example, that the various skin diseases brought together under the general term 'leprosy' come to be used as a metaphor for the corruption and the sense of uncleanness – another metaphor! – produced by sin. The most striking example occurs in Isaiah 53: '*we accounted him* **stricken,** *struck down by God, and afflicted'* (Is. 53:4); 'stricken' is Hebrew *naga*, which is cognate with the noun *nega*, used over sixty times in the instructions concerning leprosy in Leviticus 13-14. David's language for his sense of guilt and sin in his post-Bathsheba psalms (32, 38, 51) is permeated by imagery of his kind.

In the Gospels, it is Matthew who overtly exploits this metaphor, quoting the same verse from Isaiah 53:

> *That evening they brought to him many who were possessed with demons; and he cast out the spirits with a word, and cured all who were sick. This was to fulfil what had been spoken through the prophet Isaiah, 'He took our infirmities and bore our diseases.' (Matthew 8:17)*

In this quotation, the word 'infirmity' is striking. It is used by Jesus himself when speaking to the crippled woman in Luke 13: '*Woman, you are set free from your* **ailment**' (Luke 13:12). The Greek word, *astheneia*, means essentially 'weakness', and it is no coincidence that Paul uses the related adjective *asthenes* when he refers to mankind's weakness as a result of sin: '*For while we were still* **weak**, *at the right time Christ died for the ungodly'* (Rom. 5:6). Similarly, he uses the related verb *astheneo* when he says that the Law was '*weak-*

148

The Mission of Jesus

ened by the flesh' (Rom. 8:3). It seems that Paul too saw in the 'ailments' that Jesus cured symbols of human weakness on the spiritual plane; they were apparently 'in bondage' to physical ills, social disgrace, an immoral lifestyle, or psychological distress, but the truly destructive force in the lives of the people that Jesus encountered was sin, the all-too human values and concerns that ruled their lives.

Jesus' teaching, both in public and in private, repeatedly reflects his awareness of this fundamental problem. As we have seen, the first four Beatitudes concerning the 'poor in spirit', those who 'mourn', the 'meek', and those who 'hunger and thirst for righteousness' depict people weighed down by an awareness of their imperfection and sin and therefore 'hungering' for release from it. Similarly, the only petitions in the Lord's Prayer are for release from two forms of hunger: *'Give us this day our daily bread. And forgive us our debts ... do not bring us to the time of trial, but rescue us from the evil one'.* (Matthew 6:11-13). If, then, the 'infirmities' represent the condition of sin, then the healings are vivid, memorable figures for the release from sin brought by the 'year of the Lord's favour' of which Jesus was the bringer. In Mark, after the rapid sequence of incidents in chapter 1, including multiple healings, the narrative focuses at the beginning of chapter 2 on the paralytic who is let down through the roof. Jesus' immediate response makes the link between sin and sickness: *'Son, your sins are forgiven'* (Mark 2:5). In the following incident, the same link is made, this time 'in reverse': in reply to criticism of his consorting with tax-collectors, Jesus says: *'Those who are well have no need of a physician, but those who are sick; I have come to call not the righteous but sinners'* (Mark 2:17).

It is important to recognise, therefore, that Jesus' principal 'weapon' in this 'warfare' against sin is neither simple power nor authority over 'evil spirits' but rather the forgiving grace of God, expressed both in words and in his own person. Jesus' approach was not accusatory; instead, he proclaims the possibility of forgiveness, as he did in Nazareth. The God that he reveals to men is more than ready to forgive. Nowhere is this clearer than in Jesus' parables: in the parable of the unforgiving servant in Matthew 18, we see two ways of dealing with 'debt', i.e. wrongs done to another. The slave's way is the human way, demanding restoration or compensation, or, in a non-monetary situation, some form of retribution: the offended party causes the hurt to 'rebound' on the one who inflicted it. Not so the lord in the parable: when asked, he forgives without compensation or repayment – he bears the hurt, 'takes the hit' in modern parlance, not allowing it to 'rebound'.

The same is still more evident in the story of the Lost Son in Luke 15.

Jesus – yesterday, today, for ever

There, both sons fully expect that the erring son, the 'sinner', in other words, will have to endure some form of penalty, such as the loss of his former status. The only person who does not share that view is the father, the one who has been deeply wounded, not only emotionally, as a father, but also in his social standing; instead, imposing no penalty, he bears the pain and absorbs the loss. His joy at having regained a son he thought lost far outweighs whatever damage to his finances or to his reputation he may have suffered. Such is the model of forgiveness that speaks to us from Jesus' teaching.

This was not, or should not have been, a new idea for Israel. Throughout the Old Testament, the English word 'forgive' actually renders the Hebrew *nasa*, whose primary meaning is 'lift up', 'carry', or 'bear'. Its first occurrence comes in the words of Cain: *'My punishment is greater than I can bear!'* (Gen. 4:13); in Genesis 18, it is twice used when the Lord promises to 'spare' Sodom (v. 24, 26). Jacob's sons are said to 'carry' their father down to Egypt (Gen. 45:27; 46:5; 47:30; 50:13), but almost immediately after, we find the following: *'Say to Joseph: I beg you, **forgive** the crime of your brothers and the wrong they did in harming you.' Now therefore please **forgive** the crime of the servants of the God of your father.'* Further examples of *nasa* as 'forgive' can be found, for example, in Ps. 25:18; 32:1, 5; 85:2; 99:8. These examples suggest that a wrong that has been inflicted is either simply 'borne' or even that it is 'carried away' – simply removed, as though it had never been. The latter idea was graphically represented in the ritual of the Day of Atonement:

> *Then Aaron shall lay both his hands on the head of the live goat, and confess over it all the iniquities of the people of Israel, and all their transgressions, all their sins, putting them on the head of the goat, and sending it away into the wilderness by means of someone designated for the task. The goat shall **bear** (nasa) on itself all their iniquities to a barren region; and the goat shall be set free in the wilderness. (Leviticus 16:21-22)*

It is also expressed in a variety of Old Testament metaphors:

> *... you have cast all my sins behind your back. (Isaiah 38:17)*

> *You will cast all our sins into the depths of the sea. (Micah 7:19)*

> *... as far as the east is from the west, so far he removes our transgressions from us. (Psalm 103:12)*

This does not mean, however, that Jesus presents God as a 'pushover', whose forgiveness can be turned on like a tap if the right words are said. We find in the Bible as a whole, and particularly in Jesus' teaching, little use of the

The Mission of Jesus

word or the idea of 'confession', a practice that is essentially backward-looking. Instead, Jesus, like John the Baptist and later the apostles, speaks rather of 'repentance'. Accordingly, we find in Jesus' encounters with individuals that he seeks to do two things: to bring people to repentance by making them aware of their wrong, and to assure them of the reality of God's forgiveness.

The balance that Jesus strikes between these two things varies, depending on his knowledge of the state of heart and mind of the person before him – it may be some knowledge of this kind that explains his words to the paralytic in Mark 2:5. To the lame man whom he has already healed by the pool of Bethesda Jesus says in rather admonitory fashion: *'See, you have been made well! Do not sin any more, so that nothing worse happens to you'* (John 5:14). In other cases, however, the sinner is already publicly disgraced and no doubt stricken with shame at their own behaviour. These are the 'bruised reeds' and 'dimly burning wicks' of Isaiah 42:3, or the 'weary' of Isaiah 50:4. What such people needed was above all to be *'sustained with a word'* (Is. 50:4) – to receive the reassurance that their sins were not unforgivable and did not place them beyond the scope of God's mercy, even if men condemned them. Thus, to the woman in Luke 7 Jesus says: *'Your sins are forgiven … Your faith has saved you; go in peace'* (Luke 7:48, 50). We notice, though, that he does not simply confirm the reality of the forgiveness: he also urges the woman to change her life – in other words, to repent in the sense of the Hebrew *shub* that we considered in chapter 4. Otherwise, the present forgiveness will have no lasting effect. The same applies, in more obvious fashion, to his words to the adulterous woman in John 8: *'"Woman, where are they? Has no one condemned you?" She said, "No one, sir." And Jesus said, "Neither do I condemn you. Go your way, and from now on do not sin again"'* (John 8:10-11).

It is sometimes asked how we should understand what is meant when Jesus declares someone 'forgiven' or 'saved' – is that person 'saved' in the sense intended when, for example, Peter and Paul quote the words of Joel, *'Everyone who calls on the name of the Lord shall be saved'* (Joel 2:32; see Acts 2:21; Rom. 10:13)? Do Jesus' words imply a decisive and permanent change of status comparable to that of the baptised believer? It is, ultimately, not the prerogative of anyone to state categorically what Jesus meant, but we can and must attempt to understand his words. It seems to me unlikely that we should be able to equate anything that happens prior to Jesus' death and resurrection with the consequences of faith based upon those events. Rather, we should perhaps view these incidents, and in Jesus' words in particular, in three interlocking ways:

- The individuals who were thus restored by Jesus in the ways that we have outlined, whether socially, physically or spiritually, were given the opportunity for a renewed, right relationship with God in the immediate present. a chance here and now to live other, better lives, directed henceforth to living for God and their fellows rather than for self.

- These incidents are reported by the Gospel writers with the intention that they should serve as visible, enacted models of the larger and definitive process of conversion and faith yet to come – a process in which they themselves were active and which they hoped to forward by writing their Gospels.

- Their experience of Jesus and of his healing power and mercy might prepare them for a still future time when the message concerning his death and resurrection and the gospel of grace through him would reach their ears. One can readily imagine how people healed by Jesus or who had encountered his compassionate understanding might have reacted on hearing that the hostility aroused by his activities in Galilee had finally led to his death. Might they not have said something along the lines of 'He suffered all that for me' – can one conceive of a better starting-point for faith in Jesus?

'Shalom'

As we have seen, the notion of 'release' is the key to all Jesus' dealings with individuals in the Gospels. The essential objective is summed up in what he says to the repentant woman in Luke 7, already quoted: *'Your sins are forgiven ... Your faith has saved you; go in peace'* (Luke 7:48, 50). Again, it is helpful to go behind the Greek text to consider what Jesus said in the original Hebrew/Aramaic. 'Saved' is the Greek verb *sozein*, meaning to 'save' or to 'make whole'; this woman has been saved from social ignominy and personal shame as well as from sin, while 'peace' (*eirēnē*) probably reflects the Hebrew word *shalom*, which is described by Charles Talbert as follows:

In the Jewish culture from which Christianity came, peace (*shalom/ eirēnē*) meant basically wholeness, the normal state of life that corresponds to the will of God. Such wholeness would characterise the basic relations of life:
- the relations of persons and God,
- the relation of persons with one another,
- the relation of persons with the natural world, and
- one's relation with oneself.

The Mission of Jesus

This wholeness meant well-being in contrast to evil in any form. It was the gift of God. Given human sin, however, this wholeness was lost. Peace, then, became an eschatological hope and the messianic figure the prince of peace.[5]

When Jesus speaks, as he does in the Sermon on the Mount, of the *'lilies of the field'* and the *'birds of the air'*, he is evoking pictures of such untroubled existence – creatures and plants which, free of the competitive instinct, instinctively know where they belong in the ordered world of God's creative intentions and which live in a condition of *shalom*, in the right relationship with their environment.

The Gospels, by contrast, show us Jesus in a world of men and women who knew no such wholeness. Many of them, as Jesus indicated in the Nazareth address, were broken, bruised, oppressed – by disease or deformity, by social stigma and rejection, by poverty and indebtedness, by moral failing and spiritual blindness. So we can quite properly say that one central aim of Jesus' mission was to restore wholeness, to be that 'prince of peace'.

It is instructive in this connection to note how Peter subsequently described the ministry of Jesus:

*'Jesus of Nazareth was a man accredited by God to you by **miracles, wonders and signs**, which God did among you through him, as you yourselves know. This man was handed over to you by God's set purpose and foreknowledge; and you, with the help of wicked men, put him to death by nailing him to the cross.' (Acts 2:22-23)*

*'You know the message God sent to the people of Israel, telling **the good news of peace** through Jesus Christ, who is Lord of all. You know what has happened throughout Judea, beginning in Galilee after the baptism that John preached — how God anointed Jesus of Nazareth with the Holy Spirit and power, and how **he went around doing good and healing all who were under the power of the devil**, because God was with him. We are witnesses of everything he did in the country of the Jews and in Jerusalem. They killed him by hanging him on a tree ... ' (Acts 10:36-39)*

'The good news of peace', consisting, apparently, in *'miracles, wonders and signs'* and in *'doing good and healing all who were under the power of the devil'*, is exactly what the Synoptic Gospels describe for us.

---

5 Charles H. Talbert, *Reading Luke. A Literary and Theological Commentary on the Third Gospel*, Macon, Georgia 2002, p. 34

Jesus – yesterday, today, for ever

Jesus and the Sabbath

This fundamental concern that underlay Jesus' entire ministry is well brought out in two consecutive episodes in Mark 2-3.[6] At the end of chapter 2, Jesus is criticised for permitting his disciples to take *peah*, the grain left for the poor at the edge of the fields. As such, the practice was permitted under the Mosaic Law (see Lev. 19:9-10) – but the action of rubbing the ears of corn was deemed to be work and therefore forbidden on the Sabbath. In reply, Jesus, cites the incident in 1 Samuel 21, where David and his men take and eat the 'shewbread' or 'bread of the Presence', which according to the Law was to be eaten only by the priests. This illustration already suggests that, in Jesus' view, the Law should not be interpreted and applied in ways that ran counter to basic human needs. According to Matthew and Luke, Jesus then says: *'The Son of Man is lord of the Sabbath'* (Luke 6:5; cf. Matt. 12:8), which sounds like a simple assertion of his personal authority to set aside the Law if he judges it necessary. In Mark, however, he says something else, which Matthew and Luke may perhaps have thought too daring: *'The Sabbath was made for humankind, and not humankind for the Sabbath'* (Mark 2:27).

These remarks shed a flood of light on Jesus' teaching and practice. He says that the purpose of the Law of Moses, and by implication, all other divine commands and regulations, is not to restrict and to limit the development and exercise of the powers and abilities with which God has so richly endowed human beings, nor to reduce them to slavish obedience so that he alone might be magnified – this was the erroneous notion that the serpent in Genesis 3 foists upon Eve and then Adam: that God wishes to keep them in subjection: *'... for God knows that when you eat of it your eyes will be opened, and you will be like God'* (Gen. 3:5).

Rather, he wishes his creatures, the pinnacle of his creation, to flourish and exploit their gifts – but with and for him and each other, rather than in continuous, ruinous competition. Hans Küng puts it like this:

> God wills nothing but man's advantage, man's true greatness and his ultimate dignity. This then is God's will: man's true well-being. From the first to the last page of the Bible, it is clear that God's will aims at man's well-being at all levels, aims at his definitive and comprehensive good: in biblical terms, at the salvation of man and of men. God's will is a helpful, healing, liberating, saving will. God wills life, joy, free-

---

6   The following discussion of these incidents is indebted to Maurice Casey's argument in his *Jesus of Nazareth*, pp. 262-266 and 320-325.

The Mission of Jesus

dom, peace, salvation, the final, great happiness of man: both of the individual and of mankind as a whole.[7]

Viewed in that light, what Jesus then says about being 'lord of the sabbath' may be an assertion, not simply of his own authority but ultimately of that of humanity, whose vital interests take precedence over such detailed regulations as those imposed by the scribes and Pharisees – and who are, by God's creative design, destined to *'have dominion'* (Gen. 1:26-27).

In the following incident, the healing of the man with the withered hand, Jesus is again accused of infringing Sabbath laws. His reply is deceptively simple: *'Is it lawful to do good or to do harm on the Sabbath, to save life or to kill?'* (Mark 3:4). This response may well look back to an incident during the Maccabean wars when some pious Jews refused to fight on the Sabbath and as a result lost their lives. It was thereafter agreed by Israel's spiritual leaders that the saving of life took precedence over the Sabbath law, and Jesus may have been invoking this principle as a justification, both in this case and in the previous incident.

However, his reply is more complex that it might appear. Strictly speaking, Jesus was not 'saving a life', for the man's life was patently not in danger. However, Casey points out that in Aramaic the word translated as 'life', in Greek *psuche*, also means 'person'. That suggests that for him the principle applies not only to 'saving a life' in its most extreme form, i.e. saving from death, but also to saving a person, in the sense of enabling true life, free of such handicaps as a paralysed, useless arm.

We need also to note Mark's words in v. 2: *'They watched him to see whether he would cure him on the Sabbath, so that they might accuse him'*. This probably relates to the fact that the Jewish authorities had decided that a man should not be condemned for a single offence against the Sabbath laws but simply warned; only after a second offence could the death penalty required by the Law be invoked against him (Ex. 31:14; 35; 2) – that is probably why Mark has, apparently deliberately, juxtaposed these two Sabbath incidents. So Jesus' phrase *'to save life or to kill'* is intended to contrast his action, enabling a man to live in the way that God intended for his creatures, with the Pharisees' murderous intentions towards him: *'The Pharisees went out and immediately conspired with the Herodians against him, how to destroy him'* (v. 6).

The same principles are also involved in another Sabbath incident. Jesus justifies the healing of the crippled woman in Luke 13 by saying:

---

7 Hans Küng, *On Being a Christian*, translated by Edward Quinn, London 1978, p. 251.

Jesus – yesterday, today, for ever

'Does not each of you on the Sabbath untie his ox or his donkey from the manger, and lead it away to give it water? And ought not this woman, a daughter of Abraham whom Satan bound for eighteen long years, be set free from this bondage on the Sabbath day?' (Luke 13:15-16)

It is contrary to God's will for mankind that they should be 'in bondage' to any 'infirmity' (v. 11-12) – this was the 'release to the captives' that Jesus proclaimed in his Nazareth address (Luke 4:18).

In his account of the meaning of *shalom*, Talbert says something similar, echoing Küng to some extent:

The recovery of wholeness in human relationships, which is due to God's acts in Jesus, reflects honour to God. In other words, what is good for human beings glorifies God; what glorifies God is good for human beings. Glorifying God and recovering human wholeness are not mutually exclusive: they are an insoluble whole.[8]

'Glorifying God and recovering human wholeness are not mutually exclusive: they are an insoluble whole' – it was this fundamental truth, buried by centuries of ever more intricate and oppressive interpretations of the Mosaic Law, that Jesus came to proclaim and to practise in his dealings with his fellows.

Jesus and the Law of Moses

These two incidents on the Sabbath illustrate Jesus' approach to the Law throughout his ministry. Whenever he disputes with Pharisees and scribes about the Law, he reveals himself to be well aware of differing views about the various schools of thought among them – his reference to 'saving life' in Mark 3 and to untying donkeys and oxen on the Sabbath and leading them to water (Luke 13:15) are evidence of this. He sought, though, to provide a better conception of what 'righteousness' should mean, one that did not *'load people with burdens hard to bear'* (Luke 11:46; Matt. 23:4), requiring either adherence to impossibly rigorous regulations or a condition of permanent inadequacy and guilt. He wished the burden to be 'easy' and 'light' (Matt. 11:30).

The essence of the running controversy between Jesus and the religious leaders of the day is well brought out in his parable of the 'unjust steward' or 'shrewd manager' (NIV, NLT). Many interpretations of this at first puzzling parable have been advanced, all of which appear to miss the significance of the word 'manager' or 'steward' (*oikonomos*): it occurs only eight times in the New Testament, three of them in this parable. The other occurrences are

---

8 *Ibid.*, p. 36.

The Mission of Jesus

significant: all but two of them refer to people who administer God's spiritual riches for the benefit of his people. Thus we find in two letters: *'For a bishop, as God's steward ...'* (Titus 1:7) and *'Like good stewards of the manifold grace of God ...'* (1 Peter 4:10). More obviously significant, though, are Paul's words to the Corinthians: *'Think of us in this way, as servants of Christ and stewards of God's mysteries. Moreover, it is required of stewards that they be found trustworthy'* (1 Cor. 4:1-2). Here Paul also uses the word *pistos* ('faithful' or 'trustworthy') that is used by Jesus in his comments on the parable afterwards: *'Whoever is faithful in a very little is faithful also in much ... If then you have not been faithful with the dishonest wealth, who will entrust to you the true riches?'* (Luke 16:11-12).

Most significant of all, though, are Jesus' own words a few chapters earlier in Luke, when he talks to his disciples about their responsibilities as his servants: in reply to Peter's question whether he is talking about them, Jesus says:

> *'Who then is the faithful [pistos] and prudent manager [oikonomos] whom his master will put in charge of his slaves, to give them their allowance of food at the proper time? Blessed is that slave whom his master will find at work when he arrives. Truly I tell you, he will put that one in charge of all his possessions.'* (Luke 12:42-44)

The issues involved in this exchange parallel closely those that underlie the parable: the responsibilities of religious leaders towards those whom they lead. Do they provide for their spiritual needs, or do they pursue their own interests? – the latter is the charge that Jesus repeatedly levels against the Pharisees and scribes.

Given this context, it seems likely that the dishonesty of the 'steward' lies in exaggerating the debts of his master's debtors; his master's subsequent commendation for his panicky course of action may imply that the Pharisees and scribes would do well, now that they have been 'found out' by Jesus, to adopt a very different approach to the difficulties faced by the poorer and less well educated people in attempting to keep the Law. In his further comments on the parable, he contrasts the old way (the old garment and the old wineskins, as in Mark 2:21-22) with his new message of release, true repentance and forgiveness (the new cloth and the new wine): *'The law and the prophets were in force until John; since then, the good news of the kingdom of God has been proclaimed, and everyone is urged to enter it'* (Luke 16:16, NET), or perhaps *'... and everyone is eager to get in'* (NLT), or *'everybody enters it enthusiastically'*

(ISV).[9] The words are notoriously difficult to translate, but everything about Jesus' life and teaching, as well as his other comments here, suggest that he is referring either to his 'light burden', his own altogether more welcoming, forgiving way of speaking of the kingdom of God, or to the eager response of many among the poor and the 'sinners' – or perhaps to both things!

It seems clear that Jesus' attitude to the scribes and Pharisees – and later to the priestly hierarchy in Jerusalem – was shaped by his anger at the way in which the religious elites treated the ordinary people. We can see, as we read his denunciation of them, how closely he must have observed their behaviour: the carefully posed displays of piety in public places (Matt. 6:1-18), their enjoyment of the honour and reverence shown them, and their exploitation of the gullibly pious for personal gain (Mark 12:38-40; Luke 20:45-47). But worse even that their hypocrisy was the disdain for, and indifference to, the true spiritual wellbeing of those for whom they were ostensibly responsible.

It is not the case, though, that Jesus simply disregarded the Law – his very next sentence in his comments on the parable underlines this: '*But it is easier for heaven and earth to pass away, than for one stroke of a letter in the law to be dropped*' (Luke 16:17). In the Sermon on the Mount he explicitly denies any such assertion:

> '*Do not think that I have come to abolish the law or the prophets; I have come not to abolish but to fulfil. For truly I tell you, until heaven and earth pass away, not one letter, not one stroke of a letter, will pass from the law until all is accomplished. Therefore, whoever breaks one of the least of these commandments, and teaches others to do the same, will be called least in the kingdom of heaven; but whoever does them and teaches them will be called great in the kingdom of heaven. For I tell you, unless your righteousness exceeds that of the scribes and Pharisees, you will never enter the kingdom of heaven.*' (*Matthew 5:17-20*)

What is happening, rather, is that the Law is being re-understood by Jesus, laying bare the intention of God that lay behind it: it was not intended to make its observance impossible, but, in the first instance, to 'educate' a largely untutored people and lay the foundation for a knowledge of the God whom they had bound themselves to worship – this was the intention behind the self-revelation of God at Sinai that was implicitly echoed at the time of Jesus' baptism, as we saw in chapter 4. The Law had been, as Paul puts it to the Ga-

---

9   Renderings similar to these are also found in the *Christian Standard Bible* (CSB), the *Common English Bible* (CEB), the *Holman Christian Standard Bible* (HCSB), and *The Living Bible* (TLB)

The Mission of Jesus

latians, a *paidagogos* for Israel – the slave who taught the basic rules of behaviour to the children of the rich and watched over their adherence to them. But that phase of Israel's spiritual development was now over: *'But now that faith has come, we are no longer subject to a disciplinarian'* (Gal. 3:23-25). What Israel now needed, Jesus is saying, was to understand and live by the principles that the Law's plethora of commandments symbolised rather than focus on a painstaking observance of the symbolism itself.

The Gospels show us Jesus carrying out this re-interpretation of the Law: he substitutes for its ritual demarcations – clean and unclean, holy and unholy – the true distinction of which those ritual boundaries were intended to be educative symbols, one based on the realities of spiritual qualities such as faith and humble penitence before God. Apart from the recurrent issue of Sabbath observance, the most powerful example in the Gospels is the question of ritual handwashing in Mark 7 and Matthew 15. Here, Jesus rejects the formal distinction which deemed 'common' (*koinos*) hands to be 'defiled' (Mark 7:2); it is what comes from within that determines what is 'clean' and 'holy' and what is not (Mark 7:18-23). It is, of course, no accident that this incident is immediately followed in both Gospels by Jesus' encounter with the Gentile woman, whose petition is granted, not just because of her quickwittedness, but above all because of the faith that it revealed. It is no coincidence either that in Acts 10 we see the same movement of thought from clean and unclean foods and hands to clean and unclean people. The woman of Mark 7 thus presages the acceptance into the new Christian community of Cornelius, the centurion, and so many Gentiles like him.

This brief analysis of Jesus' approach to the Law confirms what we said earlier about the fundamental aim of Jesus' coming, lying behind everything that he did and said: to enable his fellows to know the God that they claimed to worship, but whom the teaching and practice of Israel's teachers – scribes, Pharisees, and priests – had largely obscured from view. It is a salutary reminder to us that a zealous study of the minutiae of God's word and calls for an ever more rigorous obedience to his commands can easily obscure from us his true nature and intentions.

The shadow of the cross

The Synoptic Gospels leave us in no doubt about the impact of Jesus on his fellow-Israelites. Repeatedly, they mention 'crowds', 'multitudes' and 'the people'. For the most part, it appears, their enthusiasm was fired by his miracles of healing – perhaps also by the evident note of compassion and understanding in his teaching. Sadly, it led in only a few cases to any insight into the meaning of his coming, though on several occasions he is referred to by the crowd as 'a prophet', mainly because of his miracles (cf. Matt. 14:5; 21:11, 46; Mark 6:15; Luke 7:16; John 6:14; 7:40; 9:17). Yet it was not the popular response that would determine the success or otherwise of his mission; that responsibility lay with those in authority, which is why spiritual leadership is so awesome a task (see Luke 12:47-48). And among those groups – Pharisees, scribes, priests and teachers – Jesus was from the beginning viewed negatively, as a false, unqualified teacher who was leading the people astray.

To the modern Christian reader, it may appear incomprehensible that so patently good a man as Jesus should be rejected and ultimately crucified. That it is so is testimony to the influence that he and his teaching have exerted over the past two millennia since he lived and died. Yet from the point of view of Israel's religious leaders at the time, he obviously represented a threat to the entire religious and social order of God's people. There was undoubtedly a personal dimension to the opposition that Jesus encountered, a jealousy at his popularity among 'the people', to which the Gospels give ample testimony, which must have appeared to threaten their own authority. However, more was obviously at stake: for it was not only in relation to the Sabbath and the purity laws that Jesus set himself against the accepted interpretation of the Law and the practices that were based on it. In virtually every area of the Israel's religious life he called into question the teaching of the religious hierarchy, laying claim, moreover, to an authority that allowed him to say: '*You have heard that it was said to those of ancient times ... But I say to you ...* ' (Matt. 5:21-22). Marriage and divorce, fasting, the taking of oaths, the management of the Jerusalem temple, the right of retribution, the defence of Jewish national identity – in all these too, Jesus' teaching was different.

Two features of his teaching must have appeared particularly shocking. First, the principle that we have noted in relation to the Sabbath: as Hans Küng puts it: '... did he not make man the measure of God's precepts by identifying God's cause with man's, God's will with man's well-being?'[10] Secondly, his message of grace and forgiveness undermined the hitherto established scale of values which enabled some to be classed as 'righteous' and others as 'sinners'. What was the world coming to if, for example, a notorious woman of the streets or a tax-collector was judged more righteous than a Pharisee (Luke 7:36-50; 18:9-14)? – and what was to become of Pharisees' and scribes' sense of their own dignity and their right to honour and respect?[11]

---

10 Hans Küng, *On Being a Christian*, p. 292. In this section of his book, Küng lays out helpfully the ways in which Jesus shocked and offended many of his contemporaries, enabling the reader to better grasp why the hierarchy were so intent on destroying him.

11 For a discussion of 'status reversal' of this kind in Luke's Gospel, see Justo L. Gonzales,

The Mission of Jesus

In these fundamental issues, as in everything about Jesus' mission, what was ultimately at stake was Jesus' understanding of, and witness to, the nature of God, which he knew to be radically at odds with all human standards, even those which purport to be derived from God's word. What John Barclay says of Paul's teaching on grace as God's unmerited gift applies, not surprisingly, to Jesus' teaching too:

> "I want you to know that the good news announced by me is not in accord with human norms" (Gal. 1:11). This negation ... signals a relation of misfit, even contradiction, between the "good news" and the typical structures of human thought and behaviour. The good news stands askance to human norms because its origin lies outside the human sphere ... Paul's [not in accord with human norms] signals the capacity of the good news to challenge every value-system and every pre-formed tradition, including Paul's own.[12]

All the Gospels make it clear not only that Jesus encountered opposition right from the beginning of his ministry, but also that it is this opposition that culminated finally in his crucifixion, even if the chief priests are in the end the primary agents in Jesus' arrest, trial and execution. As early as the beginning of his second chapter, Mark brings together a series of 'conflict-stories' in which Jesus is subject to criticism, challenge and hostility; the series is rounded off by Mark's comment, already quoted: '*The Pharisees went out and immediately conspired with the Herodians against him, how to destroy him*' (Mark 3:6). Luke begins his account, as we have already noted, with Jesus' proclamation in the Nazareth synagogue, which ends with the attempt to kill him there and then. John, for his part, places almost at the beginning of his Gospel Jesus' 'cleansing of the temple', in which he challenges his critics to 'destroy this body'. Complex though that dialogue is, it is clearly intended as a first pointer to the cross. As a result, the shadow of the cross falls across these accounts of Jesus' ministry almost from the beginning; their writers are at pains to show us that his crucifixion arises directly out of his ministry and his message. So threatened do his adversaries feel by his proclamation of 'the gospel of God' – a very different picture from the one that they had derived from their scriptures – that they decide ultimately that he must die.

It thus becomes clear, even from the early stages of Jesus' ministry, that

---

The Story Luke Tells, Grand Rapids, Michigan 2005, pp. 24-44; Joel B. Green, *The Theology of the Gospel of Luke*, Cambridge 1995, *passim*, and my *Luke's Pauline Narrative*, pp. 122-126.

12 John M.G. Barclay, *Paul and the Gift*, Grand Rapids, Michigan 2015, pp. 355-356.

Jesus' death must under no circumstances be separated from his life; it arises out of the conflict and controversy provoked by his proclaiming and demonstrating in his actions an understanding of God that was, as Barclay translates Galatians 1:7, 'not in accord with human norms'. From this in turn it follows that, contrary to so much that is said and theorised about the cross, Jesus' death was *not* something demanded and imposed by his Father as a punishment for sin – a notion which would run entirely counter to the portrayal of God that we have seen in Jesus' parables in Matthew 18 and Luke 15. Rather, it was altogether the work of men, who carried it out for their own reasons and by their own methods. That is certainly how Jesus describes it in the parable of the wicked tenants that he told shortly before his death (Mark 12:1-12; Matt. 21:33-44; Luke 29:9-18): the father in the story sends his son to plead with the tenants, well aware how dangerous a mission it was, and the son, no less aware, accepts it. Nor was it a precondition for forgiveness imposed by God. It was, obviously, foreknown and permitted by God and clearly has an essential function in the reconciliation and remaking of humanity – but not this one![13] The human conventions of 'justice' or 'honour', which have been used to explain 'the atonement', are totally at variance with the nature of God as Jesus portrays him. Atonement theory has, in effect, often made God in man's image, ascribing to him our notions of penal justice and retribution.

Where is the man Jesus in all this?

As we read the Gospels' account of Jesus' Galilean ministry, it is easy to forget that this is the carpenter's son from Galilee and that only a few months previously he had been living, outwardly at least, an 'ordinary' human life as part of a family and going about his daily work. How could he behave with such apparent certainty and authority? How did he know or decide what to do or say at any moment? Perhaps we should as readers ask ourselves what made Jesus do or say what he did, try to imagine the inner life out of which his actions sprang – in other words, try to think of him as a real person, having to deal with his emotions, facing decisions, albeit of a very special kind, as all men and women do. As we said earlier, it is impossible for us to have access to the inner life of Jesus, as so many commentators have pointed out; it seems to me important, though, to remember that he had one!

Some may think it an illegitimate enterprise even to seek to understand Jesus' inner life: most Gospel scholarship takes it as a given that we have no access to the self-consciousness of Jesus and that it is pointless, or even wrong, to seek it. John A. T. Robinson was doubtless right when he wrote:

---

13 I shall comment further on this vital issue in chapter 8.

The Mission of Jesus

The materials clearly fail for reconstructing Jesus' self-consciousness in psychological terms, for analysing his psyche, its history or its type. The Gospels are no more in the business of supplying answers to psychological questions than they are to sociological or economic questions.

However, I think he was also right to continue as he does: 'But this does not mean that they presuppose there was no development in his apprehension of God or himself, or that his was a static perfection.' He then adds, referring specifically to John, the immediate subject of his writing: 'In John ... there is even less attention to questions of psychic development or to the human factors that obedience involved. Yet they can be read between the lines in a number of passages.'[14]

The Gospels do give us some pointers. They do, for example, refer at times to Jesus' emotions: seven times they refer to his compassion in his dealings with men and women and once to his anger (Mark 3:5). Then, of course, there are the expressions used in John 11 to describe his reactions at Lazarus' tomb: '... *he was greatly disturbed [embrimaomai] in spirit and deeply moved [tarasso] ... Then Jesus, again greatly disturbed, came to the tomb*' (John 11:33, 38).

The mention of 'anger' on Jesus' part is particularly significant: imagine the degree of frustration and irritation that he must have experienced, not only at the failure to understand and respond as he would wish, but also, and especially, at the manifest hostility of those who opposed him. Here is a man evidently resisting successfully the natural impulses to which we all succumb; that alone would be enough to make Jesus utterly human – and yet utterly unique, the first true man as God intended. We recall the case of the first angry man, Cain: '*Why are you angry, and why has your countenance fallen? If you do well, will you not be accepted? And if you do not do well, sin is lurking at the door; its desire is for you, but you must master it*' (Gen. 4:6-7). Sadly, Cain was unable to – with dire consequences. Among those consequences, five generations later, was Lamech, the archetypal 'angry man' who boasts of his vengeance: '*Lamech said to his wives: "Adah and Zillah, hear my voice; you wives of Lamech, listen to what I say: I have killed a man for wounding me, a young man for striking me. If Cain is avenged sevenfold, truly Lamech seventy-sevenfold"*' (Gen. 4:23-24). Jesus, we have to remember, shares this man' legacy, as we all do. His reply to Peter's question about forgiveness points up the contrast: '*Then Peter came and said to him, "Lord, if another member of the church sins against me, how often should I forgive? As many as seven times?" Jesus said to him, "Not seven*

---

14   John A.T. Robinson, *The Priority of John*, London 1985 pp. 354-355.

times, but, I tell you, seventy-seven times' (Matt. 18:21-22).

But what of the cognitive side of his mind? He must have had to make choices and decisions and to respond instantly to new circumstances. Must he not also have had moments of doubt and uncertainty? Mark's spare, at times enigmatic narrative in particular, containing no overt comment or interpretation, may leave us with the impression that Jesus did everything almost automatically, as if every action were pre-determined, yet that seems scarcely compatible with his being the young man from Nazareth. Jesus' contemporaries are said to have asked on various occasions: *'Where did this man get this wisdom?'* (Matt. 13:54) or *'Where did this man get all this? What is this wisdom that has been given to him?'* (Mark 6:2), and we might ask that too. The phrase '... given to him' should not lead us to think that the words simply 'came to him' by some kind of divine telepathy. One can only surmise that he had a continuing awareness of the presence of the Father with him, on which he drew in his times of prayer and meditation – probably a more or less continuous process of 'consultation' with the Father during which he reflected on each day's events and on what lay ahead.

The Synoptic Gospels allow us occasional glimpses of this process:

And after he had dismissed the crowds, he went up the mountain by himself to pray. When evening came, he was there alone ... (Matthew 14:23)

In the morning, while it was still very dark, he got up and went out to a deserted place, and there he prayed. (Mark 1:35)

After saying farewell to them, he went up on the mountain to pray. (Mark 6:46)

... he would withdraw to deserted places and pray. (Luke 5:16)

Now during those days he went out to the mountain to pray; and he spent the night in prayer to God. (Luke 6:12)

Once when Jesus was praying alone, with only the disciples near him, he asked them, 'Who do the crowds say that I am?' (Luke 9:18)

He was praying in a certain place ... (Luke 11:1)

By contrast, in John's Gospel Jesus is portrayed as speaking freely of his intense personal relationship with the Father:

'And the one who sent me is with me; he has not left me alone, for I always do what is pleasing to him.' (John 8:29)

The Mission of Jesus

'*Father, I thank you that you have heard me. I knew that you always hear me.*' (*John 11:41-42*)

'*Very truly, I tell you, the Son can do nothing on his own, but only what he sees the Father doing; for whatever the Father does, the Son does likewise. The Father loves the Son and shows him all that he himself is doing; and he will show him greater works than these, so that you will be astonished.*' (*John 5:19-20*)[15]

It seems to me, then, that what we find in Jesus' words and actions is the fruit of his own mental processes, in which three elements interact:

- his own intense of awareness of God, developed through his times of prayer and reflection;

- his uniquely perceptive understanding of the Old Testament;

- his observation and profound understanding of the people and the society among whom he had moved before his ministry began.

And all this was heightened and clarified by the Spirit of God at work in him, helping him to find the words and the images in which to proclaim his teaching in so penetrating and memorable a way. We have to understand, I think, that as a result of this enriching and transforming process Jesus was able to respond naturally, even instinctively, as it were, in every new situation – to every new encounter and challenge.

Jesus and the Gentiles – a learning process?

I suggested in chapter 3 that if Jesus was truly a man, then his life, even including his ministry, must have involved learning and development. Possible evidence of such learning may be seen in the references in the Gospels to Jesus' forays into predominantly Gentile areas. The implication of Mark 4:36 is that he went to the 'country of the Gerasenes' (5:1) in order to find brief respite from the unremitting pressure that he was under in Galilee, rather than to preach. The same appears to be true of his visit to 'the region of Tyre and Sidon' – Mark says that '*he entered a house and did not want anyone to know*' (Mark 7:24). When the Syro-Phoenician woman comes seeking help for her

---

15 '...there is reason to believe that Jesus really did have an unusually deep awareness of God's transcendent majesty and of his all-embracing regard for mankind' (John Ashton, *Understanding The Fourth* Gospel, Oxford, Clarendon Paperbacks, p. 327). I find helpful on this subject the comments of John Robinson in the final section, 'The Person of Christ' in his *The Priority of John* (see note 14), p. 343 ff. I attempted to express my own understanding of Jesus' inner life in my *The Word Became Flesh*, 2016, pp. 172-178.

Jesus – yesterday, today, for ever

daughter, Jesus' initial response is: *'Let the children be fed first, for it is not fair to take the children's food and throw it to the dogs'* (7:27), or, as Matthew paraphrases it: *'I was sent only to the lost sheep of the house of Israel'* (Matt. 15:24) – an answer paralleled by his instruction to the disciples: *'Go nowhere among the Gentiles, and enter no town of the Samaritans, but go rather to the lost sheep of the house of Israel'* (Matt. 10:5-6). The conventional conception of an infallible Jesus suggests that in the former case Jesus was seeking, deliberately and with humour, to draw from the woman an expression of her faith, and that the instruction to the disciples reflected his awareness that it was by his Father's will that his mission should for the present be confined to Israel – on the principle enunciated by Paul: *'to the Jew first and also to the Greek'* (Rom. 1:16).

It seems not impossible, however, that the Gospels show us Jesus modifying his practice as a result of experience. His first venture into non-Jewish territory ends, after the healing of the Gerasene demoniac, with a request to leave: *'Then they began to beg Jesus to leave their neighbourhood'* (Mark 5:17), whereupon he and the disciples return to the western, Jewish shore of the Sea of Galilee. After his encounter with the Syro-Phoenician woman, by contrast, he makes a further excursion into Gentile territory: *'Then he returned from the region of Tyre, and went by way of Sidon towards the Sea of Galilee, in the region of the Decapolis'* (7:31), and this is followed by the healing of a deaf man and then the feeding of a predominantly Gentile crowd of 4,000 (Mark 7:32-8:9). Was it the woman's faith and receptiveness that encouraged Jesus to spend more time among Gentiles, even going back to the area that had previously seemed unwilling to receive him? David Rhoads comments as follows:

> ... [the woman's] insight and persistence serve to change Jesus' mind (heart), and he goes directly back to Decapolis ... From this point in the narrative, Jesus no longer treats the Jew/Gentile distinction as a boundary either for separation or for delay.[16]

The apparent change is the more striking since it follows upon the dispute with the Pharisees over the washing of hands, which leads Jesus to the far-reaching conclusion that it is what is within a human being, not the outside, that determines their 'cleanness' or otherwise (Mark 7:1-23). Peter had to be taught that principle by his vision upon the roof before being sent to preach the gospel to the Gentile Cornelius (Acts 10:1-16); for Jesus, it was the encounter in 'Tyre and Sidon' that provided a dramatic practical confirmation of the conclusion to which his disputation with the Pharisees had just led him. If that reading of these events is correct, it provides a picture of a thoroughly

---

16   David Rhoads, *Reading Mark, Engaging the Gospel*, Minneapolis 2004, p. 112.

The Mission of Jesus

human Jesus, who, in constant communication with God, reflects on his experiences, good and bad, and draws conclusions from them that shape his future course of action – as should be the case with all believers!

Self-effacement

A further feature of Jesus' behaviour emerges strongly from Mark's Gospel in particular. Here, Jesus repeatedly forbids those who benefit from his healing powers to speak of what he has done:

> *He also drove out many demons, but he would not let the demons speak because they knew who he was. (Mark 1:34)*

> *Jesus sent him away at once with a strong warning: 'See that you don't tell this to anyone.' (Mark 1:43-44)*

> *But he gave [the evil spirits] strict orders not to tell who he was. (Mark 3:12)*

> *He gave strict orders not to let anyone know about this. (Mark 5:43)*

> *Jesus warned them not to tell anyone about him. (Mark 8:30)*

> *Jesus gave them orders not to tell anyone what they had seen until the Son of Man had risen from the dead. (Mark 9:9)*

Why did Jesus behave in this way? It is so unlike the contemporary practice of telling the world of one's latest doings, via Facebook, Twitter, Instagram and the like! Surely, we may think, if he desired followers, wished people to believe in him, then he must have wished to be known and recognised?[17] Many reasons have been advanced to account for Jesus' reticence: publicity might have been dangerous because of the opposition that it would provoke; the resulting conflict might have brought his ministry to a premature end. Or it might be that Jesus wished to avoid the kind of dangerously simplified publicity that we find in today's tabloid headlines.

Perhaps the essential problem lay in the associations attached to any of the terms in which people might speak about him; the word 'Messiah' in particular came loaded with preconceptions – of political or military action, power and glory – which ran counter to the mission in which Jesus was engaged. Rowan Williams puts it like this: 'Throughout Mark's Gospel Jesus holds back from revealing who he is because, it seems, he cannot believe that there are

---

17 This feature of Mark's Gospel has been much discussed since the appearance in 1901 of Wilhelm Wrede's book, *Das Messiasgeheimnis in den Evangelien* (English title: *The Messianic Secret*).

Jesus – yesterday, today, for ever

words that will tell the truth about him in the mouths of others. What will be said of him is bound to be untrue ...'[18] We shall have more to say about the question of Jesus' identity, and especially about how Mark deals with it, in the next chapter.

There is, however, one aspect of this issue that relates directly to the question of Jesus' thinking and consciousness. It may appear strange to suggest that one who went around performing amazing deeds was self-effacing, yet in the Synoptic Gospels Jesus is exactly that – he never seeks honour and glory for himself. He clearly realised that his actions, above all his healing miracles, were certain to provoke curiosity (to say the least!), but his expectation, in the Synoptic Gospels at least, is that the result will be *repentance* towards *God* rather than belief in himself: '*Woe to you, Chorazin! Woe to you, Bethsaida! For if the deeds of power done in you had been done in Tyre and Sidon, they would have repented long ago in sackcloth and ashes'* (Matt. 11:21; cf. Luke 10:13). In the one case in Mark where he invites someone, the Gerasene demoniac, to speak of the healing that he has received, he tells him: '*Go home to your friends, and tell them how much the Lord has done for you, and what mercy he has shown you'* (Mark 5:19), again pointing away from himself to God, the true source of the healing. Whatever 'strategic' purpose might lie behind it, this feature of Jesus' behaviour is consistent with his dedication to the realising of his Father's will, completing the mission to which he had been called, and fulfilling his role as 'Servant'. It is of a piece, too, with his rejection during his time in the wilderness of all temptations to sensationalism and self-dramatisation (see chapter 4). And to recall that initial episode in this context is to remind oneself that those temptations must have presented themselves again and again throughout his ministry.

Why, then, did people frequently complain that Jesus assumed too much authority – 'took too much upon himself', as we might say? This reaction occurs very early in his ministry: '*Why does this fellow talk like that? He's blaspheming! Who can forgive sins but God alone?'* (Mark 2:7). Similarly, the responses to his teaching when he went back to Nazareth amounted to something like 'Who does he think he is?' (Mark 6:1-6). Such a reception, like the behaviour of his family, for example in Mark 3:21, must have been a bitter experience for him. The difficulty for him was that he was profoundly conscious of the unique importance of his role as God's servant and empowered agent, and that awareness inevitably emerges in things that he says. Matthew in particular records many such sayings: '*... something greater than the temple is here'* (12:7); '*... something greater than Jonah ... than Solomon is here'* (12:41-42).

---

18 Rowan Williams, in *Christ On Trial*, Grand Rapids, Michigan 2000, p. 6.

The Mission of Jesus

As we saw in looking at Luke's account of Jesus' appearance in Nazareth, he draws attention to his own role as the one anointed to proclaim good news; elsewhere, his teaching makes clear that salvation depends on people's attitudes to him and his teaching (Matt. 7:23-24). He even declares those blessed who are persecuted *'on my account'* (Matt. 5:11), and implies that he, and possibly his followers, should be exempt from the temple tax because he and/or they are the children of the king (Matt. 17:25-26).

What is happening in all these cases, of course, is that Jesus speaks and acts in such moments as God's *shaliach*, his empowered representative, who to all intents and purposes *is* the one who sent him. Jesus is not claiming authority or such decisive importance for himself as Jesus of Nazareth, but as God's appointed and anointed one. That he should arouse such negative responses at times was perhaps inevitable; not many people possessed the insight into the principle of delegated authority possessed by the Roman centurion in Matthew 8:5-13.

Jesus' practice of referring to himself in the third person as 'son of man' – no one else used the phrase about him – was another facet of this self-effacement. Though this title may well have possessed messianic implications for many in Israel, it also had the simple meaning of 'man', as we saw in chapter 2; Matthew directs our attention to this dual sense of the term when he describes the healing of the paralytic who was let down through the roof:

> *'But so that you may know that the **Son of Man** has authority on earth to forgive sins' – he then said to the paralytic – 'Stand up, take your bed and go to your home.' And he stood up and went to his home. When the crowds saw it, they were filled with awe, and they glorified God, who had given such authority to **human beings**. (Matthew 9:6-8)*

Jesus, his use of the title suggests, sums up in himself all humanity: his development and his 'career' are the collective career of mankind as a whole, so that when such authority as is exhibited in this healing is given to Jesus, it is, in principle, and will ultimately be in practice, given to all humanity. The other side of the coin is that Jesus embraces within himself *all* men, not just the strong, the healthy and the righteous, but also the outcasts, the marginalised and the despised – in short, 'the poor'.

As usual, it is in the Gospel of John that we find the most succinct description of Jesus' attitude: *'Those who speak on their own seek their own glory; but the one who seeks the glory of him who sent him is true ...'* (John 7:18). Before the raising of Lazarus, he says to Martha: *'Did I not tell you that if you believed, you would see the glory of God?'* (John 11:40).

It may seem paradoxical to quote John's Gospel in speaking of Jesus' self-effacement, because there he repeatedly suggests that the works that he performs should lead men and women to recognise *him* as God's self-revelation:

'... the very works that I am doing, testify on my behalf that the Father has sent me.' *(John 5:36)*

'But if I do them, even though you do not believe me, believe the works ...' *(John 10:38)*

'... believe me because of the works themselves.' *(John 14:11)*

Yet here too, Jesus' claim is that the works testify, not to his own greatness but to the relationship with the Father, who performs *his* works *through* Jesus – that *'the Father has sent me'* (5:36) or that *'the Father is in me and I am in the Father'* (10:38). In fact, they are *'the works of my Father'* (10:37).

It is Jesus' self-effacement, this putting God before self, that ultimately will lead Jesus to the cross. It finds its ultimate expression, not in John, for once, but in Jesus' words in the Synoptics' account of his prayer in Gethsemane: *'Abba, Father, for you all things are possible; remove this cup from me; yet, not what I want, but what you want'* (Mark 14:36) – Mark's version, unlike Matthew's and Luke's, includes the Aramaic *Abba*, allowing us to hear, surely, the authentic voice of the man Jesus himself. But of this, more in a later chapter.

A revelation of God

In trying to think about Jesus' inner life and in reflecting on his obedience and dedication as man to God, it is easy to lose sight of the other essential dimension of the Gospels' picture of him. We saw in chapter 4 that Mark's description of the heavens being 'torn' (Mark 1:10) is an echo of Isaiah 64:1, which is itself a prayer for a new self-revelation on God's part comparable to the events at Sinai. The connection thus established between Jesus' public ministry and Sinai directs us to see his life, including, of course, his death and resurrection, as that longed-for new self-revelation. We are obliged, then, to view him not only as a new and better Adam, as Paul in particular invites us to regard him (see chapter 2), but also as one in whom God is revealed, in fact as 'Immanuel', that is, 'God with us' (Matthew 1:22), and as *'the image of the invisible God'* (Col. 1:15) – see chapter 1.

Achieving the right balance between Jesus' humanity and his mission to show God to mankind is far from easy. It seems to me that much that is said and written about Jesus has things precisely the wrong way round: while portrayed as possessing *God-like* qualities, he is viewed almost solely as the representative *man*, the one who, facing God, has to 'conquer sin' on behalf of

The Mission of Jesus

humanity, thus 'earning' (for want of a better word) eternal life for himself and God's forgiveness for those who believe in him.

In fact, the Gospels present him primarily as facing mankind, as God's emissary toward us. The need to deny the promptings of human passions and needs is not an end in itself; it is necessary in order to allow God to be revealed in him. He is not a man intent on 'passing a test' but one focused on the task of showing God to his fellows – and that task will allow no pursuit of private motives, no indulgence of human passions. It is his dedication to his calling that makes possible his sinlessness – it leaves no room for self-indulgence. He *'make[s] no provision for the flesh, to gratify its desires'* (Rom. 13:14). What God asks of men and women is a 'binocular' vision that both sees God in him *and* sees the real man that he is – that recognises 'God with us' in the man from Nazareth: *'And this is eternal life, that they may know you, the only true God, and Jesus Christ whom you have sent'* (John 17:3). And, having once seen him like this, they recognise too that he represents what we are all intended to be, men and women in God's image.

But how *can* a man be a revelation of God's true nature – not just in some inspired utterances and miraculous powers but in the totality of his person and character? Several answers to this question must, I think, be dismissed. As I suggested in chapter 3, the Trinitarian view of Jesus appears to offer an easy solution to the dilemma by permitting its adherents to focus now on the one 'nature' of Jesus, now on the other – but does so at the expense of any sense at all of Jesus as a truly unified being.

But, as we also discussed in chapter 3, even those who do not subscribe to that view easily slip into a way of thinking which, doctrinal formulations notwithstanding, is not so very different from it. Jesus' humanity is recognised and asserted, both in his moments of emotion and the occasional references to his physical needs, and in his suffering, but when he speaks or acts, he is thought and spoken of as though he were God in human form. The effect is to make Jesus little more than a body whose thoughts and actions God directs. That is why the term 'self-effacement' may be misleading: it might be understood to mean that Jesus is an empty vessel that God is able to fill.

Equally inadequate, though, is a third view which emphasises Jesus' obedience in ways that give the impression of one grimly obeying orders, as implied perhaps by the words of the centurion in Matthew 8:9 that we quoted earlier: *'For I also am a man under authority, with soldiers under me; and I say to one, 'Go,' and he goes, and to another, 'Come,' and he comes, and to my slave, 'Do this,' and the slave does it'.* The centurion is commended for his faith and insight, but Jesus does not present himself as simply acting under orders, like

Jesus – yesterday, today, for ever

a soldier or a slave. He was God's 'servant' of course, but Isaiah's Servant is far from being a mere creature of his master. His relationship to his master is more like that of the servant depicted in Exodus 21, who says: *'I love my master, my wife, and my children; I will not go out a free person ... '* (Exodus 21:5). He is, in a sense, 'under orders' – but in a very different way: *'No one takes [my life] from me, but I lay it down of my own accord. I have power to lay it down, and I have power to take it up again. I have received this command from my Father'.* What he says of his followers applies first of all to himself: *'I do not call you servants any longer, because the servant does not know what the master is doing'* (John 15:15).

No, the compassion that Jesus shows is God's compassion – he is, after all, 'God with us'. But it also *his* compassion, arising out of his own heart and mind – can compassion really be anything else? – and therefore a man's compassion too. One is led to the conclusion that the inner human life of Jesus has been so suffused with the mind and the being of God that its spontaneous responses are as God's are. His aims are God's aims; he loves and desires what God loves and desires.

I have referred several times to the difference between John's Gospel and the Synoptics in relation to Jesus' inner life and have suggested that it is in John that we find statements that sum up features of Jesus' words and actions that remain implicit and unspoken in the Synoptics. That is not accidental: John is writing, not a historical, factual account of Jesus' life but rather an *interpretation* of it from a post-resurrection perspective. Sure enough, it is in John that we find the words that best express this unity – not a metaphysical unity but one at the level of heart, mind and will. The words are inevitably metaphorical – abstract psychological language would be of no use – but they serve to illuminate the mystery of this *practical* identity of two:

> *'Do you not believe that I am in the Father and the Father is in me? The words that I say to you I do not speak on my own; but the Father who dwells in me does his works.' (John 14:10)*

> *'I do as the Father has commanded me, so that the world may know that I love the Father.' (John 14:31)*

> *'... you, Father, are in me and I am in you ... ' (John 17:21)*[19]

---

19 Jesus' relationship to the Father as the Son, as 'the word become flesh', and as the one whom God has 'sent', his *shaliach* or empowered emissary, is, of course, the central concern of John's Gospel. In consequence, his relationship to the Father is the principal theme, not only in the numerous 'I am ...' statements but in all Jesus' discourses.

The Mission of Jesus

'In his image'

Our attempts to understand to some degree the relationship of Son to Father brings us back to the words in Genesis 1: *'Let us make humankind in our image, according to our likeness'* (v. 26) that we examined back in chapter 1. The three ways of describing that relationship that I have judged inadequate are all, in one way or another, expressions of despair at the seeming impossibility that any human being might ever truly be 'in God's image', or, to put it another way, that God might ever be revealed in a human life. Yet what the Synoptic Gospels *show* us, and John's Gospel *explains*, is that it *is* possible. Why else did God endow these strange human creatures with such extraordinary gifts, such potential for spiritual understanding, practical achievements and emotional sensitivity? It is what we are made for – and Jesus is the model. And it is also what he came for: the object of his mission was ultimately to bring about the realisation of the seemingly unattainable purpose of God in creation that we considered in chapter 1:

> *It was fitting that God, for whom and through whom all things exist, in bringing many children to glory, should make the pioneer of their salvation perfect through sufferings. For the one who sanctifies and those who are sanctified all have one Father. For this reason Jesus is not ashamed to call them brothers and sisters ... (Hebrews 2:10-11)*

Chapter 7

From Caesarea Philippi to Jerusalem

At Caesarea Philippi, at the foot of Mount Hermon, north of the northern border of Galilee, Jesus did three things that, as far as we know, he had not done before: first, he asked his disciples about popular reactions to his ministry – who people thought he was. Second, he asked them what *they* thought of him; and thirdly, and most momentously, he told them for the first time that he was to die – at the hands of the Jewish religious authorities in Jerusalem – and then rise again: *'Then he began to teach them that the Son of Man must undergo great suffering, and be rejected by the elders, the chief priests, and the scribes, and be killed, and after three days rise again'* (Mark 8:31; cf. Matt. 16:21; Luke 9:22).

It is hardly surprising, then, that the Synoptic Gospels present this episode as a turning point in Jesus' ministry – the end of the ministry in Galilee and some surrounding areas, and the beginning of a journey to Jerusalem and to death. Matthew in particular presents it as a new departure, parallel to the beginning of Jesus' ministry (compare Matt. 4:17 and 16:21). They do not actually say that the journey to Jerusalem begins at that point; Luke alone explicitly marks the beginning of the journey (9:51), but he places several events, notably the Transfiguration, between that and the announcement of his coming death (9:22).

The details of the journey are both vague and varying. Matthew devotes four chapters to it (ch. 17-20), though one of them is actually a collection of teachings about relations between believers in the as yet still future church, while Mark covers essentially the same ground in just two chapters, 9-10. Luke, by contrast devotes over a third of his Gospel to this journey, though the chronology and the geography of the journey are far from precise.[1] This

---

1 David Wenham states confidently in his *Jesus In Context*, Cambridge 2021 (p. 180) that 'The route of Jesus' final journey to Jerusalem with his followers was evidently the one most frequently used by Galilean pilgrims, avoiding Samaria by travelling south on the east side

From Caesarea Philippi to Jerusalem

entire section of Luke is unique to him: he leaves the order of events found in Mark at Luke 9:50 (= Mark 9:40) and rejoins it at 18:15 (= Mark 10:13). When Luke writes that *'When the days drew near for him to be taken up, he set his face to go to Jerusalem'* (9:51), he is perhaps referring primarily to the new direction in Jesus' thinking rather than the journey itself.

One further feature of this new phase of Jesus' ministry also needs to be mentioned: the disciples come much more sharply into focus than in the earlier stage – indeed, they are frequently centre-stage, rather than mere companions of Jesus. They are prominently involved in every episode in Mark's two chapters, sometimes by their reactions to events, at other times through conversations with Jesus, initiated either by Jesus or by the disciples themselves.

At Caesarea Philippi

Jesus' questions

Why does Jesus' ministry take this new turn? Why does he begin, apparently suddenly, to speak about his death and resurrection? The crucial conversation at Caesarea Philippi is begun by Jesus' question: *'Who do people say that I am?'* (Mark 8:27; cf. Matt. 16:13; Luke 9:18). A possible explanation of this question may be that Jesus wished to take stock of his ministry, to assess how effective it has been. It is noteworthy that the sequence of events just before the Caesarea Philippi scene are bracketed by two deeply symbolic events: the healing of a deaf man (7:31-37) and of a blind man (8:22-26). These two miracles may have particular reference to the disciples' obtuseness (7:18; 8:14-21), but they probably reflect also that of the people: *'Then he called the crowd again and said to them, "Listen to me, all of you, and understand ...'* (7:14).

The disciples' answer to Jesus' question remains within the range of Jewish expectation as shaped by the Old Testament: *'John the Baptist; and others, Elijah; and still others, one of the prophets'* (Mark 8:28 – Matthew adds the name of Jeremiah). When John the Baptist was questioned about himself, he too mentioned Elijah and 'the prophet' (possibly a reference to Deuteronomy 18:15-22), but he had added one very significant alternative, *'the Messiah'* (John 1:20-21). The Synoptic Gospels repeatedly mention the popular response that Jesus may, or even must, be 'a prophet' (see Matt. 21;11; Mark

---

of the Jordan river and then, near Jericho, turning westwards towards Jerusalem.' This view would account for his passing through or near Jericho shortly before reaching Jerusalem, as mentioned by all three Synoptic Gospels (Mark 10:46 and parallels). If correct, it would make it difficult to explain Luke's references to Samaria and Samaritans (Luke 9:52; 17:11) and would render rather less convincing Austin Farrar's thesis that the second set of twelve healings that he finds in Luke took place in Samaria.

6:15; Luke 7:16, 39; John 6:14; 7:40; 9:17), but speculation that Jesus might be 'the Christ' (i.e. Messiah) is mentioned only by John (1:21; 4:29, 42; 7:41; 10:24). The disciples' answer can therefore not have been surprising or disappointing to Jesus, especially in view of his self-effacement that we referred to in the previous chapter, to say nothing of the secrecy with which, according to Mark, he apparently sought to surround his identity.

Far more significant for the outcome of Jesus' ministry than these popular responses, however, was the outright opposition that Jesus had encountered from the religious leaders, Pharisees, scribes, and the lay leaders of synagogues. Whatever enthusiasm there might be elsewhere for Jesus and especially his miracles, it was these influential people who would determine whether Jesus' call to Israel to turn to God in response to his message of 'release' would be effective. And by now it was clear that this opposition would continue; even before the decisive episode at Caesarea Philippi, Jesus had twice been rejected in Jewish synagogues, both in Capernaum (Mark 3:1-6) and in Nazareth (Mark 6:1-6 = Luke 4:16-30), and he had also received ominous news of the execution of his forerunner, John the Baptist, by Herod Antipas. Increasingly, Jesus and those who follow him are seen in locations *outside* the towns and villages of Israel: in a 'desolate place' (Mark 6:31), in Gentile territory (Mark 7:24-8:10), and on a boat (Mark 8:14-21). At least in Luke's rather uncertain chronology, it is not long after Caesarea Philippi that Jesus denounces first 'this generation' and then, more specifically, both Pharisees and 'lawyers' for their failure to recognise that *'something greater than Solomon is here'* (Luke 11:31).

It may be, of course, that Jesus had long known that his mission, as it appears throughout the Galilean phase, was certain to fail as a result of such opposition; the Old Testament echoes at his baptism, his profound understanding of the Old Testament, not least the Servant passages, and his periods of intense prayer and reflection must, one supposes, have left him in no doubt. But if that is so, one is tempted to wonder why the mission was undertaken in the first place. From the divine point of view – if we may presume to speculate about that – it is easy to conclude that it had to be done as a witness against Israel before disaster fell upon them. However, it seems to me that the answer probably lies elsewhere: it was not simply that Jesus was to die, nor was it the simple *fact* of his death that would finally be decisive. What mattered was rather the meaning that men and women would be able to discern in it – and crucial to that meaning was that it was to be a form of suffering and death that arose out of human rejection, not the result of some narcissistic desire for martyrdom, nor a punishment arbitrarily imposed by the Father. The cross

From Caesarea Philippi to Jerusalem

had, in short, to make unmistakably clear 'the sin of the world'. We shall need to return to this later, when we come to the crucifixion itself.

From Jesus' point of view, we might suppose that he went ahead with his mission out of simple obedience to the Father – or perhaps because he realised how much practical good he would be able to do among the people in and around Galilee. Or he might well have undertaken his mission hoping against hope, as it were. Yet, whatever his thoughts and feelings may have been, the Servant passages suggest that he must have had at some point a sense of failure or disappointment, however momentary. For the second of them includes, as part of the Servant's 'soliloquy', the following words that we have already referred to earlier: *'But I said, "I have laboured in vain, I have spent my strength for nothing and vanity'* (49:4).

Human and natural though such a feeling would be in such a situation, the words that follow in Isaiah suggest strongly that Jesus not only knew where his path was to take him, but also understood the purpose that lay behind it: *'... yet surely my cause is with the* LORD, *and my reward with my God'*. He was not to be a servant who blindly carries out orders but rather the empowered *shaliach*, who understands and shares his master's intentions, the 'friend' to whom everything is made known (John 15:15) – or rather, the Son, with whom the Father shares everything (Luke 15:31; John 17:10). He grasped, I imagine, at some point that, paradoxically, his mission *needed* to fail; it was his rejection, suffering and death at the hands of men that would achieve what all his words, like those of the prophets before him, would not achieve. The fourth 'Servant song' in particular, in Isaiah 52-53, must have led him to understand that it is the Servant's unmerited suffering and death that elicit the insight and repentant confession that we hear in the 'we' passage in Isaiah (53:4-6 – see the discussion of these passages in chapter 2). At the same time, those passages gave him the ultimate assurance that, whatever lay ahead of him, it was encompassed within the loving, gracious purposes of the Father – his future, though unknown in one sense, was foreknown, made secure by God's unchanging, steadfast love. His experiences as he sought to call Israel back to God, and especially the opposition that he had encountered, would surely have removed any doubts that he might have had about the accuracy of Isaiah's portrait of the Servant.

Given all of this, Jesus was also clearly aware, by this time if not before, that the ultimate realisation of his mission was going to be delayed. I doubt that he knew how long that delay would be; when he spoke in the 'Olivet prophecy' about the future in a way that clearly presupposed a time of absence followed by a return, he was careful to disclaim precise knowledge: *'But about that day or hour no one knows, neither the angels in heaven, nor the Son, but only the Father'* (Mark 13:32). However, the very fact of delay meant that his disciples were to play a significant part in the continuation of the work that he had begun. That is surely the reason for the greater attention paid to them, both by Jesus and by the Gospel writers, from this point on. Indeed, it may well be that Jesus asked his question about other people's view of him only as a preliminary to speaking to the disciples about the end to which his ministry was leading.

Jesus and Peter

This new focus on the disciples begins at Caesarea Philippi, when Jesus turns his attention to them: *'But who do you say that I am?'* (Mark 8:29). The answer that Peter gives, probably on behalf of all the Twelve, *'You are the Messiah'* (or 'Christ'), is a vast step forward compared with those current among the people, for it recognises his uniqueness: he is not 'a ...' but 'the ...'. The term 'Messiah' ('anointed one') was far from precise, however: it suggested above all divine selection and appointment for a special role, whether as king or as priest, or even as 'the prophet' – contemporary Jewish expectation was far from unanimous as to who or what precisely the 'coming one' would be.

> Messianic expectations were as diverse as any other part of inter-testamental Jewish thought, if not more so. These matters were "the centre of a vast mass of confused, involved and even contradictory notions, from which there arose few certainties that were acknowledged by all."[2]

Thus, like the answers that they had given about the people, the disciples' response remained within the framework of contemporary Jewish thought and faith; it was a good start, but not enough. No less importantly, it remained within the compass of human conceptions of greatness, focused on power and glory – precisely the values that Jesus had learned during his temptation to reject. The fluidity of Old Testament language and imagery about 'the coming one' had become frozen into terms like 'Messiah' which, imprecise though it was, was now the key word that summed up all Israel's longing for power and glory that would enable them at last to lord it over their oppressors. And if the disciples were ultimately to carry on his work after his death and resurrection, their conception of what 'Messiah' meant needed now to be corrected; that, surely, was the ultimate reason for Jesus' two questions.

---

2   Scott, *Jewish Backgrounds*, p. 307, quoting Henri Daniel-Rops, *Daily Life in the Time of Jesus*, trans. P. O'Brian, New York 1962, p. 409. C. D. Elledge points out that the Dead Sea Scrolls suggest 'the expectation of dual messiahs, one royal and one priestly', in Green & McDonald (eds.), *The World of the New Testament*, p. 239.

From Caesarea Philippi to Jerusalem

This is why Caesarea Philippi is so decisive a moment in Jesus' life. It is not just that it marks the change of direction that we have already considered; above all, it reveals at last what is fundamentally at stake in Jesus' ministry and indeed in his whole life. We referred in the previous chapter to Jesus' self-effacement, to his apparent secrecy about himself; now, after Peter's confession that he is the 'Messiah', Jesus again forbids the disciples (Mark 8:30) to tell anyone about him. It is as if the words that he might use and that they might pass on to others would be tainted by their use in the pursuit of human interests and consequently understood according to the values and preconceptions of this world – in terms of power and dominion. So how can Jesus make them 'see'? As with the blind man in Mark 8:22-26, it will not be accomplished at once. What he cannot yet show them he will tell them – and so he describes to them what lies ahead: '*… the Son of Man must undergo great suffering, and be rejected by the elders, the chief priests, and the scribes, and be killed, and after three days rise again'*.

All this must have seemed to them both shocking and inconceivable: that he, the Messiah, was to be put to death by his own people but then rise – impossibility piled upon impossibility. Little wonder, then, that Peter should reply as he did: *'Peter took him aside and began to rebuke him'* (Mark 8:32) – to which Matthew adds Peter's actual words: *'God forbid it, Lord! This must never happen to you'* (Matt. 16:22). Jesus' reply is astonishing in its severity: *'Get behind me, Satan! You are a stumbling block to me; for you are setting your mind not on divine things but on human things'* (Matt. 16:23). Rebuke for rebuke: the word *epitimao* in Mark 8:32 and 33, the same word used when Jesus 'rebukes' the sea and the storm and when he 'drives out' the 'unclean spirits', suggests a severe reprimand.

The 'Caesarea Philippi principle'

Why, exactly, did Jesus respond so fiercely? He cannot have been surprised at the disciples' limited comprehension; during the events leading up to Caesarea Philippi he had already spoken in some exasperation, it would appear, about their lack of understanding:

'Why are you talking about having no bread? Do you still not perceive or understand? Are your hearts hardened? Do you have eyes, and fail to see? Do you have ears, and fail to hear? And do you not remember? When I broke the five loaves for the five thousand, how many baskets full of broken pieces did you collect?' They said to him, 'Twelve.' 'And the seven for the four thousand, how many baskets full of broken pieces did you collect?' And they

said to him, 'Seven.' Then he said to them, 'Do you not yet understand?'
(Mark 8:17-21)

Was it that Peter, and presumably the others too, had not rightly understood the Old Testament and did not perceive the necessity of the Messiah's dying? That may be so, but it is, I think, far from being the whole story. We need to understand what Jesus meant by 'divine things' and 'human things' (literally, 'that which is of God/of man'). What lay behind Jesus' rebuke emerges best, perhaps, in what follows, when Jesus speaks directly not only to the disciples but also to the crowd (Mark 8:34). Here, he turns what he has said about his own fate into a general principle for all who wish to follow him:

If any want to become my followers, let them deny themselves and take up their cross and follow me. For those who want to save their life will lose it, and those who lose their life for my sake, and for the sake of the gospel, will save it. For what will it profit them to gain the whole world and forfeit their life? Indeed, what can they give in return for their life? Those who are ashamed of me and of my words in this adulterous and sinful generation, of them the Son of Man will also be ashamed when he comes in the glory of his Father with the holy angels. (Mark 8:34-38)

The verses 35 and 36 present two pairs of opposites: first, 'save their life' v. 'lose their life', each leading ultimately to an exactly contrary outcome, which are then contrasted in the second pair, 'gain the whole world' v. 'forfeit their life'. These contrasted pairs represent the essential difference between 'human things' and 'divine things'. On the one hand, there are 'the human things', the instinctive human desire to preserve one's life at all costs – self-preservation is, after all, the most basic of human instincts – and, as an extension of it, the desire to 'gain', perhaps not the whole world but whatever status, possessions and advantages can be acquired to feed natural human self-interest and self-importance. Peter takes this to be a universal, self-evident human impulse – no wonder he was horrified at the notion that Jesus would accept death, apparently willingly. Jesus, however, is saying that, though self-preservation – looking after oneself first – seems natural or necessary, self-evidently the right thing to do, its outcome will ultimately be the loss of everything, including life itself.

On the other hand, there is the way of Jesus, clearly ready to 'lose his life' for the sake of the gospel, that is to say, in the fulfilment of his mission to bring to mankind the message of the mercy of God and his call to repentance. This willingness to bear all the ill that men do to him without seeking vengeance is the essence of the 'divine things'. It is Jesus' way, but it is also God's way, for it

From Caesarea Philippi to Jerusalem

was from the Father that he had learned it, and it is Jesus' embracing of it and his willingness to enact it that make him what we discussed in chapter 2, the man 'in God's image'. Whatever he did or did not know prior to his baptism, he knew and understood his calling now.

Moreover, as Jesus is 'after God's image', or, as Matthew tells us, 'God with us', it follows that what he does or says, God says and does – what he endures, God endures. That means that if Jesus was preparing himself now to bear all the rejection and consequent hatred from mankind that was predicted of the Servant, then in the person of his beloved Son the Father too was to bear human beings' rebellion and disobedience against himself (cf. 'the gospel of God' and the Hebrew word *nasa* that we discussed in the previous chapter).

In the light of Jesus' comments in these lines, we can see that Peter's words were not simply the result of a failure to understand the scriptures correctly. Rather, they represent the very essence of human thinking and values: self-preservation and the pursuit of one's personal advantage. What's more, Peter does not simply speak for himself: he assumes that Jesus must surely be governed by the same basic impulses. In effect, he was subjecting Jesus all over again to the temptation that he had decisively rejected during his forty days in the wilderness – hence, perhaps, the vehemence of his words, the reference to a 'stumbling block' (*skandalon*), and the use of the term 'satan' to describe the hapless Peter. Jesus' reference to 'gaining the whole world' is an obvious echo of the third of the temptations (in Matthew's order). By implication, Peter was attempting to 'correct' Jesus' judgment, blocking his path, diverting him from his chosen course. No, says Jesus, your place is behind me, following where I lead.

Worse still, though, Peter implicitly ascribes such ideas to God himself. He imposes man's values on God and so 'makes God in man's image'. That means in effect that there is no gospel – no 'gospel of God' – for God is then not the self-giving, all-merciful one that Jesus has been proclaiming, but just another power in the interplay of competing powers that make up this world – more powerful, perhaps, but fundamentally one who plays by the same rules as the 'rulers' and 'great ones' (Mark 10:42) of this world.

It is important to notice, too, that the contrast that Jesus presents is not operative only at the level of individual lives. The ideas of 'saving oneself' and 'gaining the whole world' are equally evident – and equally damaging – at national level. The popular notion of 'Messiah' was the characteristic Jewish expression of them: the great leader who would restore Israel to its former glory and to its rightful place above all other nations.[3] Jesus' rebuke of James and

---

3 It is not difficult to recognise parallel expressions of the same fundamental drive in the

Jesus – yesterday, today, for ever

John when they suggest calling down fire on a Samaritan village in possible emulation of Elijah: *'You do not know what kind of spirit you are of'* (Luke 9:52-56 NASB), is omitted by most modern translations and is not supported by the best sources. Nevertheless, one cannot but feel that such a rebuke, if genuinely expressed by Jesus, would reflect not only his attitude to the use of physical force and his readiness to bear without retribution such slights and injuries as the Samaritan villagers were guilty of, but also his rejection of nationalism and exclusivism.

But we notice, too, that in describing his future Jesus yet again spoke in the third person, using the 'Son of man' title. If we recall the implications of that term that we explored in chapter 2, we see that Jesus was inviting the disciples – and us – to see him as the prototype of a new humanity, one that abandons 'the human things' to embrace 'the divine things', renouncing self-interest as the driving force in human life. Sure enough, Jesus proclaims that those who wish to follow him must take that same step. But he also reassures them that the ultimate result would be for them as it would be for him: just as he would 'save his life' by an act of God that reverses the actions of men against him, so ultimately would they.

From this moment on, Jesus' declaration at Caesarea Philippi, the 'Caesarea Philippi principle' as I think of it, stands at the centre of his ministry. It is probably not by accident that this episode is located almost exactly at the mid-point of Mark's Gospel. It is against this criterion that Mark focuses so heavily on the disciples in his chapters 9-10, and it is the decisive issue that contrasts Jesus and his disciples at the climax of the story, when Jesus is arrested and dies, in accordance with the principle – while the disciples flee. Thereafter, it becomes the governing principle in the apostles' conduct as we see it in Acts and, in varying formulations, is central to their teachings and writings, for example in the following:

> *Let each of you look not to your own interests, but to the interests of others. Let the same mind be in you that was in Christ Jesus ... (Philippians 2:4-5)*

> *If we have died with him, we will also live with him; if we endure, we will also reign with him ... (2 Timothy 2:11)*

> *Since therefore Christ suffered in the flesh, arm yourselves also with the same intention (for whoever has suffered in the flesh has finished with sin) ... (1 Peter 4:1)*

---

world today, 'Making ... great again' is one obvious example.

From Caesarea Philippi to Jerusalem

The Transfiguration

The three Synoptic accounts of the Caesarea Philippi incident all conclude with words which explicitly link it with what follows next, the 'transfiguration' of Jesus, probably on nearby Mount Hermon. The links are unmistakable: Jesus had spoken of *'coming in the glory of his Father'* (Mark 8:38) – and now he appears with his face *'shining like the sun'* (Matt. 17:2) and his clothes dazzlingly white. He is transformed – Matthew and Mark use the Greek verb *metamorphoo*, which implies a change from one form of existence to another, from human finitude to divine eternity. Mark's apparently rather homely comparison, *'such as no one on earth could bleach them'* is actually very explicit: what has occurred is outside the earthly realm, beyond all human experience.

The Transfiguration can readily be recognised as a follow-up to the events at Caesarea Philippi, but what exactly was the purpose of the extraordinary happenings on the mountain – and for whose benefit did they take place? For Jesus himself, they must have provided reassurance. The calm, decisive manner in which at Caesarea Philippi he announces what is to happen to him may well prevent us from seeing what it must have cost him. Hitherto, he had played the part of the prophet, proclaiming a message and performing works of compassion and mercy – not an easy role but one for which there were models aplenty in Israel's history. But now he has had to commit himself, publicly for the first time, to a very different and lonely path: after Caesarea Philippi, there was no going back. No wonder Luke writes that *'he set his face to go to Jerusalem'* (9:51) – the word 'set' suggests the inner struggle involved – echoing the words of the Servant in Isaiah 50: *'... therefore I have set my face like flint'* (v. 7). The immediate context in Isaiah probably tells us in what frame of mind Jesus took this decision: *'The Lord GOD helps me; therefore I have not been disgraced ... and I know that I shall not be put to shame; he who vindicates me is near'* (v. 7-8). The moments on the mountain were evidence of the Father's nearness that the Isaiah passage promised, providing for him a confirmation that he was not pursuing some imaginary goal, that the mission that he had embraced was truly from God, and that the consequent rising again, of which he had spoken to his disciples a week earlier, was no illusion. This presupposes, of course, that the Transfiguration was not simply something that the disciples *saw*, but was an event that Jesus himself experienced, nothing less than an anticipation of the promised participation in the divine life through the transformation of his very body. Thus, tempting as it may be to think of the Transfiguration as subjective vision, that cannot apply to what Jesus experienced.

That conclusion may not apply, however, to the appearance of Moses and

Elijah. No particular significance can be attached to the use of the word 'appear' (*optanomai*), but it seems *prima facie* unlikely that dead men would be momentarily raised to life in order to fulfil what was essentially a symbolic function. Luke suggests that some kind of conversation took place between them and Jesus, but he also says that the disciples with Jesus were *'weighed down with sleep'* (Luke 9:32). More specifically, Luke says that they spoke with him about *'his departure, which he was about to accomplish at Jerusalem'*; 'departure' (*exodos*) could simply refer to Jesus' death, though it seems plausible that it looks back to an 'exodus' in the biblical sense, a deliverance comparable to that which Moses 'accomplished' from Egypt; such a sense would be an echo of Jesus' proclamation of 'release' in the Nazareth synagogue. Whatever the reference, however, one wonders what either of these two Old Testament figures could possibly tell Jesus that he did not know far better than they.

It therefore seems to me more likely that their appearance, and indeed the Transfiguration as a whole, took place primarily for the disciples' sake. They must have been deeply shaken by Jesus' words at Caesarea Philippi, the more so as he had not merely spoken of his own death but had also demanded of them that they too should 'take up the cross' – which in Jesus' day was no casual reference to burdens that men and women have to bear in the course of their life, but rather an all too explicit reference to an extremely painful and ignominious death. The Transfiguration was, therefore, an act of extraordinary kindness and understanding on the part of Father and Son, who had, it would appear, agreed that it should take place before Jesus spoke the mysterious words of Mark 8:38. Jesus, one supposes, had foreseen the dismay and puzzlement of his disciples and asked the Father that he might provide some form of reassurance for them. For the overriding sense of the Transfiguration was clearly that what Jesus had said about his glory was true, and that there was thus no conflict between his being 'Messiah' and the death that he had predicted.

Whether the disciples grasped all this at that moment is uncertain; all three Synoptic Gospels speak of their fear at this spectacle so far removed from human experience; Mark and Luke also tell us that Peter *'did not know what to say'* (Mark 9:6; Luke 9:33), when confronted with the sight of Moses and Elijah with Jesus. But why did these two figures appear? It is normally assumed that they are there as representatives of 'the Law and the prophets', thus confirming that what Jesus had said about himself at Caesarea Philippi was in fact in accord with the Old Testament predictions that we considered in Chapter 2; we remember how much weight Jesus attached to this understanding in Luke 24 when he opened the eyes and the minds of his bewildered

From Caesarea Philippi to Jerusalem

disciples after his resurrection.

Their presence gains added point, however, if we recall the responses to Jesus' question: *'Who do people say that I am?'*. Elijah and 'the prophet', i.e. a new Moses, were the two most common answers mentioned – and now here they were, witnesses of a glory that far surpassed their own. Peter's suggestion, *'... let us make three dwellings, one for you, one for Moses, and one for Elijah'* (Mark 9:5; cf. Luke 9:33; Matt. 17:4), may have meant that they should try to erect three 'tabernacles', one for each of the three – *skene* is used in this sense in the New Testament. Or perhaps he had in mind some kind of temporary shelter – it can be cold on mountain tops! A voice then speaks from heaven, probably in response to Peter's suggestion: *'This is my Son, the Beloved; listen to him!'*

This announcement carries several meanings. First, it is in all three Gospels a clear echo of the voice from heaven at Jesus' baptism; Matthew makes this explicit by adding the phrase *'with him I am well pleased'*. The three disciples now hear for the first time the stunning proclamation of Jesus' identity – we notice that the voice now speaks of Jesus in the third person, addressing the disciples rather than Jesus, whereas at his baptism it had said 'You are ...'. It is a declaration that far surpasses anything they they had previously understood, including the term 'Messiah' that Peter had used at Caesarea Philippi.[4] Second, the following phrase, 'listen to him', has about it something of a rebuke: there could be no question of equality between the Son and any Old Testament figures, however great. He above all must now be heeded. The sudden disappearance of Moses and Elijah as the scene comes to an end seems to symbolise their eclipse in the glorious presence of Jesus. Thirdly, as Son, he cannot be contained within any pre-existing framework of ideas that Israel had derived from the Law and the prophets – hence the inadequacy of all the responses given to Jesus' questions a week before. And fourthly, and probably most importantly, the disciples must listen to what he had said at Caesarea Philippi, incredible and perhaps unpalatable though it may have seemed.

Towards Jerusalem

These two episodes, which together mark the turning point in Jesus' ministry, largely determine the character of the phase of Jesus' ministry between the Transfiguration and his arrival in Jerusalem. In Matthew and Mark, as we have

---

4   The announcement during the Transfiguration appears to make it unlikely that Peter identified Jesus as 'Son of the living God' at Caesarea Philippi, as Matthew appears to suggest (Matt. 16:16) – or at least, that he used the term in the sense that Christians have come to understand it. If Peter had made so momentous a confession, Mark and Luke would surely not have omitted it.

already noted, the focus shifts away from Jesus' encounters with individuals and groups to his conversations with the disciples.

Luke and his parables

First, though, we need to consider Luke's much longer account, which comprises almost entirely events and teaching not found elsewhere. In part, these chapters, Luke 10-18, resemble the Galilee mission: Jesus continues to heal (we noted in the previous chapter Farrer's theory of a further twelve healings, mirroring those in the earlier section, but which he portrays, without much evidence, as taking place in Samaria), to speak to individuals and to crowds, to accept hospitality (11:37 ff.; 14:1 ff.). He has not abandoned his mission to 'seek and to save' (Luke 19:10) in favour of a martyr's death: rather, he pursues his mission towards the ending that had long been foreshadowed, ever since '*The Pharisees went out and immediately conspired with the Herodians against him, how to destroy him*' (Mark 3:6). The death that lies ahead is the result of that mission, its inevitable climax.

There is not much by way of geographical detail in Luke's account of the journey; the account is held together rather by the occasional 'notices of travel' (e.g. 10:38; 13:22; 17:11) and by what David Moessner calls Jesus' 'continuity of resolve'. He shows, Moessner writes, '... the flint-like purpose of the prophet-'servant' of Isaiah 50:4-11 to accept humiliation from his own people as he announces good news ... [and] exhibits "unbending determination" to complete his "taking up" by moving resolutely towards Jerusalem'.[5]

However, the distinctive feature of this section of Luke is the series of wonderful parables: the Good Samaritan, the Great Supper, the Lost Coin, the Lost Sheep, the Lost Son, the Dishonest Manager, the Rich Man and Lazarus, and the Pharisee and the Tax-collector. In their different ways, all these parables contrast social and religious 'insiders' and self-consciously righteous people with repentant sinners and despised outsiders. They are, in effect, depictions of Israel's response to Jesus' message of compassion for suffering and of grace and forgiveness of sinners, contrasting the reactions of the self-righteous and hard-hearted with those of the needy and the merciful. There are figures who feel no need of grace (the Pharisee, the invited guests, and the elder son), those in confessed need of pardon (the tax-collector and the younger son), those who show compassion (the Samaritan, the host at the

---

5   David P. Moessner, 'How Luke Writes' in Markus Bockmuehl & Donald A. Hagner (ed.), *The Written Gospel*, Cambridge 2005, p. 157, and 'Reading Luke's Gospel as Ancient Hellenistic Narrative', in Craig G. Bartholomew, Joel B. Green & Anthony C. Thiselton (ed.), *Reading Luke. Interpretation, Reflection, Formation*, Milton Keynes/Grand Rapids, Michigan, 2005, p. 139.

From Caesarea Philippi to Jerusalem

Supper, and the father of the two sons), and those without compassion and grace toward others (the elder son, the rich man, and the unjust manager). Finally, there is one in whom the terrible consequences of self-righteous indifference to others are seen: the rich man suffering the imagined torments of exclusion from 'Abraham's bosom'.

This recurrent contrastive pattern in Luke can be viewed in several ways: first, it represents, at its simplest, a warning to the self-righteous and the powerful. Second, all these stories involve a stunning reversal of fortune, in which Jesus lifts up the fallen and the marginalised while shaming or casting down the powerful and the comfortably off; he thus passes an implicit judgment on the social and moral order created by the dominance of 'the human things' and asserts against it the values of the reign of God. Thirdly, the figure of the rich man in particular prefigures the fate that will overtake Israel if its collective disobedience is maintained: their place in Jesus' new people will be taken by the most despised of all outsiders, the Gentiles. If the parables of Matthew 13 and Mark 4 may be seen as a kind of commentary on responses to Jesus' mission as it was taking place, these parables are like snapshots of the process at a later stage, when the differing responses that we see in the Galilee section have congealed into a more or less fixed form, from which there will be no going back and whose outcome is now inevitable. The influence of Paul, Luke's 'mentor', with his concern for witness to Gentiles and his analysis of 'salvation history', notably in Romans 11, can clearly be recognised here.[6] Jesus' commission to the seventy-two (10:1), found in Luke only and distinguished from the sending out of the twelve (9:1), should perhaps be seen as a foreshadowing of the world-wide mission that would follow Israel's rejection.

It is worth noting too that all these parables, except the Good Samaritan, have been preceded by Jesus' condemnation of 'this generation' (Luke 11:29-32, 51) and particularly of their spiritual leaders (11:42-54), while the whole section is 'book-ended' by the two sections in which Jesus foretells his death for the second and third times (Luke 9:44-45 and 18:31-34), the parallels to which are found in Mark 9:9:30-32 and 10:32-34. Beautiful and inspiring though these parables are, the context within which they sit reveals a Jesus engaged in a continuous process of reflection on the impact and ultimate consequences of his mission. In telling these stories, he shows himself well aware, not only of where events were inexorably leading him personally, but also of the outcomes that would follow: forgiveness and release for some, but tragedy for his own people. His frame of mind, resolved to continue his mission to the end but saddened by one of its consequences, can be seen, surely, at the

---

6 I argue this more fully in my *Luke's Pauline Narrative. Reading the Third Gospel*.

Jesus – yesterday, today, for ever

beginning and end of chapter 13:

'*Do you think that because these Galileans suffered in this way they were worse sinners than all other Galileans? No, I tell you; but unless you repent, you will all perish as they did ... Yet today, tomorrow, and the next day I must be on my way, because it is impossible for a prophet to be killed outside of Jerusalem. Jerusalem, Jerusalem, the city that kills the prophets and stones those who are sent to it! How often have I desired to gather your children together as a hen gathers her brood under her wings, and you were not willing!' (Luke 13:2-3, 33-34)*

Luke's record may rejoin the story as told by Mark at Luke 18:15, but it is noticeable that he ends his account of Jesus' ministry as a whole, before he reaches Jerusalem, not with the healing of Bartimaeus, as do Mark and Matthew, but with another incident unique to him, Jesus' visit to the home of the tax-collector Zacchaeus (Luke 19:1-10). This episode thus functions as the counterpart of the visit to the Nazareth synagogue which marks the beginning of the ministry. In both, we find a programmatic statement of the overall intention of Jesus' coming; the announcement of 'good news' for the poor and the 'year of the Lord's favour' in Luke 4:18-19 is balanced by Jesus' summing up of his visit to Zacchaeus: '*For the Son of Man came to seek out and to save the lost*' (19:10). The link with the Nazareth incident is confirmed by the use of the word 'today' (19:9), just as in 4:21.

Focus on the disciples

We return now to the story as told by Mark and Matthew – and by Luke when his 'special section' ends. Leaving aside Matthew's chapter devoted to the future church (Matthew 18), and two or three other incidents – the question about divorce (Mark 10:1-12), the question about the temple tax, and the parable of the labourers in the vineyard (Matt. 17:24-27; 20:1-16), the focus is on the disciples, as we saw earlier. How will they be affected by the revelations at Caesarea Philippi and on the mount of Transfiguration? How will they respond to the choice that Jesus has put before them between 'the human things' and 'the divine things' and the challenge to 'follow me'?

In Mark, the very first pericope after the healing of the epileptic boy (Mark 9:14-29) sets the tone for the rest:

They went on from there and passed through Galilee. He did not want anyone to know it for he was teaching his disciples, saying to them, 'The Son of Man is to be betrayed into human hands, and they will kill him, and three

From Caesarea Philippi to Jerusalem

> *days after being killed, he will rise again.' But they did not understand what he was saying and were afraid to ask him. (Mark 9:30-32)*

Jesus did not wish to be interrupted because he was focused on helping his disciples to understand and accept the 'Caesarea Philippi principle', not only in its application to himself but also in relation to them. He speaks of his suffering twice, in this passage in Mark 9 and parallels and in chapter 10:33-34. We should not forget, though, that the disciples presumably also heard Jesus tell the parables in Luke that we have just been considering. All of them confirmed in different ways the incompatibility between the world as organised by men and the divine way. Thus, the story of the Lost Son illustrates the contrast between the assumptions of the elder son (and of the younger son too) and the judgment of the father; all worldly notions of 'justice', the whole system of merit, of rewards and punishment and of earned rewards, is overturned by the father's forgiveness and grace.[7] The same fundamental principle emerges also in Matthew's wonderful parable of the Labourers in the Vineyard, where the landowner gives a reply that undermines the entire basis on which the human world is organised: *'Am I not allowed to do what I choose with what belongs to me? Or are you envious because I am generous?'* (Matt. 20:15).

The passage from Mark 9 quoted above is followed by a whole series of pericopes which give the reader the impression that, despite Jesus' teaching, the disciples have been so dazzled by what three of them had heard and seen on the mountain that it has obscured the unpalatable recollection of what they had heard at Caesarea Philippi:

- they argue about who was the greatest (9:33-37);

- they seek to exclude others from any share in their work (9:38-41);

- they try to turn away people bringing their children to Jesus – was he in their eyes perhaps too great for such trifles?

- following Jesus' encounter with the rich young man, Peter asks what their reward is to be for having 'left everything and followed you' (10:28);

- James and John seek to elicit from Jesus a promise that they will have places of pre-eminence 'in your glory' (10:35-44) – the irony that colours this entire section reaches its pinnacle here as the reader remembers the places that are going shortly to be available on Jesus' right and

---

7   Cf. the notion of 'incongruous grace' in Barclay's *Paul and the Gift*, mentioned in the previous chapter.

Jesus – yesterday, today, for ever

left hands (15:27).

The section ends with two moments that put these issues into the sharpest focus: first, Jesus is moved by their scrambling for eminence and power to repeat the message of Caesarea Philippi: *'... whoever wishes to become great among you must be your servant, and whoever wishes to be first among you must be slave of all. For the Son of Man came not to be served but to serve, and to give his life a ransom for many'* (10:43-45). After this, he calls blind Bartimaeus to him, ignoring those who were trying to silence him, and restores his sight. Jesus thus provides not only the final example of his compassion but also the most eloquent, though unspoken, rebuke to his still unseeing disciples. And Bartimaeus, with no ifs and buts, *'followed him on the way'*.[8] But even before this, Mark, with the understated compositional skill that marks his entire narrative, has provided the perfect cameo that sums up the disciples' hesitation between the two ways: *'They were on the road, going up to Jerusalem, and Jesus was walking ahead of them; they were amazed, and those who followed were afraid'* (10:32).

The picture of the disciples that emerges from Matthew's and Mark's accounts of this stage of Jesus' ministry may appear irredeemably negative, yet we have to remember that alongside the instances of incomprehension and the as yet unresolved conflict in basic values, there was also the continuing pattern of shared experiences – the walking, talking and eating together. Jesus does not dismiss them as beyond hope, nor do they abandon him as one bent on pointless sacrifice. They may not understand him, but they grasp, however incompletely, that he is 'from God' and thus to be listened to above all, as the voice from heaven had said on the mountain. Some writers have likened Jesus' journey from the mount of Transfiguration to Jerusalem to Moses' spiritually lonely journey from Horeb towards the Promised Land. Yet Jesus, we may be sure, appreciated the human companionship that they gave him; this is revealed later, at the Last Supper, when, according to Luke, Jesus says to them, after another display of the all too human mindset: *'You are those who have stood by me in my trials'* (Luke 22:28). Nor should we forget that the travelling company included, for part, if not all, of the time *'The women who had followed him from Galilee'* (Luke 23:49, 55).

Coming to Jerusalem

And so Jesus comes to Jerusalem – not just the destination of their journey from Galilee, but the goal towards which Jesus' ministry has been carrying

---

8   The way in which the word 'follow' echoes through Mark 9-10, following on from Jesus' words at Caesarea Philippi, is further evidence of Mark's skilful use of irony.

From Caesarea Philippi to Jerusalem

him from the beginning – '*... because it is impossible for a prophet to be killed outside of Jerusalem*'. In one respect, however, Jesus' arrival in Jerusalem sees a remarkable change of strategy on Jesus' part almost more profound than at Caesarea Philippi. For over three years (if we accept John's chronology) he had carefully avoided making any specific claims for himself, apart from any inferences that people might draw from his actions; he had forbidden people to speak of what he had done or to air their convictions about his identity. Yet now, abruptly, he not merely announces himself as the 'coming one' but by implication lays claim to authority over Jerusalem and its temple. He is careful, though, not to do so in words; instead, he relies on eloquent symbolism based on Israel's scriptures:

> *Then they brought the colt to Jesus and threw their cloaks on it; and he sat on it. Many people spread their cloaks on the road, and others spread leafy branches that they had cut in the fields. Then those who went ahead and those who followed were shouting, 'Hosanna! Blessed is the one who comes in the name of the Lord! Blessed is the coming kingdom of our ancestor David! Hosanna in the highest heaven!' (Mark 11:7-10; cf. Matthew 21:7-9; Luke 19:35-38; John 12:12-15)*

Words could be treacherous, all too easily pressed into the service of 'the human things', the ambitions for power and dominion. In this connection, the choice of mount – a colt rather than a horse – was itself significant. A horse would have hinted – or more than hinted – at possible warlike intentions; an ass's colt gave quite a different impression.[9] He came in peace, as Matthew's quotation from Zechariah 9 emphasises, but it was still a kingly arrival, as the parallels with Solomon's accession to the throne (1 Kings 1:33-40) and Jehu's acclamation by his fellow-officers (2 Kings 9:11-13) indicate.

So Jesus' 'coming' to Jerusalem was, in effect, a *parousia*, the term widely used at the time for the arrival of a ruler of an important official and which the New Testament writers take up to describe the arrival of king Jesus – four times in Matthew 24, for example, and four times in 1 Thessalonians. When such a coming occurred, there was, of course, a welcoming party, who went *eis apantesin*[10] – to meet and greet the arriving dignitary – and that is the role

---

9 It is hard to be sure just what kind of animal it was. Mark and Luke say simply 'a colt'; Matthew and John, however, speak of an 'ass' (Matt. 21:2; John 12:14), doubtless wishing to underline the link with Zechariah's prophecy (Zech. 9:9).

10 'The ancient expression for the civic welcome of an important visitor or the triumphant entry of a new ruler into the capital city and thus to his reign' (*IDNTT*, p. 325). It is used in this sense to describe the coming of Jesus in 1 Thess. 4:17; the only other New Testament

Jesus – yesterday, today, for ever

fulfilled by the crowd on this occasion.

Why did Jesus now begin to invite identification as the promised 'Messiah'? As early as Luke 9:51, Jesus evidently had the sense that the time had now come to make his way to Jerusalem to die, as was predicted and purposed for him: *'When the days drew near for him to be taken up, he set his face to go to Jerusalem'* (Luke 9:51).[11] He obviously believed that his death should coincide with a Passover feast and he by now knew which one. He expresses this sense that the time had come more explicitly in the last day or two before Passover: *'He said, "Go into the city to a certain man, and say to him, 'The Teacher says, My time is near; I will keep the Passover at your house with my disciples'"* (Matt. 26:18). There are, of course, repeated references throughout the Gospel of John to Jesus' 'hour', which appears to mean the time of his 'glorification', i.e. the time of his death and resurrection: *'Jesus knew that his **hour** had come to depart from this world and go to the Father ... "Father, the **hour** has come; glorify your Son so that the Son may glorify you ... "'* (John 13:1; 17:1). And, if the time was now come, perhaps a provocative step was necessary to ensure that the expected end did occur.

In thus inviting his enemies finally to act against him, Jesus made two things clear: first, that though he would be the victim of human beings' animosity against him, yet his suffering would not simply be inflicted on him – though others would perform the action, he was giving himself, as he says in John, *'For this reason the Father loves me, because I lay down my life in order to take it up again. No one takes it from me, but I lay it down of my own accord'* (John 10:17-18). He wished, it seems, to remain in control of events – as he does throughout the events of his Passion.

Secondly, the change of strategy reflects Jesus' changed situation: hitherto, his role had been essentially that of a prophet, proclaiming the gospel of forgiveness and grace by word and deed. That is how Peter describes his mission in Acts 10, as we saw earlier:

> *'You know the message he sent to the people of Israel, preaching peace by Jesus Christ – he is Lord of all. That message spread throughout Judea ... how God anointed Jesus of Nazareth with the Holy Spirit and with power; how he went about doing good and healing all who were oppressed by the devil, for God was with him.' (Acts 10:36-38)*

---

usages occur in Matt. 25:1, 6 and Acts 28:5.

11 'Taken up' translates the noun *analepsis,* which occurs here only, but it is cognate with the verb *analambano,* which is used fairly frequently in the New Testament, five times in connection with Jesus' ascension.

From Caesarea Philippi to Jerusalem

Now, however, Jesus was no longer to be the *proclaimer* of grace – he was to *embody* it. He would longer speak of 'the divine things' – he would enact them with his own body.

Yet, however we attempt to explain it, the manner of Jesus' arrival at Jerusalem appears totally out of character; such self-dramatisation is so far removed from the reluctance to speak of himself that he had shown hitherto. What does it tell us about him as he approached the city where he was shortly to die? It was clearly *not* the case that he harboured any secret hopes that Israel might yet welcome him now at last as their promised saviour. In the passage that immediately follows his account of Jesus' approach, Luke provides a unique and precious insight into his state of mind:

> *As he came near and saw the city, he wept over it, saying, 'If you, even you, had only recognized on this day the things that make for peace! But now they are hidden from your eyes. Indeed, the days will come upon you, when your enemies will set up ramparts around you and surround you, and hem you in on every side. They will crush you to the ground, you and your children within you, and they will not leave within you one stone upon another; because you did not recognize the time of your visitation from God.' (Luke 19:41-44)*

This, after all, was Jerusalem, the city of God, and as a faithful Israelite, how could he not grieve to see it so far removed from its high calling that its temple could only be described as a 'den of robbers'? According to John's Gospel, Jesus had visited the city on several occasions during his ministry, only to be challenged and impugned each time by hostile representatives of the religious establishment. And how could he not be distressed at the events that would befall it within a generation as a result of its fallen condition?

But if such was the case, why the dramatic, kingly gesture? It might be that he wished to provide this enacted testimony to his identity as a last witness against the city and its people, as if to make their rejection of him the more flagrant. I wonder, though, whether there were not other, more personal motives behind the gesture. For three years he had not permitted himself to talk publicly about his identity, allowing those who met him to draw conclusions from his teaching, his actions and his character, however much he may have wished at times to speak plainly. But these must have been deeply emotional moments for him – as the lament over Jerusalem makes apparent – and he must have felt the overwhelming need to reveal himself. It was a truth that could not, must not be concealed for ever; his words at the close of Luke's account of these events points in that direction: '... *if these were silent, the stones would shout out'* (Luke 19:39). And so his arrival at Jerusalem becomes something like a public version of the Transfiguration – revealing and challenging to others, deeply reassuring and satisfying to Jesus himself.

But it would be wrong to view these events as a mere gesture; Jesus was not just asserting his status in a vain act of defiance against the city and against the entrenched powers that were bent on his destruction. It was an assertion – that, though now he was to die, there would come a time when he would approach as king and be welcomed as saviour. It was essentially a prophetic act, looking to the moment when mankind, including Israel, would greet him with the words from Psalm 118 that the crowds used on this occasion:

> *This is the Lord's doing;*
> *it is marvellous in our eyes.*
> *This is the day that the Lord has made;*
> *let us rejoice and be glad in it.*
> *Save us, we beseech you, O Lord!*
> *O Lord, we beseech you, give us success!*
> *Blessed is the one who comes in the name of the Lord.*
> *We bless you from the house of the Lord. (Psalm 118:23-26)*

All the Gospels include in their account of the crowd's behaviour words closely resembling the first line of v. 26, while all but Luke mention the word 'hosanna', which is essentially a transliteration of the Hebrew of the 'Save us' or 'Save now' in v. 25, though by the time of Jesus the word is thought to have become a cry of triumph parallel to 'hallelujah'. Like the palm branches, its use is thought to have been associated more with the Feast of Tabernacles than with Passover. Some authorities think that the language of these verses originally referred to the idea of David leading the people to the house of God, which would account for the references to David in Matthew's and Mark's accounts.

For Jesus, though, these echoes of Psalm 118 must have brought to mind, if that was necessary, the preceding verses:

> *I shall not die, but I shall live,*
> *and recount the deeds of the Lord.*
> *The Lord has punished me severely,*
> *but he did not give me over to death.*
> *Open to me the gates of righteousness,*
> *that I may enter through them*
> *and give thanks to the Lord …*

From Caesarea Philippi to Jerusalem

> I thank you that you have answered me
>   and have become my salvation.
> The stone that the builders rejected
>   has become the chief cornerstone. (v. 17-22)

The cries of the crowd would thus have confirmed for him what lay immediately ahead was not to be the end, but only a beginning – that he would come through and that the triumphant arrival depicted in the psalm would one day be realised. The most obvious confirmation that Jesus viewed his arrival and the crowd's response in this light is seen in his defiant statement at the end of Matthew 23, where he takes up the cry with which he has been greeted and declares that it will be heard again, even from the lips of those who now oppose him: *'For I tell you, you will not see me again until you say, "Blessed is the one who comes in the name of the Lord"'* (Matt. 23:39).

One further detail of this episode remains to be noted: the three Synoptic Gospels, which have earlier foregrounded the disciples' lack of understanding and preoccupation with 'human things', now all suggest that it is the actions of the disciples in spreading their garments on the colt and, at least according to Luke, on the road before him, that trigger the crowd's acclamation – John focuses rather on the raising of Lazarus as the reason for the crowd's enthusiasm (John 12:17-18). In this way too, it is a remarkable moment: all the misunderstandings and reproaches, and, one may surmise, the moments of ill-feeling on the part of the disciples, are put to one side in this display of admiration, honour and reverence for their lord and master. They may have been uncomprehending at times and all too human in their aspirations, yet their loyalty to Jesus is unquestionable. His appreciation of this loyalty emerges later in Luke's record of the Last Supper: *'I have eagerly desired to eat this Passover with you before I suffer'* (Luke 22:15, 28). At this moment, though, the spectacle of his disciples at the heart of the 'welcoming party' must have added yet another strand to the swirl of conflicting emotions at this climactic moment in Jesus' ministry.

In Jerusalem

It was probably surprising to many, including the disciples, that, having arrived in kingly fashion, Jesus then made no effort to assert power over the city, to consult with the authorities, or to lead a popular uprising against the regime. He chose, clearly, to sleep outside the city, among friends in Bethany, presumably at the home of Martha, Mary and Lazarus, apparently returning to the city each day. The main focus of his activities in Jerusalem was the temple; Mark describes his first action, on the day of his spectacular entry, as if it were a kind of inspection: *'Then he entered Jerusalem and went into the temple; and when he had looked around at everything, as it was already late, he went out to Bethany with the twelve'* (Mark 11:11). And an inspection it was indeed: *'the Lord whom you seek will suddenly come to his temple'*, Malachi had said (3:1) – it was the 'visitation' implied by the use of the word *episkopē* in Luke 19:44, the word from which is derived, of course, the word *episkopos*, 'bishop' or 'overseer'. The cognate verb *episkeptomai* is used twice by Zechariah in his song of rejoicing (Luke 1:68, 78) and by the crowds in Luke 7:16; Israel did not realise that when God came to redeem them, as they hoped and believed, it of necessity involved a searching scrutiny too. If my suggestions in chapter 3 are correct, that scrutiny had begun much earlier, when Jesus had first come, aged twelve, but now he pronounced the result of his findings and his judgment:

> *And he entered the temple and began to drive out those who were selling and those who were buying in the temple, and he overturned the tables of the money changers and the seats of those who sold doves; and he would not allow anyone to carry anything through the temple. He was teaching and saying, 'Is it not written, "My house shall be called a house of prayer for all the nations"? But you have made it a den of robbers.'* (Mark 11:15-17)

Mark in particular gives the impression that the temple was effectively Jesus' base during the week leading up to his crucifixion. Maurice Casey argues that the phrase *'he would not allow anyone to carry anything through the temple'* in effect meant the interruption of all the trading and commercial activities from which the temple, and thus the Jewish hierarchy, obtained their vast wealth. It would, Casey suggests, have interrupted also the cultic activities in the temple, though it would not have prevented poor people from fulfilling their religious duties. As a result, the temple would for a short time have become what it was intended to be, a place of peace and worship; in particular, the outermost court, where much of the trading was done, would have been restored to its intended use as a place of prayer for Gentiles.[12] The authorities, the chief priests and the elders were, not surprisingly, outraged at Jesus' action; there is little doubt that it was this action, far more than the triumphal entry into the city, that decided the authorities finally that Jesus must die.

But Jesus' enthusiastic support among the poor made it at first impossible for them to take action against him: *'And when the chief priests and the scribes heard it, they kept looking for a way to kill him; for they were afraid of him, because the whole crowd was spellbound by his teaching'* (Mark 11:18). Unable to take action against Jesus directly, the various sections of the religious leadership

---

12   Casey, *Jesus of Nazareth*, pp. 411-415.

From Caesarea Philippi to Jerusalem

resorted to presumably concerted questioning of Jesus, probably in the hope of drawing from him answers that might be used to incriminate him in the eyes of both the authorities and the masses. There are three, or possibly four, such encounters: the question about authority (Mark 11:27-33 and parallels), the issue of paying taxes to Caesar (Mark 12:13-17 and parallels), the question about resurrection (Mark 12:18-27 and parallels), and, perhaps, the question about the greatest commandment, though this, at least according to Mark, may have come from a genuine desire on the part of a Pharisee (Matthew) or a scribe (Mark) to hear Jesus' opinion.

Jesus' replies are in all four cases masterly in their scriptural insight. However, in all but the last case he avoids responding directly to the question as put. This alerts us to the fact that in all four cases it was not simply a matter of differing or competing interpretations. It was firstly a question of 'authority', the issue raised in the first of these scenes; the scribes and Pharisees clearly saw Jesus as unqualified to teach, let alone interfere with temple arrangements, because he had not enjoyed a scribe's normal training – '… *when he has never been taught?'* (John 7:15). Jesus' implied response is the claim to derive his authority from a closer and more profound relationship with, and knowledge of, God. His answer to the Sadducees' question about resurrection must have enraged all his adversaries but actually sums up his critique of the Jewish 'authorities': *'Is not this the reason you are wrong, that you know neither the scriptures nor the power of God?'* (Mark 12:24).

The second issue arises out of the first and takes us back to the antithesis that Jesus referred to at Caesarea Philippi: the scribal interpretations all sat within the tradition of teaching and training that they had received – they belonged to the world as viewed through the prism of 'the human things'. Jesus' answers, by contrast, came from outside that tradition and were shaped by his affinity with, and understanding of, 'the divine things'. The antithesis is laid bare in the discussion about Roman taxes, where Jesus explicitly sets 'Caesar' over against God. Deny it though they might, the scribes, Pharisees and high priests were closer to Caesar than they were to God.

It is striking that after the first three controversies (Mark 11:27-12:27), Mark places the conversation with a Pharisee about the commandments, where we hear from Jesus the principle that governs his life and his way of understanding the Jewish scriptures:

Jesus answered, 'The first is, "Hear, O Israel: the Lord our God, the Lord is one; you shall love the Lord your God with all your heart, and with all your soul, and with all your mind, and with all your strength." The second is this, "You shall love your neighbour as yourself."' (Mark 12:29-31)

He then records Jesus' commentary on the series of disputes, in which he points to the essential underlying issue:

> 'How can the scribes say that the Messiah is the son of David? David himself, by the Holy Spirit, declared, "The Lord said to my Lord, 'Sit at my right hand, until I put your enemies under your feet." David himself calls him Lord; so how can he be his son?' (Mark 12:35-37)

The secret that runs through the whole of Mark's Gospel in particular, spoken, apart from two demoniacs, only by the voice from heaven at Jesus' baptism and at the Transfiguration, lies entirely outside the scope of scribal thinking. It is this, Jesus' sonship, that is the source of his understanding and his closeness to God, which are displayed to such brilliant effect in all his dealings with his adversaries. Yet even his disciples, those to whom it had been revealed, did not grasp its implications.

The Parable of the Wicked Tenants

It was after the first of these disputes with Jewish leaders that Jesus told his parable of the Wicked Tenants (Matt. 21:33-46; Mark 12:1-12; Luke 20:9-19). It offers an unparalleled insight into how Jesus viewed his ministry as far as his crucifixion, surpassing even the parable of the Sower and confirming a number of points that we have already considered:

- The parable places Jesus' coming firmly in the context of God's relationship with Israel. The figure of the vineyard and its description in Matt. 21:33 explicitly echo Isaiah's use of the same figure (Is. 5:1-2), where the metaphor is explained: 'For the vineyard of the LORD of hosts is the house of Israel, and the people of Judah are his pleasant planting) (v. 7).

- As in Isaiah's parable, Israel has been 'unfruitful' – it has not yielded what God expected of it: 'he expected justice, but saw bloodshed; righteousness, but heard a cry!' (v. 7) – the 'cry' probably refers to a cry for help of the oppressed and afflicted.

- Like Isaiah's parable, which focuses on the oppressive, exploitative conduct of the powerful in Judah, as the immediately following passage in Isaiah indicates, Jesus' parable is directed at the ruling elites in Israel. As Matthew says: 'When the chief priests and the Pharisees heard his parables, they realized that he was speaking about them' (v. 45). The phrase in Mark, 'the inheritance will be ours' (Mark 12:7), refers to a custom at that time which permitted tenants of an absentee landlord who had no heir, or whose heirs failed to register their claim to the property, to claim ownership for themselves.

From Caesarea Philippi to Jerusalem

Not that Israel's leaders would have seen it like that: they would argue that Israel was still God's people, subject to his law – but that would mean their continued control of Israel in accordance with their understanding, with the striving for power and eminence, the injustice and oppression that characterise 'the human things'.

- Though we must not press the detail of the story too far – the description of the owner's reaction (Matt. 21:41) should not be regarded as portrayal of a vengeful God – the parable confirms, within the constraints of the fictional narrative, what Jesus had already said in Luke 19:43-44 about the consequences of his rejection and about Jerusalem's and Israel's fate at the hands of the Romans.

- The other statement about the consequences, '... *and give the vineyard to others'* (Mark and Luke) or *'lease the vineyard to other tenants who will give him the produce at the harvest time'* (Matthew) should likewise be read with caution. Jesus is clearly not saying that the present set of rulers will simply be replaced by another. It is best understood in the terms of the gloss that Jesus provides in Matthew's version: *'the kingdom of God will be taken away from you and given to a people that produces the fruits of the kingdom'* (Matt. 21:43).

- Perhaps most important of all, Jesus here shows us how he saw himself. He implicitly breaks his secrecy surrounding his identity and identifies himself as a son who is sent by his father after all other means of calling back his rebellious people have failed. In Mark's and Luke's versions, Jesus echoes the words that he had heard at his baptism: *'a beloved son'* (Mark) or *'my beloved son'* (Luke); yet the father sends him on a dangerous mission – to men who have already maltreated or killed other servants – armed with nothing save the expectation that he will be 'respected' because he is the Son. As John expresses it in his Gospel *'God so loved the world that he gave his only son ... '*. And he, the Son, has accepted the mission: Father and Son are in agreement that the Son is to be his Father's servant, his *shaliach*, who comes for and as his Father. In sending him, the Father was making his ultimate appeal to rebellious human beings, not just with a prophet's words but with the person and the life of his Son.

- Jesus thus sees his mission as squarely in line with Israel's prophets, as he frequently suggests elsewhere. He confirms that his task was not to achieve any abstraction such as 'to conquer sin' or 'to die as a sacrifice' but, quite concretely, to call Israel and, by inference, all mankind back to God, risking his life to bring them his message of repentance, forgiveness and grace. Death would indeed be the immediate outcome, but while that would lead to disaster for the tenants, there would also be created a new people who would *'produce the fruits of the kingdom'*.

Preparing for the future

One can only be amazed by the way in which Jesus, facing so terrible an ordeal and fully aware of what was to come, was able to devote so much time and thought to the needs of his disciples, on whom would fall so great a task and responsibility – and this despite both past disappointments and the knowledge of future failures. His concern for them takes several forms: there is, first, the brief overview of the future that we call the Olivet Prophecy. It is anything but detailed: in Matthew's version, for example, it outlines broadly the kinds of events that the disciples will have to face, the same kinds of disasters of which human history is full (Matt. 24:4-14), before focusing on two major crises, the fall of Jerusalem (v. 15-22) and his return (v. 29-31).

How was Jesus able to predict the siege and fall of Jerusalem in AD 70 so accurately, both here and especially in Luke 19:41-44? It is easy simply to assert that this is an example of inspired prophetic foreknowledge. If we accept his unique status as divinely appointed Messiah and as Son of God, we are bound to accept the possibility of his possessing knowledge of future events such as other men do not have. However, it did not in fact require great prescience, especially for one as perceptive in his understanding of human motivations and impulses, to see that the tension between Jewish nationalism and Rome's determination to hold on to its power in what we now call the Middle East was likely to lead sooner or later to a Jewish uprising and a terrible Roman response. Jesus also perceived, I am sure, that the forces behind that nationalism, the usual human drives for self-preservation and self-aggrandisement, were the same impulses that drove the Jewish leaders' opposition to his call for repentance. There was thus an obvious link between his rejection and death at their hands and the uprising against Rome and its consequences. Nor did it take much privileged knowledge to predict what the outcome of that conflict would be like for the losers, any more than it would for modern readers to imagine the consequences of impending conflicts in our own world.

However, the essential key for understanding Jesus' predictions in Luke 19 and 21 is probably to be found at 21:22 *'these are days of vengeance, as a fulfilment of all that is written'*. His knowledge of the Old Testament not only told him that Israel and, specifically, Jerusalem would be conquered: it also provided terrible images of the fearful events that would accompany that

From Caesarea Philippi to Jerusalem

conquest. The dreadful predictions of Deuteronomy 28 might have been fulfilled in the Babylonian conquest in 586 BC, but Jesus could see that the definitive destruction and scattering still lay ahead and that the Romans were the *'nation from far away'* that would repeat or even surpass the fate meted out to Jerusalem by Nebuchadnezzar:

> *The* LORD *will bring a nation from far away, from the end of the earth, to swoop down on you like an eagle, a nation whose language you do not understand, a grim-faced nation showing no respect to the old or favour to the young. It shall consume the fruit of your livestock and the fruit of your ground until you are destroyed, leaving you neither grain, wine, and oil, nor the increase of your cattle and the issue of your flock, until it has made you perish. It shall besiege you in all your towns until your high and fortified walls, in which you trusted, come down throughout your land; it shall besiege you in all your towns throughout the land that the* LORD *your God has given you. (Deuteronomy 28:49-52)*

Moreover, the grim detail of what such a catastrophic conflict would entail could easily be imagined and thus predicted from the accounts found in the final chapters of 2 Kings, 2 Chronicles and Jeremiah, and also in Lamentations.[13]

In fact, though, Jesus stresses in the Olivet prophecy not so much the events but rather the need for watchfulness, for faithfulness and patience on the disciples' part – it is the pastoral rather than the prophetic dimension that predominates. The repeated use of the word 'watch' (*gregoreuo*) in both Matthew and Mark sums up the purpose of the entire discourse. According to Luke in particular, Jesus had already spoken repeatedly to his disciples about watchfulness. In Luke 17 he speaks of *'the day that the Son of Man is revealed'* (17:30), comparing it to the Flood and to the destruction of Sodom and Gomorrah; elsewhere, he does so through parables about servants awaiting the return of their masters (Luke 12:35-48; 19:11-27). These passages all presuppose a period, of unspecified length, during which he would no longer be with his disciples but during which they would have the task of forwarding his cause, after which he would return, assess their service, and reward those who had been faithful.

It is difficult to imagine what his disciples made of such teaching; there is no indication that they expected such a period of absence – as they had not been able to receive the message about Jesus' death, that is hardly surprising

---

13   This argument is made by C.H. Dodd in his 'The Fall of Jerusalem and "the Abomination of Desolation"', *Journal of Roman Studies* 37 (1947), pp. 47-54.

Jesus – yesterday, today, for ever

– and their talk about their places in his glory suggests a much more immediate expectation. Matthew, like Mark, holds back parables about Jesus' coming until the time in Jerusalem. Mark includes just one brief word picture (Mark 12:34), but Matthew has a series of parables, first that of the Wedding Feast (Matt. 22:1-14) and then the four parables in Matthew 24-25. It is not possible here to look at these parables in detail; it is noteworthy, though, that from a picture of servants being judged by their master (24:45-51), we move finally to a picture in the parable of the Sheep and the Goats, of people who have served without realising it or without specific command. They have behaved as he would – they have internalised his way of thinking, becoming men and women in his image as he is in the image of God, while he has become *the first-born among many brothers and sisters* (Rom. 8:29, *Christian Standard Bible*).

As usual, John's Gospel presents Jesus' way of preparing his disciples for his absence in quite a different manner. The 'discourses' of Jesus in John 13-16, followed by his prayer in chapter 17, are quite without parallel in the Synoptic Gospels, yet one must suppose they reflect in some way things that Jesus said to his followers in the time leading up to his crucifixion, albeit developed and extended by John in the light of Christians' experiences and struggles later in the first century. In these discourses, the disciples' incomprehension regarding Jesus' forthcoming absence is much more frankly depicted, as is Jesus' awareness of it. We shall have more to say about the discourses in John in the next chapter, in the context of the crucifixion itself.

We quoted earlier in this chapter, as evidence of Jesus' determination to retain control of events even when apparently reduced to the status of a victim, Jesus' words from John 10: *'For this reason the Father loves me, because I lay down my life in order to take it up again. No one takes it from me, but I lay it down of my own accord'* (John 10:17-18). We cannot leave the question of the 'preparation' of the disciples without referring to their sequel. Chapters 13-16 of John begin with the most powerful and unforgettable symbolic action by which Jesus sought to impress upon them the 'Caesarea Philippi principle' as the epitome of the new way to which they were being called. All readers of the New Testament are surely familiar with the account of the washing of the disciples' feet. It was a deeply symbolic action:

> *Jesus knew that the Father had put all things under his power … so he got up from the meal, took off his outer clothing, and wrapped a towel around his waist. After that, he poured water into a basin and began to wash his disciples' feet, drying them with the towel that was wrapped around him … When he had finished washing their feet, he put on his clothes and returned to his place. 'Do you understand what I have done for you?' he asked them.*

From Caesarea Philippi to Jerusalem

> *'You call me 'Teacher' and 'Lord,' and rightly so, for that is what I am. Now that I, your Lord and Teacher, have washed your feet, you also should wash one another's feet. I have set you an example that you should do as I have done for you. Very truly I tell you, no servant is greater than his master, nor is a messenger greater than the one who sent him. Now that you know these things, you will be blessed if you do them. (John 13:3-5, 12-17)*

The action was clearly intended by Jesus to provide a vivid, memorable illustration of the principle of non-hierarchical, mutual service which he wished to prevail in the future community of his followers. Not looking after oneself, nor seeking to 'gain the whole world' would be its distinguishing mark, as he points out in v. 13-17. But beneath the surface lay an additional sense which John is careful to point out to us: when he writes in v. 4 that he *'took off his outer clothing'*, he uses the same verb *tithemi* that also occurs in the words back in John 10:17 when Jesus says that he will 'lay down' his life. Similarly, when Jesus *'put on his clothes'* (v. 12), John uses the verb *lambano*, just as in 10:17: 'take it up again'. So the model that Jesus puts before his disciples here for imitation is that of the ultimate form of 'service' – nothing less than laying down his life for his followers. But not only laying it down, but also 'taking it again' – here was the 'Caesarea Philippi principle' in action: losing one's life and thereby gaining it.

We are here, manifestly, well beyond the story of Jesus' ministry that the Synoptic Gospels seek to relate, and we shall need to look further at the discourses later, when we attempt to think about Jesus 'today', the risen, exalted Lord. Yet they do, surely, reflect, in John's own special way, Jesus' evident care for his bewildered, frightened disciples in those last few days in Jerusalem, a city probably not well known to this group of men and women from Galilee, who must have been wondering what they had got themselves into and where it was all leading. It seems most unlikely that he would have spoken to them only of terrifying events on the world stage, of future responsibilities and judgment. Whether the actual words are his or John's, his talk with them must have included something like what John records: *'I do not give to you as the world gives. Do not let your hearts be troubled, and do not let them be afraid'* (John 14:27).

Chapter 8

The Passion – and After

The accounts of Jesus' suffering and death are the most detailed sections of the Gospels; they are also more similar to each other than any other sections – it is widely thought that they may all have drawn upon a record of events that was made very early on after Jesus' ascension. They are also, and with good reason, the most intensively studied sections, for they contain a series of events of vital importance to Christian faith: the Last Supper, Jesus' prayer and arrest in Gethsemane, his trial, the roles played by Peter and Judas, and, of course, the crucifixion itself. The accounts of the resurrection and after are in a different category, for they differ widely from each other. I shall look at them in the next chapter – they belong, in any case, to the new world of 'today' that comes into being with Jesus' new life.

Given the amount of detail in these accounts and their crucial importance, in both senses, it is not possible here to deal with them all in depth. I shall be trying to focus, as I have throughout, on Jesus himself as the Gospels portray him and on his role in events of decisive significance for the saving purpose of God, through which Jesus himself moves from the 'yesterday' of mortal human life to the 'today' of participation in the life of God after his resurrection. Rather than following the course of events chronologically, we shall be looking at aspects of Jesus' conduct – first, at his relation to the authorities who arrest and try him, then at his behaviour towards his disciples, Israel and the world, and finally at Jesus himself, at his inner life, as far as it can be surmised, and his relationship to his Father.

The authorities

From the moment of his arrest, Jesus is no longer a free agent; one indication of this is the recurrent use, no less than fifteen times in Matthew 26-27, of the verb *paradidomi* ('betray' or 'hand over'); Jesus is first betrayed by Judas, then 'delivered' by the soldiers to the Jewish authorities, who in turn 'hand him over' to Pilate, who finally 'delivers him' to the soldiers who will carry out the crucifixion. The change is also indicated by the very syntax of the nar-

The Passion – and After

rative: hitherto, Jesus has been the main mover of the events in the Gospels and is accordingly the subject of many of the verbs. But with his arrest, he suddenly becomes the object, to whom things are done, as the following passage illustrates:

> *So he released Barabbas for them; and after **flogging Jesus**, he **handed him over** to be crucified. Then the soldiers of the governor **took Jesus** into the governor's headquarters, and they gathered the whole cohort around him. They **stripped him** and **put** a scarlet robe **on him**, and after twisting some thorns into a crown, they **put it on his head**. They **put a reed in his right hand** and knelt before him and **mocked him**, saying, 'Hail, King of the Jews!' They **spat on him**, and took the reed and **struck him** on the head. After **mocking him**, they **stripped him** of the robe and **put his own clothes on him**. Then they **led him** away to crucify him. (Matthew 27:26-31)*

To all of this Jesus submitted, apparently with no attempt at resistance; as the Servant passages predicted, he *'gave [his] back to those who struck me, and [his] cheeks to those who pulled out the beard; [he] did not hide [his] face from insult and spitting'* (Is. 50:6).

Yet that verb '**gave** his back' is a clue to what is really happening: though overtly passive, Jesus was active still. If he was in the hands of the authorities, it was because he invited his own arrest, first by coming to Jerusalem, and in so public a manner, then by taking dramatic action against the misuse of the temple, and finally by going to Gethsemane despite being aware that Judas would know where to find him. We recall the words quoted in the previous chapter: *'No one takes it [my life] from me, but I lay it down of my own accord. I have power to lay it down, and I have power to take it up again. I have received this command from my Father'* (John 10:18). John draws attention to Jesus' active role in these events when he describes him setting out for Golgotha: *'Carrying **his own** cross, he went out to the place of the Skull'* (John 19:17).

There are some discrepancies between the Gospels' accounts of the 'trials' that Jesus was subjected to – 'trials' because none of them is, properly speaking, a trial in the modern sense of the term. *Matthew* and *Mark* both speak of some kind of informal interrogation at night by Caiaphas and others of the 'chief priests' and the 'Council', i.e. the Sanhedrin, at which the decision to seek Jesus' execution is taken (Matt. 26:57-68; Mark 14:53-65). That decision was then rubber-stamped early the following morning by the whole Council, formally constituted (Matt. 27:1-2; Mark 15:1-2). *Luke* reports that Jesus was brought to the High Priest's house but makes no mention of any deliberations there; he confines himself to a very brief account of the Council proceedings the next morning (Luke 22:66-71) – writing, as he was, for a Gentile audience, Luke perhaps decided to focus almost solely on the trial before Pilate, though he does include, alone among the Gospel writers, Jesus' brief and essentially pointless appearance before Herod, who was in Jerusalem at the time. *John's* account is different in two ways: he says that Jesus was first taken to the house of the ex-high priest Annas, the father-in-law of the present incumbent, Caiaphas (John 18:12-14, 19-23). Only then is he sent to Caiaphas himself and thus to Pilate (18:24, 28) – with no mention of a formal sitting of the Council or any decision by the Jewish authorities. This is perhaps best explained by the fact that John is interested, not in the outward, visible aspect of things, but in their inner truth – and for him, the decision to seek Jesus' death had long since been taken, after the raising of Lazarus:

> *Then the chief priests and the Pharisees called a meeting of the Sanhedrin. 'What are we accomplishing?' they asked. 'Here is this man performing many miraculous signs. If we let him go on like this, everyone will believe in him, and then the Romans will come and take away both our place and our nation.' Then one of them, named Caiaphas, who was high priest that year, spoke up, 'You know nothing at all! You do not realise that it is better for you that one man die for the people than that the whole nation perish' ... So from that day on they plotted to take his life. (John 11:47-53)*

Brief and slightly confusing as these accounts are, they are highly dramatic. The drama does not lie solely in what happens – the outcome of the trials – but above all in the encounter between Jesus and the powers that be, or rather, were. Jesus is confronted in turn by the supreme Jewish authorities, by king (or tetrarch) Herod Antipas, the puppet-ruler of Galilee and Perea, and by Pilate, the representative of the most powerful man in the ancient world at that time, Caesar Augustus. In one sense, it is 'no contest': Jesus is powerless before their juridical, political and military power. But on another level, the trials bring together, face-to-face, two worlds, the two contrasted value-systems that Jesus first identified at Caesarea Philippi. Caiaphas, Herod, and Pilate are the very embodiment of 'the human things', or as John puts it, 'the world', and the Gospel narratives allow us to see their pragmatic, not to say cynical, calculation of political and personal advantage.

'The world' reveals itself in a variety of forms: Caiaphas' choice for political expediency in order to save, as he thinks, Jewish national existence and religious heritage, and, of course, his own favourable position within them (John 11:50); the chief priests' manipulation of the crowd and ruthless blackmailing of Pilate (Matt. 27:20; John 19:12); Herod's reduction of his judicial and

The Passion – and After

political powers to mere curiosity (Luke 23:8); Pilate's choice of political and personal expediency against the claims of principle and justice (Matt. 27:24; Mark 15:15; Luke 23:24; John 19:12). It also reveals itself in less sophisticated ways: in the fickleness of the crowd, and the casual cruelty and mockery of the soldiers, who are just 'carrying out orders'. Sad to say, two of Jesus' own followers become caught up in a similar way of behaving: Judas by deliberate decision, for whatever reason, and Peter in moments of weakness, when fear, so much a theme in Mark, and the same impulse for self-preservation which had earned Jesus' rebuke at Caesarea Philippi, assert themselves against all his protestations of undying loyalty. Over against all this stands Jesus, resolved to 'lose his life' for the gospel's sake, in obedience to his Father's will and for the saving of men and women.

Apart from the lack of any specific charge against Jesus, the most striking feature of the trials as related in the Synoptic Gospels is the almost complete absence of dialogue. Jesus remains silent in face of various dubious witness statements and speaks only when required, under oath, according to Matthew, to respond to the question whether or not he is *'the Christ, the Son of the Blessed One'* (Mark 14:61). To this Jesus replies: *'I am … And you will see the Son of Man sitting at the right hand of the Mighty One and coming on the clouds of heaven'* (Mark 14:62). Essentially the same thing happens in Matthew and Luke too, though in a somewhat different order in Luke.

Jesus' reply is all the more striking in view of the silence that he has maintained not only during the questioning but through his ministry, as stressed particularly by Mark. It is worth quoting here the comments of Rowan Williams:

> Jesus before the High Priest has no leverage in the world; he is denuded of whatever power he might have had. Stripped and bound before the court, he has no stake in how the world organizes itself. He is definitively outside the system of the world's power and the language of power. He is going to die, because that is what the world has decided. It is at this moment and this moment only that he speaks plainly about who he is. He names himself with the name of the God of Israel, 'I am', and tells the court that they will see the Human One [i.e. the Son of Man] seated at God's right hand, coming in judgement. Humanity does not live in this world of insane authorities, but with God. When God's judgement arrives, it will be the unveiling of a true human face as opposed to the masks and caricatures of the High Priest's world.[1]

---

1 Rowan Williams, *Christ on Trial. How the Gospel Unsettles our Judgement*, London 2000,

Jesus – yesterday, today, for ever

It is, in other words, 'the time for truth', as Williams calls it. The only other utterances of Jesus recorded by the Synoptics have to do, precisely, with the possibility or impossibility of speaking truth in the language of the world: '*You have said so*', he says to Caiaphas (Matt. 26:64), or, more fully, in Luke: '*If I tell you, you will not believe; and if I question you, you will not answer*', and then, when the question is repeated: '*You say that I am*' (Luke 22:67-70). Williams explains Jesus' silence and these few utterances like this:

> How, in such a world, could there be a language in which it could truly be said who Jesus is? Whatever is said will take on the colouring of the world's insanity; it will be another bid for the world's power, another identification with the unaccountable tyrannies that decide how things shall be. Jesus, described in the words of this world, would be a competitor for space in it, part of its untruth.[2]

Before Pilate the pattern is the same. Jesus remains silent, save when asked directly whether he is 'the king of the Jews', to which, in all three Synoptic Gospels, Jesus gives a two-word answer that again focuses on what happens to truth in the worlds of one such as Pilate: '*You say so*' (Mark 15:3).

As so often, John's account apparently differs widely from the others but in fact presents, in probably imagined words, things that remain unspoken in the others. We have already noted that John includes no hearing before Jewish authorities, but his version of Jesus' appearance before Pilate articulates precisely those issues that we have identified in the other Gospels. When Pilate asks Jesus whether he is 'the king of the Jews', the charge that has been brought against him, he replies: '*My kingdom is not from this world. If my kingdom were from this world, my followers would be fighting to keep me from being handed over to the Jews. But as it is, my kingdom is not from here*' (John 18:36). In saying this, Jesus confirms the fundamental contrast between 'the world' (in John's language), organised in accordance with 'the human things', and the 'kingdom of God', the realm of 'the divine things', of which Jesus is the future head and its present embodiment, here in the dangerous world of men.

The following exchange illustrates the other issue that we have identified. Pilate, failing to understand what Jesus is saying, hears only the word 'king' and points out its unreality in the world as at present constituted: '*Your own nation and the chief priests have handed you over to me*' (v. 35). To this Jesus replies that kingship, in Pilates's sense, is no part of his mission; rather, '*For

---

p. 6-7.

2 *Ibid.*, p. 6.

The Passion – and After

this I was born, and for this I came into the world, to testify to the truth. Everyone who belongs to the truth listens to my voice' (v. 37) – the 'this' at the beginning of this quotation points forward to *'to testify to the truth'*, not back to the previous phrase *'You say that I am a king'*. To this Pilate replies with the weary cynicism of politicians everywhere: *'What is truth?'*.[3] His disregard for justice, demonstrated in his bending to Jewish blackmail, and his concern for his own position, confirms that truth is of little account in his thinking and practice.

In their further brief exchange in John 19, a similar 'dialogue of the deaf' takes place: Pilate attempts to pressurise Jesus into explaining and defending himself, appealing to just that self-interest that Jesus has renounced: *'Do you refuse to speak to me? Do you not know that I have power to release you, and power to crucify you?'* (19:10). Jesus' reply to this is somewhat enigmatic: *'You would have no power over me unless it had been given you from above; therefore the one who handed me over to you is guilty of a greater sin'* (19:11).[4] It is, I think, perhaps the most deflating thing that Jesus could have said: that far from being the arbiter of life and death, as he claims to be, Pilate is actually no more than a small cog in the great interlocking machinery of individual self-interests that make up the world of men.

And so 'justice' takes its course; Pilate yields to the pressure and 'hands over' Jesus for crucifixion. And Jesus, *'carrying the cross by himself'*, makes his way to Golgotha, doubtless already weakened and bloodstained, yet dignified and spiritually upright, the only true, whole man in all these shameful events. With that, the world has done its worst, and we hear virtually nothing more of the authorities' actions, apart from Matthew's account of the watch that is set at the grave and the subsequent story of the stolen body (Matt. 27:62-66; 28:11-15).

The disciples

We have seen that at Jesus' trials, the fundamental issue was not anything that he might have *done*, but who he *was* – his identity. That is also the fundamental question in relation to all the other participants in these events, all of whom are revealed in their 'worldliness'. Jesus is remarkably without rancour

---

3   Various alternative senses of this phrase have been offered, but there is, it seems to me, no escape from the obvious – the doubting of any meaning or value to the notion of truth in the world of *Realpolitik*. This sense is confirmed, it seems to me, both by the question's surrounding language in the other Gospels and by Pilate's subsequent behaviour. The behaviour of many present-day political leaders reminds us that little has changed in the intervening centuries!

4   Perhaps Jesus does also imply that the prior responsibility lies with the Jewish leaders, 'the Jews' as he calls them, those 'blind leaders of the blind'.

Jesus – yesterday, today, for ever

towards all of them; he appears to speak calmly, if searchingly, to Pilate; he even begs forgiveness for the soldiers crucifying him – and perhaps others too (Luke 23:34).

The question about identity is put in sharper fashion to Jesus' disciples. This is most obviously the case with Peter: Mark, in one of his characteristic 'sandwich' constructions, cuts between the questioning of Jesus, including his affirmation of his identity, and Peter's ordeal at the hands of his questioners, ending, of course, in the triple denial of his identity. The juxtaposition could not be clearer: *"Are you the Messiah, the Son of the Blessed One?" ... "I am"'* and *"'Certainly you are one of them; for you are a Galilean." ... "I do not know this man you are talking about"'* (Mark 14:61-62, 70-71). But in fact, all the disciples, not just Peter, had deserted him, according to Matthew and Mark, seeking to 'save their life' by obeying the instinct for self-preservation that is the epitome of 'the human things'. This desertion, and the betrayal that it implied – and that was exhibited by Peter – must have been exceedingly painful to Jesus, foreknown though it was (Mark 14:27); not only had they spent many months together and shared all kinds of experience, but he had lavished time and care on them, trying to teach them to share his ways. When he arrived in Jerusalem, they had touchingly displayed their loyalty and their enthusiasm for him, but less than a week later, in Gethsemane, he had reproached them for their inability to stay awake with him during his time of greatest anguish: *'Simon, are you asleep? Could you not keep awake one hour? ... Are you still sleeping and taking your rest?'* (Mark 14:37, 41). Peter's denial in particular, though he had predicted it, must have been more painful even than Judas' betrayal, yet Jesus appears to respond to it with only a probably reproachful glance (Luke 22:61). So now Jesus was left alone, 'handed over' to the tender mercies of his enemies; the words of Psalm 69 may well reflect his feelings: *'I looked for pity, but there was none; and for comforters, but I found none'* (Ps. 69:20).

John, however, tells us that Jesus, even in the hour of his arrest, sought to spare his disciples any part in his fate: *"I told you that I am he. So if you are looking for me, let these men go." This was to fulfil the word that he had spoken, "I did not lose a single one of those whom you gave me"'* (John 18:8-9). These words, attributed to Jesus at this of all moments, are testimony to his sense of responsibility for them, as a shepherd for his flock (cf. Mark 14:27; John 10:1-18, 27-28). They also point to something else, however: his certainty that there was a future for these disciples, despite his present plight and their seeming weakness – that there would be a community of believers which would result from their future loyalty to him and their continuation of his

The Passion – and After

work. God desires many children, not just one, and the realisation of that intention depended not only on him, but also on these apparently inadequate disciples.[5]

Nor was it simply a question of creating a body of adherents who would receive and believe his teaching. His own task had been to proclaim the grace of God and the possibility of rebirth to a new life, as he had done in the Nazareth synagogue, and that same message now had to be spread more widely – and for this, more was needed than simply passive recipients of his message. It would need men and women who would proclaim it, not only with their words, but with the whole of themselves, with their lives and, if necessary, with their deaths, as he was about to do. Jesus sums this up in his prayer: *'As you have sent me into the world, so I have sent them into the world'* (John 17:18).

It was the most challenging task imaginable. We saw in the previous chapter how Jesus endeavoured to prepare them for what lay ahead, and he continued to do that even during the last hours of his mortal existence. He was profoundly aware of the enormity of the responsibility that would fall upon his disciples and of the pressures to which they would be exposed from a largely indifferent or hostile world, even after they had recovered from the fear that would shortly cause them to flee in the face of danger – he had already seen with his own eyes how easily they became fearful. His care for them is seen in many ways: his acceptance of Mary's extravagant gesture of love and his rejection of any criticism of her (Mark 14:3-9; John 12:1-8), his reassurance to Peter that though he will fail the test that lies ahead, he will not be rejected but will be enabled to 'turn again' (Luke 22:32), and, of course, his concern for his mother in his dying moments (John 19:26-27).

One thing he could not do, however: he could not speak to them of his own courage in the face of the prospect of arrest and a terrible death, though he would, of course, offer them that supreme example. We see its power only later, not only in Acts, where they display a courage not unlike his, but also in Peter's words, written much later, in which he may well be alluding to his own personal failure and the chance that he had been given to 'turn again' – 'return' in the final line (*epistrepho*) is the same word that Jesus uses in Luke 22:32:

> For to this you have been called, because Christ also suffered for you, leaving you an example, so that you should follow in his steps. He committed no sin, and no deceit was found in his mouth. When he was abused, he did

---

5   See Hebrews 2:5-18.

*not return abuse; when he suffered, he did not threaten; but he entrusted himself to the one who judges justly. He himself bore our sins in his body on the cross, so that, free from sins, we might live for righteousness; by his wounds you have been healed. For you were going astray like sheep, but now you have **returned** to the shepherd and guardian of your souls. (1 Peter 2:21-25)*

It is above all in the 'discourses' of Jesus in John 13-16, followed by his prayer in chapter 17, that we see evidence of Jesus' attempts to prepare his disciples for the future. What these utterances show above all is his awareness of their fallibility – he had experienced it, of course, within himself, although we see so little of it – and of his efforts to counter it. In these discourses, the disciples' incomprehension regarding Jesus' forthcoming absence is much more frankly depicted, as is Jesus' awareness of it. He is also conscious of the rivalries and jealousies that existed among them; they had become so apparent after the Transfiguration and persisted even in the last hours before his death (Luke 22:24). The teaching that he gave them in his last hours, at least according to John, is obviously intended to counter such tendencies; he repeatedly bids them 'love one another' – not just 'love', but *'love as I have loved you'* (John 13:34). Jesus trusted in the transforming power of what they were to witness in the next few days – we shall return to this at the end of this chapter. He also gives them a simple yet unforgettable picture of what they should be, a single vine taking its life and its character from him, the stem (John 15).

Nor was it only a matter of words; he enacted before them what such love means when he washed their feet – an unforgettable experience that was surely more powerful than any words or metaphors could be, no matter how eloquent. His action epitomised the love and care for each other rather than for self that Jesus sought to inculcate in them. It also presented a model of what they were henceforth to be: a community without hierarchy, where there is no 'least' and no 'greatest'.

What else could he offer them to encourage and support them? He does not talk here, as he does in the parables in Matthew 24-25, for example, about servants working for their master and encountering his scrutiny on his return. Instead, the focus is precisely on the time following his 'departure'; Jesus offers them perhaps the most precious thing that they could hear: the promise of his own presence with them. He would not 'leave them as orphans' but would 'come to them' (John 14:18). So it would not be an empty time, characterised by absence; rather, they would enjoy a new, richer relationship with him, their Lord, and with each other, symbolised in the figure of the vine that we have already referred to. For, though he would have 'gone away' or 'gone

The Passion – and After

to the Father', he would not be absent but would be with them through the Spirit; he would dwell with and in them and they in him. It wouldn't be 'quite like old times' because he would not be visibly present – it would be even better! They would have the support of an almighty Jesus, sharing in the divine life and with all the authority and power of the Father (John 16:7) – *and* the certainty that their prayers would be heard (John 14:13-14; 15:7; 16:23). It would bring persecution, certainly – 'the world' would hate them as it hated him – but despite that they would have joy and peace in him that none could take from them.

And finally, in John 17, Jesus prays before them, allowing them for the first time to 'eavesdrop' on his communion with his Father and, in doing so, initiates them into it. Jesus permits his disciples to hear a prayer in which their unity and mutual love is the subject of conversation and petition between the Son with the Father – that is how important it is! Their loving unity will be, he says, the most powerful witness to the world around of the truth of Jesus: *'I ask not only on behalf of these, but also on behalf of those who will believe in me through their word, that they may all be one. As you, Father, are in me and I am in you, may they also be in us, so that the world may believe that you have sent me'* (John 17:20-21).

The Last Supper

There is one further gift that Jesus gave to his disciples – perhaps the best of them all. On the evening before his arrest, trial and death, he gathered his disciples, possibly just the twelve, but probably more, including the women who had come with them from Galilee – can one imagine that he would have excluded them? – for a meal together.[6] It may or may not have been a Passover meal: the Synoptics imply that it was, while John's chronology makes that impossible; but whether it was or not, it took place during the Passover season and may well have included elements that belonged to the traditional Passover meal. There are slightly inconclusive references to Passover in Mark and Matthew's accounts (Mark 14:12; Matt. 26:17), whereas Luke says that Jesus began by saying: *'I have eagerly desired to eat this Passover with you before I suffer'* (Luke 22:15). This is still not quite as conclusive as it looks – Jesus may have meant something like 'this is my new version of Passover'. Certainly, Jesus made it a kind of Passover, exploiting the traditions that must have been in everyone's mind in order to create, it seems, a new rite for his followers that would symbolise a new and better 'release' for his followers. In doing so, he

---

6 Matthew appears to say that only 'the Twelve' were present, but his phrase *'he took his place with the twelve'* (Matt. 26:20) leaves open the possibility that others were present too.

Jesus – yesterday, today, for ever

gave them something that every united body of human beings seems to need: a ceremony or rite that symbolised the things that drew them together and confirmed their new collective identity. It was a rite that would recall for ever both Jesus, the master and lord of the new community, and the remarkable saving action out of which the community was born.

But what, exactly, did Jesus intend the simple ceremony, using no meat but only bread and wine, to mean for his disciples? Though there was no meat – which makes one wonder whether it could have been a real Passover meal – Jesus' words and actions make a distinction between the flesh and the blood, just as was done with all animal sacrifices. So it is likely that his followers would have understood his words within the framework of traditional practices involving animal sacrifices. The most basic sense, therefore, has to do with Jesus' self-giving in death; in Luke's account, Jesus says, as he divides the bread: *'This is my body, which is **given** for you'* (Luke 22:19).

Might, then, Jesus have intended his disciples to relate his impending death to any of the sacrifices described in Leviticus? His words in Matthew, where he says of the wine that it represents his blood which is *'poured out for many for the forgiveness of sins'* (Matt. 26:28), might lead us to conclude that Jesus wished them to see a parallel with the Levitical sin offerings, as though it was by his death that forgiveness was secured for human beings – a widely held view. But we have seen, as we have followed the story of Jesus' life, that he has been promising and granting forgiveness right from the start, specifically right from the healing of the paralytic in Mark 2:5. The parables that we considered briefly in the previous chapter likewise run counter to such a notion.

An alternative possible link with the sacrifices prescribed by the Mosaic law is suggested by the fact that the disciples are invited to eat the bread that represents Jesus' body. There was, of course, a sacrifice in which the worshippers ate some of the flesh of their offering, the so-called 'peace offering' or 'fellowship offering', which could be offered as part of a vow, or as an expression of thanks, or simply from a desire to offer worship (see Lev. 7:11-18). As the names 'peace offering' or 'fellowship offering' both suggest, the inclusion within this particular rite of a shared meal – part for God, part for the offerer – symbolised a condition of peace or even friendship with God.

Such an idea finds confirmation in the two sets of associations evoked by Jesus' words as he invited the disciples to share the bread and wine. First, this meal took place at Passover, the feast which celebrated and recalled Israel's release from bondage in Egypt. We recall how Luke begins his account of Jesus' ministry: twice in his quotation from Isaiah 61 we find the word *aphesis*

The Passion – and After

('release'): *'He has sent me to proclaim **release** to the captives and recovering of sight to the blind, to **set at liberty** those who are oppressed ...'* (Luke 4:18). For Israel in Egypt, that release was achieved by the slaying of lambs and the use of its blood to distinguish the dwellings of the Israelites from the rest of Egypt. Jesus had long been proclaiming such a release, and many had already experienced it. In the original Passover, the blood that so distinguished the Israelites from others was derived from the death of animals. Jesus' mission, with its message of forgiveness, was not free of cost either; the hostility that Jesus had aroused was going shortly to take his life. But Father and Son were not to be deterred by such hostility or by the attempt to silence this gracious voice. In that sense, his death was the ultimate confirmation of the reality of his message of release, of the determination of God to free men and women from the sad condition in which they had placed themselves, even at the cost of his 'beloved son' – we remember the use of that phrase at his baptism, at the Transfiguration, and in the parable of the Tenants. So, sharing in bread and wine at this Passover season was comparable to being marked with the blood that ensured survival and release; it was a way of declaring that they belonged to the people that would enjoy the saving that Jesus had brought and was about to confirm in the most solemn way known to humanity.

The other set of associations are evoked by the words that Jesus uses in all three Synoptic Gospels: *'This is my blood of the covenant, which is poured out for many'* (Mark 14:24). The idea that the solemn, binding nature of a covenant, treaty or agreement should be confirmed by using blood, the most precious thing known to man, was well known in the ancient world. We find an early example in Genesis 15, where God makes a covenant with Abraham, confirming it by passing between the two halves of slain animals:

> *He said to him, 'Bring me a heifer three years old, a female goat three years old, a ram three years old, a turtledove, and a young pigeon.' He brought him all these and cut them in two, laying each half over against the other; but he did not cut the birds in two ... When the sun had gone down and it was dark, a smoking fire pot and a flaming torch passed between these pieces. On that day the LORD made a covenant with Abram, saying, 'To your descendants I give this land, from the river of Egypt to the great river, the river Euphrates ...' (Genesis 15:9-18)*

We find another reference to this practice in Jeremiah 34:18.

However, the words of Jesus at the Last Supper surely evoke in particular the sealing of the covenant between God and Israel at Sinai, where the blood of animals was smeared both on the altar, representing God, and on the elders

215

who represented Israel:

Moses took half of the blood and put it in basins, and half of the blood he dashed against the altar. Then he took the book of the covenant, and read it in the hearing of the people; and they said, 'All that the LORD has spoken we will do, and we will be obedient.' Moses took the blood and dashed it on the people, and said, 'See the blood of the covenant that the LORD has made with you in accordance with all these words.' (Exodus 24:6-8)

It becomes clear that the symbolism of the Last Supper reflects the sequence of events in Exodus: having released his people from their bondage, God then makes a covenant with them, the beginning of a lasting relationship of friendship and fellowship. It is no accident that the immediately following verses tell that the leaders of Israel then had some kind of vision of God – and survived. They also shared food.

Then Moses and Aaron, Nadab, and Abihu, and seventy of the elders of Israel went up, and they saw the God of Israel. Under his feet there was something like a pavement of sapphire stone, like the very heaven for clearness. God did not lay his hand on the chief men of the people of Israel; also they beheld God, and they ate and drank. (Exodus 24:9-11)

It is not difficult here to recognise both the principle and the rituals of the 'peace offering': friendship between man and God, confirmed in a shared meal, which, as we have seen, is echoed in the Last Supper. What is unparalleled, however, is that the blood in which this new covenant is sealed and the food that is eaten, represent the body and blood of Jesus; God was, in effect, using the most precious thing that he had, his Son, in order to display his seriousness about his promise of release, forgiveness and peace – and Jesus was working together with his Father, allowing himself to be so used. Like the symbolism of the sealing of the Sinai covenant, then, the simple rite of the Last Supper expressed the utter commitment of Father and Son to the saving mission which had brought Jesus to this moment and to the death that was shortly to follow. So the symbolism did indeed point to a sacrifice – but not to one made in order to secure forgiveness. It spoke rather of self-sacrifice on the part of both Father and Son in order to persuade men and women of their need of such forgiveness, to prove beyond all doubt its reality, and to appeal to them, at the deepest possible level, to accept the grace and the 'friendship' that God was offering. The different layers of meaning are perhaps best summed up by Paul:

The Passion – and After

> *All this is from God, who reconciled us to himself through Christ, and has given us the ministry of reconciliation; that is, in Christ God was reconciling the world to himself, not counting their trespasses against them, and entrusting the message of reconciliation to us. So we are ambassadors for Christ, since God is making his appeal through us; we entreat you on behalf of Christ, be reconciled to God. (2 Corinthians 5:18-20)*

We must not overlook, however, the other, complementary dimension. At Sinai, Moses read out to the people the 'book of the covenant', in other words, the terms and guarantees that it provided for. But the covenant could not be sealed until the people respond: *'All that the LORD has spoken we will do, and we will be obedient'*. They too must commit themselves. So it was, manifestly, at the Last Supper: to sit with Jesus in friendship, all past errors and follies notwithstanding, as the disciples did, was a remarkable privilege, and they must have sensed the solemnity of what was happening. They too were binding themselves – but to what?

There was obviously, in the first place, the sense of belonging to and with Jesus and to the community of his followers. But there are, perhaps, two other ways in which the Gospels help us to see the nature of the commitment. First, the parallel to the book of the Law read at Sinai is best summed up in the words of Jesus, already quoted, in the discourses in John: *'If you keep my commandments, you will abide in my love, just as I have kept my Father's commandments and abide in his love ... This is my commandment, that you love one another as I have loved you'* (John 15:10, 12). But we need also to go back to those decisive moments at Caesarea Philippi: *'If any want to become my followers, let them deny themselves and take up their cross and follow me. For those who want to save their life will lose it, and those who lose their life for my sake, and for the sake of the gospel, will save it'* (Mark 8:34-35). The actions that Jesus performed with the bread and the wine and the words that he spoke were the signs that he was about to realise this principle by giving himself, losing his life for the sake of the gospel. In eating and drinking with him, sharing in a symbolic act of fellowship, the disciples were in fact committing themselves to his way. Jesus was, in effect, saying that the Caesarea Philippi principle, as I have called it, was to be the mark of his new community and of the new humanity of which he was the prototype – all those other men and women beside himself who, thanks to his action, would be reborn, re-made 'in the image of God'.

Did the disciples understand anything of this kind at the time? That seems to me highly doubtful. Their non-understanding and bewilderment are all too apparent in the Gospels, and their flight at the time of Jesus' arrest shows how unready they were to share in Jesus' way. Only later, one supposes, did they gradually come to realise just what this simple rite implied in addition to its function as a reminder of him. I suspect that the words of Jesus that John attaches to the feeding of the 5,000 in his Gospel, virtually an exposition of the meaning of the Last Supper, are an example of that subsequent developing understanding. By his action on the eve of his crucifixion, Jesus ensured that his self-giving, its meaning, and its implications for themselves, became the focal point of his followers' faith and worship. That 'the Lord's Supper', this permanent reminder of Jesus at the supreme moment of his life, at the point where all the words were about to become terrible, amazing reality, began to be observed so soon and so spontaneously is the surest evidence of the depth of the impression that this evening left in the hearts and minds of his first followers.

'It is finished' – Jesus and his suffering

At the centre of the events of that Passover festival stands Jesus, apparently the still point amid all the turmoil of those final hours. Compared with any modern retellings of the story, especially in film, the Gospel accounts are extraordinarily reticent, dealing with the horror of what happened with extreme brevity. They do, though, narrate this last stage in Jesus' life in much greater detail than all that has gone before, as we commented at the beginning of this chapter. Throughout, Jesus conducts himself with great composure and, though passive victim, is presented as being in some sense in control of events, as we have seen. But the writers do permit us one or two moments of insight into Jesus' thoughts and feelings – enough for us to gain at least some idea of how he approached and bore his terrible ordeal.

To start at the end: John records that Jesus' final utterance was 'It is finished' (John 19:30). Those few words place Jesus' crucifixion and death in the context of his mission that began at his baptism; this is the end towards which he had been moving ever since that moment. I have already suggested that Jesus might perhaps not have fully realised at the outset how his ministry would unfold, even though he understood the many hints and predictions in the Old Testament, most notably in Isaiah's 'Servant' passages; learning and developing in understanding, I have argued, must have been part of his experience if he was truly man. I have also suggested that Caesarea Philippi marks either his having come to a full awareness of what lay ahead, or a change of strategy in his teaching so that he now began to speak to his disciples about his death. As a result of his meditation on Isaiah's words and in his constant communion in prayer to his Father, he must have grasped that the goal of his mission, the changing of men's and women's hearts and minds in relation

The Passion – and After

to the sovereignty and the grace of God, could and would be achieved only through his death. His knowledge of human society and behaviour, and especially the experience of human responses to the gospel that he gained as his ministry unfolded – all this must, I think, have served to confirm the picture of the Servant – and thus of his work – that he had found in Isaiah. And so he had *'set his face'*, as Luke puts it, to go to Jerusalem to endure that terrible end.

Motivation?

What motivation drove him, this special, unique man from Galilee, to embrace and pursue unswervingly the course that lay before him? We might suggest three powerful forces that impelled him to persevere. First, to ask that question is to revert to Jesus' temptation; there, he had rejected all alternative courses of action essentially on the grounds of obedience to God: *'Worship the Lord your God, and **serve** only him'* (Luke 4:8), and *'One does not live by bread alone, but by every word that comes from the mouth of God'* (Matt. 4:4). But he was, evidently, more than just an obedient servant: he was the Son, totally identified with the Father's aims, in love with the realisation of the Father's will and with the prospect of a world in which his grace and mercy and his power to heal would finally prevail. This cast of mind was surely his from his childhood – hence his dissatisfaction with what he found in Jerusalem during his visit as a twelve-year-old – but it must have been enormously enhanced by the periods of intensive prayer that the Gospels allow us to glimpse.

It seems likely, though, that what he saw during his ministry, as he moved about in Galilee and elsewhere, bore in upon him the urgency of the need for such healing. On the one hand, he saw the poverty of many, the wretchedness of the beggars and the outcasts, and the domination of their lives by grinding economic necessity and a rigidly unspiritual travesty of Israel's true faith. On the other hand, he saw the self-satisfaction of scribes, Pharisees, and teachers of the Law; to judge from the severity of his condemnation, he was enraged by their apparent indifference to the real needs of the people who depended on them, and the obstacles that they placed in their pathway back to God. Not for nothing did Jesus liken himself to a 'good shepherd' and the people of Israel to *'sheep that have no shepherd'* (Matt. 9:36). How could he possibly abandon those who so needed the message – and the practice – of forgiveness and grace that it was his task to bring to them? And so he had come, directed by the Father, to Jerusalem.

We must mention, however, a third factor: his utter confidence in the promise of life beyond the suffering – and not just a renewal of the only kind of life that he knew, but rather a share in the divine life. It would bring with it

Jesus – yesterday, today, for ever

a relationship with God of which even his present sense of their nearness and communion was only a pale shadow, and with it powers that would enable him to further his Father's purpose, continuing on a far larger scale the saving work that he had been trying to do. It is, of course, John's Gospel that puts such probably unspoken longings into words; there, Jesus speaks not of his death but of 'going to the Father'. He also says, to the amazement of his disciples – if they heard him say it – that *'it is to your advantage that I go away'* (John 16:7): as their new *parakletos*, their invisible, yet close friend, counsellor and guide, he would be able both to support them in their work and himself *'prove the world wrong about sin and righteousness and judgment'* (John 16:8). In doing all this, he would be able to give even greater glory to the Father than he had done during his life – hence his prayer in John 17: *'... glorify your Son so that the Son may glorify you ... I glorified you on earth by finishing the work that you gave me to do'* (John 17:1, 4).

Inner struggles

Yet, despite such composure, conviction and purposefulness, the Gospels include, as already mentioned, a few moments where the veil is lifted to permit us some insight into the inner struggles that must have accompanied them. All the Gospels, except Luke, recount the meal at Bethany where *'a woman'* (Matthew and Mark) or Mary (John) anoints Jesus' head (or feet) with a very costly ointment. The disciples (or Judas) see this action, presumably an expression of gratitude and devotion, as an extravagant waste. But Jesus interprets it differently: *'she has anointed my body beforehand for its burial'* (Mark 14:8). He then adds, in defence of her action: *'Truly I tell you, wherever the good news is proclaimed in the whole world, what she has done will be told in remembrance of her'* (v. 9). That Jesus should make such a connection suggests a mind preoccupied with the ordeal that was drawing ever closer. At the beginning of his account of this incident, John includes an apparently unimportant phrase: *'The house was filled with the fragrance of the perfume'* (John 12:3). Perhaps John wishes to suggest that the forthcoming death of Jesus was 'in the air' – at least for Jesus.

In the same chapter, John describes a much more obvious indication of Jesus' state of mind. To the request of some 'Greeks' – probably Greek-speaking diaspora Jews who were in Jerusalem for Passover – to see Jesus, he replies: *'The hour has come for the Son of Man to be glorified'* (John 12:23). It seems that their request had sent Jesus' mind to the Old Testament predictions, for example the references to the 'banner' in Isaiah 11:10, 12 and to the Servant's role in Isaiah 49, for he says: *'I, when I am lifted up from the earth, will draw all people to myself'* (v. 32). But in the midst of these reflections, it

The Passion – and After

is as if Jesus is suddenly struck by the brutal reality of what that 'lifting up' will really mean: 'glorification', yes, but also the agony, the humiliation and the public shame of crucifixion. And so he says: *'Now my soul is troubled. And what should I say – 'Father, save me from this hour'? No, it is for this reason that I have come to this hour'* (v. 27). Involuntarily, instinctively, the impulse for self-preservation asserts itself. But the very utterance of the words reminds him of his own principle – that to seek to save one's life is to lose it – and he remembers for what purpose he finds himself where he is and how much hangs upon his persisting to the end. And the moment passes.

This scene in John has been regarded by some commentators as John's equivalent of the moments in Gethsemane that are so striking a part of the Synoptic Gospels' accounts. There too Jesus is 'troubled' – though that is too weak a word for the crisis of anguish and instinctive terror at what is about to happen to him; it is every human being's reaction to such an awful prospect. Jesus faces here the same issue as during his temptation, but now not as a still distant possibility but as an imminent and all-too real threat to his life. So he himself wrestles with the choice of paths that he had laid before his followers at Caesarea Philippi. The fierceness of that struggle is rendered by the Synoptics in different ways: Matthew and Luke say that he uttered fundamentally the same prayer three times over, though in Matthew's account he moves from *'My Father, if it is possible, let this cup pass from me; yet not what I want but what you want'* to *'My Father, if this cannot pass unless I drink it, your will be done'* (Matt. 26:39, 42). Luke, by contrast, refers to only a single prayer but adds graphic detail which gives a vivid impression of the physical effects of such extreme anguish: *'In his anguish he prayed more earnestly, and his sweat became like great drops of blood falling down on the ground'* (Luke 22:44). We notice, incidentally, that at this time of extreme trial Jesus expressed the need for human companionship (Matt. 26:37, 40); his disciples may have understood little of what was happening, but their very presence must have lessened the sense of loneliness

How did Jesus manage to come through this crisis and, only a few minutes afterwards, probably, face with extraordinary calmness not only the band of thugs (or, according to John, the detachment of Roman soldiers) sent to arrest him, but also the treacherous Judas? How did he control the anger, the sense of outrage and injustice at what was happening to him? How could he *'endure … such hostility against himself from sinners'* (Heb. 12:3)? The Synoptic Gospels all say that Jesus addressed God as Father, but Mark alone includes in Jesus' prayer in Gethsemane the Aramaic word *abba* that seemingly imprinted itself so strongly in the memory of Jesus' followers. It suggests, surely, that the personal, intimate relationship that had developed between Jesus and the Father was real enough to carry him through, along with the strength of his belief in, and commitment to, the Father's saving purpose. It had carried him thus far; he had long known where his journey was leading him – so how could he pull out now? He evidently understood that this had to happen: nothing but this act of surrender by both Father and Son would ever have the power to convince men and women of the depth of the Father's saving love. He therefore submits, restraining instinctive attempts by his disciples to defend him, while rebuking his captors for the unnecessary show of force and doing all he can to ensure that his followers are able to escape being rounded up along with him. From this moment on, Jesus maintains throughout his ordeal the dignified, seemingly passive silence that we have already considered.

Unique and dramatic as this scene in Gethsemane is, we should not overlook one probable implication: that what we are permitted to witness here is not unique. I believe it more likely that this scene opens a window onto inner struggles that Jesus experienced throughout his ministry. He took a decision during his time in the wilderness, certainly, but is it conceivable that he never thereafter knew a moment of doubt or regret, never felt that he would like to be free of the crushing burden of responsibility and the imperative to self-denial that he had embraced then? Were those nights in prayer filled only with sweet musings and eager questing after greater insight? Or did they sometimes include periods of wrestling with his calling, especially in the face of the crowds' superficiality, his opponents' obdurate refusal to think beyond their imagined certainties, and his disciples' incomprehension? Such a conflict is surely foreshadowed, as we noted earlier, in Isaiah's words: *'But I said, "I have laboured in vain, I have spent my strength for nothing and vanity; yet surely my cause is with the LORD, and my reward with my God"'* (Is. 49:4). The words do not envisage a conflict like that of Gethsemane, but they do suggest a man questioning, even doubting, his mission before finding renewed assurance through his faith in the Lord who had entrusted the mission to him in the first place. And then there is the very suggestive sentence that we find in Luke's account of the temptation: *'When the devil had finished every test, he departed from him until an opportune time'* (Luke 4:13). There may, one feels, have been many such 'opportune times' in Jesus' ministry.

On the cross

The accounts of Jesus' last moments on the cross may also provide insights into Jesus' thoughts. The presentation of the actual crucifixion is brief and understated in all four Gospels; John's is the longest at eighteen verses. We have already referred to Jesus' final words in John, with their emphasis on

The Passion – and After

the completion of his earthly ministry (but see 17:4-5) and to his evident care for his distressed mother. Perhaps the extra detail in John reflects the fact that he alone of the Gospel writers was an eye-witness of the crucifixion. Luke's ending is somewhat different – we shall come to that shortly. Mark's and Matthew's accounts are the starkest and most sombre, with, seemingly, no redeeming gleams of light apart from the emphasis in Matthew on the fulfilment of Old Testament prefiguring – though this is far more pronounced in John. It is in keeping with this sombre mood that Jesus' words in these two Gospels are a cry of apparent despair: *"'Eloi, Eloi, lema sabachthani?" that is, "My God, my God, why have you forsaken me?"'* (Mark 15:34; Matt. 27:46). But is that all they are? If we are to dare to attempt a look into the feelings and thoughts that lay behind that cry, we must do so with the greatest reverence and respect possible.

It seems to me that we must first see it as it appears to be: as the involuntary cry of a man tortured beyond the capacity of any human being to bear it – and since he was 'godly' in a way that no other man was, the agony was more than physical pain. It must have seemed to him at that moment that the Father had brought him to this – and left him there, at the mercy of that ingenious cruelty that only human creatures are capable of, unable, for the moment at least, to find God in the way that he had been accustomed to do. The agony, one suspects, simply blotted out all other sensations. I do not believe, however, that God deliberately 'withdrew himself' so that Jesus should know the fullness of human suffering – there seems to me to be something almost sadistic about such a notion.

These words are, of course, the opening of Psalm 22, a psalm attributed to David, though we cannot be sure what experiences may have inspired them. Was it that Jesus deliberately set himself to recite the psalm as a source of comfort and strength as his ordeal neared its climax? That seems to me a little too cold-bloodedly rational; I am more inclined to think that Jesus quite involuntarily gave voice to his anguish – but that the words that came unbidden to his lips were some that he must have known so well, that he may even have dwelt on at times, wondering whether they might ultimately refer to him.

If we assume something like this to have happened, then it might suggest that, having not quite accidentally quoted the psalm's opening, he found the rest of it flooding into his consciousness as he fought against the pain, helping him to recover his spiritual balance in his final moments. We can imagine him then thinking his way through the psalm, recognising his own experience there, moving with the movement of the psalm from despair to renewed confidence and on to the psalm's triumphant conclusion. It has been suggested

Jesus – yesterday, today, for ever

that its final phrase *'... that he has done it'* may lie behind Jesus' final words in John: *'It is finished'*. It may be no more than coincidence that the Hebrew verb *asah* ('done') in this final phrase is repeatedly used in Genesis in relation to the creation – eight times in Genesis 1:1-2:3, including the key phrase *'Let us **make** man in our image'*!

Perhaps, then, we would be right to assume that the psalm is indeed an expression of Jesus' innermost feelings in these last moments – that David's words, inspired by we know not what, may have been so shaped and guided that they come by some mysterious process to speak also for Jesus. Perhaps they did even more: they may have helped to guide his thoughts into channels that would not only strengthen him in his ordeal but enable him ultimately to emerge from it in a kind of triumph. If we make that assumption, how should we read the psalm in relation to Jesus' experience?

- It describes physical suffering in a way that could reflect the experience of crucifixion (v. 14-15)

- It depicts the shame of public crucifixion and the taunting to which Jesus was exposed (v. 6-8 (v. 16-18). The use of animal imagery (v. 12-13, 16) suggests that Jesus' persecutors have fallen away from their human status: far from being 'in the image of God', they resemble the animals over whom man was intended to 'have dominion' (cf. the use of wild beasts in Daniel's visions to represent the kingdoms and empires of the world).

- He feels himself utterly alone (v. 11). Worse than the physical ordeal and the absence of other helpers is the difficulty in 'finding' God amid his suf-ferings (v. 1-2, 11, 19). The sense of being alone is so different from the nearness that he has known since childhood (v. 9-10). In effect, he is ask-ing again the question that he put in Gethsemane – must this really be? How can you let this happen to me? Can this really be your will?

- In the verses 3-5, David, the original speaker, looks back to Israel's forefa-thers whose prayers for deliverance were heard – we might think that he was thinking of such figures as Moses, Joshua and Gideon, for example. For Jesus, thinking his way through David's words, that list would be ex-tended to include David himself. In this way, as throughout, the psalm was being actualised – past words made present. The use of the present tense means that the psalm, though referring originally to events long past, un-folds in 'real time' in Jesus' present.

- That in turn implies that in using this psalm, Jesus is lining up with David and all those forefathers of Israel. He does not set himself apart from other

The Passion – and After

men: on the contrary, their past experience of God becomes instructive for him. As Hebrews puts it: *'For the one who sanctifies and those who are sanctified all have one Father. For this reason Jesus is not ashamed to call them brothers and sisters'* (Heb. 2:11). Interestingly, the writer of this letter then himself alludes to Psalm 22.

- In a sense, the psalm is 'standing in' for the God whom Jesus cannot find – and thus enables him to find him again. Perhaps the key moment is to be seen in v. 15: *'You lay me in the dust of death'*; to say this implies that God is there after all – if he has brought Jesus to this moment, then he has not, after all, 'fallen out of the hands of the living God'.[7]

In thinking earlier of what might have motivated Jesus to persevere with his mission to the end, despite the obvious, instinctive urge to escape crucifixion we considered three factors. Psalm 22 suggests another, every bit as important and as powerful as the others. After its turning point, from despair to confidence and final triumph, at v. 21, the speaker in the psalm envisions the consequences of his deliverance: he will speak to others about his deliverance, praising God for having heeded his prayer: *'I will tell of your name to my brothers and sisters; in the midst of the congregation I will praise you … For he did not despise or abhor the affliction of the afflicted; he did not hide his face from me, but heard when I cried to him'* (v. 22, 24). This was indeed what happened later; perhaps Jesus did exactly this during his meetings with his disciples after the resurrection. It could be what the writer to the Hebrews is referring to when he says: *'… how can we escape if we neglect so great a salvation? It was declared at first through the Lord…'* (Heb. 2:3). It was certainly what happened when Jesus' resurrection was proclaimed to others by his disciples, acting as his messengers.

In the rest of the psalm, v. 25-31, the speaker imagines the result: everwidening circles of men and women, first 'the congregation', then all Israel, 'the great congregation', and finally 'all the ends of the earth' and 'all the families of the nations' – all these turning to God, worshipping him for his righteousness and acknowledging his kingship:

All the ends of the earth shall remember and turn to the LORD; and all the families of the nations shall worship before him … For dominion belongs to the LORD, and he rules over the nations … they shall come and proclaim

---

7   Inappropriate though the reference might seem in this context, I am reminded of the words of D. H. Lawrence's poem, *The Hands of God*: 'It is a fearful thing to fall into the hands of the living God./But it is a much more fearful thing to fall out of them.'

his deliverance to a people yet unborn, saying that he has done it. (v. 27-28, 31)

What words and healings alone could not do would in due time be achieved by his self-giving and the grace of God.

If Jesus truly was able to think clearly, despite his agony and the nearness of death, such a prospect would have provided the ultimate motivation to hold on to the end, for it is a vision of precisely what had from the beginning been the goal of his mission. This, surely, was *'the joy that was set before him'* which enabled him to *'endure … the cross, disregarding its shame'* (Heb. 12:2), Though expressed in different language, it is also a prospect comparable to that evoked by Paul in Ephesians 1:9-10, referred to at the beginning of this book: all things brought together under one head, Christ. If any part of what Psalm 22 speaks of were to have been Jesus' final thoughts, then it is no surprise that he was able to say 'it is finished', i.e. 'completed'. The divine will to which he had yielded in Gethsemane would be at last achieved – by his dying.

The veil rent

There is one further detail of the accounts of the crucifixion that must not be omitted. All three Synoptic Gospels mention two things at the moment when Jesus breathed his last: the veil of the temple was torn in two, from top to bottom, according to Matthew and Mark, and an awe-struck centurion on duty at the crucifixion site said something like *'Certainly this man was innocent'* (Luke) or *'Truly this man was God's Son!'* (Matthew and Mark). What was it that so impressed the centurion? Matthew suggests that it was the earthquake at that moment; popular superstition associated all such rare phenomena – earthquakes, comets, eclipses, etc. – with significant events associated with great men. Luke tells it differently: *'When the centurion saw what had taken place, he praised God … '*.

It is Mark, though, who gives these two events a meaning that wonderfully holds together his entire account of Jesus' ministry.[8] All three Gospels use the verb *schizo* ('tear') to describe what happened to the temple veil, but, as we saw back in chapter 4, Mark alone used this same verb when describing what happened at Jesus' baptism – that the heavens were 'rent' or 'torn asunder'. As Brian K. Gamel convincingly argues, Mark has created by his choice of words a parallel between these two moments, one at the opening of Jesus' ministry and one at its culmination. Gamel also argues that the tearing of the veil is

---

8   Brian K. Gamel, *Mark 15:39 as a Markan Theology of Revelation. The Centurion's Confession as Apocalyptic Unveiling*, London/New York 2017.

The Passion – and After

intended to be a parallel to the 'tearing of the heavens' in Mark 1; he refers to Josephus' description of the veil as a kind of symbolic 'heavens':

> … before these doors there was a veil of equal largeness with the doors. It was a Babylonian curtain, embroidered with blue, and fine linen, and scarlet, and purple, and of a contexture that was truly wonderful. Nor was this mixture of colours without its mystical interpretation, but was **a kind of image of the universe** … This curtain had also **embroidered upon it all that was mystical in the heavens**, excepting that of the [twelve] signs, representing living creatures.[9]

In Mark's version, the rending of the curtain is thus, symbolically, a second 'rending of the heavens', opening the way for men henceforth to approach God without the barriers and obstacles placed in their way by the Mosaic Law – and, on the other hand, allowing God out from his confinement among Israel to invade and take possession of the whole world. But we saw in chapter 4 that Mark's language in his opening chapter was a reference back to Isaiah 64 and its plea for God to reveal himself again, as he had done at Sinai. Against that background, Mark's statement about the centurion takes on added significance: *'Now when the centurion, who stood facing him, saw that in this way he breathed his last, he said, "Truly this man was God's Son!"'* (Mark 15:39). It is not the earthquake, nor even the rending of the curtain, that permits the revelation of God but the death of Jesus.

Hitherto in Mark, the only human voices that have recognised Jesus as the Son of God, probably in some sense more pagan than true, have been those of the deranged man in Mark 1 and the Gadarene man in chapter 5; what they somehow understood was probably the power that he possessed. This centurion, however, recognises him precisely in his powerlessness, in his dying. We do not know what his words meant to him – it was perhaps as pagan an utterance as those of the demoniacs – but Mark uses them to express the most fundamental truth of his Gospel: that it is here, on the cross, in his dying in furtherance of the gospel, that the Son of God has to be recognised. This is the 'secret' that until this moment had remained unspoken but is now revealed. Gamel suggests that the centurion's words are treated by Mark as effectively a voice from heaven, the result of a moment of revelation akin to that in chapter 1. But now the announcement is made not to Jesus but to the world – and to the reader, thus bringing to an end Jesus' obvious reticence about himself that is such a feature of Mark in particular.

But that is not all: the link with Sinai confirms that this is also the truest

---

9 Josephus, *Jewish Wars*, 5.5.4.

revelation of God himself, for, as we have emphasised earlier, the man Jesus is 'God with us'. When Paul writes to the Corinthians that God gives us *'the light of the knowledge of the glory of God in the face of Jesus Christ'* (2 Cor. 4:6), we may think first of, for example, the shining face of the transfigured Jesus; but it seems to me that Mark wishes us to see him here, in the face of Jesus at this moment, streaked with blood and twisted with the pain of self-giving, of losing his life to save others. That, Mark says, is our God; that is the extent of his grace and his desire to turn us back to him. And that message is the 'gospel of God' that Mark wishes to lay before us.

And afterwards?

How do we get from Jesus on a Roman cross to the amazing outcome envisaged in Psalm 22? – for apparently, the world continued on its way unchanged, having got rid of this troublesome prophet from Nazareth. The conventional answer is that Jesus bore on the cross the guilt of human sin and the penalty which it necessarily incurred, and this made possible, or opened the way to, a reconciliation with God.

For the reader of the Gospels there are three obvious problems about such an explanation. First, the Gospels themselves give no indication of any such thing, apart from the unexplained statement in Mark 10 that Jesus was going to *'give his life a ransom for many'* (Mark 10:45). In these narratives, Jesus' death is the result solely of the hostility of the Jewish authorities, with the collusion of the Roman occupiers. Jesus clearly views it as the will of God that it should be so, but it is an action conceived and performed by men.

Secondly, the Gospels show us Jesus, not as our representative, meeting demands of God on our behalf, but, on the contrary, as God's representative – as 'God with us', acting on his behalf, wielding his power and authority, and showing us what God is like.[10] And thirdly, to suggest that God wished in some sense to exact a penalty or to inflict some form of retribution as a 'price' for the sins of men against him flies in the face of the picture of God that Jesus has been presenting; in the two parables in Matthew 18, it is a man, not God, who demands 'satisfaction' or 'compensation' for debts or sins. Similarly, in the parable of the Lost Son, it is the two sons who expect some penalty to be imposed on the erring son – but not the father, who, despite critical occasional suggestions to the contrary, is unquestionably intended to represent God. The conventional notion that forgiveness came 'at a price' – the price of the death of Jesus – appears to me to be an example of human beings making

---

10 These are the functions which, back in chapter 1, we identified as three senses of the notion of being 'in the image of God': resemblance, manifestation and representation.

The Passion – and After

God in their own image.

There are two incidents in the stories of Jesus' end, both unique to Luke, that help us to understand both the meaning of Jesus' coming and, in consequence, its results. Luke tells us of an incident as Jesus made his way to Golgotha for crucifixion:

> *A great number of the people followed him, and among them were women who were beating their breasts and wailing for him. But Jesus turned to them and said, 'Daughters of Jerusalem, do not weep for me, but weep for yourselves and for your children. For the days are surely coming when they will say, "Blessed are the barren, and the wombs that never bore, and the breasts that never nursed." Then they will begin to say to the mountains, "Fall on us"; and to the hills, "Cover us." For if they do this when the wood is green, what will happen when it is dry?' (Luke 23:27-31)*

In his words to the lamenting women, Jesus makes a link between his suffering now and what they will have to endure later. Given what he had said about Jerusalem's fate, both in Luke 19:43-44 and in the Olivet Prophecy in Luke 21, it seems clear that he had in mind the disaster that would overtake the city a generation later. He knew that his personal fate foreshadowed that of the whole city – he was the 'green wood', unfit for burning, suffering an untimely end, and they the dry wood, all too ready for the flames. There is here even a hint of what is made explicit in the deliberate ambiguity of a phrase in John's Gospel, *'Destroy this temple'* (John 2:19). Which temple does he mean – his body, or the temple in Jerusalem? Probably both – his crucifixion, he implies, is the first step in the train of events that will lead to the destruction of the temple which was Jerusalem's glory. It is hardly surprising that Jesus should have wept over the city as Luke describes (Luke 19:41-44).

But wherein, exactly, lies the similarity? First, perhaps, in that they and he are both to be victims of Roman power. But does the similarity end there? On the face of it, there is a great difference between Jesus' death, suffered willingly for the sake of the gospel, and the fate of the inhabitants of Jerusalem, caught up in a war between Roman imperial power and Jewish nationalism. But if we look closer, we recognise that they, like Jesus, are the victims of mankind's restless drive to 'save their life', as Jesus put it at Caesarea Philippi, in other words, to pursue their own vital interests and its expression in the quest for advantage, power, possessions, and dominion. That is, after all, the essence of what Jesus also described as 'the human things'.

Behaviour directed by that drive is of necessity opposed to 'the divine things', the principle that had brought Jesus to his cross. In fact, the pursuit of self-interest at every level is part of humanity's collective rebellion against its Creator. Human history's seemingly endless catalogue of wars, conquests, rebellions, etc. is, in essence, the consequence of the initial rebellion encapsulated in the story told in Genesis 3. It is no coincidence that Genesis 3 is immediately followed by a chapter containing the first murder and the enacting of violent revenge (Genesis 4:23-24) – as we have said before, when men fall away from God, they fall away from each other. Conversely, it is no coincidence either that Jesus' first great commandment, to love God, is followed by a second commandment: to love your neighbour as yourself. Human aggression, lust for power and the pursuit of self-interest have many victims, especially among those who are less strong, less adept at playing the game, as these women of Jerusalem were. But in all but the rarest cases, those victims were themselves part of this destructive process, still playing the same desperate game – simply less good at it, less powerful than those who played more skilfully and more ruthlessly. And because that drive for power is part of the human rebellion against God, they are, as it were, 'collateral damage' in that too. That is perhaps why Jesus had great sympathy for the oppressed 'poor' and held their leaders largely responsible for their plight. Yet they, 'the people', for their part, though they often seemed to support him, could also be persuaded to shout for his death.

Jesus was caught up in the endless round of human conflicts too, as well as being the immediate target of men's rejection of God's authority. There is, though, still a vast difference between him and the people of Jerusalem: he had no part in human conflicts, having consciously renounced the 'natural' human way. He had freely chosen to share their plight and was about to suffer as they would; but his solidarity was not (yet) enough to cause them to move from lamentation to new insight and to repentance.

The other incident involves one whose plight was still more desperate. The criminals who were crucified with Jesus had played the game too, for reasons not known to us, but had pursued their interests with such ruthlessness and violence that they had been condemned to die – more victims of Roman 'justice'. But, according to Luke, something had evidently happened to one of these men, presumably through some kind of encounter with Jesus, perhaps only at his crucifixion, but probably also beforehand. He might previously have heard something of the teaching – but had perhaps dismissed it as just words. But now, here was the same Jesus, suffering as he was; evidently, then, his compassion for the poor, the outcasts and the 'sinners' was not just talk. And now he was suffering for it, for having been true to his calling, for having practised what he preached.

The Passion – and After

As a result, in a dialogue conducted in gasped breaths as they struggled against the effects of crucifixion, the criminal admits the folly of the path that he had chosen; he is the (still just) living proof of Jesus' teaching: *'For those who want to save their life will lose it'* (Luke 9:24). More than that, he recognises and belatedly desires to embrace the alternative way, exemplified by Jesus: *'this man has done nothing wrong'*. It is an act of repentance of the kind that Jesus had been seeking to bring about among the people of Galilee; but it is also something more: this man apparently understands that Jesus is able to grant him forgiveness – he was, after all, the man who had, back in Nazareth proclaimed *'release to the captives … to let the oppressed go free'* (Luke 4:18).

We do not know exactly what had caused this last-minute change of heart; we can only surmise that it was partly the evident emptiness of the values by which he had lived hitherto, but partly also the sight of Jesus, so manifestly a righteous man, voluntarily sharing his lot as a result of his dedication to the task of proclaiming the message of divine grace and forgiveness. He now believed that what Jesus had been preaching was the only right way: turning to God, accepting his mercy and trusting in the promise of life.

And what did this last encounter mean for Jesus? For him, it was a sign that his labour had not been in vain, as the Servant passages promised: *'… he will have a multitude of children … the LORD's plan will prosper in his hands. When he sees all that is accomplished by his anguish, he will be satisfied'* (Is. 53:10-11, NLT). That satisfaction finds expression in Jesus' last words as recorded by Luke: *'Father, into your hands I commend my spirit'* (Luke 23:46).

The extraordinary confession of the 'thief on the cross' was, of course, only a sign. To see the full outworking of Jesus' death, we need to go to the early chapters of Acts. On the day of Pentecost, and again in Acts 3, Peter, addressing a Jewish multitude, confronts them with their terrible collective action:

Jesus of Nazareth, a man attested to you by God with deeds of power, wonders, and signs that God did through him among you, as you yourselves know – this man, handed over to you according to the definite plan and foreknowledge of God, you crucified and killed by the hands of those outside the law. (Acts 2:22-23)

The God of Abraham, the God of Isaac, and the God of Jacob, the God of our ancestors has glorified his servant Jesus, whom you handed over and rejected in the presence of Pilate, though he had decided to release him. But you rejected the Holy and Righteous One and asked to have a murderer given to you, and you killed the Author of life (Acts 3:13-15)

It is a terrible indictment; it is as though the body of Jesus was hanging there

Jesus – yesterday, today, for ever

before them, with its wounds bearing witness to their sinful actions: they have not merely killed Jesus – they have denied God, rejecting the saviour that he had sent to them.

Were they now to bear a heavy penalty? Would God exact retribution for their sin? – that is, after all, the way of human justice. And so the people say in desperation: *'Brothers, what should we do?'* (Acts 2:37). From the standpoint of human thinking, the answer is astonishing: *'Repent, and be baptized every one of you in the name of Jesus Christ so that your sins may be forgiven'* (2:38). To the repentant there is no retribution, only forgiveness. And the sign that confirmed that forgiveness was that the mutilated body of Jesus, which had testified so powerfully against them, was no longer hanging on the cross: *'But God raised him up'* (2:24) *'... whom God raised from the dead'* (3:15). The cross was empty, and so was the tomb. It was as though their crime had never been. It had been blotted out, swallowed up by God's grace; in the person of Jesus, he had absorbed the blows inflicted on him by men's rebellion and, as it were, removed all trace of them. He had *'cast all our sins into the depths of the sea'*, as Micah puts it (7:19), or, in the words of Hezekiah: *'... you have cast all my sins behind your back'* (Is. 38:17). It was the reality to which the ritual of the Day of Atonement looked: the 'scapegoat' was to be *'... sent ... away into the wilderness by means of someone designated for the task. The goat shall bear on itself all their iniquities to a barren region...'* (Lev. 16:21-22).

It was fitting that it should be Peter who first publicly proclaimed this message, for he knew better than any man whereof he spoke. His denial of Jesus had been flagrant, repeated publicly – but he had, as Jesus had predicted he would, turned again, and Jesus had graciously received him, going out of his way to welcome him (Mark 16:7). He is perhaps our best model of how the death of Jesus 'works' – how the mission of Jesus succeeded through its apparent failure, how his death and resurrection had the power to convince and to transform where words and wonders could not. And let us notice: it is not the death alone that achieves such transformation, but death *and* resurrection: the first reveals the ugliness of human rebellion against God, in which all are implicated, but the latter confirms that all our misdeeds are undone by God's forgiving grace, as though they had never been: Jesus *'... was handed over to death for our trespasses and was raised for our justification'* (Rom. 4:25). And, with remarkable economy of means, the man through whom God calls upon mankind to take those two steps, of repentance first and then of faith, also provides the pattern for the vital third element: a new way of living and thinking arising from the transformation of human hearts and minds. In allowing himself to be 'used' as the means by which God displays his forgiving grace, Jesus embodies the 'Caesarea Philippi principle': the 'divine things', not 'the human things', or, as Jesus expressed it in Gethsemane, *not what I want, but what you want*' (Mark 14:36). Those who 'turn round', as Peter and the dying criminal did, do not instantly come to resemble Jesus – but they do set out on the new path, following where he has led: *'If any want to become my followers, let them deny themselves and take up their cross and follow me'* (Mark 8:34).

But what of those who were not there and who had no direct involvement in Jesus' crucifixion? It is possible to imagine, for example, those in far-off Galilee who had experienced Jesus' compassionate work and had themselves benefited from his healing or his forgiveness: the tax-collectors, the paralytic of Mark 2, the fallen woman of Luke 7, the crippled woman of Luke 13, and the adulteress of John 8. They had all seen how he suffered criticism, hostility and opposition from scribes, Pharisees, synagogue officials and the like, and in due course, they would hear that that opposition had finally led to his arrest and death in Jerusalem. *They* would understand what 'give his life a ransom for many' meant. Their reaction, I suspect, would have been something like 'He bore all that for me – to bring to me the release and the forgiveness that I so badly needed'. And it is, perhaps, that reaction that best explains how the world would get from Golgotha to the end of Psalm 22.

An afterthought

It is evident from the New Testament that Jesus' death and resurrection possessed a unique power to touch human hearts and minds – as the Servant prophecies also suggest. Given that, should our presentation of the gospel not focus more frequently on that essential message, with its implications for a right understanding of the relationship between God and man? We have seen that, for the New Testament writers, to preach the gospel was to 'preach Christ'. So too today: the narrative of Jesus is God's most powerful instrument for transforming human hearts. If his death brings into the sharpest focus human sin, in which all are complicit, his resurrection is the supreme expression of the grace of God. Whatever other aspects of God's purpose Christians may choose to highlight, and from whatever starting point they choose to approach it, Jesus must surely be constantly present as the essential Christian message.

Chapter 9

The Glorified Lord

To leave the Jesus of the past and the life recorded in the Gospels, and to attempt to think and write about the ever-living Jesus of 'today', of the present and the future, is not just a shift in focus; it also means that we move from what is, in the last analysis, history, to our own time and so also to ourselves. As believers, we readers are therefore directly involved, alongside Jesus, in what we shall be considering.

This move also raises a question as to possible sources. We might think that we are inevitably limited to other, more recent sources than those provided by the New Testament, written over 2,000 years ago, i.e. to personal, subjective experience. Yet the very word 'subjective' warns us of the need to proceed cautiously: 'subjective' experience is by definition unverifiable, no matter how real it might be for the individual whose experience it is.

In fact, we are not limited in this way. Despite their relative proximity in time to the earthly Jesus, all the New Testament writers were working in a post-resurrection context: their Jesus is already the living, risen Jesus. However much the Synoptic Gospels, unlike John, may give the appearance of simply following the unfolding story of Jesus' life, they are all written from within a world transformed by Jesus' death and resurrection and for a community of believers for whom the risen Jesus was the supreme reality in their lives. This is, of course, still more true of the rest of the New Testament; even in passages in the Letters where he is not mentioned, the very fact of his life, to say nothing of his active involvement in the church's life, exert their influence at every point. It is therefore primarily to the New Testament that we shall be looking as we attempt to develop and to express an understanding of Jesus 'today'.

Nevertheless, it is with the Gospels that we must begin, for it is there that we first see and hear the risen Jesus in those extraordinary chapters about his post-resurrection appearances to his followers. In fact, we need to go back even further. As usual, it is John who opens up to the reader aspects of Jesus' life of which the Synoptics know – or simply say – nothing. As we saw in the

The Glorified Lord

previous chapter, in John 17, Jesus' followers, and we readers, are permitted to eavesdrop, as it were, on Jesus' prayer and thus on his communion with the Father – an insight quite without parallel elsewhere. Much of this prayer, as of the 'discourses' in John 13-16, is devoted to the future. In its early verses, Jesus looks back on his ministry – as *shaliach*, he 'reports back', as it were, on the completion of his mission to the one who sent him:

> *I glorified you on earth by finishing the work that you gave me to do … I have made your name known to those whom you gave me from the world. They were yours, and you gave them to me, and they have kept your word … the words that you gave to me I have given to them, and they have received them and know in truth that I came from you; and they have believed that you sent me … While I was with them, I protected them in your name that you have given me. I guarded them, and not one of them was lost except the one destined to be lost, so that the scripture might be fulfilled. (John 17:4-12)*

The greater part of the prayer, however, focuses on the future, making requests partly for himself but primarily for his followers – though they are, in fact, things that Jesus has already promised them during the discourses in chapters 13-16. Putting the discourses and this prayer together, we can, I think, distinguish three overlapping aspects of the post-resurrection and post-ascension period, i.e. for the whole of the time prior to his Second Coming – about which, by contrast, John has little to say. These three aspects are:

- Jesus himself in his resurrection glory;
- his future work in the world in support of his followers as they bear witness to him;
- his relationship to the believers collectively and individually.

Not surprisingly, these three themes can also be discerned in the Gospels' accounts of Jesus' meetings with the disciples after his resurrection, and they provide a convenient way of approaching the teaching of the rest of the New Testament about the person and the work of Jesus in the new post-resurrection world, though it is not easy to disentangle them. Moreover, we need to keep reminding ourselves that what was true in New Testament times is not just history: it remains essentially true for ever thereafter, now as much as then. The first two of these themes are the subject of the present chapter, while the third one will be the focus of the next chapter.

The risen Jesus

It is difficult enough to understand the human, mortal Son of God whom we

Jesus – yesterday, today, for ever

encounter in the Gospels, but there we are at least able, thanks to our shared humanity, to try to enter into his experience and to imagine what his thoughts and feelings might have been. But the risen Jesus is completely 'beyond our ken' – we have no idea what it is like to be not merely immortal but also endowed with truly godlike attributes. All we can do, therefore, is draw tentative conclusions from the clues and indications that the New Testament writings offer us.

Our starting point is a sentence in Jesus' prayer in John 17: '*So now, Father, glorify me in your own presence with the glory that I had in your presence before the world existed*' (v. 5). 'Glory' is a word and an idea that are particularly difficult to define; certainly, Jesus did not mean by it simply the display of light and fire associated with manifestations of God in the Old Testament – these were, surely, simply symbolic representations of an inward quality. Nor did he mean the condition of being celebrated, praised and adored by men, however much the true glory might rightly be thus celebrated. Throughout John's Gospel, Jesus consistently rejects any desire for such adulation: '*I do not accept glory from human beings*' (John 5:41); to him, the only approval that matters comes from God:

> '*How can you believe when you accept glory from one another and do not seek the glory that comes from the one who alone is God?*' (v. 44)

> '*Yet I do not seek my own glory; there is one who seeks it and he is the judge … If I glorify myself, my glory is nothing. It is my Father who glorifies me …*' (John 8:50, 54; see also John 7:18; 12:43)

So what *does* Jesus mean by 'glory? Part of the answer lies in the phrase 'in your own presence'; Jesus has repeatedly said that he was to go 'to the Father' (John 14:12, 28; 16:10, 16, 17, 28); a similar idea is expressed by Luke when he says that Jesus set his face to go to Jerusalem '*when the days drew near for him to be taken up (analambano)…*' (Luke 9:51). This last expression is particularly revealing since it suggests that Jesus' expectation and anticipation of what lay beyond the cross was rooted in the language of the Psalms:

> *Nevertheless I am continually with you; you hold my right hand. You guide me with your counsel, and afterward you will* **receive** *(LXX: proslambano) me with honour. (Psalm 73:23-24)*

> *But God will ransom my soul from the power of Sheol, for he will* **receive** *(LXX: lambano) me. (Psalm 49:15)*

I take these various expressions to mean that Jesus was somehow to share in

The Glorified Lord

the life of God, becoming, as Peter puts it in relation to believers, a *'participant of the divine nature'* (2 Peter 1:4). That would mean not merely unlimited, immortal life but also an all-seeing, all-knowing consciousness, so widened as to encompass all time and space, and a mode of existence which, through what the biblical writers call 'the (holy) Spirit', permits him simultaneously to be everywhere – to 'walk', for example, among all the lampstands of Revelation 2-3. Revelation 3 speaks of his having *'sat down with my Father on his throne'* (3:21), while Revelation 1 offers us a visual image, using symbolism drawn mainly from the Old Testament:

> *His head and his hair were white as white wool, white as snow; his eyes were like a flame of fire, his feet were like burnished bronze, refined as in a furnace, and his voice was like the sound of many waters. In his right hand he held seven stars, and from his mouth came a sharp, two-edged sword, and his face was like the sun shining with full force. (Revelation 1:14-16)*

After Jesus' resurrection, the 'Spirit' needs to be thought of as being either 'the Spirit of God' or 'the Spirit of Jesus' – though they are, in fact, the same thing, so complete is the unity of Father and Son.

Post-resurrection appearances

The accounts of Jesus' post-resurrection appearances give us some impression of the kind of existence upon which he had entered. We see that he is able, seemingly, to materialise suddenly in the locked room where his disciples were gathered (John 20:19, 26; Luke 24:36); he is also able to disappear, equally suddenly and mysteriously, from the supper table at Emmaus (Luke 24:31). He knows what Thomas has said, though he had apparently not been present when the words were spoken (John 20:25, 27). It is possible that what is described in these episodes is some kind of interim condition prior to his ascension and to the full assumption of his godlike immortal condition. I do not think that this is what Jesus meant when he said to Mary Magdalene in John 20:17: *'Do not hold on to me, because I have not yet ascended to the Father'* – that was, I believe, simply a request to her not to cling to him as he had not yet 'gone away'. It would be unwise, though, to draw any firm conclusions from these words – we are venturing here onto terrain of which we have neither knowledge nor experience.

Yet Jesus' forty days on earth following his resurrection were some kind of 'intermediate stage', for he was going to leave them and 'go to the Father'. Why was an intermediate stage between crucifixion and ascension necessary at all? Why did Jesus appear in bodily form similar to that of any man, though he has now risen from the dead and is freed from the constraints of human existence. The first and obvious answer is that only such appearances enable his disciples to grasp and to believe the reality of his personal victory over death. 'Doubting Thomas' speaks for all of us: we all need to be persuaded that the Jesus who was crucified is now the living one.[1] And though, perforce, we were not there and have not seen with our own eyes, these appearances *and the written records of them* enable us who, as Jesus said *'have not seen'* (John 20:29) to believe none the less. As John says, explaining why he has written his Gospel: *'But these are written so that you may come to believe that Jesus is the Messiah, the Son of God, and that through believing you may have life in his name'* (John 20:31).

Needless to say, many have challenged the veracity of these accounts of Jesus' appearances, arguing that their apparent disagreements cast doubt on their truthfulness. This is not the place to engage in that discussion, but three comments may be made briefly: first, that their disagreements give the lie to any suggestion of collusion and are indicative rather of different witnesses' attempts to record events that must have left them struggling to grasp what they had seen. Second, as many writers have argued, the choice of women as the earliest witnesses to Jesus' resurrection is itself powerful evidence for the truthfulness of the accounts, given the prevailing culture of the time: who, if they were inventing the story of Jesus' rising, would have given women so prominent and crucial a role within it? Thirdly, the style of these narratives, especially, perhaps, those of Mark and Matthew, differs so markedly from what has gone before: Matthew makes no attempt to appeal to Old Testament prophecies, as he does so frequently elsewhere, because the resurrection lies outside all prior expectation, while Mark's account in its original version probably ends at 16:8 with the statement that the women *'were afraid'* – as well they might have been. It is as though Mark is saying 'no words of mine can do justice to this unparalleled, world-changing event.'[2]

---

1 Theories suggesting that the appearances were the result of hallucinations arising out of wishful thinking on the part of the disciples, or that the accounts were not intended to be taken literally but were simply metaphors for their belief that the 'spirit of Jesus' somehow survived his death – all these founder on the evidence of the disciples' complete surprise and their demand for proof. Nothing suggests that they were gullible people with fanciful ideas about a 'spiritual resurrection'.

2 There are, of course, several other ways of interpreting this abrupt ending, assuming that Mark did intend his Gospel to end in this way. That assumption has frequently been challenged, and the status of Mark 16:9-20 has been the subject of much discussion.

While the textual issues, based on the presence or absence of these verses from the most ancient sources, are inconclusive, the stylistic argument seems to me clear. A former editor of *The Christadelphian* put it like this: 'The reader with literary feeling – and especially with

The Glorified Lord

The function of the Gospel narratives as historical evidence for the bodily resurrection of Jesus is not, however, the only value of these accounts for the reader: it matters at least as much that they confirm the essential continuity between the mortal Jesus and the risen Lord. If that seems obvious, that is the result of familiarity with these accounts; one could, for example, imagine that one risen from the dead might be so entirely different as to have no connection with the person who died, or that they have entered into something like a state of *nirvana* in which individuality is swallowed up in a great sea of divine being. The closing chapters of the Gospels assure us, though, that no such thing is the case: Jesus knows and is known by his disciples – he calls Mary Magdalene by her name (John 20:16); he remembers that Peter three times denied him (John 21:15-17), for example, or that he had earlier spoken to them about his coming death in relation to the Old Testament (Luke 24:44). Banal though these details may appear, they are of the utmost importance, for they tell us that the risen Lord is still the same Lord, not only capable of knowing them but above all still retaining the memory of his personal experience of his mortal life. Everything that we can say or hope about the 'today' of Jesus depends on that essential continuity of memory and thus of identity.

That continuity must, of course, have included the memory of his own lived moments – the pain, the anguish, the humiliation of the cross. So what must it have been like for Jesus when he found himself, not merely alive but transformed into a condition similar to what he had experienced during his Transfiguration? However great his faith, however unshakeable his confidence in the promises and the love of his Father, must there not have been some kind of exultation, relief even, to find himself alive? He had gone, or, more precisely, had allowed himself to be dispatched, into the darkness of nothingness – and had emerged, just as he had trusted, and just as he had told his disciples he would. What's more, he now *knew*, in a way that no mortal being could, that the consequences for others of his suffering – all those myriads of people that Psalm 22 had taught him to see – were now secure. He *would* see the 'travail of his soul' and *would* be satisfied.

---

any experience of sub-editing – cannot escape the awareness of some kind of break after the eighth verse, and of an abrupt change in the character of the writing. There might be an explanation for this in circumstances unknown to us, and change of style is not necessarily proof of change of authorship. But that it exists, and that the last twelve verses do not bear genuine comparison with anything else in Mark, must be candidly admitted.'

L.G. Sargent was evidently unhappy with this conclusion that his own stylistic sensitivity had forced him to, for he then added: 'One thing must be certain: Mark could not have intended to end on the silence of the women. That would be a completely incredible termination to the Gospel of the Son of God ...' (L.G. Sargent, *The Gospel of the Son of God*).

Jesus – yesterday, today, for ever

Going to the Father

Returning to Jesus' prayer in John 17 and the discourses in the preceding chapters, we have to note another implication of his 'going to the Father'. It does not only mean participation in the powers of the divine life: it also refers to a condition of total intimacy and fellowship with the Father, no longer confined by the limitations of human finitude and for ever freed from its frustrations and compromises. The phrase 'in your presence' refers less to a location – as though God were here but not there – than to a relationship; it means, incidentally, that Jesus, on returning ultimately to the earth. would not then be any less in the Father's presence than he was before his return. The frequency with which Jesus, according to John's Gospel, spoke of 'going to the Father' suggests that this was his great desire, part, at least, of *the joy that was set before him'* (Heb. 12:2).[3] Whatever that particular phrase actually means, it is clear that Jesus longed for such a condition; he must have known passages in the Psalms like the following:

> *You show me the path of life. In your **presence** (Heb. panim) there is fullness of joy; in your right hand are pleasures forevermore. (Psalm 16:11)*

> *As for me, I shall behold your **face** (Heb. panim) in righteousness; when I awake, I shall be satisfied with your likeness. (Psalm 17:15 ESV)*

> *Whom have I in heaven but you? And there is nothing on earth that I desire besides you. (Psalm 73:25)*

We may wonder, too, whether the experience of the Transfiguration might have awakened, or heightened, his longing for such a condition of loving intimacy, though it is evident that it did not take that experience to make him aware of the Father's love for him. As early as John 3, before the Galilean ministry had even begun, we hear him saying: '*The Father loves the Son and has placed all things in his hands'* (John 3:35). The words of Psalm 22, to which we referred in the previous chapter, suggest that Jesus' life had from the beginning been marked by a sense of God's loving closeness: '*Yet it was you who took me from the womb; you kept me safe on my mother's breast. On you I was*

---

3   We have to note that not all translations render that phrase from Hebrews 12 in the same way. The *Mounce Reverse Interlinear New Testament*, for example, translates it as '*who rather than the joy set before him endured a cross…* ', while *Young's Literal Translation* has '*over-against the joy set before him*'. The suggestion is not lacking in evidence: the word 'for' (Gk. *anti*) usually means: 'as against' or 'instead of'; it occurs, for example in such phrase as 'an eye **for** an eye', 'recompense … evil **for** evil', 'a ransom **for** many', or 'will he **for** a fish give him a serpent?'

The Glorified Lord

cast from my birth, and since my mother bore me you have been my God' (Ps. 22:9-10).

Several New Testament passages offer images of the extraordinary transition from man of flesh and blood to divine, heavenly being that Jesus' 'going to the Father' implies. In keeping with its symbolic method throughout, Revelation offers striking images of the process by which Jesus, described as 'the Lamb' throughout Revelation, is brought into God's heavenly throne room after his death and resurrection and is there permitted to take his place at the Father's right hand, henceforth to be praised as the Father is:

> *Then I saw between the throne and the four living creatures and among the elders a Lamb standing as if it had been slaughtered … He went and took the scroll from the right hand of the one who was seated on the throne. When he had taken the scroll, the four living creatures and the twenty-four elders fell before the Lamb … They sing a new song: 'You are worthy to take the scroll and to open its seals, for you were slaughtered and by your blood you ransomed for God saints from every tribe and language and people and nation … Worthy is the Lamb that was slaughtered to receive power and wealth and wisdom and might and honour and glory and blessing … To the one seated on the throne and to the Lamb be blessing and honour and glory and might forever and ever!' (Revelation 5:6-13)*

In Ephesians, essentially the same sequence of events is described by Paul in discursive rather than dramatic language; he uses three different Greek words to give us some idea of the power and might that were required to bring about Jesus' amazing transformation:

> *… and what is the immeasurable greatness of his power (dunamis) for us who believe, according to the working (energeia) of his great power (kratos). God put this power to work (energeo) in Christ when he raised him from the dead and seated him at his right hand in the heavenly places … (Ephesians 1:19-20)*

It is not, though, simply a matter of physical power: for the God who created all things it must surely have been no great matter to raise a man from the dead and to grant him immortality. The greater miracle lies on the spiritual plane: that one who was a man should be raised up to be with the holy, eternal God, crossing the chasm that divides the fleshly, time-bound human realm from the spiritual realm where God for ever dwells. Perhaps one might add that such language would hardly be justified if the Son were simply returning to a glory that had been his before all time, as Trinitarian doctrine would have us believe.

It is hard for us to grasp the magnitude of what Paul is describing; to appreciate the scope of this event, we need to read on with Paul: '... *far above all rule and authority and power and dominion, and above every name that is named, not only in this age but also in the age to come. And he has put all things under his feet...*' (Eph. 1:21-22). The degree of exaltation bestowed on Jesus, the former carpenter from Nazareth, the man who was so tired that he sat down by the well in Samaria, fell asleep in the boat, and was hungry enough to look for figs on a fig tree out of season, elevates him to a position of honour second only to that of the Creator himself.

The same process is also described in Philippians, in a much-discussed brief passage rich with meaning:

> *... who, though he was in the form of God, did not regard equality with God as something to be exploited, but emptied himself, taking the form of a slave, being born in human likeness. And being found in human form, he humbled himself and became obedient to the point of death – even death on a cross. Therefore God also highly exalted him and gave him the name that is above every name, so that at the name of Jesus every knee should bend, in heaven and on earth and under the earth, and every tongue should confess that Jesus Christ is Lord, to the glory of God the Father. (Philippians 2:6-11)*

There are several points here that need to be noted:

- The reference to 'the form of a slave' may well confirm the importance of Isaiah's 'Servant' passages, not only for the early believers' understanding of Jesus, but also for Jesus himself.

- Paul sees that exaltation as the consequence of his obedience to the point of death – it was not a question of his simply resuming a pre-existent glory which had been temporarily laid aside.[4]

---

4 Trinitarian writers make much of the phrase 'the form of God'. It is worth noting, however, that the same word, *morphe*, also occurs in the phrase 'the form of a servant', where it unquestionably refers, not to some intrinsic ontological condition, but to a rank or status. The 'humbling' that the passage refers to is a reference, surely, to the choice made by Jesus when, after his baptism, he accepted the mission summed up in Isaiah's picture of the Servant, as we discussed in chapter 4. The NRSV rendering of the verb *ginomai* ('to become') in v. 7 as 'being born in human likeness' similarly reveals the influence of Trinitarian thinking. For an excellent detailed examination of this passage, see T.J. Barling's *The Letter To The Philippians* (see chapter 4, note 2).

The Glorified Lord

- Paul ascribes to Jesus the highest possible title imaginable in his time, 'Lord' (*kurios*); as he says, it places him above all things in God's entire creation. The extent of his exaltation is seen in the application to Jesus of the language of Isaiah 45:23-25, where it is used with specific reference to God himself, Yahweh.[5]

- The lordship that Paul ascribes to Jesus can be seen as a realisation of God's declared purpose at the time of man's creation (Gen. 1:26-27); it therefore implies that his hitherto unparalleled exaltation will not ultimately be his alone but is the destiny of many.

Excursus: Jesus as 'Lord'

The use of the title 'Lord' (*kurios*) in the New Testament is not without difficulty for the reader because it refers, sometimes to God the Father, and sometimes to Jesus. It occurs with reference to God mainly in allusions to him as Creator and in Old Testament quotations and references, where it replaces both *Yahweh*, the name of God, and the titles *adon* and *adonai*. Thus Psalm 110:1 reads *'The LORD (Yahweh) says to my lord (adoni – sing.): "Sit at my right hand, till I make your enemies your footstool"'*. In Matthew's quotation of this verse, it becomes: *'The Lord (kurios) said to my Lord (kurios), "Sit at my right hand, until I put your enemies under your feet"'* (Matt. 22:44).

It is, however, an essential part of the apostles' message that Jesus Christ is now 'Lord'. 'Jesus Christ is Lord' became, especially for Paul, the key confession of Christian faith – as, for example, in Romans 10:9 and 1 Corinthians 12:3. It was, though, no invention of Paul: in the very first proclamation of the Christian gospel in Acts 2, Peter first explains the apostles' ability to speak in tongues with a quotation from Joel 2 which culminates in the phrase *'Then everyone who calls on the name of the Lord shall be saved'* (Acts 2:21). His argument thereafter, based on quotations from Psalms 16 and 110, culminates in the triumphant conclusion: *'Therefore let the entire house of Israel know with certainty that God has made him both Lord and Messiah, this Jesus whom you crucified'* (Acts 2:36). From that moment on, Jesus is 'the Lord', the one on whose name one must call, i.e. whose lordship and power to save one must

---

5   Does this mean that Jesus too now bears the divine name, Yahweh? While the phrase *'the name that is above every name'* might suggest this, especially as the name Yahweh occurs three times in Isaiah 45:21-25, it seems to me more likely that Paul has in mind the title 'Lord'. In addition, the final phrase in the passage, *'to the glory of God the Father'*, appears to be distinguishing carefully between Father and Son rather than conflating and blurring their identities – just as the opening of the final sentence also does: *'Therefore God also highly exalted him …'*

appeal to; thus, we find Paul beginning his first Letter to Corinth like this: '*To the church of God which is at Corinth, to those sanctified in Christ Jesus, called to be saints together with all those who in every place **call on the name of our Lord Jesus Christ*** (1 Cor. 1:2).

Given this varying usage, we sometimes find references to both Father and Son as 'the Lord', often in quite close proximity:

> *You cannot drink the cup of the **Lord** (Jesus) and the cup of demons. You cannot partake of the table of the **Lord** (Jesus) and the table of demons ... Eat whatever is sold in the meat market without raising any question on the ground of conscience. For 'the earth is the **Lord's** (God the Creator), and everything in it.' (1 Corinthians 10:21, 25-26)*

It is not always easy to determine which 'Lord' is being referred to, and the context must be allowed to guide us. The following figures for three major New Testament books are based on my own assessment of the various contexts:

	God	*Uncertain*	*Jesus*
Acts	25	14	62
Romans	9 (all quotations)	3	25
1 Corinthians	6 (all quotations)	5	48

Less than infallible though they are, these figures suggest that we should, when reading Acts or the apostolic letters, take *kurios* to refer to Jesus unless the context clearly indicates otherwise.

These figures also illustrate how quickly and completely Jesus was, after his resurrection, understood and worshipped as 'Lord'. His followers apply to him a term that Greek-speaking Jews customarily used in referring to God – and which was widely used in a parallel way in a variety of cults throughout the Hellenistic world. Devout Jews who did not speak Greek probably referred to God using the Aramaic *mare*, and it seems that this term too came to be applied to Jesus, as witnessed by the survival into the New Testament of the term *Maranatha* ('Our Lord, come') in 1 Cor. 16:22. The conclusion is inescapable that his followers very soon began to place him within the realm of the divine, worthy to be honoured alongside, but not in equality with, God himself, as the passage from Revelation 5, quoted above, confirms.[6]

An additional factor leading to the use of this title for Jesus was possibly its

---

6 For a discussion of this issue and for some balanced conclusions, see James D.G. Dunn's *Did The First Christians Worship Jesus? – The New Testament Evidence*, Louisville, Kentucky, 2010.

The Glorified Lord

increasing use from about 37 AD for Roman emperors, especially Caligula and Nero, in connection with the growing cult of Caesar as a god. The language of this cult must, to the early Christians, have looked like a travesty, or a usurpation, of terms rightly belonging to Jesus alone. Thus, the emperor Augustus, or *'Imperātor Caesar Dīvī Fīlius Augustus'* (Emperor Augustus Caesar son of God) was proclaimed 'Lord' (*kurios*) and was hailed as the bringer of peace and justice, who united the whole world and claimed the allegiance and obedience of mankind. The accession of a new emperor, his birthday, or the birth of a male heir were blazoned abroad as 'good news' (*euaggelion*).

While some scholars remain sceptical as to the degree to which the language of the New Testament letters is coloured by their rejection of emperor-worship, others read parts of Paul's writings in particular against this background.[7] It is hard to imagine that much-travelled, educated Christians like Paul would have failed to be aware of the competing uses to which titles such as *kurios* were being put in their world. The challenge on a practical level that the imperial cult presented to Christian believers, especially the requirement that all should burn incense in honour of Caesar, is probably reflected in Paul's comments in 1 Corinthians 12:3.

The use of the title *kurios* in relation to Jesus is complex: the word could be used as a simple title showing respect – compare 'monsieur' in French or 'sir' in English – and as the expression of a social relationship between two of unequal social status, e.g. master and servant. Therefore, not every occurrence of *kurios* in the Gospels is of theological significance, not even when the disciples address Jesus as 'Lord', as they frequently do – these usages simply reflect their respect for him, as does their use of *rhabbi, didaskalos* ('teacher') and *epistates* ('master'). Their use of the term *kurios* becomes significant only when it occurs in third-person references to Jesus, as it does in the examples provided. It is worthy of note that only Luke among the Gospel writers himself uses the title *kurios* for Jesus in the course of his narration – see, for example, Luke 7:13, 31; 10:1; 11:39; 12:42; 13:15.[8] It also occurs frequently in his parables involving masters and servants.

We shall refer again to Jesus' status as 'Lord' in the next chapter as we consider different aspects of his present work.

---

7   See, for example, N.T. Wright's 'Paul's Gospel and Caesar's Empire' and 'Paul and Empire', both in his *Pauline Perspectives. Essays on Paul 1978-2013*, London 2013, pp. 169-190; 439-451.

8   See C. Kavin Rowe, *Early Narrative Christology. The Lord in the Gospel of Luke*, Grand Rapids Michigan 2006

Jesus – yesterday, today, for ever

A new mission

Our dependence on the New Testament for pictures of and information about the risen Jesus has one attendant danger: that we think of him primarily as the one who came, suffered, died and rose again in the past, one whom we remember – by which we tend to mean dwelling reverently on his passion, as though his work were finished. Such a view of him is perhaps reinforced by Jesus' own words in Revelation: *'To the one who conquers I will give a place with me on my throne, just as I myself conquered and sat down with my Father on his throne'* (Rev. 3:21). A similar picture is evoked by the Letter to the Hebrews: *'But when Christ had offered for all time a single sacrifice for sins, "he sat down at the right hand of God" and since then has been waiting "until his enemies would be made a footstool for his feet"'* (Heb. 10:12-13). The reference to 'sitting down', which in both passages is a conscious allusion to the language of Psalm 110: *'The LORD says to my lord, "Sit at my right hand until I make your enemies your footstool"'* (Ps. 110:1), may have strengthened the prevalent tendency to cling to the earthly Jesus, as Mary Magdalene did (John 20:17) – to *'look for the living among the dead'* (Luke 24:5), as though only the man from Nazareth is the true Jesus.

So too with Jesus' prayer in John 17: we easily gain the impression that with his death on the cross, his work was completed. He speaks of having *'finish[ed] the work that you gave me to do'* (v. 4), while in the verses 11-15 he appears to imply that his 'going to the Father' will leave his followers alone and unprotected – he asks the Father to *'protect them from the evil one'* (v. 15). In the same vein, he tells the disciples in the discourses that he will *'... ask the Father, and he will give you another Advocate, to be with you forever'* (14:16).

Yet in the immediately following verses he promises that he will himself be with them:

> *'I will not leave you orphaned; I am coming to you. In a little while the world will no longer see me, but you will see me ... They who have my commandments and keep them are those who love me; and those who love me will be loved by my Father, and I will love them and reveal myself to them ... Those who love me will keep my word, and my Father will love them, and we will come to them and make our home with them.' (v. 18-19, 21, 23)*

The 'advocate' or 'counsellor' (*parakletos*) is thus evidently Jesus himself, though no longer in bodily form. It is surely unthinkable that there might be another *parakletos* distinguishable from Jesus himself; as he repeatedly says in John 17, the disciples have been 'given' to him – the verb *didomi* is an essential key to John 17, where it occurs eleven times. It also occurs in Hebrews

The Glorified Lord

2: '*Here am I and the children whom God has **given** me'* (Heb. 2:13).

The implication, then, is that the 'mission accomplished' note in John 17 refers only to the first phase of Jesus' work. If we read carefully the opening verses of the prayer, we realise that Jesus indicates as much:

> '*... glorify your Son so that the Son may glorify you, since you have given him authority over all people, to give eternal life to all whom you have given him ... I glorified you on earth by finishing the work that you gave me to do. So now, Father, glorify me in your own presence with the glory that I had in your presence before the world existed.' (John 17:1-2, 4-5)*

Jesus asks here that, having glorified God by completing his work 'on earth', he may now glorify him in a new way, through a new form of service; he desires that, no longer confined by the limits of life 'on earth', he may be able to further the work of giving eternal life to those whom the Father has entrusted to him.

What, then, is now his task? Like his mission during his earthly life, it must obviously be directed towards the achievement of God's ultimate purpose with his created world and with man in particular. Passages such as Genesis 1:26, Ephesians 1:9-10, and Colossians 1:15-20 speak of a perfected creation, brought to unity and harmony in God through the service of Jesus, his Son, who is the prototype of a perfected humanity. During his earthly ministry, Jesus sought to further the realisation of this goal by proclaiming, first in words, then in the giving of himself, the forgiving, redeeming grace of God and by embodying that alternative model of human life. Jesus' words in John 17, already quoted: '*glorify me in your own presence with the glory that I had in your presence before the world existed*', confirm that he was fully aware of the central role ascribed to him in that purpose as the first realisation of God's intentions for human beings and the first to inherit and to experience the lofty calling of humanity. Now, in his resurrection glory, he wishes to continue the work that he had begun – no longer, though, as God's empowered agent of *shaliach*, but rather as his partner. We have, of course, no knowledge of the kind of relationships that exist between immortal, divine beings, so we of necessity use the terminology that describes relationships between humans – as the New Testament does!

We can, I think, discern two major elements in Jesus' continuing work. One is, as before, the proclamation of God's grace and the appeal to men and women to turn back to him in order to share ultimately in the life of God. In the New Testament, that dimension of his work is represented mainly in Acts, which, as its opening implies, is the continuation of the work that Jesus had been doing before his crucifixion: *'In my former book, Theophilus, I wrote about all that Jesus **began** to do and to teach ...'* (Acts 1:1 NIV).

The other dimension, to be considered in our next chapter, is the focus of Jesus' thoughts in the prayer of John 17: he desires above all that those who have already believed, however imperfectly, as was certainly the case with the disciples then, may be preserved from the evils in the world which threaten to lure them away from their faith, and may instead grow in understanding and in love, being transformed according to the pattern of Jesus until, as Paul puts it in Galatians, *'Christ is formed in you'* (Gal. 4:19). This, then, is his other great concern: to watch over those whom God has 'given' him – to be their 'shepherd' and guide.

At work in the world

How does Jesus perform his continued work of proclamation? Or, to put it another way, how is he present and active in the world despite having apparently left it? At the simplest level, he is ever-present because he is himself the essential message of the gospel and the focus of faith. I referred at the end of the previous chapter to Peter's proclamation of the gospel in Acts 2 and 3; we saw there that the heart of the message is a narrative of Jesus' life, death and resurrection. His crucifixion was the essential, once-for-all display of human fallenness, of the self-centred, potentially violent human way that Jesus had spoken of at Caesarea Philippi, and consequently an indictment of all who adhere to it. Through his crucifixion, a judgment was passed: God had *'condemned sin in the flesh'* (Rom. 8:3). But crucifixion was followed by resurrection – by a vacant cross and an empty tomb. For those willing to look at the horrifying spectacle of Jesus on his cross and recognise their own part in bringing him there, the evidence of their sin was done away, so that they found themselves, to their amazement, forgiven and accepted into the company of the risen Jesus. That, essentially, is what the apostles proclaim throughout Acts, for example in chapters 10, 13 and 26, and even also in chapter 17. And, as the Servant passages predict, those who had been his enemies, who had scoffed at his claims, were put to silence by the evidences of his rising:

> *Just as there were many who were astonished at him – so marred was his appearance, beyond human semblance, and his form beyond that of mortals – so he shall startle many nations; kings shall shut their mouths because of him; for that which had not been told them they shall see, and that which they had not heard they shall contemplate. (Isaiah 52:14-15)*

He who, in the language of John's Gospel, had been 'the word become flesh' (John 1:14), had now become 'word' again – but a more powerful word than

The Glorified Lord

any other that God had uttered, comparable to the mighty word of creation:

> *By the word of the* Lord *the heavens were made, and all their host by the breath of his mouth … For he spoke, and it came to be; he commanded, and it stood firm. (Psalm 33:6, 9; cf. Psalm 147:15)*

> *For as the rain and the snow come down from heaven, and do not return there until they have watered the earth, making it bring forth and sprout, giving seed to the sower and bread to the eater, so shall my word be that goes out from my mouth; it shall not return to me empty, but it shall accomplish that which I purpose, and succeed in the thing for which I sent it. (Isaiah 55:10-11)*

Sometimes, this central message is framed within a longer perspective, not so different from what I am attempting here, tracing the pre-history of Jesus back into the Old Testament – as, for example, Peter does in Acts 2:22-36 and 3:21-26, and as Paul does in Acts 13:16-25 and 26:22-23 – and looking forward to the future consummation of the divine purpose of which he is the focus. This we find, for example, in Acts 3:20-21; 10:42; 17:31. Yet, though Luke characterises the apostles as speaking about 'the kingdom of God' (Acts 8:12; 19:8; 20:25; 28:23, 31), it is evident that it was Jesus crucified and raised that is the focus of their message; they are repeatedly described as 'preaching Christ' (Acts 8:5; 9:20; 19:13; 1 Cor. 1:23; 2 Cor. 1:19; 4:5, etc.). Perhaps their example has something to teach present-day Christians about how best to capture the hearts and minds of those to whom they speak. The apostles evidently found that the story of Jesus possessed the power to pierce the carapace of human self-interest in a way that nothing else could – which, as we saw earlier, is what the 'Servant passages' in Isaiah would lead us to expect. Thus, from the very fact of being the focus of Christian proclamation, Jesus, once dead but now alive, is ever-present in the witness of the early church – and so it has remained.

Acting directly

In addition to being present and active simply as 'word' spoken, and later written, by the apostles, Jesus was and is able to work in other ways. As we should by now expect, he follows the example of the Father. Sometimes, the New Testament suggests, he works directly, employing the authority entrusted to him (Matt. 28:18). We cannot be sure who wrote the later verses of Mark 16, but its final verse sums up well what we see happening in Acts: '*And they went out and proclaimed the good news everywhere, while the Lord worked with them and confirmed the message by the signs that accompanied it*' (Mark 16:20). The

249

Jesus – yesterday, today, for ever

Lord 'worked with them' by empowering them to perform the 'signs' that gave persuasive force to their message, as we see especially in the early chapters of Acts – see, for example, 2:43 and the healing of the lame man in chapters 3-4, where Luke uses the same word *semeion* ('sign') to describe the healing.

Jesus' comments in John 14-16 on the role of the *parakletos* in relation to witness describe the events of Acts somewhat differently:

> *'When the Advocate comes, whom I will send to you from the Father, the Spirit of truth who comes from the Father, he will testify on my behalf. You also are to testify because you have been with me from the beginning …'*

> *'And when he comes, he will prove the world wrong about sin and right-eousness and judgment: about sin, because they do not believe in me; about righteousness, because I am going to the Father and you will see me no long-er; about judgment, because the ruler of this world has been condemned.' (John 15:26-27; 16:8-11)*

The effects of the testimony of Jesus as *parakletos* that are described here are almost a summary of what we see in Acts: human beings are convicted of sin (*'about sin'*), the resurrection and exaltation of Jesus confirm that Jesus truly was who and what he had claimed to be (*'about righteousness'*), and the world and its rulers are shown to be in the wrong because they condemned him (*'about judgment'*). But in contrast to the passage from Mark, primacy is given here to the role of the *parakletos*: the disciples, it says, *'also testify'*.

The way in which agency is ascribed to the *parakletos* gives the impression that, though his activity is usually mediated through the apostles, he may also act directly. In both Acts and the letters, there are indeed places where the action of Jesus – or the Spirit – appears to be distinguished from, or prior to, that of the apostles, as the following examples indicate (I am assuming the references to 'the Spirit' in fact refer to 'the spirit of Jesus'):

> *Then **the Spirit** said to Philip, 'Go over to this chariot and join it.' … When they came up out of the water, the Spirit of the Lord snatched Philip away; the eunuch saw him no more, and went on his way rejoicing. (Acts 8:29, 39)*

> *He fell to the ground and heard a voice saying to him, 'Saul, Saul, why do you persecute me?' He asked, 'Who are you, Lord?' The reply came, '**I am Jesus**, whom you are persecuting.' (Acts 9:4-5)*

> ***The Lord said to him** in a vision, 'Ananias.' He answered, 'Here I am, Lord.' The Lord said to him, 'Get up and go to the street called Straight,*

The Glorified Lord

> and at the house of Judas look for a man of Tarsus named Saul. … he is an instrument whom I have chosen to bring my name before Gentiles and kings and before the people of Israel; I myself will show him how much he must suffer for the sake of my name.' *(Acts 9:10-16)*

> While Peter was still thinking about the vision, **the Spirit said to him**, 'Look, three men are searching for you.' *(Acts 10:19)*

> While Peter was still speaking, **the Holy Spirit fell** upon all who heard the word. *(Acts 10:44)*

> While they were worshipping the Lord and fasting, **the Holy Spirit said**, 'Set apart for me Barnabas and Saul for the work to which I have called them.' *(Acts 13:2)*

> They went through the region of Phrygia and Galatia, having been **forbidden by the Holy Spirit** to speak the word in Asia … When they had come opposite Mysia, they attempted to go into Bithynia, but the **Spirit of Jesus did not allow them.** *(Acts 16:6-7)*

> One night **the Lord said to Paul** in a vision, 'Do not be afraid, but speak and do not be silent …' *(Acts 18:9)*

These and other passages suggest that Jesus through the Spirit intervened directly in the church's work of witness by:

- choosing his agent, as was the case with Paul in Acts 9;

- pointing the way forward, giving impetus and direction to the apostles' activity in ways that went beyond what they had themselves contemplated – this is the case with Peter's visit to Cornelius, the beginning of the first missionary journey (13:2), and the first venture into Europe in Acts 16;

- communicating directly with an apostle to provide encouragement and reassurance, as in 2 Corinthians:

> Three times I appealed to the Lord about this, that it would leave me, but he said to me, 'My grace is sufficient for you, for power is made perfect in weakness.' So, I will boast all the more gladly of my weaknesses, so that the power of Christ may dwell in me. *(2 Corinthians 12:8-9).*

In addition, there are the incidents where 'an angel of the Lord' or simply 'the Lord' is said to intervene to preserve or strengthen one of his agents, as in Acts 12:7, 17, 23; 22:10; 23:11.

Jesus – yesterday, today, for ever

Through his servants

For the most part, however, the New Testament shows us Jesus working through human agents. It appears to be a divine principle that God prefers to work in this way – as if he wishes to gain the trust and obedience of human beings, not by dazzling displays of irresistible power, but rather through their encounter with his spiritual qualities, exhibited in the men and women who represent him. Throughout his earthly mission, Jesus was accompanied and helped by people who responded to his message and believed in him, and from among whom he chose twelve to be his specially designated 'disciples'. That remains the pattern in the post-resurrection age; therefore, in thinking about the present work of Jesus, we need, almost more than anything else, to look at the relationship of 'the Lord' to his 'servants', his people.

That the Lord works through his people is not, however, simply a matter of a preferred method: it is also his joy. What greater joy and satisfaction could the exalted Jesus have than to be able to continue his saving work through men and women who, as a result of his work, were now willing to be his agents, as he had been of the Father? But it is also his 'glory': Jesus speaks in John 17 of having 'glorified' the Father by completing *'the work you gave me to do'* (v. 4) – and himself being 'glorified' in being permitted and enabled to perform that service. Now, though, that 'glory', the honour of being his chosen instruments, is given to his followers: *'The glory that you have given me I have given them, so that they may be one, as we are one'* (v. 22), while he is himself 'glorified' by their committing themselves to his service: *'All mine are yours, and yours are mine; and **I have been glorified in them'*** (v. 10). This is the measure of Jesus' exaltation – to share in the Father's glory through the willing, dedicated service of those who are themselves the fruit of his own service.

Perhaps the simplest and most memorable image of the shared work of the Lord and his apostles is the one that we find in John 21. Some of the disciples go fishing again – and catch nothing, until a figure on the shore tells them where to cast their net, whereupon they achieve a catch that surpasses all expectation. Like the two others that make up John's final chapter, this episode is symbolic of the church's future. The parallel with the episode in Luke 5, when Jesus called several of these disciples to follow him and become 'fishers of men', is obvious; however, unlike in Luke 5, the net does not break and the catch is brought safely to shore, confirming that it is a picture of the disciples' future work of witness. It is an image of men and women working under the Lord's direction; though he is no longer in the boat with them, he can see better than they where to cast their net – and he provides sustenance and strength for them in their work.

The Glorified Lord

This is surely true in a wider context than that of miraculous actions on the Lord's part. The fundamental pattern that we find in the New Testament is that of Jesus guiding, directing and supporting his followers' work for him, and this must surely be their expectation now as much as then. Whatever name it goes by, whether 'preaching' or 'outreach', the church's witness should be accompanied by explicit prayers for such guidance – which may come in many forms. Christians should expect to be surprised, to be led where they would not have expected to go, as Peter was in the case of Cornelius, and to be driven by circumstance to venture well beyond their comfort zone, as the Jerusalem church was by the success of Philip in Samaria (Acts 8) and of Greek-speaking Christians in Antioch (Acts 11).

The apostles

The apostles of whom we hear in Acts and whose letters we can read are the primary examples of the role of Jesus' servants as his representatives. It may be that they were specially empowered and fortified in ways that might appear to set them apart from other, later believers, but in essence, I believe, they are put before us precisely as exemplars, in whom the relationship of Jesus to his people is 'writ large' for our benefit. So, what do they show us? We note that it is Jesus himself who gives them their commission. First, the apostles were *chosen*, as the Twelve had been early in Jesus' earthly ministry; the foremost example from the post-resurrection period is, of course, Paul, who is described by Jesus to Ananias as *'an instrument whom I have chosen to bring my name before Gentiles and kings and before the people of Israel'* (Acts 9:15). These chosen emissaries are then inducted into the new community, sharing henceforth in *the new life of the risen Jesus* – this I take to be the sense of Jesus' symbolic action in John 20: *'When he had said this, he breathed on them and said to them, "Receive the Holy Spirit"'* (v. 22). By this single action, an obvious parallel to God's creative act in Genesis 2:7, Jesus brings into being what John describes earlier as *'the temple of his body'* (John 2:21). In the words that follow immediately afterwards, he also gives them *authority* to act on his behalf, granting to, or withholding from, others the right to be incorporated into that body: *'If you forgive the sins of any, they are forgiven them; if you retain the sins of any, they are retained'* (20:23). We see this authority being wielded by Jesus' followers in numerous places in Acts, for example, when Peter and John visit Samaria (Acts 8:14-17), when Barnabas goes to Antioch (11:23-26), when Peter encounters Cornelius (10:44-48), and when Paul meets Lydia and the prison governor in Philippi (16:15, 32-34).

In addition to such authority, Jesus grants them *power*, what he terms *'power from on high'* (Luke 24:49), which confers on the apostles the ability to speak in tongues and to heal. Whether 'tongues' refers to the ability to speak in another language or to ecstatic utterance remains uncertain; in the context of witness, the former would be of more value than the latter, as Paul appears to recognise in 1 Corinthians 14: *'If, therefore, the whole church comes together and all speak in tongues, and outsiders or unbelievers enter, will they not say that you are out of your mind?'* (1 Cor. 14:23). At the moment when this power is for the first time bestowed on the apostles, on the Day of Pentecost, it is undoubtedly command of a foreign language that is meant; the witnesses exclaim in amazement: *'Are not all these who are speaking Galileans? And how is it that we hear, each of us, in our own native language?'* (Acts 2:7-8). Probably, however, it was the ability to heal that was of greater importance to the apostles in their witness activities; at its first use, in Acts 3, it evoked a powerful reaction from the bystanders: *' ... they were filled with wonder and amazement at what had happened to [the formerly lame man]'* (Acts 3:10). The parallel event in the record of Paul's activities made a similar impact: *'When the crowds saw what Paul had done, they shouted in the Lycaonian language, "The gods have come down to us in human form!"'* (Acts 14:11).

It is important to notice that the New Testament clearly represents these powers as the gift of the risen, exalted Jesus: *'Being therefore exalted at the right hand of God, and having received from the Father the promise of the Holy Spirit, he has poured out this that you both see and hear'* (Acts 2:33).[9] The way in which Paul describes himself at the opening of the Letter to the Galatians is significant in this context: *'Paul an apostle – sent neither by human commission nor from human authorities, but through Jesus Christ and God the Father, who raised him from the dead' (Gal. 1:1).* He owes his apostleship to both Son and Father, from the former directly, on the road to Damascus, and through him ultimately from the Father.

Much later, speaking of a wider range of gifts given to all the members of the church, he makes the same point again: *'But each of us was given grace according to the measure of Christ's gift. Therefore it is said, "When he ascended on high he made captivity itself a captive; he gave gifts to his people"'* (Eph. 4:7-8). The effects achieved thanks to those gifts – not only the healings but also the transforming effects of the 'word of Christ', presented with authority by the apostles – were thus visible expressions in the world of the exaltation and lordship of Jesus, continuing his still unfinished work through the dedication

---

9   This passage implies that the Father gives to the Son, who in turn gives to his people. That is precisely what we see in the prayer in John 17 already: *' ... the words that you gave to me I have given to them ... The glory that you have given me I have given them ... '* (John 17:8, 22).

The Glorified Lord

of men and women who know themselves honoured to be his representatives. When he heals the lame man in Jerusalem in Acts 3, Peter rightly sums up the situation: '... *in the name of Jesus Christ of Nazareth, stand up and walk*' (v. 6) – he knows that he is acting 'in the name of Jesus', that is, as his agent and representative. Then, faced with the amazement of the crowd, he explains:

> 'You Israelites, why do you wonder at this, or why do you stare at us, as though by our own power or piety we had made him walk? The God of Abraham, the God of Isaac, and the God of Jacob, the God of our ancestors has glorified his servant Jesus ... And by faith in his name, **his name itself has made this man strong**, whom you see and know...' (Acts 3:12-16)

This incident is the perfect paradigm of the role of Jesus 'today': not physically present, yet active and powerful through those to whom he has 'delegated' his own authority. What Peter says about a miracle, Paul says about their witness: '*So we are ambassadors for Christ, since God is making his appeal through us; we entreat you on behalf of Christ, be reconciled to God*' (2 Cor. 5:20).

No ordinary servants

Thus, just as Jesus had been his Father's chosen 'ambassador', so now the apostles, and all those who proclaim his saving message are his. They are, of course, his 'servants'; for them, Jesus is truly the 'Lord', whose will the members of the church seek to fulfil and whose behaviour they endeavour to imitate. Jesus' disciples began to speak of him and to him as Lord, probably quite spontaneously, immediately after his resurrection:

> They were saying, '**The Lord** has risen indeed, and he has appeared to Simon!' (Luke 24:30)

> Mary Magdalene went and announced to the disciples, 'I have seen **the Lord**' ... So the other disciples told him, 'We have seen **the Lord**.' (John 20:18, 25)

> That disciple whom Jesus loved said to Peter, 'It is **the Lord**!' (John 21:7)

At this early stage, it was probably simply an expression of the awe they had already felt in his presence even before his death. Perhaps, too, it was an expression of their conviction that Jesus was indeed the promised anointed one, destined to sit on David's throne, confirmed by his own stress on the fact that David in Psalm 110 called the Christ 'lord' (Mark 12:36). It is, though, also a first indication of their growing sense that he was to be honoured in a new way. They had begun, almost instinctively, to ascribe to him a status that placed him nearer to God than to themselves, so that he became the living exemplar of the will of God for human beings. Thus, for example, their relationships with one another should mirror the pattern of Jesus: '... *live in love, as Christ loved us and gave himself up for us*' (Eph. 5:2). Perhaps Paul's best description of this relationship of service, obedience and imitation occurs in Romans 14:

> *We do not live to ourselves, and we do not die to ourselves. If we live, we live to the Lord, and if we die, we die to the Lord; so then, whether we live or whether we die, we are the Lord's. For to this end Christ died and lived again, so that he might be Lord of both the dead and the living. (Romans 14:7-9)*

Now and for ever, Paul says, believers 'belong' to Christ; they desire to give him honour, not only with their words and hymns but with the very fabric of their lives. His lordship over them is thus a force which works to transform them according to '*the image of his Son*'.

The comparison with earthly master-slave relations can be misleading, however. We remember how Paul in 1 Corinthians 9 resists the notion that he should proclaim the gospel simply because he is under obligation – he wishes to work 'of his own will' (v. 16-17). We recall too his rejection of the Law of Moses as a kind of bondage and his celebration of 'freedom in Christ', in which there is ultimately only '*a single commandment, "You shall love your neighbour as yourself"*' (Gal. 5:14). The teaching of Jesus that John records points in the same direction: '*I do not call you servants any longer, because the servant does not know what the master is doing; but I have called you friends, because I have made known to you everything that I have heard from my Father*' (John 15:15). Though he says in the preceding verse that his disciples are his friends '*if you do what I command you*', it is apparent that there is actually only one commandment, again the commandment to love, albeit here 'one another' rather than 'your neighbour'.

In fact, as one looks at the New Testament, it becomes clear that this is a lord-servant relationship of a very unusual kind; it is analogous to the relationship that we have already considered in the case of the Father and the Son. I stressed in looking at Jesus' earthly life that he needed to use his judgment, act on his own initiative – however much in prayerful consultation with the Father. The Son serves his Father and fulfils his will and purpose in a way that corresponds to the conception of the *shaliach* (see chapter 4), the plenipotentiary who, to all intents and purposes, *is* the person whose agent he or she is, totally identified with their 'sender' and yet completely free to fulfil their mission in the way that they judge most effective – totally free yet totally

The Glorified Lord

committed. In John's Gospel in particular, Jesus repeatedly describes himself as 'sent' (using the two Greek verbs *apostello* and *pempo*) and God as 'he that sent me', and asserts repeatedly his *practical* (not ontological!) identity with the Father:

'If you knew me, you would know my Father also.' (John 8:19)

'Whoever hates me hates my Father also.' (John 15:23)

'Whoever listens to you listens to me, and whoever rejects you rejects me, and whoever rejects me rejects the one who sent me.' (Luke 10:16)

'… whoever receives one whom I send receives me; and whoever receives me receives him who sent me.' (John 13:20)

'Whoever believes in me believes not in me but in him who sent me.' (John 12:44)

Jesus' words in John 20 make explicit that those whom he is now 'sending' stand in the same relationship to him as he himself did to his Father: *'As the Father has sent me, so I send you'*, and that practical identity is now extended to encompass those whom Jesus in turn sends. It is that kind of servant that Jesus anticipates in his prayer in John 17, using the same language: *'As you have sent me into the world, so I have sent them into the world'* (John 17:18).

Paul's reluctance to be merely a slave who obeyed orders suggests that he had come to understand what kind of service and what kind of servant it was that Jesus desired – and it was that kind of service that he set out to render. His own life and writings illustrate this: as he travels back from Corinth to Jerusalem at the end of what we call his 'third missionary journey', almost immediately after writing Romans, and bearing, with others, the proceeds of the collections for the poor in Jerusalem, Paul receives repeated warnings of what awaits him there:

'… the Holy Spirit testifies to me in every city that imprisonment and persecutions are waiting for me.' (Acts 20:23)

We looked up the disciples and stayed there for seven days. Through the Spirit they told Paul not to go on to Jerusalem. (21:4)

He came to us and took Paul's belt, bound his own feet and hands with it, and said, 'Thus says the Holy Spirit, "This is the way the Jews in Jerusalem will bind the man who owns this belt and will hand him over to the Gentiles."' (21:11)

Jesus – yesterday, today, for ever

The 'hired servant' might have concluded that he must not go – that the master has sent new orders and that he is therefore set free of his task. Not so Paul the *shaliach*: he uses his own judgment, seeing these messages not as orders but simply as information of what to expect. He judges the delivery of the collection vital to Jew-Gentile relationships within the young church, and his own role in its delivery no less vital, *persona non grata* in Jerusalem though he was. And so, using his own judgment and his own wisdom – and willing to risk his very life for his master's cause as Jesus had done, he goes – and the rest is history.

Something similar can also be seen in his letter to the Colossians. Near the end of the first chapter, Paul writes: *'I am now rejoicing in my sufferings for your sake, and in my flesh I am completing what is lacking in Christ's afflictions for the sake of his body, that is, the church'* (Col. 1:24). At first sight, it is a strange thing to say: how could there be anything lacking in Jesus' service? The answer can be found by looking at what Paul says in Philippians about the actions of Epaphroditus; *'Because for the work of Christ he was nigh unto death, not regarding his life, to supply your lack of service toward me'* (Phil. 2:30). 'Lack' here is the same word used in Colossians 1:24, *husterema.* Our first impression is that the Philippians had been negligent and had failed to continue their support for Paul. In chapter 4, however, Paul explains: *'I rejoice in the Lord greatly that now at last you have revived your concern for me; indeed, you were concerned for me, but had no opportunity to show it'* (4:10) – perhaps Paul was too far away, or they did not know where he was. It was, in any case, a question, not of negligence or inadequate service, but of lack of opportunity – and that, surely, is the key to Paul's words in Colossians. Jesus himself, exalted and all-powerful though he is, cannot care for the church or for its individual members in practical ways, cannot proclaim the word of his grace – except through the actions of his followers, his *shaliachim* acting on his behalf. Paul is willing to be his Lord's hands, feet, voice *'for the sake of his body'*:

> *I became its servant according to God's commission that was given to me for you, to make the word of God fully known ... It is he whom we proclaim, warning everyone and teaching everyone **in all wisdom** ... For this I toil and struggle with all the energy that he powerfully inspires within me. (v. 25-29)*

Such an attitude is about as far removed from the conventional 'servant' as one can imagine: Paul uses every scrap of understanding and judgment with which his upbringing, his experience of the world and the church, and his encounters with Jesus, not only on the road to Damascus but throughout his

The Glorified Lord

subsequent ministry, have equipped him in order to forward and to realise his Lord's wishes.

'The sharing of his sufferings'

The apostles would not have been true representatives of Jesus if their witness had been characterised only by successful witness and triumphant conquest. When Jesus spoke to the disciples before his crucifixion about what lay ahead, he included a warning: *'As for yourselves, beware; for they will hand you over to councils; and you will be beaten in synagogues; and you will stand before governors and kings because of me, as a testimony to them. And the good news must first be proclaimed to all nations'* (Mark 13:9-10). In John's version of this or a similar warning, Jesus emphasises that such persecution and suffering would occur because his disciples are as he is and therefore share his fate in some measure:

> *'If the world hates you, be aware that it hated me before it hated you. If you belonged to the world, the world would love you as its own. Because you do not belong to the world, but I have chosen you out of the world – therefore the world hates you. Remember the word that I said to you, 'Servants are not greater than their master.' If they persecuted me, they will persecute you; if they kept my word, they will keep yours also.' (John 15:18-20)*

Sure enough, Acts is to a considerable degree the record of just such sufferings: the arrest of apostles in its early chapters, the death of Stephen, persecution of believers by Saul/Paul, and the death of James. Then, of course, we come to the story of Paul, of whom Jesus himself said to Ananias: *'I myself will show him how much he must suffer for the sake of my name'* (Acts 9:16), a prediction realised in the catalogue of sufferings found in 2 Corinthians 11. It is surely no coincidence that the stories of the two figures who dominate Acts, Peter in chapters 1-12, Paul in the rest of the book, both culminate in a virtual death, followed by a miraculous deliverance. Peter, in prison and due for execution the next morning, is extricated from prison by the intervention of the angel in Acts 12, while Paul in Acts 27 undergoes an ordeal that sums up so many biblical images of death by drowning, from the Flood, via the crossing of the Red Sea, to the rite of baptism, sharing with Jesus the fate predicted of the Messiah: *'I have come into deep waters, and the flood sweeps over me'* (Ps. 69:2). In the lives of both men, the pattern of Jesus' death and resurrection is realised because they have understood and embraced what I have called 'the Caesarea Philippi principle'.

It seems more than likely that Paul's words to the Philippians, written from Rome, probably not so long after the shipwreck, reflect his understanding of

Jesus – yesterday, today, for ever

that principle: *'I want to know Christ and the power of his resurrection and the sharing of his sufferings by becoming like him in his death, if somehow I may attain the resurrection from the dead'* (Phil. 3:10-11). That connection is all the more likely in the light of the preceding verses, which appear to allude to the 'lightening of the ship' that occurred during the storm:

> *Yet whatever gains I had, these I have come to regard as loss because of Christ. More than that, I regard everything as loss because of the surpassing value of knowing Christ Jesus my Lord. For his sake I have suffered the loss of all things, and I regard them as rubbish, in order that I may gain Christ… (Philippians 3:7-8)*

However, that is not the only link with the shipwreck experience: when Paul uses here the words 'loss' (*zemia*) and 'suffer loss' (*zemioo*) on the one hand and 'gain' (*kerdaino*) on the other, he is echoing the antithesis that he had himself used during the storm: *'Sirs, ye should have hearkened unto me, and not have loosed from Crete, and to have **gained** (kerdaino) this harm and **loss** (zemia)'* (Acts 27:21 KJV). Yet those words, with their ironic use of the word 'gain', were themselves an echo of the only other place in the New Testament where we find *kerdaino* and *zemia/zemioo* brought together in this way – at Caesarea Philippi: *'For what will it profit them to **gain** (kerdaino) the whole world and **forfeit** (zemioo) their life'* (Mark 8:36).

This accord between the gospel of Jesus crucified and risen and the experience of his representatives leads us to one inescapable conclusion: that the 'word' of Jesus is most powerful and convincing when it is expressed not only in what his followers say but also in their lives. Those who follow where Jesus leads may well find that the pattern of dying and rising that we see in Peter and Paul in Acts, the 'fellowship of his sufferings', as Paul calls it in Philippians, is theirs too, not so much in the form of physical suffering or even martyrdom in the ultimate sense, but simply through the outworking in their lives of the 'Caesarea Philippi principle'. The responsibility of witness will certainly ask of them that they *'fill up what is lacking in Christ's suffering'* by becoming the voice or the hands or the feet through which the living but unseen Lord becomes a practical reality for those many who otherwise would know nothing of him. Just as Jesus during his lifetime on earth was 'the word become flesh', so now he needs to become visible, tangible 'flesh' in human beings who have placed themselves at his service out of love for their fellows.

What does all this mean as we try to think about the risen Jesus himself? We have already seen that through his participation in the divine life of the Spirit, Jesus is able to 'be' anywhere and everywhere at any time – as he had

The Glorified Lord

intimated to Nicodemus: *'The wind blows where it chooses, and you hear the sound of it, but you do not know where it comes from or where it goes. So it is with everyone who is born of the Spirit'* (John 3:8). But the conception of service to him that we encounter in the New Testament suggests something else too: that he seeks also to be present in the world through his followers; in a sense, he is not one but many, however partial and imperfect the representation of the one Jesus in all the others might be. As the song has it, 'Let me be as Christ to you'!

Chapter 10

The Risen Lord and his People

We saw in the previous chapter that as well as guiding and supporting his followers' work of witness, the risen Jesus has another purpose: he desires that those who have already believed, however imperfectly, may be preserved from the evils in the world and may instead grow in understanding and in love, being transformed until *'Christ is formed in you'* (Gal. 4:19). This is his other great concern: to watch over those whom God has 'given' him – to be their 'shepherd' and guide.

Jesus' concern for his followers is evident in the John 17 prayer: he asks the Father to *'sanctify them in the truth'* (v. 17) and then adds: *'And for their sakes I sanctify myself, so that they also may be sanctified in truth'* (v. 19). Just what is meant by *'I sanctify myself'* is not explained; it might refer simply to the act of self-dedication to God by his death. However, the Greek verb *hagiazo* used here is widely used in the LXX in relation to the 'sanctification' of holy objects under the Law and especially of the priests; perhaps, then, Jesus sees his death as the process by which he is made once and for all *'holy, blameless, undefiled, separated from sinners, and exalted above the heavens'* (Heb. 7:26) and thus able to 'save completely' those whom he first serves by giving himself for them on the cross. In other words, he has more to do yet; his work will not be truly completed until the goal that he envisages in the prayer is achieved: *'As you, Father, are in me and I am in you, may they also be in us'* (v. 21).

Jesus the 'pioneer'

However, as we look at his prayer in John 17, we see that Jesus was not only anticipating the immediate outcome of his impending death. Just as he was able in his dying moments to glimpse, with the help of Psalm 22, the future multitudes of believers, so too in this prayer he looks beyond the immediate condition of his disciples to see them as they will ultimately be, by God's grace and with his own support. It reads as though he were, in effect, already presenting to the Father the results of his ministry. First, he depicts their immediate situation:

The Risen Lord and his People

> '*I have made your name known to those whom you gave me from the world.*
> *They were yours, and you gave them to me, and they have kept your word.*
> *Now they know that everything you have given me is from you; for the words*
> *that you gave to me I have given to them, and they have received them and*
> *know in truth that I came from you; and they have believed that you sent*
> *me.' (John 17:6-8)*

But at the end of the prayer, he envisages their perfected state:

> '... *I in them and you in me, that they may become completely one, so that*
> *the world may know that you have sent me and have loved them even as*
> *you have loved me. Father, I desire that those also, whom you have given*
> *me, may be with me where I am, to see my glory, which you have given me*
> *because you loved me before the foundation of the world ... I made your*
> *name known to them, and I will make it known, so that the love with which*
> *you have loved me may be in them, and I in them.' (John 17:23-26)*

A somewhat similar sequence of thought is also found in Hebrews 1-2. The opening verses of the letter say that Jesus has become what he was always destined to be: '*When he had made purification for sins, he sat down at the right hand of the Majesty on high, having become as much superior to angels as the name he has inherited is more excellent than theirs*' (Heb. 1:3-4). The title had always been his, but only now, after his resurrection, has he 'become what he always was'. But when, after a digression in the rest of chapter 1 about Jesus' superiority to the angels, the writer returns to the theme in chapter 2, he places Jesus' glorification in the context of the entire creative purpose of God, just as Paul does in Ephesians and as Jesus does in John 17. He quotes the reflections of the writer of Psalm 8 on the paradoxical relationship between God's lofty intention for man, due to be '*crowned ... with glory and honour*', as Genesis 1 declares, and his present smallness and seeming insignificance: '*As it is, we do not yet see everything in subjection to them*' (Heb. 2:5-8). But the paradox is resolved in Jesus and in his resurrection: '*but we do see Jesus, who for a little while was made lower than the angels, now crowned with glory and honour because of the suffering of death*' (v. 9).

So this writer views the whole of Jesus' 'career', from his human condition, shared with all men, via his death to his post-resurrection glory, in relation to the destiny of mankind as a whole and to God's purpose in their creation. For him, it was God's intention that there should be not just one son who has achieved this glorious condition, but many: he wishes to '*bring many children to glory*' (v. 10). Jesus is thus the 'pioneer' or 'leader' (*archegos*, v. 10), the one who, as Jesus says in John 14, goes to the Father first; Hebrews repeats this

Jesus – yesterday, today, for ever

idea, with a change of metaphor, in chapter 6, where Jesus is described as our 'forerunner' – *prodromos,* one who runs ahead to find the way. This was the purpose of his life and death: that those many should be able to follow; in sharing their mortality, Jesus has, the writer says, 'taken hold of them' as if to lead them out of their present lowliness (2:15). 'Helps' (NRSV, ESV, NIV) seems to me a quite inadequate translation of the Greek *epilambanōmai* – the same word is used in Hebrews 8: *'not like the covenant that I made with their ancestors, on the day when I **took them by the hand** to lead them out of the land of Egypt ... '* (8:9). So Hebrews 2 re-uses the language of Isaiah 8:18 to create an image of Jesus presenting to the Father the ultimate fruit of his work, much as in John 17: *'Here am I and the children whom God has given me'* (Heb. 2:13).

It is clear, then, that the relationship between Jesus and believers involves more than their role as his witnesses that we considered in the previous chapter. It also involves their entire being in a profound identity with Jesus, just as Jesus' relationship with the Father during his earthly ministry was not only that of a *shaliach* but also that of a son.

In other ways too, the position of Jesus' followers in the new world of Acts and the Letters mirrors not so much that of the disciples in the Gospels, but rather that of Jesus himself during his earthly ministry. On the one hand, he was the Son, enjoying unique access to the Father and able to call on his power and authority; on the other, he was first 'the carpenter', and then a poor itinerant preacher, dependent on others for the necessities of life (cf. Luke 8:3). So too Jesus' followers: on the one hand, these servants of Jesus enjoyed the most exalted status possible. In Ephesians, for example, the account of Jesus' exaltation in chapter 1, quoted earlier, spills over into the next chapter, where Paul reveals the full extent of the work performed by the irresistible energy of God's working:

> *God, who is rich in mercy, out of the great love with which he loved us even when we were dead through our trespasses, made us alive together with Christ – by grace you have been saved – and raised us up with him and seated us with him in the heavenly places in Christ Jesus ... (Ephesians 2:4-6)*

It was what Jesus promised to his bewildered disciples when they first asked where he was going and then why they could not go too: *'Where I am going, you cannot follow me now; but you will follow afterward'* (John 13:36).

Yet, dazzling though these images of exaltation with Jesus are, reflecting as they do the lofty spiritual status of Jesus' people, the New Testament letters arise out of their writers' awareness that their lived reality was very different.

The Risen Lord and his People

They were subject to many kinds of external pressures, both cultural and political; still more importantly, their new life in Jesus ran counter to their all-too human impulses, not only in the individual lives but also in the collective life which was from the beginning seen, not as an optional extra to the life of faith, but as its most natural, yet most taxing expression. In all this, too, the lives of the apostles mirrored that of Jesus as we see it in the Gospels. Paul describes his situation to the Corinthians like this:

> *To the present hour we are hungry and thirsty, we are poorly clothed and beaten and homeless, and we grow weary from the work of our own hands. When reviled, we bless; when persecuted, we endure; when slandered, we speak kindly. We have become like the rubbish of the world, the dregs of all things, to this very day. (1 Corinthians 4:11-13)*

He may have been exaggerating a little – for rhetorical reasons – but only a little. As with Jesus, then, the modest outward appearance and the at times desperate circumstances of the believers in the first century gave no hint of their new spiritual status or of their present and future glory.

Already – not yet

But the New Testament writers do not fall into the trap of saying something along the lines of 'we may be poor/humiliated/powerless now, but one day ...' We notice, for example, that Ephesians does not use the future tense in the verses just quoted in speaking of their elevation, for that exaltation has already happened. The present that is already realised is at once a foretaste and a guarantee of what still remains: hope and promise. The relationship between the two is evident in Ephesians 2 itself, where Paul continues like this: '*... and raised us up with him and seated us with him in the heavenly places in Christ Jesus, **so that in the ages to come** he might show the immeasurable riches of his grace in kindness toward us in Christ Jesus*' (Eph. 2:6-7). The lives and the status of believers, especially as seen by Paul, are characterised essentially by the tension between the 'already' and the 'not yet' – between what they are already and what they shall be, between what is already theirs and what remains expectation, between firstfruits (*aparchē*) and the final harvest, or between the 'down payment' (*arrabōn*) and the 'full sum' – just as was Jesus' life during his ministry.[1] Paul reflects on this extraordinary discrepancy in 2 Corinthians 4-6: '*as sorrowful, yet always rejoicing; as poor, yet making many rich; as having nothing, and yet possessing everything*' (6:10).

---

1 For a helpful discussion of this theme in Paul, see James D.G. Dunn's *The Theology of Paul the Apostle*, Grand Rapids, Michigan/Cambridge 1998, p. 466 ff.

Jesus – yesterday, today, for ever

Images of the church

We saw in the previous chapter that Jesus' followers represented him, not only as individual believers but also through their collective presence in the world as his 'body'. Here again, however, witness is only one facet of the existence of the body of believers. Inclusion in that body plays an essential part in the experience of Christian believers and in their relationship with Jesus.

The church as a temple

The New Testament, and Jesus himself in particular, uses several metaphors for the church, each of which emphasises its role as a means through which Jesus' relationship with his followers is realised. Both Paul and Peter speak of the church as a 'temple':

> *Do you not know that you are God's temple and that God's Spirit dwells in you? (1 Corinthians 3:16)*

> *... built upon the foundation of the apostles and prophets, with Christ Jesus himself as the cornerstone. In him the whole structure is joined together and grows into a holy temple in the Lord; in whom you also are built together spiritually into a dwelling place for God. (Ephesians 2:20-22)*

> *... let yourselves be built into a spiritual house ... (1 Peter 2:5)*

We notice in all these quotations that the writers think of the church as a temple *for God* – in their minds doubtless analogous to the visible temple in Jerusalem: a tiny area of the earth's surface where God's will is done and he is worshipped. Yet this new temple is, according to Ephesians, *'in the Lord'*: if Jesus is the *'cornerstone'*, or *'the very head of the corner'* in Peter's words, no doubt remembering Psalm 118:22, then he determines its style and dimensions.

John's thinking takes him even further: at the end of his account of the cleansing of the temple in Jerusalem, Jesus implies that the temple there would be destroyed and replaced by another, *'the temple of his body'* (John 2:21). During his earthly ministry, it was already Jesus, rather than the temple of stone in Jerusalem, that was God's dwelling on earth; after his resurrection, that 'temple' was enlarged, incorporating his followers and forming a living structure in which Father and Son are present among men, while the Jerusalem temple was to be *'left to you, desolate'* (Matt. 23:38). Consequently, as men and women come to be united with Jesus, so Jesus and the Father come to 'dwell' with and in them – they too become part of this *'dwelling place for God'*: *'Those who love me will keep my word, and my Father will love them, and we will come to them and make our home with them'* (John 14:23).

The vine

Expressive as the image of the temple is in conveying the ideas of God's presence and of a unified whole characterised by Jesus, it is perhaps too static to do full justice to the animate, dynamic nature of the church and to the living relationship between the risen Lord and his people. In Jesus' own figure of the vine in John 15, by contrast, the church is a living organism. Its *raison d'être* is to bear fruit (v. 2-8) for God; the fruit is not defined, but the context suggests two ways of thinking about it: first, Jesus refers to keeping his commandments, essentially, the commandment to love as he has loved and, specifically, to *'love one another'* (v. 9-13). Second, Jesus says that by bearing fruit the vine will 'glorify' God (v. 8), and we have already seen that for John, 'glorifying God' means serving him, allowing oneself to be his instrument.

Perhaps the most important feature of this image, though, is the relationship that it implies between Jesus and the church. The vine is a single living whole, of which Jesus is the central stock, rooted in the soil and thus able to supply the rest of the vine, the 'branches', with the nutrients that keep them alive and make them fruitful. So the image suggests that from Jesus, and thus ultimately from the Father, the 'sap' of the vine circulates throughout the whole, nourishing and strengthening, and enabling the vine to grow and to be fruitful. The church is intended, then, to be a living organism, not fixed and static, and its members are not inert objects, like stones cemented into place in a building. They are themselves alive, connected with other living parts of the vine – and all of them reliant on the continuous flow of nourishment from Jesus.

The body

An equally expressive image, however, is that of the 'body of Christ'. We have already seen that Jesus identifies the new, post-resurrection 'temple' as 'his body', and when in John 20 he performs an action symbolic of 'creation', or perhaps 're-creation', by breathing on the disciples (John 20:22), he in effect brings into being that new 'body', now alive with his resurrection life.

It is Paul, though, who most makes use of this image, notably in 1 Corinthians 12, Romans 12 and Ephesians 4. In 1 Corinthians, we can observe the development of the image: first, speaking of the use made by believers of their physical bodies, specifically in their sexual behaviour, Paul reminds them that *'your bodies are members of Christ'* and that *'your body is a temple of the Holy Spirit within you'* (1 Cor. 6:15, 19). Then, in explaining to them the significance of the Breaking of Bread, he moves from the body of Jesus, first given in death and now given to them through the symbol of bread, to the church as one 'body'. Paul writes: *'The bread that we break, is it not a sharing in the body of Christ? Because there is one bread, we who are many are one body, for we all partake of the one bread'* (1 Cor. 10:16-17). In the next chapter, again speaking of the Breaking of Bread, he takes the decisive step: *'For all who eat and drink without discerning the body, eat and drink judgment against themselves'* (1 Cor. 11:29); the context here, in which Paul reproves the Corinthians for their lack of concern and regard for each other, leads us to understand that the failure to 'discern the body' relates, not to a lack of understanding of the symbolism of the bread in relation to Jesus, but rather to their failure to recognise the 'body of Christ' in their fellow-believers.

Nothing is said here about the specific role of Jesus in relation to this 'body'; Paul's thought is that all the believers together make up the body, which is thus his bodily presence in a world from which he is otherwise physically absent. In Ephesians and Colossians, however, Paul identifies Jesus with the 'head':

> *And he has put all things under his feet and has made him the head over all things for the church ... (Ephesians 1:22)*

> *But speaking the truth in love, we must grow up in every way into him who is the head, into Christ ... (Ephesians 4:15)*

> *For the husband is the head of the wife just as Christ is the head of the church, the body of which he is the Saviour. (Ephesians 5:23)*

> *He is the head of the body, the church; he is the beginning, the firstborn from the dead, so that he might come to have first place in everything. (Colossians 1:18)*

> *... and not holding fast to the head, from whom the whole body, nourished and held together by its ligaments and sinews, grows with a growth that is from God. (Colossians 2:19)*

It has been argued, rightly, that when Paul speaks of the man/husband as the 'head' of the woman/wife (1 Cor. 11:3), he is not referring to our modern use of 'head' to imply command, but rather in the sense of 'source' (as in the 'head' of a river), particularly in the sense of being the first and thus the original. That sense can also be seen in these passages, especially in Ephesians 4:15 and its parallel, Colossians 2:19 and also in Colossians 1:18. But it is hard to deny some sense of authority and command in the closing verses of Ephesians 1, where Paul relates Jesus' position as 'head' to his having ultimately all things put under him (as in Psalm 8). The thought appears to

The Risen Lord and his People

be that, while all things have not yet been put under his feet, as predicted in Genesis 1 and Psalm 8 – as we noted in Hebrews 2:8, that condition has not yet been arrived at – he *is now*, already, head over the church, already its 'lord'. It is as though the Father has entrusted to Jesus, enthroned alongside him, the church *'which is his body, the fullness of him who fills all in all'* (Eph. 1:23); he, the Son, now reigns or rules over the church as he will one day rule over the whole of God's creation.

The head of the body

So we are invited to think of Jesus as our immediate head, the one to whom the Father has 'delegated' responsibility for the care of the church. The figure of 'head' comes to suggest something like a 'command centre' from which instructions flow to the rest of the body – a very modern understanding of the central nervous system. It is not a one-way flow: every part in this body plays an active part, both giving and receiving:

> But speaking the truth in love, we must grow up in every way into him who is the head, into Christ, from whom the whole body, joined and knit together by every ligament with which it is equipped, as each part is working properly, promotes the body's growth in building itself up in love. (Ephesians 4:15-16)

How might we expect this lordship of Jesus over his church to work in practice? First and foremost, I think, his authority over the church is exercised through the power of his example. By asking his followers to practise the simple rite of eating bread and drinking wine together, he ensured that they would be confronted again and again with his pattern of self-giving; each time, we hear anew his commanding voice: *'This is my commandment, that you love one another as I have loved you. No one has greater love than this, to lay down one's life for one's friends. You are my friends if you do what I command you'* (John 15:12-14). This, he says, is how the church is to live and work – how its members should view and treat each other and all the other people that they encounter. It becomes Paul's ever repeated message, most notably in Philippians: *'Let the same mind be in you that was in Christ Jesus…'* (Phil. 2:5). The 'Caesarea Philippi principle' must be the church's one law – if it has this, it needs no other. In Philippians, Paul laments the fact that that principle is not always adhered to: *'All of them are seeking their own interests, not those of Jesus Christ'* (2:21), having *'their minds … set on earthly things'*; they are, he says in a terrible phrase, *'enemies of the cross of Christ'* (Phil. 3:18-19).

It is remarkable how little direction Jesus appears to have given for the corporate life of the church, his body; as far as we can tell from the New

Jesus – yesterday, today, for ever

Testament, what mattered to him were not specific structures and practices but rather the spiritual quality of its shared life and worship. This left – and leaves – the church free to devise its own forms of worship and fellowship. In the first-century church, Jesus' lordship was exercised primarily by those whom he had directly appointed and to whom he entrusted leadership: *'When he had said this, he breathed on them and said to them, "Receive the Holy Spirit. If you forgive the sins of any, they are forgiven them; if you retain the sins of any, they are retained"'* (John 20:22-23; cf. Matt. 16:19). The very act of choosing and empowering apostles and other leaders was one of the most obvious ways in which Jesus' position as head and Lord was expressed. Paul, for example, was conscious of a responsibility given to him by Jesus: *'the authority that the Lord has given me for building up and not for tearing down'* (2 Cor. 13:10).

There is, however, one way in which we can see the evidence of his direction of our affairs. Paul speaks three times of the 'gifts' received by believers for the benefit of the church. The list in Romans is the briefest and least detailed, but the other two, in 1 Corinthians 12 and Ephesians 4, are more specific. There are several differences between these two passages: the lists themselves vary, and in the Ephesians passage, Paul seems to say that it is the person who is 'given' to the church, whereas in 1 Corinthians the individual receives the gift for the good of all. But in both passages, the abilities possessed by believers for the good of all are seen as gifts, coming, according to Ephesians, from Christ, and, according to 1 Corinthians, from the Lord by the Spirit, but ultimately from God.

We might wonder how these gifts came to be recognised and exploited by the church; the only possible answer is that the congregation became aware of the gift because they saw evidence of it at work. It was not, then, the church that decreed that any individual should perform a certain kind of service for the church – that was decided for them, by the Lord's giving as a kind of *fait accompli* – the Lord had exercised his authority as 'head' over the church. One can only conclude that when a church or an ecclesia determines *a priori* that one section of its members, the women among them, shall not exercise various functions, irrespective of their ability – the 'gift' from the Lord – and regardless of evidence from the early church, they are in grave danger of setting aside the will of the one whom they call 'Lord'.

In addition to all these more or less 'visible' signs of Jesus' lordship over the church, the New Testament speaks of a way in which Jesus acts directly in the affairs of the church; the mechanism by which he does this is completely unknown to us but we must nevertheless acknowledge its reality. The primary evidence for it is found in the letters to the seven churches in Revelation 2-3,

The Risen Lord and his People

where Jesus speaks of himself as the one who *'walks among the seven golden lampstands'* (Rev. 2:1) and who knows their works. And he does not merely 'know' – he is also able to act:

> *'I will come to you and remove your lampstand from its place, unless you repent.' (Revelation 2:5)*

> *'I will come to you soon and make war against them with the sword of my mouth.' (2:16)*

> *'Beware, I am throwing her on a bed, and those who commit adultery with her I am throwing into great distress, unless they repent of her doings.' (2:22)*

> *'If you do not wake up, I will come like a thief, and you will not know at what hour I will come to you.' (3:3)*

> *'I am standing at the door, knocking; if you hear my voice and open the door, I will come in to you and eat with you, and you with me.' (3:20)*

Some of these statements may refer to Jesus' second coming – but surely not all. They present a picture of an active Jesus, involved in the affairs of his churches and not merely seeing but able to determine, by means unknown to us, the fortunes of each church.

Every kind of authority or leadership role brings with it temptations for its misuse. But the first-century apostles and disciples were evidently conscious of the pattern of Jesus; the opening verses of 1 Peter 5 reveal how much he, and presumably the other apostles, were influenced by their awareness that Jesus was their Lord and that their exercise of 'authority' had to be guided by the kind of leadership that he had displayed:

> *Now as an elder myself and a witness of the sufferings of Christ, as well as one who shares in the glory to be revealed, I exhort the elders among you to tend the flock of God that is in your charge, exercising the oversight, not under compulsion but willingly, as God would have you do it – not for sordid gain but eagerly. Do not lord it over those in your charge, but be examples to the flock ... In the same way, you who are younger must accept the authority of the elders. And all of you must clothe yourselves with humility in your dealings with one another, for 'God opposes the proud, but gives grace to the humble.' (1 Peter 5:1-5)*

One can imagine that those moments when Jesus washed his disciples' feet must have remained with them, a permanent pattern of a community without

Jesus – yesterday, today, for ever

hierarchy, in which the greatest can serve, and where, as Paul's image of the 'body' made clear, each member has a role to fulfil and each contribution is indispensable.

The church: God's 'new creation'

All the images used to describe the church depend ultimately on the relationship of each believer to Jesus. Their 'fellowship' is actually their 'sharing' (*koinonia*), in Jesus – and sharing equally and therefore without hierarchy. Whatever personal bonds of friendship may develop among them, they are in the last analysis secondary to, and dependent on, that first, essential bond. This in turn means that they all share in a single identity, as we said at the beginning of this chapter. It is instructive to read again Paul's letter to Philemon, in which Paul identifies himself with both Philemon (v. 19) and with Onesimus, the runaway slave whom he describes as *'my very heart'* and whom Philemon is to receive *'as you would me'* (v. 17). Such expressions may look like nothing more than persuasive rhetorical tricks, but they rest upon the fact that they are, all three, part of 'Christ' – everything is 'in Christ', a part of his life within the church.[2]

This shared identity has two consequences: first, the removal, or rather, the cancelling out of all the demarcations by which human beings are normally categorised and which are still powerfully operative in the world outside the church. It is notable in Paul's letter to Philemon that he does not insist that Onesimus the slave be set free *in the world* – but in the church he is Philemon's fellow, equally part of Jesus. Similarly, the distinction between Jews and Gentiles continued to be a feature of the ancient world – but not within the church. In both these areas, two had become one – and that one was Jesus: *'He has abolished the law with its commandments and ordinances, so that he might create in himself one new humanity in place of the two, thus making peace'* (Eph. 2:16). According to Paul, the same principle applied in relation to the third great demarcation between human beings, one that has proved almost harder to dislodge in the church than in the world, sadly, but which, it seems to me, is indefensible: that between male and female, of which Paul speaks in exactly the same terms: *'There is no longer Jew or Greek, there is no longer slave or free, there is no longer male and female; for all of you are one in Christ Jesus'* (Gal. 3:28).

The phrase *'one new humanity'* points to a second consequence: if all believers share the identity of Jesus and are somehow part of him, then they also are part of the one true man 'in God's image'. As such, they are, as a result of their

---

2 See L.S. Thornton, *The Common Life in the Body of Christ*, London 1940, pp. 38-43

The Risen Lord and his People

rebirth, part of the 'new creation'. Paul puts very clearly in 2 Corinthians:

> *From now on, therefore, we regard no one from a human point of view; even though we once knew Christ from a human point of view, we know him no longer in that way. So if anyone is in Christ, there is a new creation: everything old has passed away; see, everything has become new! (2 Corinthians 5:17).*

From a human point of view, Onesimus may be just a troublesome slave – but 'in Christ', as part of his body, he is Paul's equal as a fellow-believer, his brother 'in Christ'.

But this is, of course, not simply an individual matter: the church as a whole is a 'new creation', or rather, 'the new creation'. It is, or should be, a microcosm of the creation that God envisaged from the beginning, through, in and for Christ. And, as Paul expresses it in Ephesians, it functions as a model for the rest of humanity of what God's new world will be, united in Jesus:

> *Although I am the very least of all the saints, this grace was given to me to bring to the Gentiles the news of the boundless riches of Christ, and to make everyone see what is the plan of the mystery hidden for ages in God who created all things; so that through the church the wisdom of God in its rich variety might now be made known to the rulers and authorities in the heavenly places. (Ephesians 3:8-10)*

The church as a whole thus becomes, Paul, says, a proclamation to the world of the wisdom of God; it represents, despite its imperfection, some approximation to his ultimate intention for mankind which, as we have repeatedly noted, Paul formulates in the first chapter of this letter, *'his good pleasure that he set forth in Christ, as a plan for the fullness of time, to gather up all things in him, things in heaven and things on earth'* (Eph. 1:9-10).

Caring and protecting

In the ancient world, the term *kurios* had many applications apart from its use in religious contexts. As well as being employed as a form of polite address, it was also used in a variety of social relationships to indicate the unequal distribution of power between the parties: the less powerful, the servant, called the other, his/her master, *kurios*. Yet, unequal though the relationship was, the term implied a two-way obligation: the servant honoured, served and obeyed the one whom he or she acknowledged as 'lord', while the latter was expected to care for and protect those who served him and supply their needs. That model can be applied to the relationship between Jesus the believers too. Having attempted to characterise how the Lord Jesus' servants represent him,

273

we therefore need now to consider how the Lord fulfils his obligation of care and protection for those who 'belong' to him.

The giver of gifts

Paul begins every one of his letters with the salutation: *'Grace be unto you, and peace, from God our Father, and from the Lord Jesus Christ'* (1 Cor. 1:3). In all these greetings, Paul asserts that the church receives the gifts of 'grace' and 'peace', which I take to sum up divine favour and blessing in all and any sphere, from both Father and Son. Similarly, he ends most of his letters – all except Ephesians, Colossians, 2 Timothy and Titus – with the words *'The grace of our/the Lord Jesus Christ be with you/your spirit'*. Perhaps the Father is the ultimate source of all good, for, as James says: *'Every generous act of giving, with every perfect gift, is from above, coming down from the Father of lights'* (James 1:17) – but the Son is the channel and mediator of the gift. The pattern for this is set as early as in Acts 2, where Peter says: *'Being therefore exalted at the right hand of God, and having received from the Father the promise of the Holy Spirit, he has poured out this that you both see and hear'* (Acts 2:33) – Jesus passes on what he has received.

The same fundamental notion, but expressed in more complex theological terms, is found also in Ephesians 4:

> *But each of us was given grace according to the measure of Christ's gift. Therefore it is said, 'When he ascended on high he made captivity itself a captive; he gave gifts to his people.' (When it says, 'He ascended,' what does it mean but that he had also descended into the lower parts of the earth? He who descended is the same one who ascended far above all the heavens, so that he might fill all things.) The gifts he gave were that some would be apostles, some prophets, some evangelists, some pastors and teachers ...*
> *(Ephesians 4:7-11)*

We cannot enter here into the complexities of Paul's use of Psalm 68:18; what matters for us is how he understands Jesus' giving: he 'ascended', first in being 'lifted up' on the cross – and at the same time descending not only into the grave but into the depths of human degradation – and was then exalted in his resurrection and ascension. The consequence of that 'ascension' is that he is now empowered to give gifts to his followers. In John 17, 'give' is a key word: he 'gives' to his disciples his words, his work, his glory and a share in his life. At his death, blood and water emerged from his side, giving new life to the believers (John 19:34); accordingly, after his resurrection he imparted his life and authority to his disciples (John 20:22). Acts 2 tells of the decisive act by which Spirit gifts were imparted to the apostles, but Paul's language here in

The Risen Lord and his People

Ephesians suggests that that was far from being the end of his giving: the believers to whom Paul is writing have all received gifts from the Lord too – and, equipped with those gifts, have been 'given' to their fellow-believers.[3]

Paul also testifies to a giving of a more intimate, personal kind. He evidently senses that Jesus, his Lord, gives him strength and encouragement amid his many trials and difficulties. Near the end of 2 Corinthians he refers to his 'thorn in the flesh', which I take to be a reference not to some physical ailment but to the seemingly unending criticism, opposition and downright persecution to which he was subject from both unbelieving and believing Jews. He repeatedly asked the Lord, he says, that he might be freed from it, but received the reply that *'"My grace is sufficient for you, for power is made perfect in weakness." So, I will boast all the more gladly of my weaknesses, so that the power of Christ may dwell in me'* (2 Cor. 12:9). Paul is everywhere conscious of the power of the risen Jesus that sustains and sometimes carries him:

> *But we have this treasure in clay jars, so that it may be made clear that this extraordinary power belongs to God and does not come from us. (2 Corinthians 4:7)*

> *To this end I labour, struggling with all his energy, which so powerfully works in me' (Colossians 1:29 NIV)*

> *I can do all things through him who strengthens me. (Philippians 4:13)*

The protector

It is clear from the discourses of Jesus in John 13-16 that he was well aware of the dangers to which his followers would be exposed when he would 'send them into the world'; he warns the disciples that they will be hated as he was himself hated (15:18) and indicates the lengths to which that hatred would go: *'They will put you out of the synagogues. Indeed, an hour is coming when those who kill you will think that by doing so they are offering worship to God'* (16:2). Accordingly, he prays for them in John 17:

> *'And now I am no longer in the world, but they are in the world, and I am coming to you. Holy Father, **protect** them in your name that you have given me, so that they may be one, as we are one. While I was with them, I **protected** them in your name that you have given me. I **guarded** them, and not one of them was lost except the one destined to be lost ... I have given them your word, and the world has hated them because they do not belong*

---

3 Cf. John Muddiman, *The Epistle to the Ephesians*, London/New York 2001, pp. 186-198.

Jesus – yesterday, today, for ever

*to the world, just as I do not belong to the world. I am not asking you to take them out of the world, but I ask you to **protect** them from the evil one.' (John 17:11-15)*

But who will do the protecting? Some agent of the Father other than Jesus, the Son, to whom they have been given? As we argued in the previous chapter, the 'other *parakletos*' can surely be no one but Jesus himself, now present and active through the Spirit, though invisible. On many, though not all, occasions, it is to Jesus the Lord that the believers looked for and received protection. It is again Peter who provides the perfect example: he is miraculously delivered from prison during the night before he is due to be executed: *'Suddenly an angel of the Lord appeared and a light shone in the cell. He tapped Peter on the side and woke him, saying, "Get up quickly." And the chains fell off his wrists.'* (Acts 12:7-17). At first in a trance-like condition as he obeys the command to get up and to leave the prison, he then realises what has happened: *'Now I am sure that the Lord has sent his angel and rescued me from the hands of Herod and from all that the Jewish people were expecting'* (Acts 12:11). We note that Peter's deliverance occurs after prayers to God for him (v. 5), yet it is to 'the Lord' that he attributes his rescue; this illustrates the closeness of Father and Son: prayer to the one is prayer to the other, but the saving action is ascribed to the one to whom the Father has entrusted the care of his people.

There are other examples too:

But during the night an angel of the Lord opened the prison doors, brought them out … (Acts 5:19)

While they were stoning Stephen, he prayed, 'Lord Jesus, receive my spirit.' Then he knelt down and cried out in a loud voice, 'Lord, do not hold this sin against them.' (Acts 7:59-60)

One night the Lord said to Paul in a vision, 'Do not be afraid, but speak and do not be silent…' (Acts 18:9)

Notice too how Paul, in the last of his letters known to us, describes his experience as he faced trial and death:

At my first defence no one came to my support, but all deserted me. May it not be counted against them! But the Lord stood by me and gave me strength, so that through me the message might be fully proclaimed and all the Gentiles might hear it. So I was rescued from the lion's mouth. The Lord will rescue me from every evil attack and save me for his heavenly kingdom. To him be the glory forever and ever. Amen. (2 Timothy 4:16-18)

The Risen Lord and his People

Yet Jesus' care for the church is not only a matter of protection from external harm. At least as important is his concern for their spiritual well-being, for their faith, their growth in understanding and love, and for the lives that they lead among their fellows. This is easily said, but the magnitude of the task is impossible to comprehend: responsibility for, and care of, hundreds of thousands of individual believers distributed throughout the world. His care extends also to the clusters of believers that we know as churches and ecclesias, each of which destined to be a microcosm of the new creation in its ultimate realisation. Nowhere is Jesus' care for those entrusted to him more succinctly and beautifully summed up than in a passage frequently quoted in order to bolster traditional views about the differing role of husbands and wives in marriage but, sadly, less often in our present context:

> *Husbands, love your wives, just as Christ loved the church and gave himself up for her, in order to make her holy by cleansing her with the washing of water by the word, so as to present the church to himself in splendour, without a spot or wrinkle or anything of the kind – yes, so that she may be holy and without blemish ... For no one ever hates his own body, but he nourishes and tenderly cares for it, just as Christ does for the church ... (Ephesians 5:25-27)*

Paul here sees Jesus first giving himself on the cross to bring the church into being, but then continuing to lavish care upon it so that it may become what he and the Father wish it to be.

High priest

The Letter to the Hebrews stands alone among the New Testament writings in the use that it makes of the Mosaic Law in order to explain to perhaps dubious Jewish readers how Jesus relates to the precepts of the old covenant with which they were familiar. He shows that Jesus' ministry can be understood in the terms of the Law which, given the evident superiority of the new covenant in Jesus, was now ready to *'disappear'* (Heb. 8;13).[4] The greater part of the extended parallel in Hebrews between Jesus and the Mosaic high priest is

---

4 It is important, when reading Hebrews, to keep in mind that the writer is simply using the language and symbolism of the Law as a means of explaining the role of Jesus in the Father's saving purpose to a particular audience – just as, for a different audience, it might be elucidated through the use of the language of law, or of honour codes, for example. In fact, we do well to remember that all the different metaphors through which the 'atonement' is expounded are just that – metaphors, drawn from a variety of cultural contexts according to the needs of the readers, in order to explain the 'why' of three interlocking historical facts: Jesus' death, his resurrection, and God's offer of forgiveness and grace.

Jesus – yesterday, today, for ever

in fact a way of speaking about the self-giving of Jesus on the cross and thus about the 'atonement'. This becomes clear in the culminating passage of his exposition of Jesus' priestly work, where the writer emphasises that this work is now done:

> *And every priest stands day after day at his service, offering again and again the same sacrifices that can never take away sins. But when Christ had offered for all time a single sacrifice for sins, 'he sat down at the right hand of God,' and since then has been waiting 'until his enemies would be made a footstool for his feet.' For by a single offering he has perfected for all time those who are sanctified. (Hebrews 10:11-14)*

So the work of Jesus as 'high priest', in this sense, i.e. as representative of humanity before God, is, according to Hebrews, already completed. The same is true also of the references to his 'intercession' on our behalf: when the writer of this letter[5] says that *'he always lives to make intercession for them'* (7:25), he means, surely, that the effects of his work are once for all and permanent; his presence at the right hand of God ensures that the throne of God is 'a throne of grace'.

There is, however, another dimension to Hebrews' sustained parallel between Jesus and the Jewish high priest which does refer to the present, to Jesus' work now and to his relationship to believers. Here too, though, there is, it seems to me, a good deal of confusion about what is meant when Jesus is spoken of in these terms. It is frequently stated, or assumed, that the high priest's role is to plead with God for mercy on behalf of those whom he represents – that he receives our prayers and presents them to the Father, who grants our requests because of Jesus' intercession. But this is, surely, not what the New Testament tells us:

- Such a view implies a God who is unwilling to hear us and who consequently requires the advocacy of the Son in order to show mercy, contrary to everything that we know about the grace of God, who is the source and prime mover of the entire work of salvation;

---

5 It seems to me in the highest degree unlikely that the writer of Hebrews is Paul. Both the style and the way in which the Old Testament is used in Hebrews are fundamentally different from what we find in Paul's letters. The clinching argument, however, rests on what the writer says in Hebrews 2:3: *'how can we escape if we neglect so great a salvation? It was declared at first through the Lord, and it was attested to us by those who heard him'*. Paul would surely never imply that he had received the gospel from others who had had direct contact with Jesus, whereas he had not. He repeatedly asserts the exact opposite – see, for example, Galatians 1:11-12; 1 Cor. 11:23.

The Risen Lord and his People

- It rests on a questionable view of the role of the high priest under the Law. It was essentially a ceremonial one, as Hebrews indicates: *'Every high priest chosen from among mortals is put in charge of things pertaining to God on their behalf, to offer gifts and sacrifices for sins ... For every high priest is appointed to offer gifts and sacrifices'* (Heb. 5:1; 8:3)

- The notion of Jesus as one engaged in continued pleading on our behalf runs counter to what Jesus himself says in John's Gospel. His statements there are puzzling, it is true, for he first says: *'If in my name you ask me for anything, I will do it'* (John 14:14), then *'the Father will give you whatever you ask him in my name'* (15:16) and *'On that day you will ask nothing of me. Very truly, I tell you, if you ask anything of the Father in my name, he will give it to you'* (16:23), and finally: *'On that day you will ask in my name. I do not say to you that I will ask the Father on your behalf; for the Father himself loves you, because you have loved me and have believed that I came from God'* (16:26-27).

- Hebrews itself says unequivocally that we need no advocacy when speaking to God; on the contrary we may *'approach the throne of grace with boldness'* (Heb. 4:16) – 'boldness' here (*parrhesia*) means freedom of speech, frankness, openness. The conclusion to which the writer of Hebrews comes at the end of his exposition of the work of Jesus in terms of the Law is then as follows:

... we have confidence to enter the sanctuary by the blood of Jesus, by the new and living way that he opened for us through the curtain (that is, through his flesh), and since we have a great priest over the house of God, **let us approach** *with a true heart in full assurance of faith, with our hearts sprinkled clean from an evil conscience and our bodies washed with pure water. (10:20-22)*

It is a picture of the believer doing what under the Law was permitted only to priests – to 'enter the sanctuary' and 'approach' – the word translated as 'approach' is one used in LXX for priests performing their sacrificial duties (see, for example, Leviticus 21:17, 18, 21, 23).

These conclusions, drawn primarily from Hebrews but also from John's Gospel, concur with what we have previously noted in Ephesians 1-2: that where their Lord is, his servants are too. Not only has he himself entered into the presence of God, but those who belong to him have likewise been *'raised us up with him and seated us with him in the heavenly places in Christ Jesus'* (Eph.

Jesus – yesterday, today, for ever

2:6). No wonder, then, that they may enter freely – they belong there![6]

In what sense, then, is Jesus our 'high priest' now? It is often forgotten that the high priest, as one who stands between men and God, faces two ways. Frequently, he is viewed almost exclusively from one perspective only, as intercessor or as presenter of sacrifices, i.e. as representative of man, facing God. But alongside that role, now completed, Hebrews points to his continuing role as representative of God, facing man, in fact as 'God with us'. It portrays him as one possessing divine authority, *'a great priest over the house of God'* (10:21) and as authorised to judge: *'He is able to deal gently with the ignorant and wayward, since he himself is subject to weakness'* (5:2). It is not without significance that Jesus, as he is described in Revelation 1, is dressed in a way that gives him the appearance of a priest; it is therefore quite appropriate that he should then be depicted as walking among the churches and inspecting them, exercising his role as *'great priest over the house of God'* (Heb. 10:21). According to the Mosaic Law, the high priest's responsibilities included a judicial function – it was, for example, his task to declare someone, or sometimes a building, leprous or cleansed (Lev. 12-14), and it is this role that we see Jesus performing in Revelation 2-3, as we saw earlier in this chapter.

However, it is not only the high priest's authority and role as judge that is emphasised when Hebrews applies this title to Jesus. It shows him as, in effect, the face of God turned to us, able to grant forgiveness and impart strength to fallible human beings:

> *For we do not have a high priest who is unable to sympathize with our weaknesses, but we have one who in every respect has been tested as we are, yet without sin. Let us therefore approach the throne of grace with boldness, so that we may receive mercy and find grace to help in time of need.* *(Hebrews 4:15-16)*

There are few passages more precious to the believing Christian than this. We learn from the Old Testament of God's omniscience in relation to our inner lives:

> *O LORD, you have searched me and known me. You know when I sit down and when I rise up; you discern my thoughts from far away. You search out my path and my lying down, and are acquainted with all my ways. Even before a word is on my tongue, O LORD, you know it completely … Such*

---

6   For a broadly similar view of this topic, see the section headed 'The Intercession of the Son of God' in Neville Smart's *The Son of God Is Come*, Shipston on Stour 1998, pp. 72-75.

The Risen Lord and his People

knowledge is too wonderful for me; it is so high that I cannot attain it. (Psalm 139:1-6)

Yet the knowledge that Jesus has known life as a man, that he saw, in himself, in his family and in his working life, the extraordinary range of human experience and the choices and temptations that it puts before us, is uniquely comforting. He knew and knows how hard it is to lead a godly life. We have, I think, to count this an amazing mercy on the Father's part that he has given us this Lord to be our *parakletos*, the one who is our most immediate reference point, the one to whom we speak, to whom we confess our faults and seek for help. It is not necessary for his own sake – what the Son knows, the Father knows. No, it is to us that it makes a difference. The words from Hebrews 4 just quoted need to be put back into their context:

And before him no creature is hidden, but all are naked and laid bare to the eyes of the one to whom we must render an account. Since, then, we have a great high priest who has passed through the heavens, Jesus, the Son of God, let us hold fast to our confession. For we do not have a high priest who is unable to sympathize with our weaknesses, but we have one who in every respect has been tested as we are, yet without sin. Let us therefore approach the throne of grace with boldness, so that we may receive mercy and find grace to help in time of need. (Hebrews 4:13-16)

The train of thought here suggests, surely, that the one *'to whom we must render an account'* is this uniquely experienced high priest. The writer reinforces this in the opening verses of chapter 5, where, looking back now to the Law, he says that *'... every high priest chosen from among mortals ... is able to deal gently with the ignorant and wayward, since he himself is subject to weakness'* (Heb. 5:1-2). And that is, surely, pre-eminently a description of Jesus as our *parakletos*.

It is impossible to encompass all that the Lord, the risen Jesus, is able and desires to do for those who confess his lordship. What is important is to remember that everything that he does and will do is directed to the ultimate achievement of the divine intention first stated in Genesis 1: the bringing into being of a perfected humanity *'conformed to the image of his Son, in order that he might be the firstborn within a large family'* (Rom. 8:29). That is the purpose for which *'All authority in heaven and on earth has been given to me'* (Matt. 28:18) and which determines all the many activities that the New Testament ascribes to the risen Lord.

Jesus – yesterday, today, for ever

The teacher

In describing to his puzzled disciples the work of the future *parakletos*, i.e. his own future work, Jesus says the following: *'But the Advocate, the Holy Spirit, whom the Father will send in my name, will teach you everything, and remind you of all that I have said to you'* (John 14:26). It has become customary to explain (or explain away!) these words by seeing in them simply a promise that the Gospel writers would be enabled to remember the teaching of Jesus accurately. This interpretation takes no account of the fact that such recall of events is far from being all that is required in the composing of a Gospel; it also disregards the evidence in the Gospels themselves that they were not written under direction, but were the result of planning, research and reflection on the part of their writers (e.g. Luke 1:1-4). What Jesus means by these words becomes clearer later in the discourses, where he says:

> *'When the Spirit of truth comes, he will guide you into all the truth; for he will not speak on his own, but will speak whatever he hears, and he will declare to you the things that are to come. He will glorify me, because he will take what is mine and declare it to you. All that the Father has is mine. For this reason I said that he will take what is mine and declare it to you.'* (John 16:13-15)

> *'I have said these things to you in figures of speech. The hour is coming when I will no longer speak to you in figures, but will tell you plainly of the Father.'* (John 16:25)

In these words, Jesus gives an unequivocal promise that in the future the followers of Jesus will learn more of him than they knew or could understand at that time.

How and when was that promise fulfilled? We might immediately think of conversations between Jesus and his disciples in the forty days before his ascension, or of the teaching and writings of the apostles – Peter, John, James, Paul and others. It is no accident, however, that the teaching about the work of the *parakletos* is found in the Gospel of John. This Gospel is, in fact, itself a prime example of what it speaks of. The Jesus that we encounter in John speaks quite differently from the Jesus of the Synoptic Gospels: he uses a quite different form of speech, in which the concreteness, the pithy sayings, vivid pictures and mini-narratives of the Synoptics are replaced by a discursive, spiralling style dominated by abstract nouns – love, works, world, witness, light, life, etc. He speaks, in fact, the language of John in his Gospel and in his Letters.

The Risen Lord and his People

Still more importantly, while in the Synoptic Gospels Jesus refuses to speak openly about himself, uses the third-person 'the Son of man' in preference to 'I', and, especially in Mark, forbids people to reveal to others who he is, in John's Gospel he speaks almost solely about himself – about his relation to the Father and what he means or can mean for human beings. The difference between the two is summed up in his words at the end of John 16: *'I have said these things to you in figures of speech. The hour is coming when I will no longer speak to you in figures, but will tell you plainly of the Father'* (John 16:25). The Jesus of John's Gospel speaks in fact with the voice, and from the perspective of, the risen, glorified Jesus; the great 'I am' statements in this Gospel are open declarations, 'telling us plainly' what Jesus refused to say earlier. This voice speaks from the perspective of his post-resurrection glory, even though embedded in what is apparently a pre-resurrection narrative. John's words here probably reflect the subsequent experience of Christian believers; though the mortal Jesus is ostensibly the speaker here, what we are actually hearing is the voice of the risen, ever-living Jesus, the *parakletos,* speaking through John to tell believers things that they could not bear at the apparent time of their utterance, before his crucifixion: *'I still have many things to say to you, but you cannot bear them now'* (John 16:12).

It is surely impossible, though, to limit the meaning of Jesus' promise to the writings of the apostles that are found in the New Testament. In the list of gifts and functions in 1 Corinthians 12 and Ephesians 4 we find 'prophets' and 'teachers'. Just what the difference between these two categories is has been a matter of debate, but what matters to us at present is that there were, evidently, many teachers, 'given' to the church by Jesus. Clearly, the church needed them to expound the scriptures and to enable the believers to grasp the meaning and the challenge of faith. Both the churches and the individual believers needed to 'grow', as the New Testament confirms:

But speaking the truth in love, we must grow up in every way into him who is the head, into Christ… (Ephesians 4:15)

Like newborn infants, long for the pure, spiritual milk, so that by it you may grow into salvation … (1 Peter 2:2)

But grow in the grace and knowledge of our Lord and Saviour Jesus Christ. To him be the glory both now and to the day of eternity. Amen. (2 Peter 3:18)

That need is no less real today than it was then: all of us have to grow in understanding, in 'grace and knowledge' as Peter puts it, and we would prob-

Jesus – yesterday, today, for ever

ably find it impossible to name all the sources, influences, experiences and especially the voices of mature 'teachers' that have contributed to our growth, helping us to understand the scriptures better and to grasp more fully the wisdom of God and his grace to us in Jesus. It seems to me likely that this too is the realisation of what Jesus was promising in John 16 – that he would enable, not only those first disciples, but also those coming later, who 'have not seen' (John 20:29), to go beyond their first faulty and faltering understanding of who and what Jesus was and what he means to us. How foolish we would be if we thought we didn't need it!

'Indwelling'

To be even partially and imperfectly in the image of Jesus is the highest possible human aspiration. While it is easy enough to define and describe it, it is less easy to know how to approach it in practice. It would be easy to abandon it in despair at one's own apparently irredeemable egoism; it would be no less easy, alternatively, to view it as a call to monastic asceticism and self-denial, or as a goal to be aspired to with gritted teeth and clenched muscles. There are plenty of New Testament passages which portray the Christian life as one of unremitting, self-denying toil undertaken in order to achieve finally the reward of Jesus:

> *... be steadfast, immovable, always excelling in the work of the Lord, because you know that in the Lord your labour is not in vain. (1 Corinthians 15:58)*

> *I toil and struggle. (Colossians 1:29)*

> *For to this end we toil and struggle, because we have our hope set on the living God. (1 Timothy 4:10)*

> *Let us therefore make every effort to enter that rest. (Hebrews 4:11)*

At the other end of the spectrum, there are words which, taken out of context, may appear to suggest some kind of effortless, spontaneous realisation of Christ-like living, involving no sweat of the brow or clenching of one's spiritual muscles.

While there may be some degree of justification for both these attitudes, it is important to notice too that the New Testament has other language besides that of the lord/servant contrast to characterise the relationship between the risen Jesus and his followers. Certain passages in particular speak of their relationship in more inward, intimate terms. Foremost among these passages are the discourses in John 14-16, where Jesus makes repeated use of the verb

The Risen Lord and his People

mēno, usually translated as 'abide' or 'dwell':

> *'Do you not believe that I am in the Father and the Father is in me? The words that I say to you I do not speak on my own; but the Father who **dwells** in me does his works.' (John 14:10)*

> *'And I will ask the Father, and he will give you another Advocate, to be with you forever. This is the Spirit of truth, whom the world cannot receive, because it neither sees him nor knows him. You know him, because he **abides** with you, and he **will be in you.**' (14:16-17)*

> *'Abide in me as I **abide** in you. Just as the branch cannot bear fruit by itself unless it **abides** in the vine, neither can you unless you **abide** in me. I am the vine, you are the branches. Those who **abide** in me and **I in them** bear much fruit, because apart from me you can do nothing. Whoever does not **abide** in me is thrown away like a branch and withers; such branches are gathered, thrown into the fire, and burned. If you **abide** in me, and **my words abide** in you, ask for whatever you wish, and it will be done for you.' (15:4-7)*

> *'As the Father has loved me, so I have loved you; **abide** in my love. If you keep my commandments, you will **abide** in my love, just as I have kept my Father's commandments and **abide** in his love. I have said these things to you so that my joy may **be** in you, and that your joy may be complete.' (15:9-11)*

To these we can add a passage from 1 John and a sentence from John 14 in which Jesus uses the noun *monē*, cognate with *mēno*:

> *No one has ever seen God; if we love one another, God **lives** in us, and his love is perfected in us. By this we know that **we abide in him and he in us,** because he has given us of his Spirit ... God **abides** in those who confess that Jesus is the Son of God, and they **abide** in God. So we have known and believe the love that God has for us. God is love, and those who **abide** in love abide in God, and **God abides** in them. (1 John 4:12-16)*

> *Jesus answered him, 'Those who love me will keep my word, and my Father will love them, and we will come to them and make our **home** with them.' (John 14:23)*

It is clear from these passages that John uses the idea of 'dwelling in' in a variety of ways. Jesus most frequently speaks of believers 'abiding' in him or in God, which in view of their unity amount to the same thing. Sometimes, too, he speaks of 'abiding in love' or 'in my love'. These expressions might refer, at

Jesus – yesterday, today, for ever

a minimal level, to not abandoning one's faith in Jesus; however, the language has a degree of personal warmth that suggest that more than this is intended – something involving the heart and mind of the believer. It seems to imply a sense of the personal presence of Jesus and the focusing of one's mental life, in thought and feeling, on him. But this also involves 'his word', i.e. his commandments, abiding in the believer, which in turn leads to 'keeping my commandments'. It is not clear whether 'keeping my commandments' is the result of, or the precondition for, abiding in him and in his love.

But Jesus also reverses the phrasing sometimes, saying that he and/or the Father 'dwell' in the believer. Is this something additional to the sense of personal closeness, arising out of our awareness of Jesus' love and our consequent efforts to do his commandments – or is it simply a way of looking at that relationship from the other end? Do all these formulations fundamentally refer to our mental life? – does Jesus 'dwell in us' because we are ever aware of him, so that he occupies and preoccupies our thinking? Or do they speak of some action on his part in order to induce such a condition, influencing human beings with a power that comes from without?

There are two statements among those quoted above that might be thought to support this second possibility:

> *'You know him [the spirit of truth], because he abides with you, and he will be in you.' (John 14:17)*

> *By this we know that we abide in him and he in us, because he has given us of his Spirit. (1 John 4:13)*

We have to remember, too, that everything that Jesus says about the future of believers in John 14-16 is predicated upon his promise that he and the Father will 'send' the *parakletos*, who will be for them what, in his mortal life, Jesus has been to them. This seems to preclude the interpretation which says that Jesus is speaking solely of something that arises out of a human being's unaided and undirected thinking – though it surely does not refer to any divine action that short-circuits such thinking. For the 'mutual indwelling' is a result of loving, not of the exercise of any power that might overrule the will and intentions of the believers – except the power of love. The closing verses of Jesus' prayer in John 17 are very significant in this context:

> *'... that they may all be one. As you, Father, are in me and I am in you, may they also be in us, so that the world may believe that you have sent me. The glory that you have given me I have given them, so that they may be one, as we are one, I in them and you in me, that they may become completely one,*

so that the world may know that you have sent me and have loved them even as you have loved me … I made your name known to them, and I will make it known, so that the love with which you have loved me may be in them, and I in them.' (John 17:22-23, 26)

The 'indwelling appears to involve both knowing *who* Father and Son are *and* knowing *that* one is loved by them, while the final line in particular virtually equates Jesus being 'in them' with his love being 'in them'. And loving is a form of action too, especially when the love which is being referred to throughout the discourses is no mere emotion but the love that found expression at Golgotha: *'No one has greater love than this, to lay down one's life for one's friends'* (John 15:13).

However we read these discourses, our response to them must call upon all the resources of our mental and emotional life, of knowing, feeling and loving. Moreover, it must be rooted in our awareness that the life and the presence with us of the eternally living Lord is a consequence of his dying – which characterises everything that he now does. And our reading of them should help us to see that it is such a relationship of mutual love, not simple obedience to commandments, that will enable us, perhaps, to begin to resemble the Lord whose representatives we aspire to be.

'In Christ'

Things are similar, yet also somewhat different, in the thought and language world of Paul. One of his most characteristic phrases is 'in Christ', which, as we have already seen, appears to have a broad range of meanings: being a member of his community; the environment of thought and behaviour within that community; the essential character of all relationships between Christians and their lord and with each other, etc. In other words, it is a kind of shorthand term to indicate how their relationship to Jesus suffuses every aspect of their life, including, of course, a sense of a personal bond with him. Sometimes, though, it is 'the spirit of Christ' or 'the spirit of God' that is 'in' the believer, as in the following key passage from Romans:

*But you are not in the flesh; you are in the Spirit, since **the Spirit of God dwells in you**. Anyone who does not have the Spirit of Christ does not belong to him. But if **Christ is in you**, though the body is dead because of sin, the Spirit is life because of righteousness. If the **Spirit of him who raised Jesus from the dead dwells in you**, he who raised Christ from the dead will give life to your mortal bodies also through his Spirit that dwells in you … For all who are **led by the Spirit of God** are children of God. (Romans 8:9-11, 14)*

Jesus – yesterday, today, for ever

Fundamentally the same thing is meant, surely, when Paul sums all this up in a striking phrase in Colossians: '... *this mystery, which is Christ in you, the hope of glory*' (Col. 1:27).

The question posed by these and similar expressions is similar to that raised by the language of Jesus in John: does 'the spirit of Christ' or of God refer to an ethical and/or spiritual way of thinking and feeling in the believer, engendered by an awareness of their love? Are having '*the mind of the Spirit*' (Rom. 8:27), being '*spiritually minded*' (Rom. 8:6), or having '*the mind of Christ*' (1 Cor. 2:16), descriptions of a condition of human consciousness and behaviour in response to God's action in giving Jesus, and to Jesus' action in giving himself?

What speaks against such a focus on what happens within the believer is Paul's repeated reference to the believer having 'received' (*lambano*) something:

> *For you did not **receive** a spirit of slavery to fall back into fear, but you **have received** a spirit of adoption. When we cry, 'Abba! Father!' (Romans 8:15)*

> *Now **we have received** not the spirit of the world, but the Spirit that is from God, so that we may understand the gifts bestowed on us by God. (1 Corinthians 2:12)*

> *... if you **receive** a different spirit from the one you received ... (2 Corinthians 11:4)*

> *Did you **receive** the Spirit by doing the works of the law or by believing what you heard? (Galatians 3:2)*

In addition, Paul refers to a double 'sending': first God sent the Son into the world, and then he '*sent the spirit of his Son into our hearts*' (Gal. 4:4, 6). In Romans 5 we find a somewhat different way of describing this divine initiative: '*God's love has been poured into our hearts through the Holy Spirit that has been given to us*' (Rom. 5:5). This verse is all the more intriguing because Paul here uses for 'pour' the same verb, *excheo*, that is used in Acts for the outpouring of the Spirit gifts at Pentecost (Acts 2:17, 18, 33). So it is not surprising that throughout Acts we read repeatedly of people 'receiving' – again *lambano* – the holy Spirit (e.g. Acts 8:15-19; 10:47; 19:2).

Of particular importance are the words of Peter in Acts 2: '*Repent, and be baptized every one of you in the name of Jesus Christ so that your sins may be forgiven; and you will receive the gift of the Holy Spirit*' (Acts 2:38). Right from the earliest proclamation of the gospel, the apostles assume that belief and

The Risen Lord and his People

baptism are not simply actions initiated by an individual and performed for them by the church; nor is the 'new life' that new converts are urged to adopt solely dependent on the will-power and self-control of the new believer. In the light of the repeated references to 'receiving' the Spirit and the language found in Paul and John's writing, we are forced, I think, to conclude that repenting and committing oneself to the service of Jesus in the face of his death and resurrection is a spiritual act of a unique kind. It is not comparable to any other acts of repentance of which we read elsewhere in scripture, for it is elicits from God a corresponding action on human hearts and minds that brings about a profound re-orientation in their thinking and feeling. Peter's preaching of the gospel accordingly includes not only the fact of Jesus' death and resurrection and the call for repentance and baptism, but also the prospect and the promise of such a response on God's side. Not for nothing are Christian virtues described in Galatians 5 as the 'fruit of the Spirit'.

Such an idea has profound implications for our understanding of the working of the cross: far from being a piece of legal machinery designed to satisfy God's demand for 'righteousness' in those who approach him, the gospel of Jesus Christ, dead and risen, possesses a force that begins the work of transforming human beings into his likeness. This is, of course, precisely what the 'new covenant' was intended to do: *'But this is the covenant that I will make with the house of Israel after those days, says the* LORD: *I will put my law within them, and I will write it on their hearts'* (Jer. 31:33; cf. Heb. 8:8-10). It is also what Paul is referring to when he describes the gospel as *'the **power** of God for salvation to everyone who has faith, to the Jew first and also to the Greek'* (Rom. 1:16).

If we ask ourselves *why* the gospel of Jesus Christ should, uniquely, possess such power, we need only to remember that the 'spirit' is 'the Spirit of him who raised Jesus from the dead', or in Paul's terms, 'the spirit of Christ', that is, the spirit of him who died and rose again. Kenneth Grayston puts it like this:

Flesh and Spirit are powers, and to be 'in' one or the other is to be in the power (or under the control) of flesh or Spirit ... Although you cannot withdraw from the social world of your contemporaries ... you need not be dominated by the destructive pressures it brings to bear; for you can be moved by the power of the life-giving Spirit if the Spirit of God dwells in you ... It is not the Spirit of triumphant mankind or even of transformed mankind but 'the Spirit of Christ', that is, the Spirit that led him to his death in confidence that God would do what he would do ... participation in Christ's death changes the condition of the believer rather than the attitude of God ... the death of Christ ... is displayed as a constitutive, not an atoning act.[7]

It is as if there is some profound accord between the fundamental make-up of the human psyche and the gospel of Jesus – and who would know that better than the Creator? – which gives the gospel this power. It is capable, through the Spirit of God working through it, of causing men and women to 'die' in spirit with Jesus and then to bring about their rebirth as new people. Peter speaks of it too: *'You have been born anew, not of perishable but of imperishable seed, through the living and enduring word of God'* (1 Pet. 1:23). And lest we should be foolish enough to think that he simply means 'reading the Bible', he explains: *'That word is the good news that was announced to you'* (v. 25).

The New Testament provides living models of that process taking place: when we meet Jesus' fearful disciples again in Acts, they are men transformed – the death and resurrection of their Lord have done their work. The same is no less true of Paul; it is not his baptism that makes him a new man – it simply symbolises outwardly the powerful working of the cross of Jesus within him. He describes this process as 'dying with Christ' or being 'crucified with Christ', most powerfully in Galatians: *'I have been crucified with Christ; and it is no longer I who live, but it is Christ who lives in me. And the life I now live in the flesh I live by faith in the Son of God, who loved me and gave himself for me'* (Gal. 2:19-20). He knows that he is no longer the man that he was: within the 'I' that he still is, there now lives another, who is Jesus.[8]

Needless to say, though Paul is a kind of 'offshoot' of Jesus, he is initially still far from being fully 'in his image'; for that reason, the process of dying and rising after his pattern has to repeat itself again and again, as Paul's example illustrates. Though he knew that Christ now lived in him, he aspired to an ever-closer oneness with him and was therefore willing to undergo that often painful process time after time. Acts tells us something of how it happened, while his letters reveal how he understood his experiences:

---

7 Kenneth Grayston, *Dying, We Live. A New Enquiry into the Death of Christ in the New Testament*, New York/Oxford 1990, pp. 111-112, 118.

8 The way in which individuals in Acts transcend the constraints imposed by their origins, the culture in which they grew up, material, economic, social and political pressures – and even the bars and chains of imprisonment – is perhaps the best clue to the meaning of what Jesus said in his conversation with Nicodemus: *'The wind blows where it chooses, and you hear the sound of it, but you do not know where it comes from or where it goes. So it is with everyone who is born of the Spirit'* (John 3:8).

The Risen Lord and his People

> *We are afflicted in every way, but not crushed; perplexed, but not driven to despair; persecuted, but not forsaken; struck down, but not destroyed; always carrying in the body the death of Jesus, so that the life of Jesus may also be made visible in our bodies. For while we live, we are always being given up to death for Jesus' sake, so that the life of Jesus may be made visible in our mortal flesh. (2 Corinthians 4:8-11)*

> *We are treated as impostors, and yet are true; as unknown, and yet are well known; as dying, and see – we are alive; as punished, and yet not killed. (2 Corinthians 6:8-9)*

He formulated this aspiration most succinctly, perhaps, in Philippians: '*I want to know Christ and the power of his resurrection and the sharing of his sufferings by becoming like him in his death, if somehow I may attain the resurrection from the dead*' (Phil. 3:10-11).

There is one further passage that we have to consider that seems to me to confirm that the language of John and Paul about the 'spirit of Jesus' is more than just the name of a particular ethical quality – that it suggests the kind of active involvement of the Lord in the ways that I have been attempting to describe. In Romans 8, Paul talks of the incompleteness of believers:

> *I consider that our present sufferings are not worth comparing with the glory that will be revealed in us … We know that the whole creation has been groaning as in the pains of childbirth right up to the present time. Not only so, but we ourselves, who have the firstfruits of the Spirit, groan inwardly as we wait eagerly for our adoption as sons, the redemption of our bodies … In the same way, the Spirit helps us in our weakness. We do not know what we ought to pray for, but the Spirit himself intercedes for us with groans that words cannot express. And he who searches our hearts knows the mind of the Spirit, because the Spirit intercedes for the saints in accordance with God's will. (Romans 8:18, 22-23, 26-27 NIV)*

We are, Paul says, acutely aware of our divided, imperfect condition as we live amid the pressures of the present world and our our own impulses – and so we groan, just as the whole creation groans as it awaits its transformation at the coming of the Lord. We groan although, or perhaps because, we have 'the firstfruits' of the Spirit – enough of Jesus within us to make us aware of all that we not yet are. The phrase 'firstfruits of the Spirit' already suggests that we have received something, albeit in part, just as Paul says elsewhere (Eph. 1:13-14; 2 Cor. 1:22; 5:5). It means that we long for the fullness which will complete the process of transformation.

But then Paul says that 'the Spirit' helps us, interceding for us with *'groans that words cannot express'*. Whose can this voice be, since it is, apparently, not the believer's own? It is not that of Jesus in his perfection and glory, for he would surely not be limited by such inarticulacy. It would appear, therefore, that it is the 'voice' of the Spirit of Jesus implanted in the believer, on his or her side, testifying on their behalf but constrained by the weakness of human imperfection. But, Paul adds, this faltering voice is nevertheless heard and understood – by whom? The somewhat mysterious phrase *'he who searches our heart'* is presumably a reference to God himself (cf. Luke 16:15; 1 Thess. 2:4); however, a comparison with Hebrews 4 makes one wonder whether this could be a reference to Jesus in his role as 'high priest', as we suggested earlier. Whichever of these two interpretations one adopts – and in practice they amount to the same thing – Paul is saying that Spirit speaks to Spirit: the indwelling Jesus is heard by the exalted Jesus and by the Father. The mighty Jesus on high comes to the aid of the 'Christ' that is struggling to be formed in us (Gal. 4:19) – and our awareness of his experience of human existence is our greatest comfort and assurance.

We have no conception of what the personality and feelings of the risen, immortal Jesus are like, but, remembering the importance to Jesus in his dying moments of Psalm 22's vision of multitudes turning to God as a result of his story, and the concern that he showed for those who were 'given to him' in John 17, the care for his people that is implied by all these different New Testament expressions is what we would expect. If Paul thought of his converts as *'my joy and crown'* (Phil. 4:1) and *'our glory and joy'* (1 Thess. 2:20), how much more will his people be a joy to Jesus when he is finally able to present them to the Father, using the words from Hebrews that we have already quoted: *'Here am I and the children whom God has given me'* (Heb. 2:13)! Nor will it be simply a matter of personal satisfaction; this continuing care for those who are his will be that further 'glorifying' of the Father that he prayed for in John 17. By carrying forward to its ultimate completion the work that he began during his earthly ministry, Jesus is the means by which God's aim, a new humanity in his image as proclaimed in Genesis 1, will at last be achieved.

The very present Jesus

Thinking and writing about Jesus in the past, both before and after his birth, is essentially a matter of facts and their interpretation, though the conclusions that one comes to may, of course, have an impact on one's faith and conduct in the present. Such an impact is far greater and more immediate, however, when we try to understand and to give due weight to New Testament teach-

The Risen Lord and his People

ing about the risen, living Jesus of the present. How we think of Jesus now has a direct influence on our thinking at every moment, on our behaviour, on the character of our worship and on our relationship to the Father as well as to the Son.

One reason for attempting the probably impossible task of looking across Jesus' 'career', from pattern of humanity conceived before all time through to the risen Lord of the present, is my sense that frequently insufficient place is given to the Son in the personal and collective lives of believers. A great deal is said and written about him, of course; he holds a central place in doctrine and in the 'First Principles' of faith. But almost all of it is focused on the Jesus of the past, on his earthly life culminating in his death and resurrection, and then on his future role at his coming. But the present Jesus? One sometimes has the impression that he is regarded as simply 'parked', just *waiting "until his enemies would be made a footstool for his feet"'* (Heb. 10:13). I hope that the content of this and the preceding chapter may perhaps help to dispel such an approach by reminding us of his continuing activity and his centrality in the unfolding and completion of his Father's loving purpose.

The following are some of the questions than arise in my mind about our language and our practice in relation to him whom the Father has appointed as our Lord:

- Our attempts to understand New Testament references to the relationship between the risen Jesus and his followers have led us to think of him as intensively active: not only in imparting to them his many gifts, watching over them as his people, and protecting them against a hostile world, but also in entering into personal relationship with them individually, dwelling with them and in them, to make them even more conformable to his image. Do we, in our personal and collective lives of faith, give sufficient recognition to the fact that God has 'given' or entrusted us to him as our Lord? Should it not be to him that we look for care and protection, and to him, rather than to angels, that we attribute the providential care that we experience in our Christian experience? And, contrary to what is often asserted, is it not an essential part of our faith-lives that we should speak to him? How could we not do so, when he is the 'one with whom we have to do', who is the 'high priest' set over us, and whom we shall one day meet face to face? It is evident that neither Stephen nor Paul, to name but two, had any inhibitions about doing so.

  To say this does not imply, of course, a unique focus on Jesus at the expense of the Father, nor any lessening of our adoration of the Father. In the ultimate, it may make little difference to whom we address our prayers

Jesus – yesterday, today, for ever

and praises. Yet it seems to me perverse to disregard the evident will of God that Jesus should be the immediate focus of our faith; he manifestly judged it to be for our good that we should be able to relate to Jesus as one who is known to have experienced from within the joys and the anguish of human existence.

- At the level of our communal life, should we not be more aware of Jesus as our Lord and 'head'? This might involve, for example, positively seeking his guidance in our decision-making. We have no right, of course, to assume that everything that we find in the New Testament accounts of the early church must axiomatically remain the same today. Not many Christians today have or expect to have any experience of the kind of miraculous healings or the gifts of 'tongues' or of languages that we read of in Acts, and we are probably wise to be wary of the claims to have witnessed or even performed such miracles that are advanced by some Christian groups. But equally, we have no right to deny their possibility or to argue, on the slenderest possible evidence, that the gifts of the Spirit described in Acts have been 'withdrawn'; it is not for us to prescribe to the living, empowered Lord what he may or may not do. The dilemma facing believers today is that one cannot preclude some such miraculous action on the part of the Lord, yet finds it hard to *'ask in faith, never doubting'* (James 1:6).

  On balance, one cannot but feel that we would do well to be bolder and more persistent in asking the Jesus to 'work with us' (cf. Mark 16:20) as we try to proclaim his name. This is surely true in a wider context than that of miraculous actions on the Lord's part. As we saw in the preceding chapter, the fundamental pattern that we find in the New Testament is that of Jesus guiding, directing and supporting his followers' work for him, and this must surely be their expectation now as much as then. Whatever name it goes by, whether 'preaching' or 'outreach', the church's witness should be accompanied by explicit prayers for such guidance – which may come in many forms. Christians should expect to be surprised, to be led where they would not have expected to go, as Peter was in the case of Cornelius, and to be driven by circumstance to venture well beyond their comfort zone, as the Jerusalem church was by the success of Philip in Samaria (Acts 8) and of Greek-speaking Christians in Antioch (Acts 11).

- Does an awareness of Jesus as Lord over the church not also imply that we should allow the evidence of his gifts to determine who may exercise which functions in the church, rather than devising rules that sometimes

The Risen Lord and his People

set aside his declared will. If, as Paul says, *'There is no longer Jew or Greek, there is no longer slave or free, there is no longer male and female; for all of you are one in Christ Jesus'* (Gal. 3:28), then the categories that have traditionally determined the distribution of power and responsibilities in the human world have no place in the realm of Christ, and we are on slippery ground if we seek nevertheless to retain them.

- That is one example of a more fundamental principle: I have used the concept of the *shaliach* to characterise both Jesus' service to the Father and that of the apostles and others in post-resurrection times to Jesus. The *shaliach*, as we have seen, is above all free in the way in which he or she serves – free, yet directed by a personal sense of responsibility to his or her lord. Does this principle not imply that churches and ecclesias should not seek to impose rules, whether about personal conduct or forms of worship, and that decisions on such things should flow from the faith of the individual or group of believers? The teaching of Paul on this matter in Romans 14 could scarcely be clearer. He formulates just two principles: first, that our conduct should be an expression of our personal faith and is therefore subject to the judgment of our Lord and no one else: *'Who are you to pass judgment on servants of another? It is before their own lord that they stand or fall ... The faith that you have, have as your own conviction before God ... whatever does not proceed from faith is sin'* (v. 4, 22-23); and second, the principle of practical love that considers the effect of one's actions on others: *'Do not, for the sake of food, destroy the work of God. Everything is indeed clean, but it is wrong for you to make others fall by what you eat; it is good not to eat meat or drink wine or do anything that makes your brother or sister stumble'* (v. 20-21).

- And finally: do we give to Jesus the honour and the worship due to him, bearing in mind the words of John 5: *'... so that all may honour the Son just as they honour the Father. Anyone who does not honour the Son does not honour the Father who sent him'* (John 5:23), and following the example set in Revelation 5: *'To the one seated on the throne and to the Lamb be blessing and honour and glory and might forever and ever!'* (Rev. 5:14)? It must surely be our wish to add our voices to that great chorus of praise.

Chapter 11

'And for ever' … Jesus in the Future

To begin to think about Jesus in the future is to venture even further into the unknown and unknowable than in anything that I have discussed so far. For that reason, this chapter is by intention relatively brief and does not engage extensively with the many views and theories about the coming of Jesus and the nature of the kingdom of God.

The 'future' with which we are concerned in this concluding chapter refers not only to the period usually described as 'the kingdom of God', i.e. the period following the return of Jesus, when *'The kingdom of the world has become the kingdom of our Lord and of his Messiah'* (Rev. 11:15), but also to the infinities of time stretching away before us of which Paul speaks in 1 Corinthians 15:

> *Then comes the end, when he hands over the kingdom to God the Father, after he has destroyed every ruler and every authority and power. For he must reign until he has put all his enemies under his feet. The last enemy to be destroyed is death. For 'God has put all things in subjection under his feet.' But when it says, 'All things are put in subjection', it is plain that this does not include the one who put all things in subjection under him. When all things are subjected to him, then the Son himself will also be subjected to the one who put all things in subjection under him, so that God may be all in all. (1 Corinthians 15:24-28)*

The effect of this passage is to divide the future into two phases: first, a finite phase, defined, probably symbolically, in Revelation 20 as 'a thousand years', during which God's purpose with his creation will be brought to its completion, and then a time without end, of which we can really say nothing beyond Paul's phrase that God will be 'all in all'. The opening of Revelation 22 may also provide some brief indications of that age of perfection:

'And for ever' ... Jesus in the Future

> *Nothing accursed will be found there any more. But the throne of God and of the Lamb will be in it, and his servants will worship him; they will see his face, and his name will be on their foreheads. And there will be no more night; they need no light of lamp or sun, for the Lord God will be their light, and they will reign for ever and ever. (Revelation 22:3-5)*

There can, then, be little point in further speculation as to the nature of that time or of Jesus' role within it, beyond reiterating that, whatever it is, it will be 'for ever'.

In this chapter we shall, therefore focus on the earlier phase, and specifically upon two aspects of it: on the one hand, Jesus' reappearance on earth in relation to the world as a whole, including his subsequent role within the 'kingdom of God', and, on the other hand, his coming in relation to believers, i.e. the 'judgment' and their sharing in what Jesus calls in one of his parables *'the joy of your master'* (Matt. 25:21). It is uniquely difficult to say anything specific about any of this, since it is, by definition, totally unknown to us. Though the scriptures refer to this future time quite extensively, they do so, perforce, in the language and imagery of their time, and in terms derived from their own social and political reality. If we do not make allowance for this in our reading and interpretation, we are in danger of suggesting that mankind will move from the age of computer and internet back to the bronze age and early iron age – notwithstanding the fact that the development of contemporary technology was and is an inevitable consequence of the intellectual gifts with which God as Creator so liberally endowed mankind.

Jesus and the world of the future

The vengeful warrior?

To discuss the impact of Jesus' reappearance on earth on the world at large is fraught with other difficulties apart from those already mentioned. In some Christian circles, especially among some 'evangelical' Christians in the USA, Jesus' coming is often described in quite lurid terms, involving wars, conflicts and terrible slaughter and with a warrior Jesus seen as exacting vengeance upon his enemies. There are, of course, a number of Biblical passages that suggest something of the kind. In one of his earliest letters, Paul speaks of a time *'when the Lord Jesus is revealed from heaven with his mighty angels in flaming fire, inflicting vengeance on those who do not know God and on those who do not obey the gospel of our Lord Jesus'* (2 Thess. 1:7-8), while Revelation 19 describes him in these terms:

Then I saw heaven opened, and there was a white horse! Its rider is called Faithful and True, and in righteousness he judges and makes war. His eyes are like a flame of fire, and on his head are many diadems; and he has a name inscribed that no one knows but himself. He is clothed in a robe dipped in blood, and his name is called The Word of God. And the armies of heaven, wearing fine linen, white and pure, were following him on white horses. From his mouth comes a sharp sword with which to strike down the nations, and he will rule them with a rod of iron; he will tread the wine press of the fury of the wrath of God the Almighty. (Revelation 19:11-15)

Before we assume this to be a literal description of a warrior Jesus, we have to take account, not only of the symbolic character of the language of Revelation throughout, but also of specific details: the 'sharp sword' has occurred earlier in Revelation as a figure for the authority in judgment wielded by Jesus (Rev. 1:16; 2:12, 16; cf. *'in righteousness he judges and makes war'*). The fact that the scene is located 'in heaven' reminds us of the spiritual battle that takes place in Revelation 12:7, while the white horse recalls the first of the 'horsemen' in chapter 6. We have also to ask ourselves how it could come about that the robes of his followers apparently remain white, while his own is 'dipped in blood'. In addition, though, we have to notice that the entire scene owes much to another passage which is frequently taken to be a picture of Jesus and which apparently portrays him in bloody, martial terms:

Who is this that comes from Edom,
*   from Bozrah in garments stained crimson?*
Who is this so splendidly robed,
*   marching in his great might?'*
'It is I, announcing vindication,
*   mighty to save.'*
'Why are your robes red,
*   and your garments like theirs who tread the wine press?'*
'I have trodden the wine press alone,
*   and from the peoples no one was with me;*
I trod them in my anger
*   and trampled them in my wrath;*
their juice spattered on my garments,
*   and stained all my robes.*
For the day of vengeance was in my heart,
*   and the year for my redeeming work had come.*

'And for ever' ... Jesus in the Future

> I looked, but there was no helper;
>   I stared, but there was no one to sustain me;
> so my own arm brought me victory,
>   and my wrath sustained me.
> I trampled down peoples in my anger,
>   I crushed them in my wrath,
>   and I poured out their lifeblood on the earth.' (Isaiah 63:1-6)

Dramatic and colourful as this passage is, we should hesitate before seeing in it a picture of a vengeful returning Jesus. First, it is actually a picture of God himself – compare Isaiah 59:16, which includes the same figure of God's 'arm', where it is clear that the enemy is human wickedness. Here in chapter 63, as also in Isaiah 34, Edom, also known by the names of places within it such as Idumea and Bozrah, serves as the epitome of resistance to God, all the more fittingly since Edom was a persistent adversary of Israel and Judah from the time of the Exodus. The victories of David and later of Jehoram, son of Jehoshaphat, and Amaziah (2 Kings 8 and 14) may well provide the model for the graphic language of this passage in Isaiah 63.

We notice too that the 'day of vengeance' is coupled with the 'year of my redeeming work', suggesting that the passage represents the entire work of God in Christ, both judgment and redemption. When Jesus, in the Nazareth synagogue, quotes Isaiah 61 (Luke 4:18-19), he appears to separate the two aspects of God's work by omitting the reference to *'the day of vengeance of our God'* (Is. 61:2), referring to *'days of vengeance'* (i.e. AD 70) only in Luke 21:22.

Incongruity

For my own part, I find it difficult, not to say impossible, to embrace the notion, enthusiastically promoted by some, of a warrior Jesus who indulges in the slaughter apparently attributed to him by a few such passages. The idea is fraught with so many contradictions. Put simply, such a picture of Jesus seems to me incompatible with everything that we know about him from the Gospels. It is true, of course, that Jesus is at times not sparing in his condemnation of those whose influence in their often self-appointed role as religious leaders was in fact directly opposed to his mission and to the saving purpose of God. Yet these are individual judgments on the spiritual plane and their consequence is exclusion from the kingdom of God; they have nothing to do with random slaughter and bloodletting.

Moreover, Jesus explicitly rejects the use of force as the means of establishing his reign among men: *'My kingdom is not from this world. If my kingdom were from this world, my followers would be fighting to keep me from being handed over to the Jews. But as it is, my kingdom is not from here'* (John 18:36). Should one understand Jesus to be saying that he does not use violence now – but will be happy to do so later? In the ears of those to whom he wishes to appeal, that would sound cynical indeed! And would it then be possible to say that Jesus is *'the same yesterday and today and for ever'*?

Imagine, too, a future kingdom of God, a reign of Jesus on earth, originally established by means of such violence. Would it not be an enforced obedience that mankind would then give to God? And would it not teach that this kingdom was fundamentally no different from all its human predecessors, based simply on the right of the strong? Throughout his earthly ministry, Jesus sought always to win the hearts and the minds of men and women through his message, his actions, and his realisation in his own life of the grace and mercy of God; is it conceivable that he would on his return abandon that path in favour of mere force?

The bigger picture

The three passages referred to above, from 2 Thessalonians, Revelation 19 and Isaiah 63, are but a few of all those, mostly in the Old Testament, that appear to predict that Jesus' reappearance on earth will be preceded by military conflict, focused, seemingly, on the Middle East and Israel. It is a striking feature of many of them that the divine intervention in this conflict is depicted in terms of cataclysmic natural events: earthquake, pestilence, hail and fire, thunder and lightning – see, for example, Ezek. 38:19-22; Joel 2:10; 3:16; Hagg. 2:6-7, 21; Zech, 14:4-5; Luke 21:25-26; Heb. 12:26; Rev. 16:18-21. In addition, most of these passages appear to describe a war *between human forces*, to which the divine intervention puts an abrupt end: *'I will summon the sword against Gog in all my mountains, says the Lord God; the swords of all will be against their comrades'* (Ezek. 38:1-13, 21 – see also Rev. 16:14; Joel 3:11-13; Zech. 12:2-3; 14:1-2).

In fact, the purpose of the divine intervention appears to be that of putting an end to the conflict, perhaps thus saving mankind and the entire planet from a destruction brought about by the aggressive propensities of man, no longer exercised with bows and arrows but with all the destructive potential of modern technology. It is perhaps no accident that Isaiah announces: *'For thus says the Lord, who created the heavens (he is God!), who formed the earth and made it (he established it; he did not create it a chaos, he formed it to be inhabited!)'* (Is. 45:18) – the word 'chaos' (*tohu*) is defined by Strong's as 'from an unused root meaning to lie waste; a desolation (of surface), i.e. desert … confusion, empty place, without form, nothing, (thing of) nought, vain, vanity, waste,

'And for ever' ... Jesus in the Future

wilderness'. The word occurs also in Genesis 1:2, and one might conclude that Isaiah's use of the word implies a danger that without such a divine intervention the earth might revert – through men's activities – to the formless, inert thing that it originally was.

It is consistent with this view of Jesus' coming that Isaiah's and Micah's depiction of his subsequent reign, once established, focuses on the 're-education' of mankind so that their creative powers are used for fruitful ends rather than for war and conquest: *'He shall judge between the nations, and shall arbitrate for many peoples; they shall beat their swords into ploughshares, and their spears into pruning-hooks; nation shall not lift up sword against nation, neither shall they learn war any more'* (Is. 2:4; Mic. 4:3). In Isaiah, the announcement of the impending birth of the one whose name is to be 'prince of peace' also says that *'... all the boots of the tramping warriors and all the garments rolled in blood shall be burned as fuel for the fire'* (Is. 9:5). Still more succinctly, Zechariah says that *'he shall command peace to the nations'* (Zech. 9:10). Such instruction would come strangely from one who had, to use the words of Thomas Gray in his famous 'Elegy', *'wade[d] through slaughter to a throne'*.

It is pointless to speculate by the use of what power and authority Jesus will be able to put an end to the conflict already raging and then to restrain the self-assertive, competitive impulses of human beings in the way that Psalm 2, for example, describes, and to redirect them into new and more useful channels. All that we can say is that he will possess the authority and the power that will enable him to do so. It may be more helpful to focus on the way in which several psalms represent this mighty act of peace-making in terms of the quietening of raging seas: *'By awesome deeds you answer us with deliverance, O God of our salvation; you are the hope of all the ends of the earth and of the farthest seas ... You silence the roaring of the seas, the roaring of their waves, the tumult of the peoples'* (Ps. 65:5-7; see also Ps. 89:9). We can trace the use of this metaphor through scriptures, via Isaiah 57:20-21 and Luke 21:25, right through to Revelation 15:2. It becomes more compelling still, though, when we recall Jesus' symbolic enactment of this as yet future intervention when he *'commanded peace'* to the stormy seas in Mark 4:35-41. Though the thoughts of an immortal being are quite beyond our grasp, one cannot help but imagine the joy and the satisfaction that it will give Jesus when he can at last do what the symbolic action pointed to: bring peace, not to a stormy Sea of Galilee but to the teeming masses of warring mankind. He knows from his earthly life the ways of the 'rulers' and 'tyrants' (Mark 10:42), and he has seen the plight of those who, while attempting to assert their own wills and freedoms, find themselves crushed or exploited by those more ruthless and more ambitious than themselves (cf. Luke 23:28-31).

The reign of Jesus

Whatever difficulty we might have in describing the events surrounding Jesus' coming, we might think it easy to describe his reign after his establishment as 'king'. The scriptures contain, after all, many pictures of a future time of blessing, such as Psalm 72, Isaiah 11:1-9, 35 and 65:17-25, Amos 9:11-15, and Revelation 21-22 For all that, a caveat is necessary: all these pictures are very general in character; they are also either symbolic, as in the case of Revelation, or they offer isolated details as examples of the transformed conditions of human life, as in the following passage:

> *The wolf shall live with the lamb, the leopard shall lie down with the kid, the calf and the lion and the fatling together, and a little child shall lead them. The cow and the bear shall graze, their young shall lie down together; and the lion shall eat straw like the ox. The nursing child shall play over the hole of the asp, and the weaned child shall put its hand on the adder's den. (Isaiah 11:6-8)*

In addition, they are in two ways shaped by the age and the culture from which they come; first, they assume an essentially pastoral and agricultural way of life, utterly different from the world that Jesus will encounter at his coming: '... *but they shall all sit under their own vines and under their own fig trees, and no one shall make them afraid'* (Micah 4:4). Secondly, some of the pictures evoked by these passages, especially Isaiah 35 and 65, are couched largely in the form of negatives, telling us how things will no longer be:

> *... **no more** shall the sound of weeping be heard in it, or the cry of distress. **No more** shall there be in it an infant that lives but a few days, or an old person who does not live out a lifetime ... They shall build houses and inhabit them; they shall plant vineyards and eat their fruit. **They shall not** build and another inhabit; **they shall not plant** and another eat ... **They shall not** labour in vain ... (Isaiah 65:19-23)*

Given the vast material, social, and technical differences between the ancient world and the present, to say nothing of the as yet future, it seems to me wiser not to attempt to describe the reign of Jesus beyond its most basic principles. And in fact, most of these prophetic passages focus, not on material conditions as such, but rather on those features which in every age have been the aspiration of the great mass of humanity: the absence of conflict, justice, plentiful food supplies provided by a fertile earth, protection for the weak, freedom from oppression and exploitation:

'And for ever' ... Jesus in the Future

> *For he delivers the needy when they call, the poor and those who have no helper. He has pity on the weak and the needy, and saves the lives of the needy. From oppression and violence he redeems their life; and precious is their blood in his sight ... May there be abundance of grain in the land; may it wave on the tops of the mountains; may its fruit be like Lebanon...* (Psalm 72:12-14, 16)

I have already suggested that the moment when Jesus quietens the raging sea in Mark 4 serves as an enacted metaphor for his action in stilling the raging sea of humanity at his coming. It is widely recognised that his ministry as a whole represented a kind of realisation in miniature of Old Testament pictures of the kingdom of God. In particular, his healings are frequently linked to Isaiah 35: *'Then the eyes of the blind shall be opened, and the ears of the deaf unstopped; then the lame shall leap like a deer, and the tongue of the speechless sing for joy'* (v. 5-6). Jesus himself makes the connection explicit: *'But if it is by the finger of God that I cast out the demons, then the kingdom of God has come to you'* (Luke 11:20; cf. Matt 12:28). Still more obvious is his use of Isaiah 61 in the Nazareth synagogue. It is clear from the Gospels that Jesus had grasped the import of such passages and saw it as his task to realise their images of blessing by his words and actions, driven not simply by a sense of obedience, but also by having profoundly identified with the aims and values of such kingdom pictures.

What is less often noted is the obverse of this relationship: that Jesus' actions during his earthly ministry provide the template for his action on his return. What he once did for individuals he will now do for mankind and the world as a whole. Where he once made straight a woman unable to stand straight, he will make straight all that is twisted and distorted by human greed and lust for power; instead of healing individuals stricken with blindness or deafness, he will open men's and women's eyes and ears to what is true and right; where once he cleansed lepers, he will now purify a polluted planet and rid the world of the distorted values, activities and practices that endanger life and sanity in our present world. Most important of all, he will heal the world of its many forms of collective madness – aggression and war, the pursuit of wealth and possessions, unlimited growth, addiction, discrimination of every kind – instead winning anew the hearts and minds of mankind for the loving Creator who made them for better than the struggle for survival and the self-destructive practices that now disfigure the lives of so many. Isaiah and Micah share a picture of a human race that now desires to unlearn the assumptions of the present and to devote its God-given abilities to fruitful, constructive ends:

Jesus – yesterday, today, for ever

Many peoples shall come and say, 'Come, let us go up to the mountain of the Lord, to the house of the God of Jacob; that he may teach us his ways and that we may walk in his paths.' For out of Zion shall go forth instruction, and the word of the Lord from Jerusalem ... they shall beat their swords into ploughshares and their spears into pruning-hooks; nation shall not lift up sword against nation, neither shall they learn war any more. (Isaiah 2:3-4)

If one thinks of Jesus in the past, full of compassion for the poor and afflicted, one can perhaps begin to imagine his joy and satisfaction at being able now to exploit his power and authority to the full, bringing relief to mankind and giving glory to the Father by creating the *'new heavens and a new earth, where righteousness is at home'* (2 Pet. 3:13).

It is not my purpose to attempt to say *how* all this will be done – it would be most unwise to do so! Similarly, I do not wish to speculate about the actual length of the 'millennium', about how it will end, or by what process and on what basis people who are alive during that time will be able to share in the eternal life of God and the perfections of the age that lies beyond it. The scriptures focus, naturally enough, on the 'throne of David' and the role of Jerusalem, but we do well not to form too fixed a picture of the future on the basis of the past. One of the first things that Jesus is likely to have to do is to overcome the established powers – presidents, dictators, even 'democratic' governments of the world. Numerous passages depict this process, such as Psalm 2; Isaiah 60:3, 11 and 62:2; Revelation 1:5; 6:15. It will be the practical expression and display at last of the authority with which Jesus was endowed after his resurrection and that we referred to in chapter 10 – see, for example, Ephesians 1:21; Philippians 2:10; 1 Peter 3:22. He will at last have laid claim to the authority and power that are his by right: *'for you have taken your great power and begun to reign'* (Rev. 11:17).

It may be that Revelation's obviously symbolic – and poetic – image of a 'new Jerusalem' is at least as good a guide to the shape of the future. What emerges above all from the many pictures of the reign of Jesus, and especially from Revelation's closing chapters, is the idea that this perfected world will be the realisation of what is foreshadowed in the creation story in Genesis 1-3; these chapters of Revelation draw on so many of the motifs of those early scenes – see, for example, Rev. 21:1, 3-4, 23; 22:1-2, 4-5. Whether these scenes depict the world as it will be when Jesus finally presents it to the Father as completed (1 Cor. 15:25-28) or the unknown reality that lies beyond is impossible to say.

It seems clear, though, that an earth suddenly coming under the rule of

'And for ever' ... Jesus in the Future

Jesus will require some kind of administration and that Jesus will require a vast number of agents who will share with him the work of transforming not only the physical environment, but also the attitudes and assumptions of the men and women who inhabit it. The New Testament provides some pointers: in his parable of the pounds in Luke 19, the master rewards his faithful servants by putting them in charge of a number of cities (Luke 19:17, 19), while in the parable of the talents, the master says *'I will put you in charge of many things'* (Matt. 25:21, 23). Revelation is perhaps more explicit: those who sing the 'new song' say of the 'saints': *'you have made them to be a kingdom and priests serving our God, and they will reign on earth'* (Rev. 5:10). They will, one supposes, be Jesus' *shaliachim* as he himself once was for his Father.

There are other questions, too, that come to mind as we contemplate the reality of this new world: how great a population will the earth bear? And what of the endless spaces of the expanding universe? But these, and so many others, are not directly relevant to our focus on Jesus. The furthest that we can go in thinking about the Jesus of the future is the glimpse provided by Paul: *'When all things are subjected to him, then the Son himself will also be subjected to the one who put all things in subjection under him, so that God may be all in all'* (1 Cor. 15:28). We recall Jesus' own words, first in his prayer in John 17: *'I glorified you on earth by finishing the work that you gave me to do'* (John 17:4), and then with his dying breath: *'It is finished'* (John 19:30). In truth, it was only a phase of the work that was 'finished', albeit the decisive phase. But Paul's words evoke a picture of the Son able at last to declare to the Father that everything known to us of his original creative purpose, his *'plan for the fullness of time, to gather up all things in [Christ], things in heaven and things on earth'* (Eph. 1:10) is truly, in a final and absolute sense, 'finished' (*teleo*) – not simply 'over' but rather 'completed', in fact, 'complete'.

Meeting Jesus

In looking at the 'big picture' of Jesus' work in remaking the world after his coming, we have omitted one vital dimension: the meaning of his coming for those who have believed in him. We cannot be sure about the order of events at that time. Paul's words give the impression that his first action might be to raise 'the dead in Christ': *'For the Lord himself, with a cry of command, with the archangel's call and with the sound of God's trumpet, will descend from heaven, and the dead in Christ will rise first'* (1 Thess. 4:16). This reference to an archangel's call and the sound of a trumpet is paralleled elsewhere, notably in 1 Corinthians 15:52 and John 5:28, but most importantly perhaps in Matthew 24: *'And he will send out his angels with a loud trumpet call, and they will gather his elect from the four winds, from one end of heaven to the other'* (v. 31).

Jesus – yesterday, today, for ever

The similarity is particularly significant because it is one of many echoes of the language of Matthew 24-25 that can be found in 1 Thessalonians 4:13-5:11. We have no way of knowing how or in what form the record of Jesus' words, as we now have them in Matthew 24-25, were known to Paul, but the similarities are, it seems to me, too many to be dismissed as coincidence. They are all the more intriguing because Paul introduces this passage by saying: *'For this we declare to you by the word of the Lord'* (v. 15), or *'According to the Lord's own word'* (NIV), literally 'in the word of the Lord' (*en logō kyriou*), which could well be an indication that he claims to be reproducing what Jesus himself had said. Paul's version is more detailed, however; conscious of the anxieties of some believers that any of their number who died before the Lord's coming might somehow be forgotten entirely or be latecomers at this meeting, he is at pains to distinguish clearly between the raising of the dead and the subsequent gathering of all, the living and those newly raised alike, to meet the Lord.

Readings of this passage from 1 Thessalonians tend, unfortunately, to be distracted either by outlandish theories of the so-called 'rapture' or by speculations concerning the means by which this 'gathering' of 'the elect' will take place – 'unfortunately' because it deflects attention from the primary import of these passages, namely that the returning Jesus will gather his people and that they will 'meet' him. This passage in 1 Thessalonians suggests not only that it was a vital element in Paul's teaching but that it had been passed down as part of Jesus' sayings about his return by his disciples. Paul refers to it again in 2 Thessalonians: *'As to the coming of our Lord Jesus Christ and our being gathered together to him, we beg you, brothers and sisters ... '* (2 Thess. 2:1). This aspect of Jesus' coming appears to figure more prominently in the minds of the apostles than the Old Testament predictions of conflict and conquest might lead us to expect.

But what kind of meeting will it be? Foremost in the minds of most of those who are awaiting his coming is probably the notion of his 'judgment seat'. The actual term, using the word *bema*, occurs only twice: *'For we will all stand before the judgement seat of God'* (Rom. 14:10) and *'For all of us must appear before the judgement seat of Christ, so that each may receive recompense for what has been done in the body, whether good or evil'* (2 Cor. 5:10), but there are numerous passages suggesting that Jesus will come, not only as the judge and ruler of the world as a whole but also as the judge of his own people. In John 5, Jesus speaks of it in these terms: *'the hour is coming when all who are in their graves will hear his voice and will come out—those who have done good, to the resurrection of life, and those who have done evil, to the resurrection of condemnation'*

306

'And for ever' … Jesus in the Future

(John 5:28-29), an echo, perhaps, of Daniel 12:2: *'Many of those who sleep in the dust of the earth shall awake, some to everlasting life, and some to shame and everlasting contempt'*. In addition to such statements, Jesus' parables include repeated pictures of a returning master or employer who summons his servants and asks them to give account of their stewardship during his absence. In various ways, the New Testament repeatedly gives us the impression that Jesus' followers will somehow – the form and setting do not concern us – be required to face Jesus and speak for themselves. It is undoubtedly a daunting prospect, dreaded, one suspects, by many believers, who are only too conscious of their inherent shortcomings, the inadequacy of their service and the uneven nature of their faith.

Three things at least speak against such doubtless natural reactions. First, when discussing in chapter 7 the welcome that Jesus received on his arrival in Jerusalem, we noted the use by Paul in 1 Thessalonians 4:17 of the phrase *'eis apantēsin'*. It has been described as *'the ancient expression for the civic welcome of an important visitor or the triumphal entry of a ruler into the capital city and thus to his reign'.*[1] It suggests a kind of 'welcoming party' and thus complements the meaning of the word *parousia*, which, according to Walter Riggans, '… is used … for the arrival of rulers or military commanders. In the Roman world it was even used as a kind of technical term for the celebration of an emperor's visit to, and extended presence with, a particular city or community'.[2] The only other uses of the phrase *eis apantēsin* in the New Testament confirm this idea of welcome: *'Ten bridesmaids took their lamps and **went to meet** the bridegroom … at midnight there was a shout, "Look! Here is the bridegroom! Come out **to meet him**"'* (Matt. 25:1, 6); *'The believers from there, when they heard of us, came as far as the Forum of Appius and Three Taverns **to meet us**'* (Acts 28:15). All these contexts imply the arrival at last of one whose coming and presence have been long desired and who is therefore greeted with rejoicing. As Paul writes, *'… he comes to be glorified by his saints and to be marvelled at on that day among all who have believed … '* (2 Thess. 1:10).

Perhaps, one might object, these are pictures of how things ought to be, not of the actual emotions of Christians preparing to meet their Lord and judge. The most effective counter to their natural trepidation is found, perhaps surprisingly, in 1 John – 'surprisingly', because this letter appears to insist the most rigorously on the link between faith and conduct, as in the following examples: *'Whoever says, "I have come to know him," but does not obey his*

---

1 *Dictionary of New Testament Theology*, I, p. 325.

2 *Themelios*, XXI, 1, 1995.

commandments, is a liar, and in such a person the truth does not exist' (2:4; see also 4:20). Yet this same letter is not only the most realistic in its recognition of the believers' lack of consistency (e.g. 1:8-2:2), but also the most encouraging in relation to future judgment: 'And by this we will know that we are from the truth and will reassure our hearts before him whenever our hearts condemn us; for God is greater than our hearts, and he knows everything' (3:19-20). John is more explicit still in the following chapter:

> Love has been perfected among us in this: that we may have boldness on the day of judgement, because as he is, so are we in this world. There is no fear in love, but perfect love casts out fear; for fear has to do with punishment, and whoever fears has not reached perfection in love. (1 John 4:17-18)

The believer may be moved to confess that his or her love is not perfect and cannot therefore overcome the natural impulse of fear, but John appears to suggest that the fear of punishment has more to do with human beings' natural tendency to go on viewing God through the lens of human notions of rewards and penalties rather than as he truly is, as the one who is absolute love (v. 8, 16) and who by his love enables us to be freed from fear and set free to love in our turn (v. 19).

It is perhaps helpful to set alongside John's words here Jesus' parables in Matthew 25. In the story of the talents, the slave who is rejected is one who, not understanding the ways of his master, is paralysed by fear: '... so I was afraid, and I went and hid your talent in the ground' (Matt. 25:25). This dismal example is, by implication, contrasted with the 'sheep' in the third story in the chapter: these have 'kept his commandments', to use the language of 1 John, without realising that they have done so, because their actions and reactions have been reshaped by their acquaintance with the master (Matt. 25:34-40). As John says, the master is 'greater than our hearts, and he knows everything'; his judgment sees more and further than ours, and that may be to the believer's good!

The third counter to the Christian's natural tendency to fear judgment involves a more fundamental change of perspective. Instinctively, human beings see this 'meeting' from their point of view and in terms of their feelings about it. But consider it from Jesus' point of view. We may be familiar with Paul's thoughts as he contemplates that day: 'For what is our hope or joy or crown of boasting before our Lord Jesus at his coming? Is it not you? Yes, you are our glory and joy!' (1 Thess. 2:19-20). His one desire is to 'present everyone mature in Christ' (Col. 1:28), or, as he puts it elsewhere, 'to present you as a chaste virgin to Christ' (2 Cor. 11:2).

'And for ever' ... Jesus in the Future

If that was true of Paul, how much more of Jesus? His aim, Paul says, is '... *to present you holy and blameless and irreproachable before him'* (Col. 1:22). We referred earlier to the picture evoked in Hebrews 2 of Jesus 'presenting' to the Father the fruits of his labours: *'Here am I and the children whom God has given me'* (Heb. 2:13). One can perhaps have some idea of Jesus' joy on meeting face to face those whom the Father had entrusted to him – those who have lived and spoken with him; those whose thoughts and imaginations he has inhabited, on whom he has lavished so much care, whom he has carried and sustained, whose behaviour he has shaped and permeated in the way that the parable of Matthew 25 suggests – this, surely, is a major part of what Hebrews calls *'the joy that was set before him'* (Heb. 12:2). Jesus, we may be sure, will as judge be no 'soft touch'; for all that, this encounter will be not be a cool, dispassionate appraisal but rather a meeting at last of those who have long known and loved each other. And that is a reflection that adds urgency to the need of believers to speak to their Lord *now* – as they will be asked to do when at last they meet him.

'A life-giving spirit'

What will be the outcomes of this judgment? Leaving aside the account in Revelation 20, which it is difficult to reconcile with the evidence of the rest of the New Testament, every picture of this judgment suggests that there can be only two. That is seen at its starkest in the final parable in Matthew 25: *'... he will separate people one from another as a shepherd separates the sheep from the goats ... '* (Matt. 25:32). In this picture, the judge rejects those in whom he can recognise no likeness to himself. The language in which the fate of such people is expressed is fearsome – see Matthew 25:41, 46, for example – but in all these parables, it appears to imply that they are banished from his presence: *'... depart from me ... '* (v. 41); *'As for this worthless slave, throw him into the outer darkness'* (v. 30); *'... and the door was shut'* (v. 10). Similarly, Paul writes: *'These will suffer the punishment of eternal destruction, separated from the presence of the Lord and from the glory of his might ... '* (2 Thess. 1:9). Perhaps what is concealed behind this parabolic language is what Revelation 20 refers to as *'the second death'* (Rev. 20:14). Nowhere is the bitterness of exclusion expressed more powerfully than in Jesus' words after his encounter with the centurion whose servant he had healed: *'I tell you, many will come from east and west and will eat with Abraham and Isaac and Jacob in the king-dom of heaven, while the heirs of the kingdom will be thrown into the outer dark-ness, where there will be weeping and gnashing of teeth'* (Matt. 8:11-12). No one wishes to dwell on such a prospect, but it is clear from the relative frequency of such images in his teaching that Jesus deemed it necessary for his followers to be aware of the reality of such exclusion from *'the joy of your master'* (Matt. 25:21, 23).

Jesus' language in Mathew 8 and 23 is characteristic of the way in which he speaks in the Synoptic Gospels of what is in store for those who are deemed worthy: he draws on the Old Testament language which depicts the consummation of God's gracious purpose as a sumptuous banquet. In ancient Israel, to be a guest at a banquet and to partake of the richest dishes was the greatest sign of favour that one could receive, as we see in Joseph's treatment of his brothers and especially of Benjamin (see Genesis 43:34), and it was thus natural that the kingdom of God of the future should be depicted in this way: *'On this mountain the Lord of hosts will make for all peoples a feast of rich food, a feast of well-matured wines, of rich food filled with marrow, of well-matured wines strained clear'* (Is. 25:6). Jesus exploits this imagery on numerous occasions, not least at the Last Supper, when he speaks of *'that day when I drink it [i.e. the fruit of the vine] new with you in my Father's kingdom'* (Matt. 26:29; cf. Mark 14:25).

In their own writings the apostles are more explicit, though even here there are some variations. In his earlier letters, Paul attributes the granting of eternal life at Jesus' return to the Father: *'... when God's righteous judgement will be revealed ... to those who by patiently doing good seek for glory and honour and immortality, he will give eternal life ...'* (Rom. 2:5-7). In 1 Corinthians 15, he speaks of Jesus, the *'man from heaven'* as *'a life-giving spirit'* (v. 45), but this should probably be seen as part of his contrast between Jesus and Adam, who gave mankind a form of life encumbered by mortality. Later, however, he foregrounds the role of Jesus: *'He will transform the body of our humiliation so that it may be conformed to the body of his glory, by the power that also enables him to make all things subject to himself'* (Phil. 3:21). In his last letter, he is still more explicit: *'... the crown of righteousness, which the Lord, the righteous judge, will give to me on that day'* (2 Tim. 4:8). As we might expect, John's Gospel insists on the authority of Jesus to judge and to grant life, traditionally the two powers reserved uniquely to God:

> *Indeed, just as the Father raises the dead and gives them life, so also the Son gives life to whomsoever he wishes. The Father judges no one but has given all judgement to the Son ... he has given him authority to execute judgement, because he is the Son of Man. Do not be astonished at this; for the hour is coming when all who are in their graves will hear his voice and will come out—those who have done good, to the resurrection of life, and those who have done evil, to the resurrection of condemnation. (John 5:21-22, 27-29)*

'And for ever' … Jesus in the Future

None of the New Testament writers satisfies our curiosity as to the nature of 'eternal life'. They stress instead one all-important, heart-stopping fact: that those whom Jesus receives will bear his image, an idea that occurs repeatedly: *'Just as we have borne the image of the man of dust, we will also bear the image of the man of heaven.'* (1 Cor. 15:49; see also Rom. 8:29 and 2 Cor. 3:18). The use of the term 'image' links us, via Jesus, to the Father, of whom Jesus is the image (2 Cor. 4:4; Col. 1:15); at the same time, it takes us back to the beginning, to the intention of God that the human beings that he was going to create should be 'in his image' (Gen. 1:26), as we have noted on several occasions. Men and women who have borne the marred image of the rebellious Adam will ultimately arrive at their predestined goal, as Paul points out in Rom. 8:19. But the one who joins together the two ends of the vast spiritual and material distance between those two 'images', bridging the chasm to enable others to cross from the one to the other, is Jesus.

What does it mean to 'bear his image', to have a body made conformable to his glorious body, as Paul puts it in Philippians 3:21? It is not simply a question of immortality and immunity to ageing and decay. We recall Jesus' words to Nicodemus: those who are 'born of the spirit' are no longer bound by the limitations of their physical existence: *'The wind blows where it chooses, and you hear the sound of it, but you do not know where it comes from or where it goes. So it is with everyone who is born of the Spirit'* (John 3:8). The example of the risen Jesus is perhaps the best guide as we attempt to grasp the implications of his words.

However, the ultimate goal is still greater: it is that *'you may escape from the corruption that is in the world because of lust, and may become participants in the divine nature'* (2 Peter 1:4). To escape from physical infirmity, from ageing, pain and death, may seem goal enough, but Christians know other afflictions than these – not only the physical 'corruption' that his passage speaks of, but the 'lust', the wayward, rebellious desires which underlie it. To be 'as Jesus', to participate in the 'divine nature', must surely mean deliverance at last from the nagging, persistent awareness of imperfection and the sense shared by most Christians of failing to be as they would wish to be and of remaining at best 'unworthy servants' (Luke 17:10). For that reason, John's words in his first Letter are particularly appealing:

See what great love the Father has lavished on us, that we should be called children of God! And that is what we are! The reason the world does not know us is that it did not know him. Dear friends, now we are children of God, and what we will be has not yet been made known. But we know that

Jesus – yesterday, today, for ever

when Christ appears, we shall be like him, for we shall see him as he is. (1 John 3:1-2)

To be like him: in the image of God at last!

But notice how John works back from that ultimate destiny to its impact on the present: *'All who have this hope in him purify themselves, just as he is pure'* (v. 3). The ultimate reason for thinking (and writing!) about Jesus at all is not curiosity about an unimaginable future but the persuasive force of his person on our present lives. In the verse from 2 Peter 1 that precedes the one quoted above, the apostle says that *'His [i.e. God's] divine power has given us everything needed for life and godliness, through the knowledge of him [i.e. Jesus]* **who called us by his own glory and goodness'**.

And afterwards

We have already seen, earlier in this chapter, that Jesus' now immortal followers will not be idle; they will be his helpers in the most challenging but most satisfying of all tasks: the transformation of a ravaged planet into one that worthily reflects its Creator *and* helping humanity to unlearn its destructive habits of thought and action and to embrace the pattern of Jesus.

It might be possible to attempt to imagine what that task, and the endless future that lies beyond, will hold for Christ's followers, but I see neither merit nor purpose in such speculation. It must be confessed, too, that for many the boundless yet totally inconceivable prospect held out to believers can in its way be daunting by virtue of its very unknowability. For my own part, the most reassuring thought is summed up in two phrases of Paul in the key passage from 1 Thessalonians: *'For God has destined us … for obtaining salvation through our Lord Jesus Christ, who died for us, so that whether we are awake or asleep* **we may live with him'** (1 Thess. 5:9-10), and *'so* **we will be with the Lord for ever** …*'* (4:17). To borrow the words of John Keats in his 'Ode on a Grecian Urn', *'that is all/ Ye know on earth, and all ye need to know.'*

Afterword

Attempting to follow what I have called Jesus' 'career', from Bethlehem and Nazareth through to the present and beyond, has proved every bit as complex and challenging as I had expected. It is, of course, an inexhaustible subject; things overlooked and new reflections continually demand inclusion, making it close to impossible to bring the work to a conclusion. Inevitably, it has involved an element of surmise and supposition, but I hope that my suggestions are at least credible in the light of what information we do possess.

The humanity of Jesus

One reason for attempting to follow Jesus as he progresses through to his present exalted position was the belief that the relationship between the different phases would help us to recognise their coherence within the overarching purpose of God. It is hard to grasp that the young man who grew up in Nazareth and worked as a carpenter-builder is now the almighty 'Lord of all', as Peter calls him (Acts 10:36), alive for ever with the eternal life of God and everywhere present where his followers need his support. It is therefore not difficult to see why, faced with the vast difference between the two, early Christian theologians, trained in the essentialist thinking of Hellenistic philosophy, sought to explain (away) this difference by asserting that he really was always somehow God, even before the beginning of his earthly life. A 'God become man' was thought to be the only means by which such a vast gap might be bridged. James T. Dennison explains the thinking as follows:

> If the Son of God is a creature (as Arius maintained), salvation would be impossible. A creature cannot save a creature. To be rightly related (or united) to God would take God rightly related (or united) to human nature. Hence, the Incarnation for Athanasius was a paradigm of mankind's salvation: God and man united. If the Saviour is not God incarnate, there can be no salvation. Athanasius was persistent in defending the essential or consubstantial deity of the Son of God because he deemed this truth essential to the salvation of sinners.[1]

---

1 James T. Dennison, Jr. 'Athanasius, the Son of God, and Salvation'

It seems to me, however, that the exact opposite is the case. Nothing is more important in helping us to see 'the big picture' than the creative intention of God expressed in Genesis 1:26. From the beginning, it tells us, God wished to have with him, about him, creatures who would be like him, with whom he would share his life, his being, his creation. When taken up and echoed in later passages, such as Psalm 8 and Hebrews 2, this statement requires us to see Jesus in terms of that divine intention, as the first among many 'children of God' in whom that goal will finally be achieved. The effect is to root Jesus far more firmly in and among humanity; Genesis 1:26 and Hebrews 4:16 insist on his solidarity with humanity, not merely as a temporary expedient necessitated by our need of redemption, but in his essential nature. It renders superfluous all theorising about his possible heavenly origins as what John Robinson described as 'the Invader from Another World … a cuckoo in the human nest'.[2] Jesus' insistent use of the term 'son of man' points in the same direction, implying an identity between Jesus and humanity that needs to be taken with full seriousness.

If Jesus, this 'young man from Nazareth' is the 'son of man', then he is the quintessential man. That means not only that his earthly life provides the pattern for all subsequent generations of what a true human being 'in God's image' looks like: it also means that, though his manner of birth may have been unique, he reveals what human beings are capable of becoming, once they have undergone a birth of the Spirit like his, as Jesus implies in John 3:8. Notwithstanding their terrible propensity to misuse their divinely given powers, they too are, at least by God's intention, destined for a similar exaltation. The implications of that identity are breath-taking, not least in relation to the creative and spiritual potential of humanity. And only one who was truly man could be what God intended: a man in his image.

But it was precisely in being 'in God's image' that he was and is able to fulfil the other role that the Father gave him. Conventional theology has viewed Jesus' human life primarily, or even solely, as a quasi-legal requirement arising out of a theory of atonement in which a representative of mankind was required who would bear the penalty for mankind's sins – or 'conquer' sin on our behalf. It is this thinking that underlies Athanasius' view, referred to above.

It appears to me, however, as I have said more than once, that the Synoptic Gospels point in quite another direction: they emphasise, as John does too in

---

(https://opc.org/new_horizons/NH02/12e.html)

2 John A.T. Robinson, *The Priority of John,* London 1985, pp. 365-366.

Afterword

his very special way, that it was in those few brief years that, as 'God with us', Jesus showed us the meaning of divine grace within the confines and circumstances of human life and thus in a 'language' that we can understand. A man who in his actions, words and behaviour is in God's image, is, by that very fact, a revelation of God. A suffering, forbearing God is almost impossible for us to grasp, so accustomed are we to human notions of 'just deserts' and of rewards and punishments according to our imagined 'merits' and the like: a Jesus suffering crucifixion without recrimination speaks to us at the most profound level of heart and mind. It truly is a 'gospel of God' that emerges from Jesus' earthly ministry; his resurrection was and is the great sign of sin forgiven and put away, opening up new possibilities for those who believed the good news of that great event.

So it is precisely as man – but in God's image – that Jesus fulfilled his dual roles. He holds together within himself man and God – not through some unimaginable, inexplicable metaphysics, or through the bland assertion of polar opposites that we find in orthodox statements about Jesus, but in a unity that is at once functional and ethical.

This understanding of the meaning of Jesus brings home to us the importance of Jesus' true humanity, which I have been at pain to stress. As I have suggested throughout, he was not some unique creature who, although of flesh and blood, was somehow infallible and unerring in judgment, but rather one who knew doubt and uncertainty, was obliged to take decisions, to work things out – in short to 'learn obedience' as we must do. If we see him as the first realisation of Genesis 1:26 and as one who was 'tested as we are', then his likeness to us was no mere charade, nor was it confined to what is habitually described as 'the temptation of Jesus'. The word 'became flesh', not by some divine *fiat* but by the humble obedience of the man from Nazareth who, wrenched from his familiar environment, found his way, with the Father ever at his side, to the appointed goal. That is why I have repeatedly sought to envisage what the reactions and even the feelings of Jesus might be at specific points in his 'career'.

A continuing identity?

The writer to the Hebrews refers to Jesus, in the passage that I quoted in the introduction, as *'the same yesterday and today and for ever'* (Heb. 13:8). But how can he be the same? What possible similarity can there be between Jesus of Nazareth and the 'Lord of all'? The writer of that letter may have a particular, limited meaning in mind – that Jesus' care for his people, like God's steadfast love (*hesed*) in the Old Testament, is unwavering. But if we take the words at their face value, we see, I think, that this identity consists in two things.

Jesus – yesterday, today, for ever

The first of these is the eternal, unchanging nature of the divine purpose. The view of Jesus across the ages – and across the scriptures – that I have been attempting to develop reveals to us his centrality from first to last in the realisation of God's purpose in creation. As Paul expresses it in Colossians 1:16, all things were created *'in him ... through him and for him'*, which, as I have understood it in chapter 1, means that he is the *'blueprint' according to which* everything was made, the *means by which* everything is brought to its intended perfection, and the *heir for whom* in the first instance everything was made. We see him differently when our eyes are trained by words such as these, or by the passage from Ephesians that I referred to on several occasions, that ultimately God will *'gather up all things in him, things in heaven and things on earth'* (Eph. 1:10).

The other dimension of this continuing identity is the person of Jesus himself, and particularly his self-consciousness. What gives all sentient creatures their continuity of existence and thus their identity is the ability to recall, whether self-consciously, as human beings do, or not. As we look across the phases of Jesus' existence, we see that the risen Jesus recognises and is recognised by his friends. That apparently banal fact is the sign to us that the mighty, exalted Lord carries within himself, we know not how, the consciousness of what he has been and has experienced. Conversely, we see in his discourses in John's Gospel that the still mortal Jesus speaks of who and what he will be and do in the time after his resurrection, when he will apparently no longer be with his disciples. Jesus' personal continuity of identity, of mind and will, thus holds together the different phases both of his own existence and of the Father's saving purpose. In trying to follow Jesus through the different stages of his existence, we are, in effect, attempting to do trace the course of that developing continuity.

The New Testament accordingly shows us Jesus moving from human mortality to divine immortality, not returning to a status that he previously enjoyed, but achieving a destiny which was always prospectively his but attained only after and because of the mortal life that he had led – and doing so not only for himself but as our pioneer and forerunner. As a result, Christians are able to hope and believe that they too, though born 'of the flesh' as John puts it (John 1:13; 3:6), will in due time become 'participants in the divine nature' (2 Peter 1:4) as he is; like him, they will be at once free from the limitations of natural human existence as the wind is (John 3:8) and yet the same identifiable beings, 'yesterday, today and for ever'.

Crucial – *in more senses than one*

What becomes apparent in particular, when we try to follow the course of Je-

Afterword

sus' existence, is that it is the earthly life of Jesus on which everything depends and that holds everything together. On the one hand, it was the time of fulfilment, when the prophecies, prefigurings and expectations of the ages before his birth were finally realised. On the other hand, this earthly life, by virtue of his experience of the best and the worst of humanity, equipped Jesus for his future roles: as head over his church – there could be no better preparation for that task than to have led and cared for his disciples; as our compassionate 'high priest' and *parakletos*, able to *'deal gently with those who are ignorant and are going astray'* (Heb. 5:2) because he *'in every respect has been tested as we are'* (Heb. 4:15); and as *'king of kings and lord of lords'* (Rev. 19:16). And, of course, it was for his faithful service in his difficult and ultimately painful role as God's righteous son in a wicked human world that he was *'highly exalted'* and given *'the name that is above every name, so that at the name of Jesus every knee should bend, in heaven and on earth and under the earth, and every tongue should confess that Jesus Christ is Lord, to the glory of God the Father'* (Phil. 2:9-11). What Jesus is now, he is because of what he was then.

It is, then, Jesus who links together the finite, time-bound world of our present with the eternal realm. At God's right hand there is now one who has shared the human condition, with all its fears and anxieties, its joys and its follies. This is, I suspect, what Hebrews means when it says that he *'always lives to make intercession for them'* (Heb. 7:25). He who was once 'God with man' (cf. Matt. 1:23), that is, God shown to us in the life and character of a man, has become 'man with God' – for our sakes. Yet though he is there with God in the realm of eternal glory, he is also here with us in all the confusion and disorder of the present. It is in this sense, above all, that we are able to think of him as our 'mediator': in his own person he brings together, and holds together, man and God. As he intimates at the end of John 1, he is like a ladder joining earth and heaven, and it is through linking ourselves to him that we too may ascend to the unimaginable heights of being 'partakers of the divine nature'.

Two key moments: baptism and Caesarea Philippi

Thinking about Jesus and his life has brought home to me as never before the significance of two specific moments. I had not grasped before the resemblance of events at his baptism to the 'call' of prophets in the Old Testament, a fact which suggests to me that it was an event of far greater moment than I had realised. It is through this call, with the accompanying empowering gift of the Spirit, that the carpenter from Nazareth becomes teacher, master and ultimately 'Lord'. Both the wording of the temptations and the time that Jesus spent in the 'wilderness' are indicative to me of a Jesus who, divine son though he was, was having to confront and think his way through a calling to

Jesus – yesterday, today, for ever

a task and a destiny more challenging than those of any prophet.

This in turn suggests that his baptism was much more like our baptism than I had imagined. If ours marks both an ending and a beginning, a death and a rising, should we not conclude that such may have been the case with Jesus' baptism too? – that, notwithstanding his unique manner of birth and parenthood, he too had to pass through a comparable 'dying and rising' at the beginning of his ministry that prefigured its physical outworking at the end of his mortal life? Some may not agree with my suggestions that he might not have known from the beginning what his mission was to be and where it would lead; it seems vital to me, however, that we have in mind an earthly Jesus who was just that: earthly, subject to the limitations of finite human existence, no matter with what powers of thought and action he was endowed at his baptism.

If Jesus' earthly life is the centre and pivot of his entire 'career', then the events at Caesarea Philippi are the centre and pivot of that brief life. I had long been aware of that moment as a turning point in Jesus' ministry; I had not, however, grasped the importance of the words that Jesus spoke at that time. It is not just his personal commitment to the path that would lead to his death, though it is here expressed in words for the first time. His reference to 'human things' and 'divine things', later explained as the contrast between clinging to life, yet thereby losing it, and being willing to lose one's life and thereby gaining it – what I have called the 'Caesarea Philippi principle' (see chapter 7) – is, I now see, at the very heart of his life and teaching. The Gospels show him losing his life and then gaining it, just as he had said, while later sections of the New Testament illustrate the superiority of that new, 'gained' life over what went before. But the Gospels also pointedly illustrate the converse: they set over against Jesus' pattern the ambitions of James and John and the fearfulness of Peter, all three driven, like the rest of the Twelve, by 'the human things'.

This principle is also at the heart of Jesus' challenge to mankind. The 'human things' take us back to Adam; they have governed human behaviour and society ever since. The repentance that Jesus calls for means a renunciation of that fundamental orientation in favour of its alternative, the 'divine things' exemplified in Jesus. It implies a re-orientation of aims and aspirations so radical that it is best represented by baptism, an act symbolic of death and rebirth, the ending of one life and the beginning of a new life based on a diametrically opposed principle.

But does Jesus' teaching not set the bar impossibly high? The message of Jesus is one of grace – but it is no 'cheap grace', as we emphasised in chapter

Afterword

6. The behaviour of Jesus' disciples as we see them in the Gospels illustrates the natural, instinctive reactions of human beings; how can one expect them to rise to the degree of selflessness apparently demanded by Jesus, to be willing to *'lose their life for my sake, and for the sake of the gospel'* (Mark 8:35)? It certainly does look an unreasonable ask – until one takes into account the resurrection of Jesus. Faith that he is 'risen indeed' makes the unreasonable reasonable, the impossible possible. Jesus is not requiring all his followers to become martyrs in the conventional sense of the word; what he asks for is that men and women cease to live for themselves – that the self is dethroned. Instead, the will of Jesus and his Father and the good of their fellows take precedence: *'... we are convinced that one has died for all; therefore **all have died**. And he died for all, so that those who live **might live no longer for themselves**, but for him who died and was raised for them'* (2 Cor. 5:14-15). In the book of Acts we see Jesus' followers learning to live by their faith in Jesus' resurrection, facing all kinds of opposition, danger and loss for his sake and the gospel's, but receiving in return *'... a hundredfold now in this age—houses, brothers and sisters, mothers and children, and fields, with persecutions—and in the age to come eternal life'* (Mark 10:30).

The Paul who wrote those words from 2 Corinthians quoted above well knew that some found it too difficult or had never understood the faith that they had supposedly accepted: *'All of them are seeking their own interests, not those of Jesus Christ'*, he says, and as a result they *'live as enemies of the cross of Christ ... Their end is destruction; their god is the belly; and their glory is in their shame; their minds are set on earthly* things' (Phil. 2:21; 3:18-19) – the echoes of Caesarea Philippi are unmistakable. But those echoes are even clearer earlier in Philippians 3, as we pointed out in chapter 9: in v. 7-8, he takes up Jesus' contrast between gain and loss, just as he had previously done at the height of the storm in Acts 27. It is surely no accident that Acts ends with the shipwreck, in which Paul, losing everything, undergoes a 'death by baptism' of an all too realistic kind but thereby 'gains' everything, or as he puts it, *'wins Christ'* (Phil. 3:8), emerging to life on his very own 'resurrection morning' – when even a serpent's bite could not harm him (Acts 28:4-6).

Jesus for us – today and for ever

As this book demonstrates, it is impossible to encompass all the roles that Jesus has fulfilled and still fulfils in God's gracious purpose of salvation. So much depended and depends on him; as Hebrews says, he *'sustains all things by his powerful word'* (Heb. 1:3). We may dwell on his obedient realisation of all that had been written about him, on his acts and words of mercy and kindness to those that he encountered, his patient bearing of the very worst that

Jesus – yesterday, today, for ever

man could devise against him, his guidance of his servants as they began to proclaim his name, or his future role as righter of this world's wrongs. But beyond all this, he is for each of us at once our Lord and our friend, who sustains us by his strength and reassures us by his grace. He is our *parakletos*, the one called to be beside us in every moment of our lives. And not only beside us: if we will let him, he will dwell with us and in us, today and for ever. *'Listen'*, he says, *'I am standing at the door, knocking; if you hear my voice and open the door, I will come in to you and eat with you, and you with me'* (Rev. 3:20).

Bibliography

On Jesus

Robert Aron, *Les Années Obscures de Jésus*, Paris 1966

Kenneth E. Bailey, *Jesus Through Middle Eastern Eyes*, Downers Grove, Illinois & London 2008

William Barclay, *The Mind of Jesus*, London 1960

W.F. Barling, *Jesus – Healer and Teacher*, Birmingham (*The Christadelphian*) 2005

Maurice Casey, *Jesus of Nazareth, An Independent Historian's Account of His Life and Teaching*, New York 2010

Oscar Cullman, *The Christology of the New Testament*, London 1959

James D.G. Dunn, *Christology in the Making*, 2nd. Edition, London 1989

James D.G. Dunn, *Jesus Remembered (Christianity in the Making*, vol. 1), Grand Rapids, Michigan 2003

James D.G. Dunn, *Did The First Christians Worship Jesus? – The New Testament Evidence*, Louisville, Kentucky 2010

James D.G. Dunn, *Jesus According to the New Testament*, Grand Rapids, Michigan 2019

Chris Keith, *Jesus Against the Scribal Elite. The Origins of the Conflict*, London/New York 2020

Hans Küng, *Jesus*, Munich & Zürich 2013 (part of *Christ sein*, Zürich 1974; translated by Edward Quinn as *On Being a Christian*, London 1978)

Enda Lyons, *Jesus: Self-portrait by God*, Blackrock, Co. Dublin 1994

T.W. Manson, *The Teaching of Jesus. Studies in its Form and Content*, Cambridge 1963.

E.P. Sanders, *Jesus and Judaism*, London 1985

Neville Smart, *The Son of God Is Come*, Shipston on Stour 1998

Geza Vermes, *Jesus the Jew. A Historian's Reading of the Gospels*, London 1976

Cecilia Wassén & Tobias Hägerland, *Jesus the Apocalyptic Prophet*, London/New York 2021

David Wenham, *Jesus in Context. Making Sense of the Historical Figure*, Cambridge 2021

NT Wright, *Jesus and the Victory of God*, London 1996

Jesus – yesterday, today, for ever

On the Gospels

John Ashton, *Understanding the Fourth Gospel,* Oxford 1991

Richard Bauckham, 'John for Readers of Mark' in Richard Bauckham (ed.), *The Gospels for All Christians,* Edinburgh 1998

Richard Bauckham, *Jesus and the Eyewitnesses,* Grand Rapids, Michigan/ Cambridge 2006

Richard Bauckham, *The Testimony of the Beloved Disciple,* Grand Rapids, Michigan 2007

Richard A. Burridge, *Four Gospels, One Jesus? A Symbolic Reading,* London 1994

Jerry Camery-Hoggatt, *Irony in Mark's Gospel. Text and Subtext,* Cambridge/ New York 1992.

Austin Farrer, *A Study in St Mark,* Woking/London 1951

Austin Farrar, *St Matthew and St Mark,* Glasgow 1954

Brian K. Gamel, *Mark 15:39 as a Markan Theology of Revelation. The Centurion's Confession as Apocalyptic Unveiling,* London/New York 2017.

Justo L. Gonzales *The Story Luke Tells,* Grand Rapids, Michigan 2005

Joel B. Green, *The Theology of the Gospel of Luke,* Cambridge 1995

Joel B. Green, *The Gospel of Luke,* Grand Rapids, Michigan/Cambridge 1997

Graham Jackman, *The Word Became Flesh. A Theme in John's Gospel,* 2016

Graham Jackman, *Luke's Pauline Narrative. Reading the Third Gospel,* 2019

David P. Moessner, 'How Luke Writes' in Markus Bockmuehl & Donald A. Hagner (ed.), *The Written Gospel,* Cambridge 2005, p. 157

David P. Moessner, 'Reading Luke's Gospel as Ancient Hellenistic Narrative' in Craig G. Bartholomew, Joel B. Green & Anthony C. Thiselton (eds.), *Reading Luke. Interpretation, Reflection, Formation,* Milton Keynes/Grand Rapids, Michigan, 2005.

David Rhoads, *Reading Mark, Engaging the Gospel,* Minneapolis 2004

John A.T. Robinson, *The Priority of John,* London 1985

C. Kavin Rowe, *Early Narrative Christology. The Lord in the Gospel of Luke,* Grand Rapids Michigan 2006

L.G. Sargent, *The Gospel of the Son of God,* Birmingham (The Christadelphian) 1966

Charles H. Talbert, *Reading Luke. A Literary and Theological Commentary on the Third Gospel,* Macon, Georgia 2002

Rowan Williams, in *Christ On Trial, How the Gospel Unsettles Our Judgement,* Grand Rapids, Michigan/London 2000

Bibliography

On Paul

John M.G. Barclay, *Paul and the Gift*, Grand Rapids, Michigan 2015

T.J. Barling, *The Letter To The Philippians*, Birmingham (*The Christadelphian*) 1981

James D.G. Dunn, *The Theology of Paul the Apostle*, Grand Rapids, Michigan/ Cambridge 1998.

John Muddiman, *The Epistle to the Ephesians*, London/New York 2001

Brant Pitre, Michael P. Barber, John A. Kincaid *Paul, A New Covenant Jew*, Grand Rapids, Michigan 2019

Francis Watson, *Paul and the Hermeneutics of Faith,* 2nd edition, London/ New York 2016

Tom (N.T.) Wright, *Paul And The faithfulness Of God*, London 2013

Tom (N.T.) Wright, *Pauline Perspectives. Essays on Paul 1978-2013*, London 2013

Tom (N.T.) Wright, *Paul. A Biography*, San Francisco/London 2018

On the historical background

Gerd Theissen & Annette Merz, *The Historical Jesus. A Comprehensive Guide*, London 1998 (translated by John Bowden from the German original, *Der historische Jesus: Ein Lehrbuch*, Göttingen 1996)

N.T. Wright, *The New Testament and The People Of God*, London 1992

J. Julius Scott Jr., *Jewish Backgrounds of the New Testament*, Grand Rapids, Michigan 1995

Joel B. Green & Lee Martin McDonald (eds.), *The World of the New Testament. Cultural, Social, and Historical Contexts*, Grand Rapids, Michigan 2013

Josephus, *Antiquities of the Jews*

Josephus, *Jewish Wars*

On New Testament use of the Old Testament

G.K. Beale and D.A. Carson (eds.), *Commentary on the New Testament Use of the Old Testament*, Grand Rapids, Michigan/Nottingham 2007

Richard B. Hays: *Echoes of Scripture in the Letters of Paul*, New Haven/London 1989

Richard B. Hays, *Reading Backwards*, Waco, Texas 2014/ London 2015

Richard B. Hays, *Echoes of Scripture in the Gospels*, Waco, Texas 2016

Graham Jackman, *Re-Reading Romans in Context*, 2012 (Appendix B)

Jesus – yesterday, today, for ever

On Christian doctrine

D.M. Baillie, *God was in Christ. An Essay on Incarnation and Atonement,* 2nd.
Ed., London 1955

Catechism Of The Catholic Church, London 1994

Kenneth Grayston, *Dying, We Live. A New Enquiry into the Death of Christ in
the New Testament,* New York/Oxford 1990

Walter Riggans, 'The Parousia: Getting our Terms Right', *Themelios,* XXI, 1,
1995

L.S. Thornton, *The Common Life in the Body of Christ,* London 1940

Printed in Great Britain
by Amazon